# Humana Festival 2017
## The Complete Plays

**About the Humana Foundation**
The Humana Foundation was established in 1981 as the philanthropic arm of Humana Inc., one of the nation's leading health and well-being companies. Located in Louisville, KY, the Foundation seeks to co-create communities where leadership, culture, and systems work to improve and sustain positive health outcomes. For more information, visit www.HumanaFoundation.org.

Humana and the Humana Foundation are dedicated to Corporate Social Responsibility. Our goal is to ensure that every business decision we make reflects our commitment to improving the health and well-being of our members, our associates, the communities we serve, and our planet.

# Humana Festival 2017
## The Complete Plays

Edited by
Amy Wegener and Jenni Page-White

**Playscripts**
Inc.

New York, NY

Published by Playscripts, Inc.
7 Penn Plaza, Suite 904
New York, New York, 10001
www.playscripts.com

Cover Design by Mary Kate Zihar
Text Design and Layout by Kathryn Funkhouser
Cover Image Model: Kelsey Johnson
First Edition: March 2018
10 9 8 7 6 5 4 3 2 1

LCCN: 95650734
ISSN: 19354452

ISBN-13: 978-0-9819099-5-0

# Contents

# Acknowledgments

The editors wish to thank the following persons for their invaluable assistance in compiling this volume:

Vivian Barnes
Lila Rachel Becker
Sara Durham
Katie Foggiano
Kathryn Funkhouser
Melissa Hines
Bryan Howard
Laura Humble
Steve Knight
Lexy Leuszler
Meredith McDonough
Meghan McLeroy
Zachary Meicher-Buzzi
Kevin E. Moore
Hannah Rae Montgomery
Jessica Reese
Jeffrey S. Rodgers
Emily Tarquin
Paige Vehlewald
Les Waters
Justin Williamson
Sammy Zeisel
Mary Kate Zihar

Michael Finkle
Di Glazer
Seth Glewen
Max Grossman
Leah Hamos
Mark Subias
Susan Weaving
Derek Zasky

# Actors Theatre of Louisville Staff Humana Festival 2017

ARTISTIC DIRECTOR, Les Waters
MANAGING DIRECTOR, Kevin E. Moore

## ARTISTIC

Associate Artistic Director . . . . . . . . . . . . . . . . . . . . . . . . . . . Meredith McDonough
Artistic Producer . . . . . . . . . . . . . . . . . . . . . . . . . . . . . . . . . . . . . . Emily Tarquin
Artistic Manager . . . . . . . . . . . . . . . . . . . . . . . . . . . . . . . . . Zachary Meicher-Buzzi
Company Manager . . . . . . . . . . . . . . . . . . . . . . . . . . . . . . . . . . . . . . Dot King

### Literary
Director . . . . . . . . . . . . . . . . . . . . . . . . . . . . . . . . . . . . . . . . . . . . Amy Wegener
Literary Manager . . . . . . . . . . . . . . . . . . . . . . . . . . . . . . . . . Jenni Page-White
Resident Dramaturg . . . . . . . . . . . . . . . . . . . . . . . . . . . Hannah Rae Montgomery
Literary Associate . . . . . . . . . . . . . . . . . . . . . . . . . . . . . . . . . . . . Jessica Reese

### Education
Director . . . . . . . . . . . . . . . . . . . . . . . . . . . . . . . . . . . . . . . . . . . . Jane B. Jones
Education Manager . . . . . . . . . . . . . . . . . . . . . . . . . . . . . . . . .Betsy Anne Huggins
Education Associate . . . . . . . . . . . . . . . . . . . . . . . . . . . . . . . . . Lexy Leuszler
Teaching Artists . . . . . . . . . . . . . . . . . . . . . . . . . . . . . . . Liz Fentress, Keith McGill,
Talleri McRae, Letitia Usher

## ADMINISTRATION

General Manager . . . . . . . . . . . . . . . . . . . . . . . . . . . . . . . . . . .Jeffrey S. Rodgers
Human Resources Manager . . . . . . . . . . . . . . . . . . . . . . . . . . . . . . Marie Tull
Systems Manager . . . . . . . . . . . . . . . . . . . . . . . . . . . . . . . . . . . . . .Dottie Krebs
Executive Assistant . . . . . . . . . . . . . . . . . . . . . . . . . . . . . . . . . . . . Janelle Baker
Administrative & IT Services Coordinator . . . . . . . . . . . . . . . . . . . . . Alan Meyer

## AUDIENCE SERVICES & SALES

Ticket Sales Director . . . . . . . . . . . . . . . . . . . . . . . . . . . . . . . . . . Kim McKercher
Season Tickets Manager . . . . . . . . . . . . . . . . . . . . . . . . . . . . . . . . Julie Gallegos
Box Office Managers . . . . . . . . . . . . . . . . . . . . . . . . .Steve Clark, Kristy Kannapell
Customer Service Representatives . . . . . . . . . . . .Cheryl Anderson, LaShana Avery,
Matthew Brown, Marty Huelsmann,
Deva North, Chandler Smith, Veronica Thomas

### Volunteer and Audience Relations
Director . . . . . . . . . . . . . . . . . . . . . . . . . . . . . . . . . . . . . . . . .Allison Hammons
House Managers . . . . . . . . . . . . . . . . . . . . . . . . . . . . .Jeanne Becker, Tiffany Bush,
Elizabeth Cooley, Jordan Kelch, Marianne Zickuhr
Lobby Manager . . . . . . . . . . . . . . . . . . . . . . . . . . . . . . . . . . . . Tiffany Walton
Coat Check Supervisor . . . . . . . . . . . . . . . . . . . . . . . . . . . . . . . Tanisha Johnson
Coat Check Attendants . . . . . . . . . . . . . . . . . . . . . .Matt Dalton, Sandra Temgoua

## DEVELOPMENT

Director ................................................ Julie Roberts
Associate Director of Development. ....................Shannon Kisselbaugh
National Philanthropy Manager. ..........................Justin Williamson
Community Philanthropy Manager............................Carrie Syberg
Annual Fund Manager ....................................... Liz Magee
Donor Relations Coordinator............................... Susan Bramer

## FINANCE

Director ................................................Peggy Shake
Accounting Coordinator..................................... Jason Acree
Accounting Assistant........................................Jillian Innes

## MARKETING & COMMUNICATIONS

Director ................................................. Steve Knight
Public Relations Manager...................................Sara Durham
Marketing Manager........................................ Melissa Hines
Festival & Events Manager..................................Erin Meiman
Marketing & Communications Coordinator....................Laura Humble
Graphic Designer .........................................Mary Kate Zihar
Assistant Graphic Designer .................................Amie Harris
Group Sales Manager .......................................Sarah Peters
Group Sales Associate..................................... Chris O'Leary

## OPERATIONS

Director ......................................... Mike Schüssler-Williams
Operations Manager ........................................Barry Witt
Building Services Supervisor ...............................Ricky Baldon
Building Services..............................Deonta Burns, Joe Spencer,
Jeramaine Spain
Receptionist .......................................Amanda Marshbanks

## PRODUCTION

Production Manager ........................................Paul Werner
Associate Production Manager......................... Michael DeWhatley
Production Stage Manager ............................. Paul Mills Holmes
Resident Stage Managers....................... Stephen Horton, Katie Shade
Resident Assistant Stage Manager .........................Jessica Kay Potter
Production Assistant..................................... Leah Pye

### Scenic

Technical Director.........................................Justin Hagovsky
Associate Technical Director .............................. Braden Blauser
Scenic Charge............................................. Rachael Claxton
Scene Shop Manager......................................Javan Roy-Bachman

Master Carpenter. . . . . . . . . . . . . . . . . . . . . . . . . . . . . . . . . . . . . . . . . . . . . Alexia Hall
Carpenters . . . . . . . . . . . . . . . . . . . . . . . . . . . . . . . . Elliot Cornett, Emily Graver,
Eric Kneller, Matthew Krell, Winslow Lindsay,
Brooke McPherson, Nikolas Mikkelsen, Pierre Vendette
Scenic Painter. . . . . . . . . . . . . . . . . . . . . . . . . . . . . . . . . . . . . . . . . . . . . . . Liv Joyce
Deck Carpenters . . . . . . . . . . . . . . . . . . . . . . . . Caitlin McCarthy, Peter Regalbuto

## Costumes
Costume Director . . . . . . . . . . . . . . . . . . . . . . . . . . . . . . . . . . . . . . . . Mike Floyd
Crafts Master . . . . . . . . . . . . . . . . . . . . . . . . . . . . . . . . . . . . . . . . . Shari Cochran
Wig and Makeup Supervisor. . . . . . . . . . . . . . . . . . . . . . . . . . . . . . Jehann Gilman
Wardrobe Supervisors. . . . . . . . . . . . . . . . . . . . . Emily Astorian, Molly Herman
Draper/Tailor . . . . . . . . . . . . . . . . . . . . . . . . . . . . . . . . . . . . . . . . . Jeffery Park
First Hand . . . . . . . . . . . . . . . . . . . . . . . . . . . . . . . . . . . . . . . . . Natalie Maynard
Stitcher Captain . . . . . . . . . . . . . . . . . . . . . . . . . . . . . . . . . . . . . . Elizabeth Hahn
Stitchers . . . . . . . . . . . . . . . . . . . . . . . . . . . . . . . . . . . Melissa Allgeier, Faith Brown,
Lilly Higgs, Christina Marcantonio
Costume Design Assistants . . . . . . . . . . . . . . . . Maggie McGrann, Adrienne Nixon
Wig and Makeup Assistant . . . . . . . . . . . . . . . . . . . . . . . . . . . . . . Tanner Pippert
Wardrobe and Wig Assistant . . . . . . . . . . . . . . . . . . . . . . . . . . . . . Byrone Smith

## Lighting
Supervisor . . . . . . . . . . . . . . . . . . . . . . . . . . . . . . . . . . . . . . . . . . Jason E. Weber
Assistant Lighting Supervisor. . . . . . . . . . . . . . . . . . . . . . . . . . . . Dani Clifford
Master Electrician . . . . . . . . . . . . . . . . . . . . . . . . . . . . . . . . . . . . John Newman
Pamela Brown Lighting Technician. . . . . . . . . . . . . . . . . . . . . . Jacqueline Malenke
Bingham Lighting Technician . . . . . . . . . . . . . . . . . . . . . . . . . . . Lauren Gallup
Swing Lighting Technician. . . . . . . . . . . . . . . . . . . . . . . Oliver Kassenbrock
Lighting Technicians. . . . . . . . . . . . . . . . . . . . . . . . . . . . . . . Christian Bowyer,
Çolin Evans, Aaron Hutto, Riley Noble

## Sound
Supervisor . . . . . . . . . . . . . . . . . . . . . . . . . . . . . . . . . . . . . . . . . . . Paul Doyle
Assistant Sound Supervisor . . . . . . . . . . . . . . . . . . . . . . . . . . . . . Jessica Collins
Sound Technicians. . . . . . . . . . . . . . . . . . . . . . . . . . . . . . . . . . . . Rachel Regan,
Rachel Spear, Amanda Werre

## Properties
Director . . . . . . . . . . . . . . . . . . . . . . . . . . . . . . . . . . . . . . . . . . . Mark Walston
Props Master . . . . . . . . . . . . . . . . . . . . . . . . . . . . . . . . . . . . Carrie Mossman
Assistant Properties Master . . . . . . . . . . . . . . . . . . . . . . . . . . . Heather Lindert
Carpenter Artisan . . . . . . . . . . . . . . . . . . . . . . . . . . . . . . . . . . . Karl Anderson
Soft Goods Artisan. . . . . . . . . . . . . . . . . . . . . . . . . . . . . . . . . . Jessie Combest
General Artisan. . . . . . . . . . . . . . . . . . . . . . . . . . . . . . . . . . . . . . Brad Baute
Props Artisan. . . . . . . . . . . . . . . . . . . . . . . . . . . . . . . . . . . . . . Sidney Martin
Props Observer . . . . . . . . . . . . . . . . . . . . . . . . . . . . . . . . . . . . . Lindsey Sample

## Video
Media Technologist . . . . . . . . . . . . . . . . . . . . . . . . . . . . . . . . . . . Philip Allgeier

## PROFESSIONAL TRAINING COMPANY

Director . . . . . . . . . . . . . . . . . . . . . . . . . . . . . . . . . . . . . . . . . . . . . . . . . Michael Legg
Associate Director . . . . . . . . . . . . . . . . . . . . . . . . . . . . . . . . . . . . . . . . John Rooney
Acting . . . . . . . . . . . . . . . . . . . . . . . . . . . . Carter Caldwell, Andres Nicolas Chaves,
Andrew Cutler, Jenn Geiger, Abby Leigh Huffstetler,
Daniel Johnson, Kelsey Johnson, Elijah Jones,
Kevin Kantor, Sam Kotansky, Anna Lentz,
Kathiamarice Lopez, Laakan McHardy,
Alexandra Milak, Regan Moro, Grace Palmer,
Jacob Sabinsky, Anne-Marie Trabolsi, Alice Wu
Arts Administration . . . . . . . . . . . . . . . . . . . . . . . . . . . . . . . . . . . Katie Foggiano
Communications . . . . . . . . . . . . . . . . . . . . . . . . . . . . . . . . . . . . . . Kate Leggett
Company Management/Hospitality . . . . . . . . . . . . . . . . . . . . . . . Chandler Smith
Development . . . . . . . . . . . . . . . . . . . . . . . . . . . . . . . . . . . . . . Rachael Everson
Directing . . . . . . . . . . . . . . . . . . . . . . . . . . . . . Lila Rachel Becker, Sammy Zeisel
Dramaturgy/Literary Management . . . . . . . . . . . . . Bryan Howard, Paige Vehlewald
Education/Teaching Artists . . . . . . . . . . . . . . . . . . . . . . . . . . . . Elliott Talkington,
Victoria Marie Masteller
Events and Festival Management . . . . . . . . . . . . . . . . . . . . . . Allison Paige Gilman
Lighting . . . . . . . . . . . . . . . . . . . . . . . . . . . . . . . . . . . . . . . . . . . . Natasha Bray
Marketing . . . . . . . . . . . . . . . . . . . . . . . . . . . . . . . . . . . . . . . . . . . . Jenny Wilde
Production Management . . . . . . . . . . . . . . . . . . . . . . . . . . . . . . . . . Hannah Cava
Scenic Painting . . . . . . . . . . . . . . . . . . . . . . . . . . . . . . . . . . . Hannah Allgeier
Stage Management . . . . . . . . . . . . . . . . . . . . . . . . . Alexis Breese, Michael Donnay,
Emily Pathman, Katherine Thesing

## USHER CAPTAINS

Alex Ackerman, Dolly Adams, Star Adams, Shirley Adkins, Marie Allen, Katherine
Austin, June Blair, Libba & Chuck Bonifer, Tanya Briley, Maleva Chamberlain,
Donna Conlon, Terry Conway, Laurie Eiden, Doris Elder, Reese Fisher, Joyce
French, Carol Halbleib, LuAnn & Tom Hayes, Candace Jaworski, Barbara Nichols,
Teresa Nusz, Judy Pearson, Beth Phipps, Nancy Rankin, Bob Rosedale, Tim Unruh,
Joshua Van Nort, David Wallace, Megg Ward

**Actors Theatre's Company Doctor**
Dr. Andrew Mickler, F.A.C.S.

# Foreword

One of the great joys of being Actors Theatre of Louisville's artistic director is having the platform to invite so many wonderful writers to join us each year—and then seeing the worlds they imagine come to life in full production, supported by a company with an unparalleled dedication to embracing the new. The path to programming the Humana Festival of New American Plays is also infused with a sense of wholehearted, open curiosity. Our literary and artistic team reads hundreds of scripts, cultivates commissions, and casts a wide net to both keep up with writers we admire, and discover promising voices previously unknown to us. Curating an adventurous slate starts with the careful attention we dedicate to all of those efforts, and I'm proud of the way the 2017 Humana Festival brought a dynamic mix of old friends and new ones into our rehearsal halls, enabling us to share their work with theatregoers (and now, readers) from all over the country.

The energy that Actors Theatre devotes to sustaining conversations with playwrights over time has always been a source of the Humana Festival's strength, and this year we featured several vibrant returning voices. We were delighted to bring Molly Smith Metzler back to Louisville with *Cry it Out*, a play commissioned on the strength of her earlier Humana Festival debut, *Elemeno Pea*. I was thrilled to direct *The New Line*, a short play by the great Will Eno, with whom I'd collaborated on *Gnit* in 2013. Tasha Gordon-Solmon and Louisville native Basil Kreimendahl had been with us for recent festivals— Tasha with a lovely ten-minute piece, and Basil as one of the playwrights commissioned to write for the Professional Training Company. They returned with fantastic full-length plays this year, *I Now Pronounce* and *We're Gonna Be Okay*, thanks to that continued dialogue with us. The talented Jeff Augustin, already a two-time festival veteran, came on board to co-author *The Many Deaths of Nathan Stubblefield*. So did Ramiz Monsef, who participated for the first time as a writer, but has appeared on our stages as a performer, and whose work in both arenas is exciting.

It's gratifying when the Humana Festival can be a home for an artist's evolving body of work, but it's equally important that we meet new collaborators and welcome playwrights we admire into our building for the first time. Jorge Ignacio Cortiñas, whose intricate and haunting drama I directed, fits both those descriptions, and it was a pleasure to work with him on the premiere of *Recent Alien Abductions*. Chelsea Marcantel's *Airness* introduced her keen sense of humor—and the oddball allure of competitive air guitar—to audiences in Louisville, and Claire Kiechel and Sarah DeLappe, whose recent plays our staff had read and loved, made their festival debuts by joining the writing team behind *The Many Deaths of Nathan Stubblefield*. An evening of ten-minute plays also shined a spotlight on the inventive comic sensibilities of two Humana Festival newcomers: Krista Knight's *Home Invasion* brought mischievous ghosts into the mix, while Eric Pfeffinger, who's had six short pieces produced with our Professional Training Company over the years, imagined a showdown between monsters in *Melto Man and Lady Mantis*.

The Humana Festival's extraordinary capacity to encompass such a spectrum of styles, stories, and theatrical vocabularies each season results from a guiding impulse to embrace new voices and diverse viewpoints. We never quite know where the process of selecting plays will lead as we begin our search, and we never program thematically; rather, like embarking on a good road trip, we start with a full tank of gas and a sense of the route, but allow ourselves to become enthralled with surprises and uncharted destinations along the way. And with a spirit of generosity and an ongoing commitment to reading the work of friends old, newfound, and yet-to-be-discovered, we attempt to map a festival of true imaginative breadth and wide-ranging perspectives. This book represents the culmination of one such expedition, and I'm very happy to see our many friends from the 2017 Humana Festival gathered again in these pages.

—*Les Waters*
*Artistic Director*
*Actors Theatre of Louisville*

# Editors' Note

Pattern recognition is one of the most fundamental cognitive skills of the human brain: we organize our feelings, thoughts, and experiences into digestible chunks, match sensory input with information retrieved from our memories, and transform those connections into concrete decisions and behavioral strategies. And we're very, very good at it. Humans can identify an incredible range of complex patterns, which scientists posit is the essence of an evolved brain. This skill enables us to do everything from grouping apples and oranges together to writing a computer program; it may even contribute to our appreciation of music.

So it's no wonder that when we reflect on the plays of the 2017 Humana Festival, we are drawn to noticing the common threads that run through these wildly different works. Actors Theatre of Louisville never programs the festival around a theme; rather, the slate is curated with an eye towards diversity in aesthetic, voice, and cultural perspective. In retrospect, though, we can't help but detect the echoes that resonate across this anthology. Whether the characters that populate these plays are entering the world of competitive air guitar or preparing for disaster during the Cuban Missile Crisis, these stories, taken as a whole, offer a kaleidoscopic view of people grappling with the upheaval of change, and yearning to be heard and understood. Where their internal compasses point them depends on how they interpret the patterns they see around them.

In several of the plays, we meet characters confronting monumental personal change, and crossing major milestones. In Molly Smith Metzler's insightful comedy, *Cry it Out*, two new mothers bridge class divides to bond over their radically altered day-to-day lives, feeling "held hostage all day in dirty yoga pants by little larval creatures." They find solidarity, but their financial situations present divergent dilemmas as the end of maternity leave looms. Centered on another rite of passage, Tasha Gordon-Solmon's *I Now Pronounce* opens with a wedding ceremony that's interrupted by the death of the elderly rabbi officiating the marriage. The wedding party takes this as a cue to behave badly, while the bride and groom question whether they should get married at all, given the challenges of authentic human connection. In a different vein, Will Eno's ten-minute piece, *The New Line*, plays with the conventions of a fashion show, moving deftly between eloquent descriptions of clothing and profound questions like, "Who are you supposed to be?" And in another short play with a memorable punch, Eric Pfeffinger's *Melto Man and Lady Mantis* introduces two creatures who've recently undergone physical transformations caused by "industrial accidents." Now wielding destructive powers, they wage an epic battle over whether their behavior should match their monstrous images.

The plays contain many examples of characters caught up in more widespread change and powerful social forces, too: from the tectonic shifts of the 1960s and an escalating nuclear threat, to a mysteriously altered television episode cited as evidence of a vast conspiracy. In their slyly hilarious *We're Gonna Be Okay*, Basil Kreimendahl draws a parallel between the existential fear underscoring the Cuban Missile Crisis and the intense anxiety that can stem from facing cultural transition. And in Jorge Ignacio Cortiñas's darkly compelling drama, *Recent Alien Abductions*, a Puerto Rican man describes an episode of *The X-Files* that he swears has been inexplicably revised; when the play takes a leap in time, that tale becomes a window to understanding the erasure of other difficult truths. Cortiñas's play interrogates the implications of power and complicity, asking us to consider who gets silenced, and whose stories are told. The four playwrights commissioned to pen *The Many Deaths of Nathan Stubblefield* for the Professional Training Company were also galvanized by questions about erasure. The inspiration for the piece was born from Kentucky's rich history of innovators and inventors, but the writers noticed that some voices were missing from the historical record. Together, they challenged themselves to ask why.

While these plays' meditations sometimes expose troubling truths, they also teach us that moments of evolution and metamorphosis can generate new connections. Just as *Cry it Out*'s Jessie and Lina forge a friendship over the shared experience of having newborns (despite their very different backgrounds), *Airness*'s protagonist, Nina, finds herself building relationships with people she never imagined she would even like before she threw herself into the world of competitive air guitar. Chelsea Marcantel's music-filled comedy follows Nina's journey to transform herself into a rock goddess—and Nina discovers that it's only with the help of her new friends that she can become the best version of herself. Even the gleeful ghosts in Krista Knight's funny ten-minute romp, *Home Invasion*, realize that changing up their haunting tactics is the way to achieve true glory.

What do we make of the preoccupation with change and revelation that we sense echoing through the plays of the 2017 Humana Festival? It's exciting to see how the collective consciousness gathered in these pages speaks to the moment we live in, that these playwrights have put their finger on the pulse of social evolution rippling through our communities today. Then again, drama has always been deeply concerned with transformation, both onstage and in the audience. Encountering a character on the precipice of discovery reminds us that our world is always in flux; theatre can hold up a mirror or show us lives and truths beyond our own, moving us to dream of who we might become. In any case, the plays in any given Humana Festival tend to converse with one another in fascinating ways, whether or not we actively look for patterns in the extraordinary breadth of experience these stories dramatize. As you read the work in this anthology, we hope you'll be inspired to find your own connections.

*—Jenni Page-White and Amy Wegener*

# RECENT ALIEN ABDUCTIONS
## by Jorge Ignacio Cortiñas

1

## BIOGRAPHY

Jorge Ignacio Cortiñas's plays include *Bird in the Hand* (Fulcrum Theater in New York; New Theatre in Miami; *New York Times* Critic's Pick), *Blind Mouth Singing* (National Asian American Theater Company in New York; Teatro Vista in Chicago; *New York Times* Critic's Pick), and *Sleepwalkers* (Alliance Theatre in Atlanta; Area Stage in Miami; Carbonell Award for Best New Play). Awards include fellowships from the National Endowment for the Arts, New York Foundation for the Arts (three years), Helen Merrill Award, Anschutz Distinguished Fellowship at Princeton University, and the Robert Chesley Award. His plays are published by Playscripts, Dramatic Publishing and *TDR/The Drama Review*. Other works include a solo performance entitled *Backroom* (Whitney Museum of American Art in New York) and an interactive "play without a script" entitled *Pick a Card* (GLBT Historical Society in San Francisco). He is the founder of the Obie-winning Fulcrum Theater, a Usual Suspect at New York Theatre Workshop, and an alumnus of New Dramatists.

## ACKNOWLEDGMENTS

*Recent Alien Abductions* premiered at the Humana Festival of New American Plays in March 2017. It was directed by Les Waters with the following cast:

| | |
|---|---|
| ÁLVARO | Jon Norman Schneider |
| NÉSTOR | Bobby Plasencia |
| PATRIA | Ronete Levenson |
| OLGA | Mia Katigbak |
| ANA | Elia Monte-Brown |
| BEBA | Carmen M. Herlihy |

and the following production staff:

| | |
|---|---|
| Scenic Designer | Dane Laffrey |
| Costume Designer | Jessica Pabst |
| Lighting Designer | Brian H. Scott |
| Sound Designer | Christian Frederickson |
| Fight Director | Ryan Bourque |
| Production Stage Manager | Paul Mills Holmes |
| Assistant Stage Manager | Lindsay Eberly |
| Dramaturg | Amy Wegener |
| Casting | Calleri Casting |
| | (James Calleri & Paul Davis) |
| Properties Director | Mark Walston |
| Properties Master | Carrie Mossman |
| Directing Assistant | Sammy Zeisel |
| Assistant Dramaturg | Bryan Howard |

*Recent Alien Abductions* was commissioned by Playwrights Horizons with funds provided by The New York State Council on the Arts.

The play first flickered into existence during a residency at The Corporation of Yaddo.

A first draft of the script subsequently received indispensable, six-month development from Fulcrum Theater, efforts that were supported in part by the National Association of Latino Arts and Culture, the Ford Foundation and the Surdna Foundation.

The play was also read at New York Theatre Workshop as part of the Mondays @ 3 series and received aid from New Dramatists.

Additional thanks are due to Juan Ernesto Ayala, Varín Ayala, Teresa Basilio, Rafael Benoit, Andy Bragen, Dalina Burgos, Hilda Burgos, Edith Cancio, Mariana Carreño King, Joshua Takano Chambers-Letson, Tom Cole, Melissa Crespo, Migdalia Cruz, Kyle de Camp, Danielle Delgado, R. Erica Doyle, Adam Greenfield, Phillip Howze, Christian Huygen, Eng-Ben Lim, Lillian Manzor-Coates, Eddie Martinez, Ellen McLaughlin, Rosalina Perales, José Quiroga, Marlene Ramirez-Cancio, Carmen Rivera, Alejandro Rodríguez, Bess Rowen, Sarah Ruhl, Tim Sanford, Debbie Saivetz, Karen Shimakawa, Rebecca Sumner Burgos, Kathleen Tolan, Andrea Thome, Alexandra T. Vazquez, the Writer's Army (especially Gordon Dahlquist, Madeleine George and Anne Washburn), Chay Yew and José Zayas.

## THE STORYTELLERS

ÁLVARO

PATRIA, the visitor. Neuyorican. Lesbian. Speaks Spanish with an accent.

NÉSTOR, the older brother. Employed. Also plays ALIEN OLDER BROTHER.

OLGA, the mother. Has Alzheimer's. Also plays ALIEN MOTHER.

ANA, the young wife.

BEBA, a neighbor.

## LOCATION

Bayamón, Puerto Rico.

## TIME

Then and now.

## NOTES

Stage directions appear in brackets and are not spoken. Text in parentheses is spoken.

The first act is probably best treated like something akin to a melancholy ghost story. Take your time.

...escribo sobre mi país porque vengo de un país que no sabe que es país y que a veces, incluso, no quiere ser país

*...I write about my country because I come from a country that doesn't know it's a country and that sometimes, in fact, doesn't want to be a country*

—Ana Teresa Toro

Wer jetzt kein Haus hat, baut sich keines mehr.
Wer jetzt allein ist, wird es lange bleiben,
wird wachen, lesen, lange Briefe schreiben
und wird in den Alleen hin und her
unruhig wandern, wenn die Blätter treiben

*Whoever's homeless now, will build no shelter;*
*who lives alone will live indefinitely so,*
*waking up to read a little, draft long letters,*
*and, along the city's avenues,*
*fitfully wander, when the wild leaves loosen*

—Rainer Maria Rilke, translated by Mary Kinzie

*for José (1967 – 2013)*
*who helped me survive my tropics*

Jon Norman Schneider
in *Recent Alien Abductions*

41ˢᵗ Humana Festival of New American Plays
Actors Theatre of Louisville, 2017
Photo by Bill Brymer

# RECENT ALIEN ABDUCTIONS

## ACT I
### A Television Episode

*Back then.*

*A moody stage.*

**ÁLVARO.** It's time for us to talk about the 25th Episode of *The X-Files*.

FBI Agent Fox Mulder has come here, to Puerto Rico, in the hopes of finally uncovering what he believes is an intergalactic alien conspiracy. But why, if Mulder is in Puerto Rico, did the camera catch a glimpse of what appears to be a California eucalyptus tree? Doesn't this suggest the possibility that the episode is not really set here in Puerto Rico but is instead set in some producer's backyard in Los Angeles? You might think you know the reasons for this inconsistency – trust me, you don't. The real reasons are fairly complicated and frankly I don't think you're ready to hear the whole truth just yet. So for now, let's just agree – for the sake of argument – that Mulder has actually arrived in Puerto Rico, alone, without Scully, for reasons having to do with the temporary dissolution of The X-Files Unit.

Important background: Over the course of the preceding twenty-four episodes, the writers of *The X-Files* have been discreetly signaling to TV viewers that Mulder knows he is under surveillance though he can't say exactly by whom. For example, when Mulder returns to his bedroom after a long workday, he remembers how he left things and he knows no matter how many times other people deny it, that someone was in there and he knows that if he had been the sort of agent careless enough to keep a diary, the person or persons spying on him would have read it. This is likely the reason the otherwise sensitive Mulder does not keep a diary. This would also appear to be the reason we often see Mulder in the shadows or hovering in doorways, always outside looking in and with that sad expression on his face. Mulder is lonely in the way people are lonely when they are looking for someone to trust.

Question: Is it possible that the sad expression on Mulder's face is a coded appeal to viewers who know what it feels like to have their own diaries read, a way of signaling to us that Mulder is on our side?

Next the camera shows us establishing shots featuring some beat up pick-up trucks and a few dark haired men in sweaty work clothes. However,

9

also included is a detail about Puerto Rico that you wouldn't expect North American producers to be familiar with. Our island hosts the world's largest telescope and it is to that important observatory that Mulder is headed. Unclear why a studio that finds it acceptable to film an episode set in Puerto Rico in some producer's backyard would then go out of its way to grudgingly admit Puerto Rico's importance to the science of astronomy. Question: Is it possible the writers of this episode disagree amongst themselves over how Puerto Rico should be represented, and that we are seeing evidence of that disagreement? Who were these writers and why is one of them listed as "un-credited"?

You know what? Don't answer yet. Because there's more.

Since this investigation has not been approved by Mulder's supervisors, he can't officially request access to the observatory. Therefore, he has no choice but to break in. He waits until late at night and picks the lock at the gate. When he is finally inside and while covertly reviewing important computer generated data, Mulder decides he has to go to the bathroom. When Mulder opens the bathroom door, he is surprised to see a dark haired teenage boy in sweaty work clothes whimpering in the corner of one of the stalls.

Mulder tries to communicate with the teenager but the young man insists he does not speak English. Mulder must therefore switch to Spanish, a language he can, apparently, barely speak. Unclear if Mulder is speaking Spanish this poorly on purpose. Keep in mind, this is a scripted drama which means the actor playing Mulder was not improvising. One of the writers, perhaps the writer listed as "un-credited," wrote that broken Spanish. Is the viewer meant to understand that Mulder's character is earnestly trying to communicate using the remnants of high school Spanish he has available to him? – or – is Mulder mocking the dark haired teenager in sweaty work clothes? – or – or – might one of the writers be putting words in the mouth of the actor playing Mulder and might this someone else be the person who is responsible for the mocking of the dark haired teenager in sweaty work clothes?

Answer: Exactly.

The dark haired teenager in sweaty work clothes seems to be muttering something. It's hard for Mulder to make out, but the dark haired teenager is muttering something about bright lights in the night sky. Blue lights. This being *The X-Files*, the viewer has to consider the possibility that the dark haired teenager in the sweaty work clothes believes he is being targeted for alien abduction. After all, the teenager avoids eye contact, doesn't seem to have any friends and is generally what one might describe as an awkward person. The threat of alien abduction would certainly explain these symptoms of trauma.

But Mulder has learned long ago that anyone he meets could also be part of the conspiracy. After all, isn't it strange that the actor playing the dark haired teenager in the sweaty work clothes, who Mulder has just met in what is allegedly Puerto Rico, appears to be Mexican? The teenager doesn't have many lines but the lines he does have are spoken with an unmistakable Mexican accent. Perhaps the actor was told to act like a Mexican for obscure plot reasons that will be made obvious later? Mulder, for his part, maintains a neutral expression on his face which could be his FBI training kicking in as he tries to decide if he can trust this seemingly Mexican teenager who has been loitering in a Puerto Rican bathroom. Or – it's possible Mulder really doesn't speak Spanish well and that the striking differences in Latin American national accents is lost on him. You might think that this detail, like so much in *The X-Files*, is left purposefully unclear. Question: Could these anomalous details be evidence of some larger, menacing force?

Answer: Do I really need to spell it out for you?

In any case. The dark haired teenager in sweaty work clothes looks up at Mulder and decides to tell Mulder his name. His name is Álvaro.

That's right: Álvaro

Now, television producers in the United States usually name their male, Latin American characters Juan or José. Maybe, if the studio is trying extra hard, they might name the character Jorge. It's not that Álvaro is a rare name but it's not the kind of name you hear on television shows made in the United States.

And the thing is: Álvaro is my name.

When I heard my name on the television, I had this impulse to turn slowly around and make sure I was still alone in the house. I turned back to the television screen in time to hear Mulder say in perfect, accent-less English: Álvaro, my name is Mulder but you can call me Fox.

That's what he said.

Eventually, Mulder and the teenager reach an understanding. Together they will spend the night in the observatory, trying to avoid detection. Mulder (aka Fox) will continue reading the data from the large computers.

I suppose that as Álvaro and Fox work quietly together in the same room, these two strangers end up being comforted by each other's presence. They can't help it. For example, Álvaro – perhaps out of boredom or perhaps because he's trying to get Mulder to pay attention to him – occasionally does something for which Fox must gently reprimand him. Fox says: Álvaro, no gogo on el rojo – by which he means: Álvaro, please don't touch the red button. The viewer can tell Fox isn't really mad though because Fox is smiling.

Later, if I remember correctly, there is another scene in which Fox is hunched over a computer screen and Álvaro casually inquires what exactly Fox is looking for. The FBI agent looks up and says, I'm looking for proof of The Alien Conspiracy.

As Mulder says these words, the episode cuts to a close up of Álvaro's face.

The choice to use a reaction shot suggests that Álvaro is wondering if he has finally found someone who takes the danger he is in seriously. But Álvaro's expression is hard to describe. It's like he wants to believe Mulder, but caution holds him back. Maybe it strikes Álvaro as suspicious that an FBI agent would so quickly reveal the details of his investigation. During the scene, you can feel the two characters circling each other, trying to get the measure of who the other really is.

But before their relationship has a chance to (how should I put this?), develop – the aliens attack.

The alien attack makes lights flash everywhere. Flashing blue lights. The building shakes and atmospheric conditions go haywire – the island is suddenly in the middle of a hurricane combined with a hailstorm. Álvaro is so startled that he runs out into the storm. Álvaro has run right into danger.

Side note: Mulder has long believed that he is surrounded by a danger that is always there but always hiding. Worse, when Mulder cites evidence of this danger his supervisors don't believe him. They'll laugh at him or say things like, Mulder, I think you're being overly sensitive – which means Mulder has to consider the possibility that his supervisors are part of the conspiracy. Before this episode, there was only one person who had never laughed at Mulder and that's Scully. Scully listens patiently. When Mulder was with Scully he was less tense and just a more pleasant person and once Mulder even let Scully tussle his well-groomed hair.

The producers want us to believe that this bond between Scully and Mulder is proof they are in love. I have to admit, I was one of those people who used to believe that until my Older Brother said something I haven't been able to forget. It's not that my Older Brother watches the *The X-Files* (he doesn't have the patience for it, basically), but one night he happened to catch a few minutes of it. He took one look at Scully and Mulder and said, Please tell me you're not so naïve that you believe those two are ever going to end up together.

According to my brother's theory, which he explained in detail, people are only attracted to those they don't trust. Sad but true, according to my brother.

My Older Brother is full of theories like this, actually. Maybe his ideas don't make sense but then for some reason they stick in your head. And as I watched the episode, I began to remember again my brother's strange theories on how suffering changes the way we desire. Question: Is it safer in the observatory where the aliens seem to be focusing their attack or is it safer for Mulder to run into the storm, to chase a teenager who has been pretending to be Mexican? If anyone tries to tell you that they know the answer to that question, that person is probably part of the conspiracy.

Now, I was home alone the day this episode was broadcast, so there were no witnesses. I can hereby affirm that my family does not own a VCR and so there is no copy of this broadcast. But I remember very clearly that Fox Mulder was on a wet, Caribbean island holding a very large flashlight and shouting my name. Fox cares enough to run through the tropical rainforest in the middle of a hurricane / hailstorm shouting: Álvaro! Álvaro!

Just when the viewer might be expected to begin asking, where has Álvaro gone?; just when the viewer might be tempted to think that maybe it's true what Álvaro's Older Brother says about him and that Álvaro really is impossible to understand; just when the viewer is close to agreeing with Álvaro's mother that constantly threatening to move by himself to a large city in the North is proof of how selfish Álvaro is; just when the viewer would be expected to despair, and I confess that witnessing this episode at home, alone, on a Friday night, hearing my mother's recriminations in my ear, sitting on the green sofa my mother bought second hand, that I did despair. But just then Fox spots Álvaro in the distance. Álvaro is waving Fox over, struggling to make himself heard over the hurricane / hailstorm. Álvaro knows a secret way out. Álvaro knows of a tunnel dug years ago by Puerto Rican freedom fighters known by many as the Macheteros.

Now, some North American viewers may believe that Puerto Rico is actually populated by dark haired men in sweaty work clothes who drive beat up pick up trucks and speak with Mexican accents. Some North American viewers may or may not know the history of Puerto Rican resistance to United States rule and they may or may not sympathize. Therefore some North American viewers may or may not know the name of this organization. The Macheteros. But clearly some viewers knew enough (because how could I have been the only one?) to lean towards their TV sets and allow themselves to whisper, Go Álvaro go.

Álvaro apologizes to Fox. Álvaro says, I'm sorry I pretended to be Mexican. The Mexican accent was just a ruse to help hide my sympathies for Puerto Rican freedom fighters. After all, Fox, you're from the FBI. I had to be sure I could trust you. I know you've been trained to hate the Macheteros, but those freedom fighters were smart enough to dig secret tunnels and right now those tunnels are our only shot. Think about it Fox. All those years, you've been made to feel alone. Well, I've also been made to feel alone. Don't you see? That's how they wanted us to feel. I can tell you more Fox but right now there is a tunnel I very much want to show you.

Fox hesitates. When a handsome Puerto Rican teenager who has just admitted he is expert in strategies of deception invites you into a tunnel – it is reasonable to hesitate. Part of Fox wants to believe Álvaro, he wants to believe that this time Álvaro is telling the truth and that Álvaro won't mislead him again. But another part of Fox wonders if the drama and intrigue that surrounds this dark haired teenager is maybe the reason he's attracted to Álvaro in the first place. Maybe it's true that we are only attracted to those we don't trust. Fox takes a deep breath and then he decides he is going to go ahead and do something so dangerous that it violates everything he has ever been taught by the FBI: Fox follows Álvaro into the tunnel. Álvaro and Fox hold each other close and, just before the episode fades to credits, it looks like (maybe) Álvaro and Fox intend to keep each other safe.

Question: Why then when the episode was rebroadcast a year later during late-night reruns, did the episode end differently than I remember? Why have my repeated letters to the studio, sent by registered mail with proof of delivery, letters in which I request an explanation for this discrepancy, gone unanswered? Why have I not been able to find a single witness to the original broadcast, even among people more devoted to *The X-Files* than me and even more likely than me to have been home alone on a Friday night?

Question: What the fuck?

In the new, revisionist ending the alert viewer catches a detail not in the original broadcast. The appearance of this new detail may or may not be the point at which a new ending to the episode was spliced in. I refer obviously to the sight of Fox Mulder running out into the storm wearing the same t-shirt that he was wearing in the previous scene but with a now different pair of pants – a pair of khaki, cargo pants manufactured by that store that calls itself Banana Republic.

Side note: I recognized the brand because those are the cargo pants that my Older Brother wears. I am not saying that my Older Brother is necessarily aware that by wearing pants he bought from a store named Banana Republic he is essentially mocking himself, his tiny country and the aspirations of his compatriots. I am not saying that my Older Brother spending money at a store with a problematic name is or is not proof that he is insufficiently sympathetic to the cause of Puerto Rican independence. And I am not drawing any conclusions about what that may or may not say about his personality in general.

Or his principles.

Or his I.Q.

(Just like I cannot confirm or deny my Older Brother's suspicion that I end up at after school detention so consistently every afternoon, to use his phrase, "on purpose." And I am not conceding that my being in after school detention so consistently every afternoon is or is not any of my Older Brother's business.)

Sorry.

Do me a favor. Forget I mentioned my Older Brother.

My point: Why is Fox Mulder suddenly wearing a different pair of pants and why would the studio commit such a glaring continuity error? Might the costume department have been operating under orders to make sure and purchase the pants from the retail chain with the potentially inflammatory name? Question: Why would the costume department do that?

Answer: Have you ever heard of diversionary tactics?

Isn't it likely that the viewer is meant to be distracted by, on the one hand, this detail of costuming, this obviously offensive provocation, so that they then, on the other hand, more readily accept the tragic (but oddly glossed over) abduction of Álvaro by the aliens? How plausible would it otherwise be, in this new revisionist ending, that Álvaro leaves the shelter of the observatory without having an escape plan? How believable would it seem that a trained FBI agent searches thoroughly for Álvaro, shouting his name into the hurricane / hailstorm, but only manages to find Álvaro just as the teenager is being lifted up by one of his ankles into the alien spacecraft? Would we otherwise have accepted the dispiriting scene in which Álvaro reaches out for Mulder's hand just as the pull of the alien spacecraft proves to be too strong, the camera lingering on Álvaro's terrified expression as he disappears forever?

People: In the new revisionist ending they never even explain why he had a Mexican accent.

When it began to dawn on me what the studio was doing, how the original episode was being rewritten, and believe me I know how this must sound, I started to write down the details of the episode, not just the plot, but its entire sequence, shot by shot, so at least there would be a record. Then I realized how dangerous it was to keep a written record like that, because of the risk that it could be discovered. So I decided I would have to destroy the written account and memorize the original episode, recite it to myself when I was alone and carry the secret within me where no one could see it.

Every night I review to myself the events of the original broadcast trying desperately to keep them recorded in my memory. But each time I recite the episode to myself, more and more details from that original broadcast slip away and are slowly replaced by new, revisionist details. I try and remember the look of relief on Álvaro's face when Fox agrees to follow him into the secret tunnel, but lately all I can recall is the terror in Álvaro's eyes as he realizes he can't escape and is pulled into the alien spacecraft. Even if I know it's not true, even if I know it didn't happen, I can't let go of the idea that Álvaro was abducted and is alone now, in captivity, afraid and that Mulder was too late.

Of course what they never show us on television and what no one ever wants to talk about is how the alien invasion continues. How the alien invasion is happening right now, as I speak, and eventually the aliens will reprogram your television sets so that all you remember is an episode in which Álvaro disappears, is never heard from again and Mulder continues to work in the shadows with the same, sad expression on his face.

*End of Act I*

## ACT II
### A Short Play

### Scene 1.

*We are now in the present day. A modest house in Bayamón, Puerto Rico. Iron bars in the windows.*

*We begin in a small, second bedroom with inexpensive, self-assemble furniture – there is a bed and a temporary cot.* PATRIA *has just unpacked.*

NÉSTOR *watches her from the doorway of the bedroom.*

**NÉSTOR.** My mother didn't talk your ear off did she?

**PATRIA.** No, no, your mother's great.

**NÉSTOR.** She's old now. She's got a lot of difficulties.

**PATRIA.** I noticed she forgets a few things.

**NÉSTOR.** No, you know what it is? It's that, for example, if she says something, you can't assume it's true. She's old now.

**PATRIA.** We actually managed to communicate a bit.

**NÉSTOR.** She won't bother you at night. We give her medication, so.

**PATRIA.** I don't mind.

**NÉSTOR.** She snores, though.

**PATRIA.** Really, it's fine.

**NÉSTOR.** We don't have much room but we offer what we have. This way at least you can tell your friends you're having an authentic Puerto Rican experience, right?

**PATRIA.** It's changed so much. Driving in from the airport we passed a Walmart.

**NÉSTOR.** Don't they have big stores in New York?

**PATRIA.** No, I just meant that here on the island I would – Nothing. Forget it. My parents are from here.

**NÉSTOR.** Oh ok.

**PATRIA.** [*Trying again.*] Your mother said this was Álvaro's room before?

**NÉSTOR.** Both of ours, actually.

**PATRIA.** Wow. For me to be in the same room your brother grew up in –

**NÉSTOR.** Oh, before I forget, don't take photos or anything.

**PATRIA.** Ok.

**NÉSTOR.** We're a private family.

**PATRIA.** No problem.

**NÉSTOR.** I saw people writing things on the internet saying they were going through my brother's things? His private things, I guess.

**PATRIA.** Yes, sorry, we couldn't exactly ask him.

**NÉSTOR.** It's good that we're talking now.

**PATRIA.** The landlord barely gave us time to clear out the apartment, there was so much to sort through and we didn't want to throw away anything valuable or throw away anything, really. And a lot of people were asking to gather there, to touch something, to say goodbye and. That's why we shared what we did. A few of us called you but –

**NÉSTOR.** I was taking care of my mother. It's like a second job.

**PATRIA.** No, I know.

**NÉSTOR.** I couldn't just leave her alone and fly to New York.

**PATRIA.** I'm sure.

**NÉSTOR.** My wife sent flowers. To the funeral home there?

**PATRIA.** They were beautiful.

**NÉSTOR.** Probably we all seem really different from how Álvaro described us, right?

**PATRIA.** Sure, I guess.

**NÉSTOR.** It's good that we're finally talking.

[*Beat.*]

**PATRIA.** Do you remember, I'm just curious. What the layout was, when your brother – I mean both you and your brother – were growing up in here?

**NÉSTOR.** Layout of what?

**PATRIA.** The bedroom. I'm wondering where his bed used to be. I'm wondering what he looked at when he lay down to sleep.

**NÉSTOR.** No one is going to remember stuff like that.

### Scene 2.

*Another day. The living room.* OLGA *in her wheelchair.* ANA *is feeding* OLGA *flavored yogurt, with a spoon.*

**OLGA.** Is it time for my pill?

**ANA.** The pill is for bedtime. Right now it's noon.

**OLGA.** Who hired you?

**ANA.** I married your son, remember?

**OLGA.** My son is dead.

**ANA.** Not Álvaro. Your other son.

**OLGA.** You married Néstor?

**ANA.** You were at the ceremony.

**OLGA.** But you're so old.

**ANA.** Is that what you think?

[*Beat.*]

**OLGA.** Is it time for my pill?

**ANA.** It will be, if you don't start being nice.


### Scene 3.


BEBA, PATRIA *and* NÉSTOR, *mid-conversation. They may be watching* BEBA *make coffee. Everyone is standing.*

**BEBA.** Where is he buried?

**PATRIA.** He was cremated, actually.

**BEBA.** No, because I thought maybe one day I would go visit where he's buried, but I didn't know where that was.

**PATRIA.** Cremation is what Álvaro wanted.

**NÉSTOR.** How do you know that?

**BEBA.** We're just curious.

**PATRIA.** It's fine. He mentioned it, in passing.

**BEBA.** Me? I want to be put in the ground. I want to feel the dirt on top of me. Some Puerto Ricans, if they move to the United States, they say they want to be brought back and buried here when they die. On the island. But that's a personal decision.

**NÉSTOR.** Where are his ashes, if you don't mind me asking?

**PATRIA.** We scattered them in the harbor.

**BEBA.** It's a personal decision.

**NÉSTOR.** To me it sounds sad to end up like that. In the water, roaming.

**BEBA.** But you two were always different. Some say water and vinegar, but I always said Clorox and ammonia. Always arguing. When did that start, Néstor?

**NÉSTOR.** [*To* PATRIA.] You have to realize, my little brother had a lot of conflicts.

**BEBA.** He and I got along. He would come next door and watch me smoke. And we talked…

[*A gesture indicating long conversations.*]

**NÉSTOR.** He fought with you also.

**BEBA.** No, never.

**NÉSTOR.** You fought after the dog fights.

**BEBA.** Maybe we fought. But I don't know why. Because I agreed with him. Really, I was on his side.

**PATRIA.** What's this about dog fights?

**BEBA.** Néstor, forget about the dog. No come here, because I wanted to ask you about the permissions. When are you going to sign the permissions?

**NÉSTOR.** Now you want to change the topic?

**BEBA.** She traveled all this way. And signing those permissions takes two minutes. You read, you sign.

**NÉSTOR.** [*Off.*] Anita! All of a sudden, our neighbor doesn't like to gossip. Now all she wants to do is talk about contracts!

**PATRIA.** He should take the time he needs. The deal was I could come and visit and we would discuss the possibility.

**NÉSTOR.** Thank you.

**BEBA.** [*To* NÉSTOR.] And I didn't take Álvaro to a dog fight just because. I drove him there because I thought it would be good for him. I don't know, to meet new friends.

**NÉSTOR.** [*Dubious.*] Ahhh.

**BEBA.** [To PATRIA.] You don't know what it was like. You didn't know him then.

**NÉSTOR.** Let's just say, he didn't make it easy on his family.

**BEBA.** That Álvaro should always keep his distance from this one, that I could understand. But by the time he started at La Yupi – he was dressing like no one else dressed. He wore sandals that supposedly were designed by the Tainos, a rope for a belt...

[*A gesture indicating the full list of accessories.*]

**NÉSTOR.** La Yupi is the university here.

**PATRIA.** No, I know.

**BEBA.** And maybe part of me admired Álvaro – to a point. Because for example, he helped to publish a little newspaper that somehow was going to achieve independence for Puerto Rico. Only students read that newspaper, but Álvaro took it seriously. Except he also took things too far. If he found a spider in the house, he would carry it outside because didn't we realize that spider was just as Puerto Rican as any of us. And that the Tainos were peaceful and so we had to be peaceful and...

[*A gesture indicating the full party line.*]

And the rest of the students, well, I got the impression they made fun of him a little.

**NÉSTOR.** It's fine to have beliefs but what if nobody has heard of those beliefs?

**PATRIA.** He was an outsider.

**BEBA.** Not always. Because there's a detail here. No, listen. At that time, anything that came from the lower classes was in fashion. The students believed that the more barefoot and uneducated something was, the more remote the little shit of a town where it happened, then the more Puerto Rican it was. And for that reason some of the male students used to go into the interior, to see dog fights.

**PATRIA.** I can't imagine Álvaro going to a place like that.

**BEBA.** Well, let me tell you. One day, some of those students called Álvaro and they left a message on the machine. They said, Look, the bus left without us and now we're stranded here, growing roots, with no way to get to the dog fights. Call us back if you have a car.
And I said, Álvaro, come on. I'll drive you and your friends.
He said, No. If I go, I'll be like this –

[*Covers her eyes in aversion.*]

I told him, Those are your comrades. (I don't talk like that usually, but on that day I did.) I told him, Those are your comrades and they need your help. And I convinced him. And you know what? He was like this –

[*Opens both her eyes wide as they can go, with her fingers.*]

I don't know if from interest or fear, but he was like this.

[*Opens both her eyes wide as they can go, with her fingers.*]

And the other students they bought him rum and put their arms around his shoulders and said Álvaro isn't so bad. We like him now. So on that day at least, Álvaro tasted acceptance.

Problem was, after that Álvaro went to see dog fights all the time. And he got his own dog that he started to train. A little puppy that he named Monster. And when I would drive Álvaro to the center, because at that time I was still working as a beautician, we would drive past dogs on the street and he would say, Oh Monster would kill that dog in two minutes. Or that other one – maybe Monster would need five minutes to kill. He classified every dog we passed according to the time it would take for his pit bull named Monster to kill it.

It should have made me happy that he was fitting in more – but I don't know. He was saying all the things that men who like dog fights say – but he didn't seem himself. He didn't seem – happy.

**PATRIA.** And what did you tell him?

**BEBA.** Me? But what could I say?

**PATRIA.** I mean, you were the one who took him to the dog fight.

**BEBA.** It's that I wanted him to have new experiences! Meet people!

[*Beat.*]

You don't believe me?

**PATRIA.** He must have been very lonely to have tried impressing people that way.

[*Beat.*]

**BEBA.** You just put into words what I never got a chance to say to him.

[*To* NÉSTOR.]

See? That's why she was friends with Álvaro.

**PATRIA.** Better you don't tell me what happened to that dog.

**BEBA.** Ah, but don't lose faith in Álvaro. The day before Monster's first fight, he took that dog, drove across the island and gave it to an aunt of his who lives in Ponce or somewhere.

**NÉSTOR.** Tía Elsa.

**BEBA.** And he dropped out of La Yupi. Got a job at one of the big hotels. Saved every cent until he had the airfare to fly to New York. He was gone before Christmas. Like that.

[BEBA *snaps.*]

If only I could talk to him now.

[*Beat.*]

Did he ever mention any of this to you?

**PATRIA.** No, he didn't.

**BEBA.** I wasn't sure. Because he left and...

[BEBA *shrugs.*]

**NÉSTOR.** But the dog fights back then were better, no? Now the police are cracking down like crazy and you have to keep the fights secret.

**BEBA.** Have you heard a word we said?

**NÉSTOR.** What? If I like dog fights I'm not allowed to talk?

[*Off.*]

Anita, if we get a dog can we name it Monster?

[*To* BEBA.]

I had forgotten how much I like that name, Monster.

[ANA *is at the door of the room.*]

**ANA.** You said something?

**NÉSTOR.** We should get a dog.

**BEBA.** See? He misses the point.

[ANA *has crossed and exited towards the other end of the kitchen.*]

**NÉSTOR.** Was it named Monster or not?

**BEBA.** You don't change.

**NÉSTOR.** Maybe I don't. But you change in the sense that you lost your looks. What? A joke! Come on. With Anita at least I lucked out.

[*Off.*]

Isn't that right Anita?

**BEBA.** Néstor, focus. The permissions. Wouldn't it be nice to walk into a store and be able to buy Álvaro's book?

**NÉSTOR.** Wouldn't it be nice if you let me finish reading the stories first, so I can decide?

[ANA *re-enters with a small trash bag, dumps it and exits.*]

**BEBA.** I think you'd feel better if you signed.

**PATRIA.** [*To* BEBA.] I can't stop thinking about that story you shared, about Álvaro and the dogs?

**BEBA.** Neither can I.

**PATRIA.** Have you read his stories?

**BEBA.** I want to. What are they about?

**PATRIA.** Each story is about a different television episode, but not really. The stories connect and you learn things about the family at the center of them.

**BEBA.** Néstor was saying the stories are mostly about *The X-Files?*

**PATRIA.** *The X-Files* are a motif, I guess.

**BEBA.** I imagine with a book like that you have to sit down and savor it, before you understand.

**PATRIA.** That's, yeah, exactly what you said.

**BEBA.** Maybe this one can lend me the stories to read. And then after you and I can talk about them. (I never get to talk about things like that.)

**PATRIA.** That would make me very happy. When I met you right away I –

**NÉSTOR.** [*To* PATRIA.] You're wrong. About what you said before.

[*Beat.*]

Because if Álvaro was so lonely, then why did he spend years pushing people away? To me that makes no sense.

**BEBA.** Néstor, I think maybe –

**NÉSTOR.** You know what? Can other people speak now? Because she doesn't know the history, but you? You should know better than to make him sound like such an angel.

[*To* PATRIA.]

You know I looked for news about him on the internet a few times? Just randomly. And I was proud ok, to discover newspapers that had written articles about him. Because despite everything, that was my little brother. And I read this one interview, ok. Where he was saying that he didn't have any photographs of himself as a child. That he left Puerto Rico without any photographs from when he was little. And I got the stupendous idea of acting like a brother and putting an old photo of Álvaro in an envelope and –

[*An airmail gesture.*]

– mailing it to him. A photo of him and me, standing together, when we were this high. He was wearing glasses and corduroy pants and so much pomade in his hair. I didn't write a letter or anything because to be honest I can't express myself the way that he could. I just put the photo in an envelope and –

[*The airmail gesture.*]

And I thought, oh, maybe one day my brother will let me hug him again and I'll smell that pomade and it will be like smelling our childhood.

[*The airmail gesture.*]

Nothing. Never heard back.

[*A beat, then* PATRIA *decides to say –* ]

**PATRIA.** I know the photo you mean.

**NÉSTOR.** What are you talking about?

**PATRIA.** He showed it to me. You both had book bags?

**NÉSTOR.** Yeah. We were standing right in front of that door.

**PATRIA.** I saw the photo.

**NÉSTOR.** He hung it up or something? Don't tell me he had it up on his wall?

[*Off of* PATRIA's *reaction.*]

What?

**PATRIA.** He didn't have it up.

**NÉSTOR.** Why do you say it like that?

**PATRIA.** Nothing, he – nothing.

**NÉSTOR.** Did he use it for toilet paper?

**PATRIA.** No, no, it was, he showed it to me but it was painful for him.

**NÉSTOR.** OK.

**BEBA.** Néstor, he kept the photo.

**NÉSTOR.** No, because of the way she said it. Like, I don't know.

**PATRIA.** It was painful for him.

**NÉSTOR.** I gave him a present and that was painful for him?

**PATRIA.** He just –

**NÉSTOR.** He just asked for a family photograph on the internet, to make himself look sad I guess?

**PATRIA.** He didn't ask, he was just –

**NÉSTOR.** But I'm the one who sent it!

[*Pause.*]

**PATRIA.** [*Carefully...*] I think he had trouble trusting the gesture because –

**NÉSTOR.** Trust me, I knew him longer than you did.

**PATRIA.** But more recently, in the past few years, it's not like you and he were exactly –

**NÉSTOR.** We grew up together.

**PATRIA.** I, I know I could never know him like you knew him, but. It's like you – when you talk about him moving away and withdrawing, ok but sometimes it sounds like you're blaming him.

**NÉSTOR.** [*Very loud.*] FOR WHAT?!

**BEBA.** Néstor.

**NÉSTOR.** WHAT ARE YOU INSINUATING? WHAT? Instead of talking to his family like a normal person, instead of coming here to say what he wanted to say he moves away and talks bad about his family to strangers? No. Ok, no.

**BEBA.** The judge talked to you about this, about the way you get –

**NÉSTOR.** But after I invite her into my house she can talk to me like I'm garbage. And no, I'm sorry. There are limits. We're not garbage.

**BEBA.** Look, she can move next door with me if you prefer.

**NÉSTOR.** Move?

[*Deadpan.*]

Why would she move? I invited her here so she could see for herself. So let her see.

We're a normal family. But she has to understand my brother had conflicts and he made up lies. Then when people didn't believe him, well you know how it ended. And my mother – even after the things he said – she keeps his photo by her bed? People talk about him like he was so smart? Strangers call here saying drop everything and fly to New York? No, I'm sorry. Who was here taking care of my mother? Did he even think, for a minute, what I would have to go through when I told my mother the news that her youngest son jumped in front of a train? He wasn't even considerate enough to wait, I don't know, just a few more years until she dies. Because that is all he had to do, just tough it out a few more years.

I'm the one who lives in this house and watches our mother fall apart. Ask our neighbor here. There was the time, no, no, why even tell you. Did you know she used to spend the night calling his number in New York? She would call, forget she called, then call again. All night. Pleading for him to call his own mother. You should have seen how many pages that phone bill was. And me, trying to do the right thing. I didn't want her to suffer. So I had to take the phone extension out of her room. And my own mother looks at me and says, Why? Why are you taking away my phone? Are you jealous? That's what she said to me. But instead you believe my brother. Who abandoned her. While I'm here trying not to drown.

[NÉSTOR *is crying.* BEBA *gets up to wipe his face and hug him. She is firm.* NÉSTOR *mostly resists her.*]

**PATRIA.** I never said that I thought —

**NÉSTOR.** And I send him a photograph in the mail and he doesn't even respond?

**PATRIA.** I was just trying to explain —

**NÉSTOR.** No, you just take the side of someone who told half of New York how messed up my family was. Running around, writing science fiction stories nobody wanted to read.

[*Beat.*]

And you know what? Maybe I'll let you publish those stories. Because I'm an idiot. And part of me thinks, Oh maybe my little brother is stuck in purgatory and looking down at us and maybe he'll see me being generous and he'll finally apologize to some stupid angel or something. Maybe.

**BEBA.** Blow your nose.

**NÉSTOR.** So I'm like 90% that I'll say yes and sign your piece of shit contract. But respect this house. Respect our way of making decisions.

**PATRIA.** I do. Completely. I do.

**NÉSTOR.** I'll let you know when I decide.

**PATRIA.** Thank you.

**NÉSTOR.** We're not garbage.

[ANA *enters. She's holding a few pieces of clean laundry.*]

**ANA.** Your mother can hear the yelling.

**NÉSTOR.** Where the fuck have you been? I've been talking into the other room like an idiot. You don't answer now?

**ANA.** I was changing your mother.

[ANA *crosses to place down the laundry. She turns around and faces the group. Beat.*]

**ANA.** What did you want?

**NÉSTOR.** I'm getting a dog. Guess what his name is going to be?

## Scene 4.

*Late at night.*

*From underneath the door to the second bedroom, we see a light is on.*

*In the living room,* ANA *sits in a chair with* NÉSTOR *sitting on the floor between her feet, next to a lamp.* ANA *is going through* NÉSTOR's *hair, picking out the gray ones.*

**NÉSTOR.** Ow.

**ANA.** I swear, these gray hairs are multiplying.

**NÉSTOR.** You love them.

**ANA.** We could just color them.

**NÉSTOR.** You want to keep your voice down?

**ANA.** I just bought a box if you don't mind having the same color as me.

**NÉSTOR.** Can we move into our bedroom? Some privacy?

**ANA.** Did you fix the lamp in there yet?

[*Given that the answer is no,* ANA *resumes her work.*]

**NÉSTOR.** Ow.

Ow.

[NÉSTOR *grabs* ANA's *wrist.*]

Wait.

[*Beat.*]

Is she up?

**ANA.** Then don't be so loud.

**NÉSTOR.** I don't want her to walk in and see.

[NÉSTOR *releases* ANA's *wrist.*]

**ANA.** The way you let her come in here and try to run things? I wouldn't trust her.

**NÉSTOR.** I have it under control.

[ANA *plucks a gray.*]

Ow.

**ANA.** How do you know she gave you all the stories to read? She could have held some back.

**NÉSTOR.** Where do you even get an idea like that?

**ANA.** If I were her, that's what I would do.

[ANA *plucks a gray.* NÉSTOR *doesn't react. Beat.*
ANA *plucks another.* NÉSTOR *doesn't react.*]

**ANA.** Now you got quiet.

**NÉSTOR.** Why do you put thoughts in my head?

[ANA *looks for another gray hair.*
NÉSTOR *grabs her wrist, holds it tightly away from his head.*]

**ANA.** Ah ah. Don't bruise me.

**NÉSTOR.** You didn't say you love them.

[ANA *tries to pull her arm away,* NÉSTOR *holds it tight.*]

**ANA.** When?

**NÉSTOR.** Before, when I said you loved me having grey hairs.

**ANA.** I love them.

[NÉSTOR *releases her.* ANA *massages her wrist then resumes looking for gray hairs.*
NÉSTOR *is thinking the thought* ANA *put in his head.*]


## Scene 5.


*Morning.*

OLGA *in her bed, on her back.* ANA *and* BEBA *preparing to change* OLGA's *adult diaper.*

**ANA.** Olga, we're going to change you now, ok? Beba is going to help.

**OLGA.** It's not my fault.

**BEBA.** No one said it was your fault.

**OLGA.** Let me go to the bathroom by myself.

**ANA.** You can't, you fall.

**OLGA.** When did I fall?

**BEBA.** You haven't told me your opinion of your visitor.

**ANA.** Can you get me that box of wipes – these are almost out.

**BEBA.** How many?

**ANA.** You always want a full box. You never know how many you're going to need.

[BEBA *hands her a box of wipes.*]

**OLGA.** When did I fall?

**BEBA.** Tell me your impression of her because mine is maybe positive.

**ANA.** Néstor doesn't like her.

**BEBA.** Never mind him, what do you think?

**ANA.** Why should I have an opinion? No one asked me before they invited her. Olga, can you straighten your legs for me?

[ANA *uncrosses* OLGA's *knees.*]

**OLGA.** It's not my fault.

[ANA *lays down a blue, disposable underpad on* OLGA's *far side, tucking it in some, then starts to unfasten the diaper.*]

**BEBA.** Well your visitor – don't think I'm nosey but – do you think she's divorced?

**ANA.** With that personality, what do you think?

**BEBA.** I think she's interesting. She's an artist.

**ANA.** Please, divorced or an artist: What's the difference? Either way, women like that end up alone. Then they go around sticking their nose in other people's business. No offense.

**BEBA.** No, no offense.

**ANA.** Before I forget – grab Olga's pillow for me.

[BEBA *hands* ANA *the pillow.* ANA *places the pillow next to* OLGA's *head, on her far side.*]

I'm going to turn you on your side now, ok Olga?

**OLGA.** Later I'm going to dress myself.

[ANA *turns* OLGA *onto the blue bed pad and the pillow.* OLGA *is now on her side and* ANA *has a clear line of sight to* OLGA's *bottom.*]

**BEBA.** How does that rate?

**ANA.** Not too bad. I know it's a good sign when she shits but on days when she doesn't – honestly – I'm glad. I'm wiping ok, Olga? It won't take long. Can you hold her? Make sure she doesn't roll back?

**BEBA.** Please don't tell me you ever do this alone.

**ANA.** I have my method. I roll up the comforter and push it in here, behind her back, like a barrier.

**BEBA.** And then she can't move?

[ANA *is wiping* OLGA's *bottom, always front to back, going through a series of wipes.*]

**ANA.** Ay no Olga, come on, lift your knees for me ok?

**OLGA.** Why?

**ANA.** Exercise Olga, exercise.

**BEBA.** But your visitor she's smart, no?

**ANA.** You know who she reminds me of?

**BEBA.** Tell me.

**ANA.** Those girls who go to university and become anti-everything.

[ANA *rolls up the soiled diaper with the used wipes. Once the diaper has been bagged up,* ANA *begins applying ointment to* OLGA's *bottom.*]

**BEBA.** We're almost done Olgita.

**ANA.** Don't let her lower her knees.

**BEBA.** Is that a bed sore?

**ANA.** If they're not bleeding, the clinic doesn't even want to hear about them. Look, you have to admit, that woman is antagonizing my husband on purpose.

[ANA *is laying out a fresh diaper.*]

**BEBA.** Is Néstor going to sign finally?

**ANA.** Not if she keeps antagonizing.

**BEBA.** I've been trying to explain to your husband that he should do the right thing.

**ANA.** Careful, because you're having the opposite effect. If you push Néstor, he just digs in. With a man like that, it's better to use psychology.

**BEBA.** Then maybe I can mention, I don't know, that she can be a little assertive but that she means well.

[*Off of* ANA's *hmph.*]

What?

**ANA.** No, it's just that supposedly you never talk bad about anyone.

**BEBA.** But you just told me to use psychology.

**ANA.** Please, I barely encouraged you.

**BEBA.** But –

**ANA.** Do me a favor. You see this blue line here? Where the lining starts? Beba, pay attention.

**BEBA.** I see it.

**ANA.** When we roll her back we want that line to stay above her crack ok?

**BEBA.** So one and two…

**ANA.** But hold her straight. She has to be straight. Ok and three.

[ANA *and* BEBA *have rolled* OLGA *onto her backside again.*]

**BEBA.** Not so bad right, Olgita?

**OLGA.** I didn't do anything wrong.

**BEBA.** Shit happily Olgita, it's normal.

[ANA *is taping up the diaper straps, making adjustments.*]

**ANA.** I try and make the diaper as even as possible on both sides, otherwise it chafes and she fidgets.

**BEBA.** Of course.

[ANA *is showing* BEBA *how snug the diaper fits.*]

**ANA.** Every time I change her I give myself a grade. Usually I get at least a B-. Today, I don't know. C? C-? I'm distracted today.

**BEBA.** What do you think Olga? Should Néstor sign the permission?

**OLGA.** It's not my fault.

**BEBA.** No one said it was. But what about your son's stories?

**OLGA.** I know about the stories. They're not my fault. They're not my fault. They're not my fault.

**ANA.** Don't upset her. Later she can't sleep and I'm the one who pays the price.


## Scene 6.


*Twilight, after the afternoon rain. The front door is open and just outside it* BEBA *sits in a chair, placed on the grass, smoking. In the living room,* NÉSTOR *is going through photos on his phone.* OLGA *in her wheelchair in a corner, sleepy.* PATRIA *on the sofa.*

**BEBA.** Also, if you decide, you could make it as a temporary installation. I mean, if you haven't picked out the style you want. Just a few big tiles,

[*Indicating the size.*]

the heavy stone ones, no?,

[*Indicating the placement.*]

ping, pam, poom.

[*Ponders a second.*]

Maybe also another row of ting, tam, toom. There. Easy.

**NÉSTOR.** Do you mind if I decorate my own house?

**BEBA.** No, of course. I'm just remarking because you agreed a porch was a good idea. Since two years ago you said.

**PATRIA.** When your mother appears in Álvaro's stories, which is like in half of them, a lot of times she's outside in a garden. Trimming, watering, always with plants.

**BEBA.** That's the way she was – just what you said. She liked things you plant in one spot and then they stay in that spot. Things with roots.

**NÉSTOR.** [*In reference to the photos on his phone, but without showing anyone.*] See, this is the kind of dog I want a puppy from.

**BEBA.** But the way this house is there's no walkway. You step outside and grass. Mud.

**NÉSTOR.** This dog was a champion fighter before she lost an eye.

**BEBA.** And now, with her in that chair there's no way. She hasn't sat outside in her own garden in, don't even ask me.

**NÉSTOR.** They should give that dog an eye-patch.

**BEBA.** Olga, don't you wish we could wheel you outside anytime you wanted? So you could see the lemon tree?

**NÉSTOR.** Supposedly her ovaries still work.

**BEBA.** Olgita, are you sleepy? Hey, did Anita give her a pill?

**PATRIA.** I could build you a porch.

[*Beat.*]

**NÉSTOR.** What? You can build?

**PATRIA.** Nothing complicated. Concrete. A brick wall if you want. Before I ran a little contracting business with my girlfriend. I retiled your brother's bathroom. He lived in a rental, but.

**NÉSTOR.** Thank you, we're fine.

**PATRIA.** I wouldn't charge you.

**BEBA.** What a relief, no? So basically at this time of day, when it's not so hot, we can wheel her outside so she can touch the plants. Or if I'm smoking I don't have to shout across the room and –

[NÉSTOR *is not dealing with his phone right now.*]

**NÉSTOR.** I finished reading the stories.

**PATRIA.** Oh. Great.

**NÉSTOR.** There weren't that many stories, when you think about it.

**PATRIA.** It depends, I guess, I mean –

**NÉSTOR.** Not that many pages at all. Which surprised me.

[*Beat.*
PATRIA *looks away from* NÉSTOR.]

**BEBA.** Can you make a smooth porch, so there's no steps?

**PATRIA.** Yeah, easy.

**NÉSTOR.** I know what you're doing.

**PATRIA.** Sorry?

**NÉSTOR.** You're trying to make us feel grateful to you.

**PATRIA.** No, I'm –

**NÉSTOR.** So then we owe you.

**PATRIA.** I was offering for your brother. That's all. I was offering for his sake.

[*Silence.*
BEBA *takes a drag, looks away. She looks back in the living room, then back out.*
*No one says anything.*]

**BEBA.** It'd be better without steps. Because with the wheels on that chair.

[NÉSTOR *stands abruptly and walks over to* OLGA. *He bends his knees to crouch down, grips the arms of her chair and speaks to her, his face at the same level as hers.*]

**NÉSTOR.** You want to go outside? These people say you're being neglected because you don't go outside enough.

[NÉSTOR *lifts his mother's head.*]

Are you being neglected? I know I never moved away to New York and that I see you everyday but maybe you feel neglected?

[*Beat.*]

You want a porch?

[*Beat.*]

Ok, come here. Put your arms around my neck,

[NÉSTOR *takes his mother's arms and drapes them over his shoulders.*]

there, and hold on to me, ok. Are you ready? Ready for a ride?

**BEBA.** Néstor, she's barely awake.

**NÉSTOR.** And up you go. I got you. I got you.

[NÉSTOR *has lifted* OLGA *up off her chair and is walking her towards the front door. He stands in front of* BEBA, *who is still seated.*]

Move.

[BEBA *gets up off her chair so* NÉSTOR *can set* OLGA *down.*]

**NÉSTOR.** [*Playfully, pinching her waist.*] Hey, you've gotten heavy. You put on some weight. You want to go on a diet?

[NÉSTOR *kisses his mother on the forehead, returns to where he was seated, sits down.*]

**NÉSTOR.** There.

[BEBA *puts out her cigarette, she is unsure where to stand.*

NÉSTOR *has resumed looking at the photos on his phone. He addresses* PATRIA.]

I've decided we can't sign the release. People want to read those stories now because my brother killed himself, not because the stories are any good. Sorry you wasted a trip.

**PATRIA.** But you said –

**NÉSTOR.** I changed my mind.

[*Silence.*

NÉSTOR *has returned his attention to the photos on his phone.*]

**PATRIA.** I'll go into town tomorrow and change my ticket.

**NÉSTOR.** Our neighbor here can give you a ride.

**PATRIA.** I wish we could talk about this.

**NÉSTOR.** [*To* BEBA.] Beba, has Ana texted you back?

**BEBA.** Not yet.

**NÉSTOR.** [*Without showing anyone.*] I want to show her these photos.

**BEBA.** Néstor, you think it's a good idea to get a dog like that in this house, with your mother?

**NÉSTOR.** Trust me, if I'm happy, she's happy.


## Scene 7.

*The next morning. The second bedroom.*

OLGA *is in her wheelchair. She is wearing a comfortable pair of pants with a drawstring waist. She pulls at the end of these drawstrings, trying to tie the ends into a knot. Her hands shake and her expression is one of deep concentration but she keeps her eyes closed during this process.*

PATRIA *watches her, from the cot.*

*Sounds of bustle from the kitchen.*

**PATRIA.** She's getting your breakfast now. We don't have a lot of time, if we want to talk.

[PATRIA *waits a moment but there is no response. She then kneels before* OLGA.]

Hello.

[*No answer.* OLGA *continues to try and tie the knot.*
PATRIA *gently approaches, puts her hand on* OLGA's *forearm.*]

Why do you keep your eyes closed if you're trying to tie a knot?

[*No answer.* OLGA *continues to try and tie the knot.*]

Here. Let me do it. No, just. It's ok.

[*Once* PATRIA *manages to get hold of the ends of the cord, she effortlessly ties the knot.*]

There. Is that better?

[*Beat.*]

Will you open your eyes for me?

[OLGA *opens her eyes.*]

**OLGA.** Who hired you?

**PATRIA.** No one hired me.

**OLGA.** I told my son we can't afford to hire people.

**PATRIA.** My name is Patria, remember? I'm a friend of your other son's.

**OLGA.** Which son?

**PATRIA.** Álvaro. The writer.

Have you read your son's stories?

**OLGA.** If he sent them to me then I read them.

**PATRIA.** There are some people who want to publish the stories your son wrote.

**OLGA.** Yes.

**PATRIA.** They want to publish his stories in a book.

**OLGA.** Will anyone read the book?

**PATRIA.** I believe they will.

**OLGA.** Don't tell his older brother. He gets jealous.

**PATRIA.** All I need is the family's permission.

**OLGA.** I always say, a mother can't choose favorites.

**PATRIA.** Álvaro loved you.

      *[Beat.]*

Did you hear what I said? Álvaro loved you.

**OLGA.** [*Clear-eyed.*] How do you know that?

**PATRIA.** Because you always show up in his stories. Because he always wrote about you.

**OLGA.** Álvaro wrote about me?

**PATRIA.** I didn't know if I should bring this up. I've been so nervous about it since I got here. I mean, I brought this document but I didn't know if I should ask you. Because I want to make sure you know what you want. Néstor doesn't want you to sign it but I think you can make your own decision, can't you?

**OLGA.** Yes.

**PATRIA.** If you sign this document, then we would have permission.

**OLGA.** My handwriting isn't steady.

**PATRIA.** But you agree that we can publish your son's stories, don't you?

      [OLGA *is pulling at the drawstring around her pants again.*]

Hello. Did you hear me?

**OLGA.** Yes.

**PATRIA.** You would tell me if you felt forced or if you didn't want to sign, wouldn't you?

**OLGA.** Yes, yes.

**PATRIA.** So you'll sign?

**OLGA.** Yes.

**PATRIA.** You're saying we can publish your son's stories?

**OLGA.** Yes. Yes.

**PATRIA.** That's such a relief.

**OLGA.** Yes. –

**PATRIA.** – I can't tell you –

**OLGA.** – Why are you crying?

**PATRIA.** It's just, thank you. Thank you. Do you want to read it first? Before you sign?

**OLGA.** My hands shake.

**PATRIA.** It's ok.

**OLGA.** No one can read my handwriting anymore.

**PATRIA.** Can you pick up this pen? Can you pick it up with your fingers?

**OLGA.** Will you do me a favor?

**PATRIA.** Of course.

**OLGA.** Can you untie this knot? It's scratching my belly.

**PATRIA.** Sorry, did I tie it too tightly?

**OLGA.** Untie it. Hurry up.

**PATRIA.** This might take a minute.

**OLGA.** What do you think we pay you for?

**PATRIA.** No, remember, I'm Patria. I'm not –

**OLGA.** If my son finds out you can't do your job he'll fire you. I can't defend you because I've always said we can't afford to hire anyone.

[*Beat.*]

**PATRIA.** If you want me to untie this knot, you have to sign your name here. Those are the rules. Here. Sign your name.

[PATRIA *holds* OLGA's *hand in place and* OLGA *signs the document.*]

**OLGA.** Like this?

**PATRIA.** Thank you.

[PATRIA *begins to fold up the document, then stands.*

OLGA *reaches up suddenly and grabs* PATRIA's *forearm.*]

**OLGA.** No one wants to tell me where my face is.


### Scene 8.


*In the living room,* NÉSTOR *is building a dog cage. He is sweating. He has three of the four walls up and is trying to attach the fourth wall, the front.*

*He succeeds, the cage is steady now.*

NÉSTOR *opens the door of the cage, then closes and locks it. Then he opens the door of the cage again, then closes and locks it. Opens it.*

NÉSTOR *looks up and sees that he has left the newspapers across the room. He gets up, crosses, retrieves the newspapers, returns and begins laying down layers of newspaper on the floor of the cage.*

NÉSTOR *feels the floor of the cage, now covered in newspaper. He closes the front gate. Locks it. Nods in approval.*

NÉSTOR *starts to attach the roof to the cage.*

ANA *enters from the rear of the house, quickly, with purse. She rushes to the door. She stops at the door, looks through her purse. Can't find her keys.*

ANA *crosses again, disappears into the rear of the house. Comes back out with her keys in her hand and crosses towards door. Opens the front door.* PATRIA *is there.*

**PATRIA.** Oh hi.

[ANA *rushes past* PATRIA *without saying anything.* PATRIA *hovers in the door, wonders if saying something would make things better or worse.*

PATRIA *steps into the house, closes the door behind her and crosses towards the second bedroom as we hear the sound of a car pulling out of the driveway.* NÉSTOR *doesn't look up from his work.*

PATRIA *stands in the doorway of the second bedroom, concerned about what she sees inside.*]

**PATRIA.** Did someone go through my luggage?

**NÉSTOR.** I did.

[*Beat.*]

My mother told me that the new girl I hired, the foreign one she called you, wanted her to sign some piece of paper. My mother has her moments of clarity, you know.

[*Silence.*

NÉSTOR *gets up, goes to the front door and turns the deadbolt. He leans his back against the front door.*

NÉSTOR *and* PATRIA *stare at each other across the room.*]

**NÉSTOR.** I figured you could do me a favor and maybe stand in front of me there and eat that piece of paper. Then you could digest it during your flight and shit it out when you get back to New York. How's that sound?

[PATRIA *reaches into her pocket, takes out her wallet. She pulls out the signed form, which she has folded into quarters.*

*She unfolds the form. She walks it over to the coffee table in the middle of the room and places it there.*

PATRIA *walks back to her end of the room.*

*Beat.*

NÉSTOR *walks to the coffee table. Picks up the contract, inspects it. Maybe shakes his head at the arrogance of it.*]

**PATRIA.** Won't you even let your brother have this?

[NÉSTOR *begins to very methodically tear the contract up, in long, irreparable strips.*]

**NÉSTOR.** How much did it cost you to come up with such a fancy document? And in English and everything. Then you fly down here and try to steal from my family?

**PATRIA.** [*Sardonically.*] Family? You weren't the ones who took care of him. We were. You weren't the ones who built a life with him. We were –

**NÉSTOR.** WHAT LIFE? HE KILLED HIMSELF!

**PATRIA.** Because of you!

[NÉSTOR *throws an object right at* PATRIA. PATRIA *dodges it. The object is smashed or the wall is dented.*]

**NÉSTOR.** Where are the missing stories? I want all the stories.

**PATRIA.** What difference does it make now?

**NÉSTOR.** They belong to his family –

                                        **PATRIA.** No.

– the copyright belongs to his
family –                               No.

– his legal family –

                                        He wrote them in New York –

– his blood family –

                                        – I didn't even bring them to
                                        Puerto Rico –

– you have to surrender them.

                                        YOU DON'T EVEN READ!

[*Beat.*

NÉSTOR *starts to walk to the television that is set against the wall of the living room.*]

**PATRIA.** I'm sorry.

[NÉSTOR *turns on the television.*

NÉSTOR *turns up the volume of the television, high.*

NÉSTOR *watching* PATRIA.]

If you're going to watch television, I'll repack and get out of…

[*Beat.*

PATRIA *makes a sudden dash for the front door.* NÉSTOR *leaps towards the center of the room, cutting her off and tackling her.*

*The ensuing is brutal, fast and messy.* PATRIA *is kicking* NÉSTOR *trying to break free. The coffee table shatters. The dog cage collapses.* PATRIA *manages to stand and almost makes it to the front door before* NÉSTOR *grabs her, spins her around and punches her in the face, quite hard.*

PATRIA *coils up in pain.* NÉSTOR *grabs one of her ankles and drags her to the center of the room. Once there, it appears as if* NÉSTOR *is going through* PATRIA's *pockets until it becomes clear that he is intent on removing her pants.* PATRIA *does not recover until* NÉSTOR *has all but succeeded.* NÉSTOR *is trying to rape her.*

PATRIA *recovers sufficiently to start kicking wildly. They struggle, entangled.* PATRIA *is trying to get her hands free to defend herself. She succeeds and jams the palm of her hand into* NÉSTOR's *nose in an upward motion.* NÉSTOR *recoils, screaming. There is a lot of blood.*

PATRIA *is free. She grabs her pants and rushes the front door, turns the deadbolt and runs out.*

*The front door is open, the bright afternoon light pours inside the house.*

*The television is on, loud.*

NÉSTOR *is on the floor, holding his face, bleeding.*]


### Scene 9.


*Late night. The broken coffee table has been swept into a pile. The dog crate is there, dismantled from being knocked about.* BEBA *is doing what she can to clean up. At some point,* BEBA *walks over to the collapsed dog crate and starts trying to reassemble it. We watch her efforts for a bit.*

PATRIA *enters from the second bedroom, pulling her carry-on. She is bruised on her neck, on her face, but she is mobile.*

BEBA *stops working. They consider each other.*

**BEBA.** I made coffee.

**PATRIA.** No thanks.

[PATRIA *leaves her luggage near the door to the second bedroom and walks over to the window. She peers out the window.*]

**BEBA.** They'll honk.

**PATRIA.** It's so late.

**BEBA.** They don't care. They'll honk.

**PATRIA.** Are you here to make sure I don't steal anything? Vandalize the place?

**BEBA.** Olga can't be left alone.

**PATRIA.** Sorry. Right.

**BEBA.** You can sit down. It's fine.

**PATRIA.** It hurts if I sit.

> [*Beat.*
>
> BEBA *goes back to working on the dog crate.*]

**BEBA.** I wish you'd steal this dog crate actually. I wouldn't stop you.

**PATRIA.** I'm not checking luggage. There's no – .
Listen to me.

**BEBA.** You could throw it out. Offer it to the taxi driver.

**PATRIA.** You could do those things.

> [*Silence.*
>
> BEBA *steps away from the dog crate, which is still not fully repaired. She sits in a chair.*
>
> *Headlights in the window.* PATRIA *starts for her luggage.*]

**PATRIA.** Ok, well. This is it then.

> [*The headlights have moved past. It wasn't the taxi.*]

**BEBA.** They'll honk.

> [*Beat.*]

Anita called. They're waiting on an X-ray. They bandaged his nose and well. They have to wait. There's maybe other tests, I'm guessing.

> [*Beat.*]

I told her you had already left. I told her your plane was gone so there was no point in her calling the police.

**PATRIA.** Did you tell her that what she should do is call the police on her husband?

**BEBA.** If I said something like that, it would only make things worse.

**PATRIA.** Worse than what?

**BEBA.** I'm not trying to start an argument.

> [*Beat.*]

**PATRIA.** There was a moment there when he was trying to force me. No, you have to hear this. I'm certain of it. He took off my pants and if things hadn't – If I hadn't –

**BEBA.** I know what he tried to do.

**PATRIA.** You know what, exactly?

**BEBA.** I believe you.

**PATRIA.** He admitted it?

**BEBA.** Néstor? Admit something? No.

> [*Beat.*]

When I heard him yelling for help I came over from next door and saw him staggering on the lawn. He was angry and. Saying that there was blood on his phone so he couldn't make out the numbers. There was so much blood. He said you had — It doesn't matter what he said because —

**PATRIA.** No, tell me, I want to —

**BEBA.** Listen.

When I finally came inside here to check on Olga I noticed the television was on and that the volume was so loud — louder than anyone would have needed it to be. And, I recognized that trick right away. I've seen him do that before.

Turning up the volume like that? That was something Néstor use to do with Álvaro. This was a long time ago — Néstor would move the television into the bedroom they shared and then Néstor would drag Álvaro in there with him and lock the door. I can't remember what year it started, it —. Néstor kept the volume so loud that no one could hear what was happening inside that room.

Nobody realized it at the time. What I'm telling you now is something I pieced together over the years. And today when I came in and saw the television blaring I...

I'm sorry.

[*Beat.*]

**PATRIA.** It would have meant so much for Álvaro to hear you say that.

**BEBA.** You don't think I realize that? Go on, say whatever insult you want to say to me. It can't be worse than what I've called myself. Go on.

**PATRIA.** That's not why I came to Puerto Rico, is it?

[*Beat.*]

**BEBA.** What's going to happen now, with Álvaro's stories?

**PATRIA.** I don't know.

Sorry, I lied. I know exactly what's going to happen. They won't get published. A few friends of his will pass the stories around, maybe, for a while. And decades from now, when the copyright expires, no one will remember enough to give a shit.

**BEBA.** Don't say that.

**PATRIA.** You prefer I lie?

**BEBA.** Isn't there anything you can do? There must be a way, no?

[*Beat.*]

**PATRIA.** Should I call the dispatcher again?

**BEBA.** Where did you find this cab company?

**PATRIA.** There was a logo with the three horses. It's not like I hailed one off the street.

**BEBA.** It's that you hear reports, on the news.

**PATRIA.** I'll be fine.

> [*Headlights in the window. A honk.*]

**PATRIA.** So. For real this time.

**BEBA.** Wait. Before you go, you need to know that Álvaro's mother didn't know either – she couldn't have. She can't defend herself anymore but –. No. Not the Olga I knew.

What?

**PATRIA.** Nothing.

**BEBA.** Do you believe me?

> [*More honking.*]

**PATRIA.** I have to go.

**BEBA.** Here, I'll walk you to the taxi.

**PATRIA.** There's no need.

**BEBA.** But that way the driver overhears me say that I'm going to stay up until I receive your call from the airport. It will make me feel better.

**PATRIA.** Please don't.

> [PATRIA *retrieves her carry-on, exits and closes the front door behind her.*
> *Eventually the sound of a car door slamming shut and the headlights pull away.*
> BEBA *stands there.*
> *Eventually she sits back down near the dog cage. She holds the pieces in her hands. She considers her options. Is she going to rebuild the dog cage?*
> *From the next room we hear...* ]

**OLGA.** [*Off.*] Álvaro.

> [*Beat.*]

Álvaro.

**BEBA.** Is there something you need Olga?

**OLGA.** [*Off.*] Álvaro.

**BEBA.** What's wrong?

**OLGA.** [*Off.*] I can't untie this knot.

### *End of Act II*

## ACT III
### Another Television Episode

*Twenty-four years before the end of Act II.*

ÁLVARO *facing the audience, isolated in light. Initially,* ÁLVARO *is all we can see. There might be a figure next to him in the dark, but we can't see who. He might be in a room but we can't make out the details.*

**ÁLVARO.** There is, allegedly, a subsequent episode of *The X-Files* that was never broadcast. There are all sorts of rumors about this lost episode – second-hand reports from people who know someone who definitely saw it.

What I've heard, ok, because I'm not commenting on whether I did or did not see this lost episode, but from what I understand the episode opens some time after Álvaro's abduction by the aliens.

**ALIEN MOTHER.** But the aliens are trying their best to convince the teenager that he hasn't been abducted at all and that he still lives at home with his family. After all, haven't these aliens taken the trouble to build a perfect replica of his living room? Doesn't the coffee table look exactly the same and isn't the alien speaking in a casual tone of voice about a casual subject, like the fact that today happens to be Presidents Day? So really, if you consider this from the alien's point of view, the only thing that looks out of place is that sullen expression on the dark haired teenager's face.

[*The light on* ÁLVARO *has slowly expanded until we see that we are in the living room in Bayamón as it was at the top of Act II. Sitting on the couch in the living room is the* ALIEN MOTHER, *leafing through a Sears catalog. She is wearing the same clothes as* OLGA, *but is larger and is an alien.*]

**ÁLVARO.** When he was first abducted, Álvaro had made a point of reminding the aliens that they weren't fooling him. Resisting that way made him feel better at first, but it didn't change anything. Lately, he's been wondering if his memories of the storm and the night he met Mulder are all some sort of misremembered dream. Lately, Álvaro has been wishing he had someone to talk to.

**ALIEN MOTHER.** The alien is leafing through a Sears catalog like there isn't anything to worry about. She's saying something about Presidents Day not being her favorite holiday but that, still, a holiday is a holiday and that it's hard to argue with a three-day sale at Sears and that if the dark haired teenager in sweaty work clothes wants something from the catalog he could maybe have it, maybe a pair of jeans for school say, if the price is reasonable because it's not as if they're a wealthy family, but first the dark haired teenager has to improve his attitude because why does he still look so sullen? And she's maybe teasing him when she says that, but maybe not.

**ÁLVARO.** Álvaro is so discouraged that all he can do is mutter something about Presidents Day not being a Puerto Rican holiday.

**ALIEN MOTHER.** The Alien Mother doesn't even look up from the catalog as she asks, True or False: weren't you home all day on account of schools in Puerto Rico being closed today? So regardless of any confusion you may feel, isn't it likely, she says, that Puerto Rico just had a holiday?

**ÁLVARO.** Álvaro hears a flicker of impatience in her voice. So it almost sounds like he's apologizing when he says, It doesn't matter really. He was only trying to explain that it doesn't make sense for them to be celebrating another country's presidents.

**ALIEN MOTHER.** The Alien Mother shifts her weight and she sighs. But she isn't mad, no, it's more like – well, like she just can't understand this stubbornly sullen attitude the teenager has.

**ÁLVARO.** Álvaro watches the alien.

**ALIEN MOTHER.** The Alien Mother looks back down and turns a few more pages, but she's too hurt now to concentrate on the catalog. So she closes it. And she shakes her head, gently. Like she doesn't know how she can keep going with so little help from her children.

Then she looks at the dark haired teenager in sweaty work clothes and says, Maybe I'm not as clever as you but the way I see it, we finally had one day when I didn't have to work and you didn't have to go to school. So tell me, why is it that all you could manage to do was invent reasons for ruining the day? It's hurtful, she says. It's hurtful.

**ÁLVARO.** Álvaro wonders, did he just see the alien's face tremble with emotion as she said those things, the same way a mother's face would?

**ALIEN MOTHER.** What is it your mother has done to make you push her away like this?

**ÁLVARO.** Could it be that this alien is sincere about wanting to be *like* a mother to him?

**ALIEN MOTHER.** Won't the dark haired teenager in sweaty work clothes help her be a better mother? Won't he help her even just a little?

**ÁLVARO.** So Álvaro says it.

He can't remember the exact wording – he forgets the verb he used – but he brings up the topic he had been warned never to bring up again, the topic that has no place inside a family.

**ALIEN MOTHER.** [*Suddenly very stern and very loud.*]
ARE YOU STARTING AGAIN?

Tell me, she wants to know, if you're starting again?

[*Beat.*]

**ÁLVARO.** Álvaro doesn't say anything.

**ALIEN MOTHER.** How can you repeat such a thing about your brother?

**ÁLVARO.** No one moves.

**ALIEN MOTHER.** And after a while she says, Honestly, there must be something wrong with you. The way you take everything and twist it into something negative.

Then she puts down the catalog and she gets up. She begins to cross the living room and walk over the clay tile. This is usually the hour she goes into her room, and the way she sees it, why should she let the dark haired teenager make this evening different from any other evening? And when she reaches the door to her bedroom, she turns back and says, I'm leaving the catalog there, in case you want to look through it. Tomorrow is the last day of the sale so we could go after school. You'll have to apologize to me first, obviously.

Then she must have closed her bedroom door behind her. Because that was her way of adding a period to the end of her sentence.

[ALIEN MOTHER *is gone.*]

**ÁLVARO.** Álvaro is left alone in the living room. He stares at the front door for a while, as if he's measuring his own resolve.

And then Álvaro gets up, opens that door right there, and walks out. He's surprised as he does it that no one tries to stop him.

As Álvaro walked through the strange replica of his old neighborhood, he was astonished at how faithfully the aliens had recreated the details of Puerto Rico. The way the roots of the alien-built banyan trees had broken apart the sidewalks. It all felt familiar, just like the island where he used to live.

Hours went by and Álvaro was still wandering. Just before dawn, it occurred to him that he had been walking in circles and that he had never gotten further than a five block radius. Not knowing what to do with his disappointment in himself, Álvaro carried it back to this house.

[*The* ALIEN OLDER BROTHER *is there.*]

**ALIEN OLDER BROTHER.** Perhaps.

Or perhaps the real reason the dark haired teenager came back to the house is because humans often end up circling the places they claim they want to leave.

**ÁLVARO.** The other alien is there now, the one they are trying to make Álvaro believe is his older brother.

**ALIEN OLDER BROTHER.** The Alien Older Brother is standing in the doorway. Behind him, you can see the blue light of the television set, because he's moved it into the bedroom that they share. Later he'll turn up the volume. Louder than anyone would need the volume to be.

**ÁLVARO.** And I suppose that was when I developed the idea that the best strategy was not to say anything anymore. And that instead of trying to communicate with the aliens, I would just wait. Because if I waited long enough, one day I'd be sure to find a way out.

*End of Play*

## A NOTE ON COSTUMES

Costuming in the third act should avoid the cliché of aliens depicted as waifs with oversized eyes and heads shaped like upside down tear drops. Try instead to emphasize their corporealness. Not ethereal, but large and heavy.

# THE NEW LINE
## by Will Eno

## BIOGRAPHY

Will Eno is a fellow of Residency Five at the Signature Theatre in New York and of the Edward F. Albee Foundation. His play *Wakey, Wakey* premiered at Signature in 2017. *The Open House* premiered at Signature in 2014, and received the Obie, the Lucille Lortel, and Drama Desk Awards. It will appear at the Theatre Royal Bath and the Print Room in England in 2017-18, directed by Sir Michael Boyd. *Gnit*, an adaptation of *Peer Gynt*, premiered at Actors Theatre of Louisville and was directed by Les Waters in the 2013 Humana Festival. His play *The Realistic Joneses* premiered at Yale Repertory Theatre in 2012 and appeared on Broadway in 2014, where it was named Best Play on Broadway by *USA Today* and the *Guardian* and was on the *New York Times'* "Best Plays of 2014" list. *Thom Pain (based on nothing)* was a finalist for the 2005 Pulitzer Prize, has been translated into many languages, and was made into a film starring Rainn Wilson that Eno co-directed with Oliver Butler. Mr. Eno's plays are published by Samuel French, Oberon Books, Theatre Communications Group, Dramatists Play Service, and Playscripts. He lives in Brooklyn with his wife, Maria Dizzia, and their daughter, Albertine.

## ACKNOWLEDGMENTS

*The New Line* premiered at the Humana Festival of New American Plays in April 2017. It was directed by Les Waters with the following cast:

MASTER OF CEREMONIES ............................... Beth Dixon
KATE ......................................................... Kathiamarice Lopez

and the following production staff:

Scenic Designer .................................................. Justin Hagovsky
Costume Designer ................................................ Alice Tavener
Lighting Designer ................................................ Steve O'Shea
Sound Designer .................................................... Christian Frederickson
Stage Manager .................................................... Stephen Horton
Assistant Stage Manager ...................................... Lindsay Eberly
Properties Director .............................................. Mark Walston

49

## CHARACTERS

MASTER OF CEREMONIES, female, 40-60

KATE, female, 20-30

## SETTING

Theater, event hall. MASTER OF CEREMONIES will be lit in a fairly tight spotlight, with some fill light so that we are seeing a beautifully but specifically-lit person. KATE will be lit in a separate larger area.

## WARDROBE

MASTER OF CEREMONIES wears a simple and conservative outfit, perhaps a dark suit with a white shirt. KATE wears the outfit described, which should be simple, tasteful and fashionable.

## THOUGHTS ON PERFORMANCE

MASTER OF CEREMONIES is entirely capable of running the show, on her own terms, without much fuss or anxiety. She can move easily between the two modes of High Fashion MC, and a human being who is simply and seriously asking people some real and specific questions. She may refer to notes from time to time. She should feel as if she's very comfortably present with the audience, i.e., she sees individual people and looks into the audience, sometimes even kind of searching in it.

KATE's movements should be choreographed in such a way that, at first, they seem entirely natural and suited to the occasion, but should slowly begin to depart, here and there, from the movements of a model in a fashion show. At some point, she sits down, both to listen to the Master of Ceremonies, and to slyly and shyly, and with some curiosity, watch the audience. While sitting, KATE will adjust hair, maybe send a text or do some other normal human things (though they might be done in a sort of formal or slightly stylized way). She may also leave the stage to make some minor change with the outfit or add a simple accessory. Ideally, all KATE's movement and "acting" is very simple, plausible, unpretentious, but also movingly expressive of some different aspects of humanness.

Beth Dixon and Kathiamarice Lopez
in *The New Line*

41st Humana Festival of New American Plays
Actors Theatre of Louisville, 2017
Photo by Bill Brymer

# THE NEW LINE

MASTER OF CEREMONIES *enters. She stands at a podium, facing the audience, and looks at her notes. She has a private moment of profound sadness, maybe 10 seconds or so. She might even cry, in a very quiet and private way, as she takes in the audience. Then* KATE *enters, barefoot, and we begin, with text and accompanying music.* KATE *strides in, exactly as if in a fashion show, and at the appropriate moments will make all the requisite twirls and stops and poses (see indicated recommendations).* MASTER OF CEREMONIES *begins speaking upon* KATE's *entrance, in an even and professional voice, in the formal tones of a fashion-show MC. Of course, at times, she will find herself speaking with vulnerability and simplicity. She will refer to her notes from time to time. The above should all happen in a gentle easy flow. MC enters, has her very sad moment, then* KATE *enters, and MC smoothly and professionally begins the show. SOUND NOTE: some bouncy EDM music, at a low level, will begin with* KATE's *entrance/MC's text.*

**MASTER OF CEREMONIES.** Katherine is wearing a dirt-white blouse in washed Irish linen, with a down collar and princess seams. A deep silhouette and side splits heighten drapability and make for maximum delicacy with a minimum of pretension. Below, a blue-dark and on-white bias-cut georgette skirt in soft cloth—tension and torsion, together at last, for a thing that practically sways by itself. All finished over-noticeably with an M-60 bullet belt, and two faded green cotton wristbands. (KATE *stands sideways to the audience, puts her hands on her hips, looks out.*) An ensemble that just whispers, "Good evening, love." Fabrics that murmur, "I thought this would be different." Clothing that screams, "I am begging you people." Quite a vocabulary, quite a range, a hundred percent human-made. (*Perhaps here, music comes down to an even lower level, or drops out abruptly.*) But don't feel threatened—it's just some material sewn together that says, very implicitly, "I am dressed in this." (KATE *moves.*) Look how it moves. The majesty of the fold. (*MUSIC, perhaps a pastoral classical music piece, at a low volume.*) It puts one in mind of Europe. There you are, in Brussels, looking for coffee in the Old Town—the gray sky, the cobblestones, a single muddy work-boot spattered with blood, sitting by a fountain. Then you're on an airplane on its freezing way toward Newfoundland, a down jacket over your head, with Europe at your back. (*Subtle and seamless change of MUSIC, perhaps a version of the same classical piece, but on banjo or guitar.*) And suddenly, here you are home in the States, charmingly ruffled from the flight and perfectly dressed for an early morning picnic in the tall and slowly moving grasses of Antietam, Bull Run, the Chickasaw Bayou. The gently fenced-off meadows of the American Civil War. Morning! (KATE *adjusts collar. Music cross fades, into a sustained tone* *that slowly eases into slightly eerie Ambient music or a sort of an abstracted soundscape of a hospital [hums, footsteps, some beeping, etc].*) Or, talk about versatility, turn up the collar and spend the evening in the emergency room of the closest big city, running from nurse to nurse to bystander, looking for the right line to wait in, while the worse-off are rushed past and the lights buzz and the late shift comes in, the later shift. This is wherever, whatever, whyever, clothing. It's designed and made by other people, but you'll make it your own, fill it with your own memories, your own happiness, sadness, and personal aroma. (*SOUNDSCAPE shifts to lapping water, maybe an owl in the distance, at some point.*) You were born, and they swaddled you, perhaps, in a tiny blanket and hat. (KATE *checks her hair in a small compact mirror, re-touches lipstick, maybe does a split-second imitation of a baby in distress.*) You were married, perhaps, and they put you in white or a rented tuxedo or some bright color you never would have imagined. Then there's the funerals, and they lay you down in luxurious satin or down-home pine, as the survivors sit quietly, even smugly, resplendent in tear-soaked black. We sometimes seem not to get much choice in the matter, and then all the perhapses are behind us and we and our clothes are put in a kiln. But oh, the accidental style and ceremony of it all, the elegant look of the wrong garment at the right time! Buying milk and cigarettes at some earthly hour at a gas station in an evening dress or a four-piece suit. Doing lawn-work in a lucky shirt, watching a movie marathon in our unlucky sweatpants, falling in love in a bathing suit or a McDonald's uniform. The choices we make, while we still can, in the morning, in our lives. The different things we put on, as we look forward to or brace for a particular future, or present. (*Very brief pause.* KATE *sits down and looks out, with a neutral expression. All SOUND abruptly stops.*) Like this second, right now. This—what shall we call it—moment. (*Very brief pause. To AUDIENCE:*) What are you dressed for? What are you prepared for? For what event? For what world? Is it this world, or another one? Who are you supposed to be? (*Very brief pause.*) If you want to make some changes, in your wardrobe, in your self, if you aren't the person you hoped you'd be, fear not, there's hope. Fear, ladies and gentlemen, not. I think we should believe that there is time and that we can change. (*Brief pause.*) Katherine is wearing— (*To* KATE:) would you mind standing up again, dear? Thank you, you don't have to move around. I just want everyone to see you. (*EDM MUSIC fades up.* KATE *stands still, looking at audience. A return to MC Fashion Show mode:*) Katherine is wearing a wonderfully mysterious and human expression, one that bespeaks the beauty and wonder of our indescribable fate. She is standing upright, in the slowly-developed style of the most magical and gifted animal the world has ever known. 100,000 miles of blood vessels run through her body, supported by 20 pounds of bones, (KATE *puts a hand on her hip.*) and now she's put her hand on her hip, because she wanted to! A string around her finger reminds her of something important she's supposed to do, maybe call her sister or do her taxes, and while she's looking at you her brain is making 38 thousand trillion calculations per second. C'est magnifique! There's hope and there's time. (*Brief pause. EDM MUSIC out.*) Add a hat (KATE *puts a hand on her head, like it's a hat.*) and you're ready for the boat races or the most ferociously rising sea level. (*Perhaps swelling orchestral music, at a low volume, as always.*) Yes, so put on this outfit, or any outfit, or no clothes at all, and stand there, stand up nice and straight. Take a few breaths. The whole world is before you like a little child, asking you what you feel and think, asking you what you want to do, and waiting for your response. The world is a two-year-old in her mother's high heels. Try to be kind and forgiving. The world is saying to you, "Excuse me?" People and all the species of the world are nudging you, looking up at you. Wear your heart on your sleeve and put on your biggest smile. The world is saying, "Hello? Hello? Hello?" (*She looks at her notes.*) Everything you see is also available in Ash. (*A pause for a few seconds. Both* MC *and* KATE *are still.* KATE *turns slightly toward* MC.)

BLACKOUT

*End of Play*

# I NOW PRONOUNCE
by Tasha Gordon-Solmon

## ABOUT *I NOW PRONOUNCE*

*This article first ran in the* Limelight Guide *to the 41ˢᵗ Humana Festival of New American Plays, published by Actors Theatre of Louisville, and is based on conversations with the playwright before rehearsals for the Humana Festival production began.*

A wedding is a rite of passage, a beautiful and meaningful ceremony celebrating the union of soulmates. Or maybe that's just Hallmark propaganda. Maybe a wedding is more like a hand-me-down sweater that doesn't really fit and itches in weird places. For Adam and Nicole, it might be a little bit of both.

In Tasha Gordon-Solmon's comedy *I Now Pronounce*, Adam and Nicole's marriage gets off to an inauspicious start when the elderly rabbi officiating their wedding drops dead during the ceremony. The members of the wedding party struggle heroically to turn around the mood at the reception, but they're much too preoccupied with their own flailing relationships to keep the festivities running smoothly. Meanwhile, the flower girls are distracted by the possibility that the rabbi is now a bloodthirsty ghost. But Adam and Nicole have bigger issues to tackle than a wedding gone awry. With death staring them in the face, they can't help but wonder: should they even be getting married?

According to Gordon-Solmon, the inspiration for the opening scene of the play was hilariously literal, sprung from a momentary daydream she had while attending a wedding. "The person officiating the wedding was coughing," she explains, with signature deadpan humor. "And I got bored and started thinking—what if this person *died*?" Out of that fleeting thought, this imaginative writer spun a story that goes to deeper and stranger places, wrestling with questions not only about the institution of marriage, but also about why we find authentic human connection so difficult anyway.

Though their wedded life together has only just begun, Adam and Nicole already feel hemmed in. And the bride and groom aren't the only ones in this play struggling with the balance between intimacy and independence. Bridesmaids Eva and Michelle and groomsmen Seth and Dave have relationship problems of their own: Eva tends to overshare; Michelle's vision of true love is too far removed from reality; Seth is hung up on the wife who jilted him; and Dave's bad-boy attitude keeps people at a distance. And like Adam and Nicole, they are unsettled by the creeping feeling that being in a romantic partnership requires conforming to prescribed roles and behaviors—none of which inspire enthusiasm for the phrase "till death do us part." In explaining why this sentiment appears in a play set during a wedding celebration, Gordon-Solmon says, "I tend to write plays from a place of, 'What's a kind of play or trope that

I don't like?' This is sort of my *take* on a wedding play, in reaction to wedding plays. And hopefully that's a jumping-off point to ask some bigger questions about the world."

Gordon-Solmon's version of a wedding play is filled with unexpected delights. One of this comedy's many charms is the trio of flower girls who add to the sense of chaos at the reception. While they're still reeling from the shock of the rabbi's death, these girls also witness the turbulence of adult relationships— and they're not sure which experience is more traumatizing. "I think there's something cool about seeing different stages of life together," reflects the playwright. "In a lot of my plays, and in this play in particular, I'm interested in the question of how we learn to be in the world. Children keep finding their way into my plays, even if I think it's not going to be a play about kids."

Of course, learning about human connection doesn't stop after childhood. The play also features two brief but poignant appearances by members of an older generation. As Adam and Nicole listen to their speeches, it's hard for them to resist the notion that true intimacy is built on a lifetime of shared experience. Gordon-Solmon observes, "There's a lot of my grandparents in this play—that was not a conscious choice when I was writing it. I'm learning more and more that they're in there. I think they're the hope in the play: an example of what a lovely partnership could look like. My grandparents were married for over 60 years. And I remember when my grandfather passed away, my grandmother said to me, 'It wasn't enough time.'"

In *I Now Pronounce*, the hope for profound intimacy built on the foundation of a marriage contract lives side-by-side with cynical reservations about what marriage might entail. As Gordon-Solmon describes the impulse behind that contradiction, "There's something beautiful, but also pretty problematic about the institution of marriage—the reasons it exists historically, the gender roles implicit in its structure. It's a question I have: if I keep my name, and I have my own life and my own friends and my own world, can I still have that sort of idealized connection that we're brought up to revere? Or is that only possible if we live according to this outdated set of rules?"

The answers to those questions don't come easy for Adam and Nicole, and it's hard to know if eternal love will win out in the end. Gordon-Solmon reports that people's reactions to the play have been as diverse as their thoughts about marriage. She explains, "It's funny: people have read the same draft of this play, and some of them say, 'I'm so happy for them.' And some people say, 'That is *so* dark.' And I love that."

—Jenni Page-White

## BIOGRAPHY

Tasha Gordon-Solmon's plays have been developed and produced at Actors Theatre of Louisville (*Coffee Break* at the 2016 Humana Festival), Clubbed Thumb, Ars Nova, Northern Stage, the Perry-Mansfield New Works Festival, Dixon Place, New Georges, INTAR Theatre, and The Flea Theater. She is a recipient of the Dramatists Guild Fellowship, a member of the BMI Advanced Musical Theater Workshop, a New Georges Affiliated Artist, and an alumna of the Ars Nova Play Group, Clubbed Thumb Early Career Writers' Group, and Project Y Playwrights Group. Gordon-Solmon's directing credits include Ensemble Studio Theatre, The Tank, The Brick, The Cell, InViolet Theater, Pipeline Theatre Company, Columbia University, Studio Tisch, the New York Fringe Festival, the Fire This Time Festival and the Young Playwrights Festival at the Eugene O'Neill Theater Center. She received her M.F.A. at New York University and is a proud 52nd Street Project volunteer.

## ACKNOWLEDGMENTS

*I Now Pronounce* premiered at the Humana Festival of New American Plays in March 2017. It was directed by Stephen Brackett with the following cast:

| | |
|---|---|
| RABBI/MRS. GOODMAN | Ray DeMattis |
| EVA | Satomi Blair |
| MICHELLE | Clea Alsip |
| NICOLE | Alex Trow |
| SETH | Forrest Malloy |
| DAVE | Jason Veasey |
| ADAM | Ben Graney |
| FLOWER GIRLS | Carmen Tate, Mary Charles Miller, Brylee Deuser |

and the following production staff:

| | |
|---|---|
| Scenic Designer | William Boles |
| Costume Designer | Kathleen Geldard |
| Lighting Designer | Tyler Micoleau |
| Sound Designer | Stowe Nelson |
| Stage Manager | Katie Shade |
| Dramaturg | Jenni Page-White |
| Casting | Paul Davis, Calleri Casting |
| Medical Consultant | Yvette Ramirez |
| Dance Supervisor | Ashley Thursby |
| Fight Supervisor | Eric Frantz |
| Properties Master | Heather Lindert |
| Production Assistant | Leah V. Pye |
| Directing Assistant | Katie Foggiano |
| Assistant Dramaturg | Bryan Howard |
| Child Talent Guardian | Hannah Cava |

*I Now Pronounce* was developed at the Perry-Mansfield New Works Festival, June 2016.

## CHARACTERS

RABBI / MRS. GOODMAN

EVA

MICHELLE

NICOLE

SETH

DAVE

ADAM

FLOWER GIRLS

While the Humana Festival production cast three wonderful young actors as the flower girls, it is possible to double these roles with rotating members of the bridal party (Seth, Dave, Eva and Michelle). This need not be done naturalistically.

## NOTES ON STYLE

This piece should feel fluid
Transitions between scenes should be smooth
Actors may move from one scene right into the next
There need not be lights up and down each time
Similarly, there is a fluidity to the space
The manifestation of the physical world need not be realistic in the slightest
Everyone should feel involved in the space
That doesn't mean we're all guests
We're an audience looking in
But things should feel real
And not real
In a way that feels real
Got it?

Alex Trow and Ben Graney
in *I Now Pronounce*

41st Humana Festival of New American Plays
Actors Theatre of Louisville, 2017
Photo by Bill Brymer

# I NOW PRONOUNCE

## PART I

### 1

*Lights up*
*Or maybe a spotlight*
*On a man alone onstage*
*But are we ever alone*
*Onstage*
*Or in life*
*Your answer may depend on your religion*
*In this case*
*We're talking a man of god*
*A* RABBI *to be exact*
*An old rabbi*
*Possibly pushing 80*
*Probably pushing 90*
*And he looks his age*
*Or older*
*Like the smallest breeze might blow him away*
*He clears his throat*
*He pauses sometimes to do this*
*Clear his throat*
*Or pause*
*To remember what he's supposed to say next*
*Or silently take note of the fact that he is somehow*
*Miraculously*
*Still alive*
*Told you he's a man of god*
*Apparently it pays off*

**RABBI.** Good evening.
Welcome.
It is my pleasure today to marry
Adam and Nicole.
To celebrate their love and join two families.
This is especially meaningful
Because I married Nicole's parents
Twenty five

Thirty
Five
Years Ago.
Adam and Nicole
Because they share a special bond
When they met
They realized they had much in common.
Adam is close with his family
So is Nicole
Adam took a class on religions in college
To learn about his Jewish heritage
So did Nicole
Adam grew up outside of Boston
In Massachusetts
So did Nicole
Adam played sports
So did Nicole
Adam liked music
So did Nicole
Adam

> *A cell phone ringer goes off somewhere in the audience*
> *Eventually it stops*

Nicole and Aaron are very happy to be joined on the
Altar today
With their families
Nicole's mother
Is here
Along with her father
And his sister
And brother
Her grandmother
Another grandmother
Her bridesmaids
Who are her friends
All of them are here
On the altar

Aaron
Is accompanied by his family
They are all here
You can see them

Welcome

As I said
It is my pleasure to welcome you all here
And it is my pleasure to partake in the
Officiation
Of this ceremony

There is a saying in the bible
Blessed Art Thou
...
Blessed Art Thou the eternal
Because god is eternal
Now is the time in the ceremony
Where the couple will exchange rings
Andrew
Take Nicole's hand
Please place the ring on Nicole's finger
Yes get the ring
Good
And say

Good yes take the ring from your brother
Uncle
Nephew
Him
And place it on her finger
Nicole do the same
Good

The couple has exchanged rings
Alan will now stand where he is
And Nicole will walk around him
Thirteen times
It is the tradition to do it
Thirty times
But we will do thirteen
            *He waits and watches them do this*
            *Maybe four times?*
That's Enough

Now
We will proceed
To the rings
Arthur

Take Nicole's hand
Ah the ring is already there
Good

Nicole take
Good you have one too
Now you will take one another's hands
Both of them
And look at each other

Good

Blessed art thou
Who has brought us to this day today
To marry Anton and Nicole
Anton is that a Jewish name?
Of course
I almost forgot
Anthony has come to Judaism
After a long process of conversion
He has accepted this faith
And
Converted
This is very holy in the Jewish faith
And because I married Abraham's parents
Twenty
Thousand years ago
This conversion is especially meaningful

It is worth noting

Today is a very special day

Welcome to you all

Now hold one another's hands

Let go

Take one another's hands

Good

Now you kiss the
Yes take off the veil first

Good
And
You

Kiss
You

Good
That was a good kiss

At moments like these
It is important to take a moment
To
Thank god
Everyone
Thank god
Now

Let's say thank you
And say it
To god
Everyone say it

Say it to yourself in your mind

Good
Good

Okay

And now
You may kiss the
Yes go ahead
These two are shy
There's a saying about that

Yes
Thank you
I was getting to that
This is the glass
The
He
Will break the glass
By standing on it

He will step
And break
In a moment

This is a symbol of
Many things
In Judaism

This is a Jewish wedding
It is unusual
To have both
Converting

Welcome

> *He totters a little*

> *A loud crash*
> *The sound of the glass being stomped on*
> *A beat*

Now
You are married

> *The* RABBI *collapses to the ground*
> *Not dramatically*
> *Not slowly*
> *Like the ground was pulled out from under him*
> *Fast*


## 2


> *A fancy bathroom*
> EVA *and* MICHELLE *are both in blue dresses*

**EVA.** Sweetie it's okay

**MICHELLE.** It's totally okay

**EVA.** You looked so beautiful

**MICHELLE.** You did

**EVA.** The music when you walked down the aisle with your parents
So beautiful

**MICHELLE.** Totally

**EVA.** Lady in Red was exactly you
But in white

**MICHELLE.** Totally

**EVA.** Adam's grandma is fine

**MICHELLE.** She only fainted
It's not like she dropped—

> *Look from* EVA

Your dress looked amazing

**EVA.** Sweetie
At some point you're going to have to come out

The room looks great
It's all set up
Everyone is enjoying the cocktail hour
**MICHELLE.** It's true they're drinking a lot
And only a few people left so—
    *Look from* EVA
**EVA.** The cocktails are delish
They match our dresses perfectly
And they're delicious
**MICHELLE.** They are I had like five
**EVA.** The appetizers are great
There is so much food
**MICHELLE.** Nobody's eating so there is so much
    *Glare from* EVA
**EVA.** I know Adam wants to see you
He's waiting right outside
**MICHELLE.** I don't think he is
I haven't seen—
**EVA.** He is
And your parents want to see you
They're done with all the
business
**MICHELLE.** It's all cleaned up
They got rid of the body and everything
So fast
It was kind of
Amazing
I was talking to the ambulance guys and I was like
Have you done this before
And then I was like
Of course you have
That's your job
But I meant like specifically dead people
Or dying people
The Deceased
It was amazing
Like how do they practice that you know
Before their first time
There's gotta be a first time
And before that, they've gotta practice
And I'm thinking

They must do a shit ton of Light as a Feather Stiff as a Board
Because
They were so fast
And one of them
His name is Carlos
And after they put everything in the ambulance
He came back
And he told me he would show me how they practice
If I wanted
And asked for my number so he could take me on a date
And I said
I have this wedding I'm going to
And I don't have a date
So why don't you be my date to that
And he said sure when is it
And I said now
And he said well my shift isn't over 'til 10
And I said I'll still be here at 10
So he should come
And then I giggled
And he was like what's so funny
And I said
When I said you should come I meant come to the party like this wedding
party that we're at now, or that's like happening in a bit, I didn't mean come
like
(Sexually)
So please don't take it the wrong way
This is my friend's wedding
And he was like
I didn't mind it anyway
And I was like
I don't mind it every way
And then he had to get back on the ambulance

**EVA.** Go outside

**MICHELLE.** What

**EVA.** Go outside

**MICHELLE.** Nikky needs us
Nikky I'm here for you
I'm not going anywhere
Even if you stay in there all night
And even if Carlos comes back
(And even if he is still wearing that uniform)

**EVA.** Not helping

**MICHELLE.** Nikky I'm helping right?

**EVA.** Nik

She can leave

If you want it to be just you and me

You tell me what you need

Okay Nik?

**MICHELLE.** Nikky

Nikky dickylicky

Remember when everyone called you that in high school?

**EVA.** //Nik

Listen to me Nik

Nik

Nik

Nik

**MICHELLE.** //Nikky

Nikky dicky licky

Licky dickky Nickky

> *A loud primal scream from someplace that we can't see*
> *It lasts longer than you'd think*
> *Perhaps through the whole transition into the next scene*

### 3

> THE FLOWER GIRLS *congregate in a corner*
> FLOWER GIRL 3 *is younger than the others*

**FLOWER GIRL 1.** My mom says he's fine

**FLOWER GIRL 2.** He's dead

**FLOWER GIRL 1.** No way

**FLOWER GIRL 2.** He died

**FLOWER GIRL 1.** My mom said he was sick and they took him to the hospital

**FLOWER GIRL 2.** Your mom was LY ING to you

**FLOWER GIRL 3.** You guys

Is he a ghost?

**FLOWER GIRL 1.** There's no such thing as ghosts

**FLOWER GIRL 2.** There is

**FLOWER GIRL 1.** Isn't

**FLOWER GIRL 2.** Is

**FLOWER GIRL 1.** Is–N't

**FLOWER GIRL 2.** Yes There Is

**FLOWER GIRL 3.** Maybe it's like that movie when the dad ghost comes back to teach his son hockey

**FLOWER GIRL 1.** I don't think rabbis play hockey

**FLOWER GIRL 2.** Not dead ones

> *Beat*

**FLOWER GIRL 3.** I'm scared

**FLOWER GIRL 2.** You're fine

**FLOWER GIRL 1.** My mom said it's totally fine

**FLOWER GIRL 2.** Your mom doesn't know anything

**FLOWER GIRL 1.** Yah she does

**FLOWER GIRL 2.** No she doesn't

**FLOWER GIRL 1.** She does

**FLOWER GIRL 2.** No She Does Not

Dumbass

**FLOWER GIRL 3.** What if his ghost is floating around and he's gonna kill us

**FLOWER GIRL 1.** Why would he kill us?

**FLOWER GIRL 2.** Because he's a ghost?

**FLOWER GIRL 1.** So you don't kill someone for no reason

**FLOWER GIRL 2.** You do if you're an angry ghost

**FLOWER GIRL 1.** Why would he be angry?

**FLOWER GIRL 2.** Maybe because you don't know anything so he's pissed and he's gonna come and get you

**FLOWER GIRL 1.** Not funny

**FLOWER GIRL 3.** Maybe he's angry because he died

> *The girls contemplate this*

---

## 4

> *Outside in the parking lot*
> ADAM *is on the curb wheezing, maybe blowing into a paper bag*
> SETH, DAVE *and BEER*

**DAVE.** We're like the T-birds

**SETH.** What

**DAVE.** The motherfucking T-birds
In the parking lot
Tearing it up
Just guys
Our whole lives ahead of us

**SETH.** He doesn't look good

**DAVE.** Adam, are you good?

**SETH.** The T-birds, as in *Grease?*

**DAVE.** He's good

**SETH.** I'm 30 and I'm wearing a tuxedo
I am not a "T-bird"

**DAVE.** Adam
If you don't want this
If you don't want to do this, say the word and we're out of here
You are a single man
A free man
One word
Say Dave, I'm out of here
Or Out
Or Go
Or Yes or No
Any word, and we're gone

**SETH.** He's already married

**DAVE.** If you want to leave, we can leave

**SETH.** Don't worry
He said the same thing to me at my wedding

**DAVE.** And don't you wish you'd listened?

**SETH.** It makes you think doesn't it?
About the things that are important, how long we have...

**DAVE.** Adam, are you thinking about that right now?
Don't think about that
He was old

**SETH.** My grandfather died of a heart attack at 45
It can happen any time

**DAVE.** So we gotta live while we can

**SETH.** His father died at 40
Stroke

**DAVE.** You don't have to have a wife
If that's not what you want

**SETH.** It really makes you think
What am I doing?
What are we all doing?

**DAVE.** We're sitting in a parking lot
Adam, why are we sitting in a parking lot when we could—

**SETH.** My uncle died in a parking lot
Car crash
Out of nowhere
38

**DAVE.** You need another drink

**SETH.** I'm good

**DAVE.** (*To* ADAM) Don't worry buddy, I will get you a drink and we will
figure this out
I've only had a few, and I've got the car
We can go anywhere you want

> *He takes out keys and puts them on the ground in front of* ADAM

The keys to your freedom
Think about it

> *To* SETH

Don't be depressing

> DAVE *leaves*
> SETH *sits beside* ADAM *as he breathes*
> *They sit in quiet*
> *The sound of* ADAM's *rhythmic breathing*

**SETH.** It makes you think, doesn't it?
How lucky were you to find Nicole
And
I can't be in my thirties and get divorced
That gives me what
10, 15 years tops, to start all over again and get it right?
Maybe less than a decade if I don't exercise, and who has time to exercise?
When I was where you are I was so in love
Forever in love
This Is It love
This Will Never Blow Up in My Face and Ruin My Already Far Too Short
Life love
I know I know
People change, people grow, people change the way they grow
But how much can you change in six months?
You don't even change your oil in six months
She needs space

I'm giving her space
She needs time
Maybe it's a good
It's gonna be fine
She's having a thing
It's a thing
She needs a space time thing and I should
…

> *He doesn't start to cry*
> *He has something in his eye or something*

You are gonna be just

> SETH *abruptly exits and* ADAM *is left alone*
> *He slowly removes the paper bag*
> *Practices breathing*
> *On his own*
> *Slower*
> *Calmer*
> *He looks at the car keys*

### 5

> MICHELLE *and* EVA *walk slowly*
> *Each balancing a very full blue drink*
> MICHELLE *stops walking*

**MICHELLE.** Wait

**EVA.** What

**MICHELLE.** It's okay

> *They start walking—slowly—again*

**MICHELLE.** This was a good idea
Giving her some space and time
Getting her a drink

**EVA.** Uh huh

**MICHELLE.** It's good you came with to help

**EVA.** You wouldn't leave if I didn't

> *They walk again*
> *Still slowly*

**MICHELLE.** Wait

**EVA.** What

**MICHELLE.** I need a second

**EVA.** Take your time
I'll bring this to Nik

**MICHELLE.** No I'm fine I'm coming with

**EVA.** You don't need to

**MICHELLE.** I want to
Nikky needs us she's upset

**EVA.** Because of you

**MICHELLE.** How is it

**EVA.** You compounded her stress

**MICHELLE.** I was consoling her

**EVA.** You stressed her out

> *They keep going*

**MICHELLE.** Wait

**EVA.** Take your time
I'll go back

**MICHELLE.** No I'm fine

I need to sit down

> MICHELLE *hands her blue drink to* EVA

**EVA.** There are chairs by the bar
Why don't you go back there and I'll

> MICHELLE *gets on the floor*

> EVA *softens a little*

Are you okay?

**MICHELLE.** Yah

> MICHELLE *lies down*

> EVA *stands there holding the drinks*

**EVA.** Do you want some water?

**MICHELLE.** No

> *Beat*

**EVA.** Do you want to find a couch you can

**MICHELLE.** I'm fine here

> EVA *sits down next to* MICHELLE

## 6

*In the bathroom, the* FLOWER GIRLS *face the mirror (the audience?)*
*They take a breath, preparing for something*

**FLOWER GIRL 1.** It's not gonna work

**FLOWER GIRL 2.** It is

**FLOWER GIRL 1.** It's not

**FLOWER GIRL 3.** You guys

**FLOWER GIRL 2.** We say it three times and that makes the ghost go away

**FLOWER GIRL 1.** I thought you say it three times to summon Bloody Mary

**FLOWER GIRL 2.** Yah and we're trying to summon Bloody Mary

**FLOWER GIRL 3.** That's two times already
Stop

**FLOWER GIRL 2.** It doesn't count unless you say it three times in an exact
row

**FLOWER GIRL 1.** How is her ghost gonna make his ghost go away

**FLOWER GIRL 2.** Because she's a ghost that makes other ghosts go away

**FLOWER GIRL 3.** I don't wanna see a ghost

**FLOWER GIRL 2.** You won't
She sucks ghosts into her mirror and traps them there

**FLOWER GIRL 1.** In the mirror?

**FLOWER GIRL 3.** You guys!

**FLOWER GIRL 1.** All she does is tell you when you're gonna get married
And if you don't ask her, then she'll kill your baby one day

**FLOWER GIRL 2.** Do you believe everything you're told?
Like EVERYthing?

**FLOWER GIRL 1.** It's true That's why she's a ghost

**FLOWER GIRL 2.** I thought you don't believe in ghosts

**FLOWER GIRL 1.** I don't

**FLOWER GIRL 2.** She is a lady who was in a car accident and her face got
so messed up that she died when she saw herself in the mirror
And now she's stuck there forever
Everyone knows that

**FLOWER GIRL 1.** Not me

**FLOWER GIRL 2.** You don't know anything

**FLOWER GIRL 3.** Do you guys wanna get killed by a ghost??
And die before you even get your period?

*A rustling or creaking*

**FLOWER GIRL 1.** What was that?

**FLOWER GIRL 2.** The ghost, Genius

**FLOWER GIRL 3.** Can somebody please say it?

**FLOWER GIRL 1.** Not me

**FLOWER GIRL 2.** Not it

*Another faint rustle?*

**FLOWER GIRL 3.** All together?

**FLOWER GIRL 2.** Fine

**FLOWER GIRL 1.** Are we saying it like on three?

**FLOWER GIRL 3.** K

**FLOWER GIRL 1.** 1, 2

**FLOWER GIRL 3.** Are we saying it before the three or on the three?

**FLOWER GIRL 2.** When do you ever say it on the three?

**FLOWER GIRL 3.** All the time

They do it on TV all the time

**FLOWER GIRL 1.** TV rots your brain

My mom said

**FLOWER GIRL 2.** 1, 2, 3

**FLOWER GIRL 3.** Bloody Mary

You guys!

**FLOWER GIRL 2.** 123 like we're gonna start counting for real

Or 1, 2, 3 and then say the thing

**FLOWER GIRL 3.** Say the thing!

**FLOWER GIRL 1.** You didn't say anything, chicken

**FLOWER GIRL 3.** One

Two

Three

**ALL.** Bloody Mary

Bloody Mary

**FLOWER GIRL 2.** Bloody Mary

You were supposed to do it too!

**FLOWER GIRL 1.** Now you know how it feels

*A creaking sound*

*A shadowy figure emerges behind them*

*They see a reflection in the mirror and run out of the bathroom*

NICOLE *emerges in her wedding gown, her face a mess of tear stains and running makeup*

## 7

MICHELLE *and* EVA, *where we left them*
*Maybe they have been onstage this whole time*
MICHELLE's *head is now on* EVA's *lap*

**MICHELLE.** Do you think Carlos is going to come back?

**EVA.** Who

**MICHELLE.** Carlos
Carlos Carlos
From the ambulance
I think he will

Do you think there's a heaven?

EVA *sips a blue drink*

I think maybe it's less
Heaven
Than like
A world of angels
I think maybe all the religions are there together
And everyone is happy and pretty
And all the animals get made into babies again
Even if they're old and missing legs and need to roll around on those things
Wouldn't it be amazing if there was a way to make puppies and kitties so that
they stayed puppies and kitties forever?
You could get a pet and it would always be cute
And at shelters none of the animals would be old or gross
And they'd all get adopted
And no one would abandon them in the first place
Because they'd stay cute forever

SETH *enters*

**SETH.** Sorry didn't mean to interrupt

**EVA.** You're not

**SETH.** Okay

**MICHELLE.** Nice to meet you

**SETH.** We walked down the aisle together

**MICHELLE.** Oh
You're great at walking

**SETH.** Well I should get back to Adam

**EVA.** Where is he?

**SETH.** With Dave out—

**MICHELLE.** I know who Dave is

**EVA.** Out where?

**MICHELLE.** Dave has a flask

**SETH.** Out back in front of the parking lot

**MICHELLE.** He has a flask with bourbon in it
Maybe that will help you find him

**EVA.** Can you stay with her?

> EVA *leaves*

**MICHELLE.** Wait I can help
I can totally

> *She doesn't move*

You're Adam's friend

**SETH.** Yup

**MICHELLE.** I forget what you said you
You have a job

**SETH.** Yup

How do you know Nicole

**MICHELLE.** High school

**SETH.** Wow

**MICHELLE.** We weren't close
We were close
But not that close
We got closer after
And now we're like
Really close
I feel so bad for her
She did all the planning you know
I feel like it's way worse when you like
Try with something
And then it doesn't happen the way you wanted
When you tried so hard
That sucks

**SETH.** Yes it does

**MICHELLE.** She planned for everything

**SETH.** You can never plan for everything

**MICHELLE.** The flowers, and the place cards
Or
How there's a basket in the bathroom with tampons in case you know
Or

How Adam has a friend and his wife cheated on him, and she told Nicole she
wants to leave her husband for the affair guy, like she told the husband Let's
just separate for a bit, but really she's gonna leave him for good, and Nik had
to beg her to wait until after the wedding, and the wife was like But I want
to bring my new guy and Nicole was like You're uninvited
Because what is worse for a wedding than a groomsman whose wife left him
and brought her new boyfriend as her date
Probably someone dying in the ceremony
But I always think you have to see the positive in things
And the party will still be so fun
So it all worked out
Did you try the blue drinks?

**SETH.** I think I need to sit down

**MICHELLE.** Yah they'll do that to you

> SETH *lies down on the floor too*


## 8


> DAVE *sits outside where the guys were before*
> *He is drinking alone*

**EVA.** You shouldn't drink out here

**DAVE.** Thanks for the tip

**EVA.** It's illegal
Drinking outside

**DAVE.** Private property

**EVA.** Do you think maybe you should be inside anyway?

**DAVE.** Uh
Nope

**EVA.** It's your friend's wedding

**DAVE.** Is that what this is?

> *Beat*

**EVA.** Have you seen him?

**DAVE.** Who

**EVA.** Adam

**DAVE.** Nope

**EVA.** Thanks

> *She turns to go*

**DAVE.** He's not in there

**EVA.** Do you know where he is

**DAVE.** I do not

**EVA.** Great

*She turns to go again*

**DAVE.** You won't find him

*Beat*

**EVA.** Okay

I am trying to save a marriage here

Put eternal love back on track

And I can't make that happen without a groom

And I will stay out here until you tell me

**DAVE.** He went for a drive

**EVA.** Where

**DAVE.** I don't know

I left him my keys

**EVA.** And

**DAVE.** And now they're gone

**EVA.** Do you care at all

**DAVE.** About...

**EVA.** Any of this?

**DAVE.** You should probably care a little less

**EVA.** I don't need

Don't tell me what

I am going to fix this

And be a good friend

And good human

And you can keep

Wasting space

And

Breaking the law

**DAVE.** Not breaking the law

*She leaves*

*She comes back*

**EVA.** What kind of car?

**DAVE.** You can't force them to be together

**EVA.** How else would people be happy if they weren't forced into it?

*She leaves*

## 9

*The* FLOWER GIRLS *enter*
*Out of breath*
*Perhaps through the audience*

**FLOWER GIRL 3.** What do we do now

**FLOWER GIRL 1.** I don't know

**FLOWER GIRL 3.** We didn't ask her for help

**FLOWER GIRL 1.** Did you see her?!?

**FLOWER GIRL 2.** She's gonna kill us

**FLOWER GIRL 3.** I don't want to die

**FLOWER GIRL 1.** We're not gonna die

**FLOWER GIRL 2.** We are if she finds us

**FLOWER GIRL 3.** What do we do

**FLOWER GIRL 1.** We need to tell someone

**FLOWER GIRL 2.** And get murdered on the way?

**FLOWER GIRL 1.** I want my mom

**FLOWER GIRL 2.** She could already be dead

**FLOWER GIRL 1.** Don't say that

**FLOWER GIRL 3.** You guys

**FLOWER GIRL 2.** She could be

**FLOWER GIRL 1.** You don't know what you're talking about

**FLOWER GIRL 3.** You guys

**FLOWER GIRL 2.** An evil ghost is on the loose who has probably started killing everyone and is looking for us

**FLOWER GIRL 3.** You guys

*The other girls finally see what she is pointing to:*

MICHELLE *and* SETH *lying on the floor*
*Maybe we see their shadows*

*The girls freeze, staring at the motionless bodies*

## 10

*Outside*
*By a door, under an awning perhaps*
ADAM *is smoking*
EVA *approaches and they stand there for a bit*

**EVA.** That really is a disgusting habit

**ADAM.** Do you remember that time we hooked // up?

**EVA.** I don't

**ADAM.** It was when Nicole and I broke up for // five hours at that party

**EVA.** Five hours at Meg's engagement party I know

**ADAM.** You were the last not Nicole person I will ever
Anything
Unless she dies first
At which point my options aren't going to be very attractive

**EVA.** Maybe you'll die first

**ADAM.** That is more probable statistically
I'll die and this will be my life
A wedding that began in death
A marriage that was a slow progression toward death
And then
Death

**EVA.** People live longer if they're married, they've done studies

**ADAM.** You can't live your life in numbers
I do and it's
I don't know what I'm doing half the time
There are so many variables, I pick some at random
Move them around until I get a number that won't get me in too much
trouble if it goes wrong, but could make me a decent amount if it goes right
Is that a life?

**EVA.** I think a life is made up of a lot of

**ADAM.** Sure
Family, vacations, human connection
But if you think about it, that all comes down to one person
How can one person be responsible for your whole happiness

**EVA.** I think what you're feeling right now is tota—
Completely normal

**ADAM.** I don't think I'm normal Eve

**EVA.** Eva

**ADAM.** I question things
I look at the world around me with a keen and critical eye
I am able to ask
What else is there?
I think that makes me worthy of finding the answer

**EVA.** If you left
Hypothetically

Forget the wedding, statistics
Where would you go

**ADAM.** Belize

**EVA.** Where is that again?

**ADAM.** I don't remember exactly

**EVA.** You don't know where the place you want to go is?

**ADAM.** You said hypothetical
I don't need specifics in the hypothetical

**EVA.** Okay what would you do
Generally
In Belize

**ADAM.** Surf

*Beat*

**EVA.** You surf?

**ADAM.** I'd learn
And I would teach others
Circle of life

**EVA.** I wish you luck then

**ADAM.** You're humoring me

**EVA.** I think you should go
Strike out all on your own

**ADAM.** I wouldn't be alone

**EVA.** I'm sure

**ADAM.** You don't think I'd make friends?
I have a room full of friends in there
I had a room full of them earlier today
Some of them are still there I think
The point is I can make friends

**EVA.** But eventually they'd all get married and have children and where would that leave you?

**ADAM.** With new, cooler friends

**EVA.** Okay, and then the new cooler friends get married and have kids

**ADAM.** I will make friends who aren't doing that

**EVA.** Other old dudes, waiting for the slow progression of their lives to end in death?
That sounds pretty alone to me

**ADAM.** It's different

**EVA.** I don't doubt it

**ADAM.** You are trying to scare me
But I didn't decide to get married because I was scared
I am deeply and passionately in love with my soul mate

**EVA.** Except you're already thinking of cheating on her with the elderly

**ADAM.** She's dead
It's not cheating if
You are abusing the hypothetical

**EVA.** Sorry

**ADAM.** If I go in there, it is not because I am scared to die alone

**EVA.** I know

**ADAM.** This day has been very stressful for me

**EVA.** I know

    *A beat*

**ADAM.** You're good
Having me think what it would be like
I'm never going to find someone as beautiful and sweet as Nicole
I can't imagine life without her
And the purpose of life
The purpose of life is to be with somebody you love who loves you back
And I'm not going to be with anyone else but her
We will die at the exact same time
I'll make sure of it

**EVA.** So
You won't be needing the car?

    *Beat*

**ADAM.** I wasn't

**EVA.** (*Genuinely*) I know
If you wanted to go you would have

**ADAM.** It's a rental
I don't know what it looks like so it was impossible to find
Maybe I could have
I got tired of looking

    *He hands her the keys*

I hope you find someone
I know you worry
The failed relationships, all your issues
Nicole tells me
One of the amazing things about love is how completely open you are
And you'll have that one day
You just have to get out there more, you know?

Put yourself out there
Send it into the universe and really focus
It'll come when you least expect it
When you're not even trying
**EVA.** Thanks
**ADAM.** Thank you, Eve

> *He exits*
> *Leaving* EVA *there alone*
> *Like always*

## 11

> NICOLE *is still in the bathroom, a bundle of energy with no place to go*
> *So she's taking it out on her face—or rather, the makeup on it*

> MICHELLE *enters, heading for a stall*

**NICOLE.** Michelle
Michelle
I am so glad you're here
**MICHELLE.** Mmhmm
**NICOLE.** I need you to tell me what to do
What should I do
**MICHELLE.** Um
**NICOLE.** I should go out there
Except
Except
Except
Should I even be getting married
Was this all some sign
Of course not
But if I'm interpreting it as a sign
Does that mean there are other things going on in the back of my mind
Reservations
Are these reservations?
I felt a little relieved
That there's an out, that I don't have to do this anymore
Is that terrible?
I should be with him
Of course I should be with him
Is there somebody else better for me than him?

Maybe
Maybe I need some alone time to figure myself out
I will never be alone again
He will be there
All the time
Every day
Every single Of every single
Which is what I want
Right?

**MICHELLE.** Totally

**NICOLE.** You're right
And we do make a great couple
Everyone says that

**MICHELLE.** Totally

**NICOLE.** I could kill him
The way he just stood there while
I could literally take my hands to his throat and
I shouldn't be so hard on him

> *Beat*

There are times when I think
Weeks where I wake up every day and look at him, really look at him, and think
Do I love you
And I wonder if it will turn into months at a time, and then years
But that's normal, right?
After such a long time?

> MICHELLE *nods*

**NICOLE.** And other times I look at him and I'm like
Yes
And we want to have kids
We will make great kids
And his proposal was so romantic
Remember how he proposed
With all the
And the goldfish

> MICHELLE *nods*

**NICOLE.** We planned this for like a year
And we love each other
It would be crazy to
I would be so crazy
Thank you
You are the best

NICOLE *leaves*
MICHELLE *vomits into the sink*


## 12


*The* FLOWER GIRLS *run through an empty hall*
**FLOWER GIRL 2.** Hurry up
**FLOWER GIRL 3.** I can't
**FLOWER GIRL 2.** We need to move faster
**FLOWER GIRL 1.** Where are we going
**FLOWER GIRL 2.** Away from murdering ghosts?!?
**FLOWER GIRL 1.** Stop
Stop
*They stop and* FLOWER GIRL 3 *catches up*
We need a plan
**FLOWER GIRL 3.** Garlic?
**FLOWER GIRL 1.** Like vampires?
**FLOWER GIRL 2.** What?
**FLOWER GIRL 1.** Garlic protects you from vampires
**FLOWER GIRL 3.** We need protection
**FLOWER GIRL 2.** These are ghosts not vampires
**FLOWER GIRL 1.** Same thing?
**FLOWER GIRL 2.** Where are we gonna find garlic?
**FLOWER GIRL 3.** The fridge!
**FLOWER GIRL 2.** We need to get someplace safe
**FLOWER GIRL 1.** We need to go to where the party is and find our parents
**FLOWER GIRL 2.** That's the first place the ghosts will go
We should go outside
**FLOWER GIRL 3.** In the woods?
**FLOWER GIRL 2.** It would keep us hidden
**FLOWER GIRL 3.** In the dark??
**FLOWER GIRL 1.** I know where we can hide
**FLOWER GIRL 2.** Where?
**FLOWER GIRL 1.** Come on
*And they keep running*

## 13

> ADAM *and* NICOLE *both enter the bridal room*
> *A hesitant moment when they see each other*
> *Then they laugh*

**NICOLE.** You okay?

**ADAM.** You?

**NICOLE.** We should have gone with the woman

**ADAM.** You wanted him

**NICOLE.** I wanted the progressive woman rabbi

**ADAM.** He was your guy

**NICOLE.** My parents'

**ADAM.** That counts as you

**NICOLE.** That's my family

**ADAM.** That's the same thing as you

**NICOLE.** Well you're my family now so I guess that means it's your fault too

**ADAM.** Is this the part where we laugh again

**NICOLE.** You didn't do anything

**ADAM.** What was I supposed to do?

**NICOLE.** I don't know
Take charge in a crisis
Do something
Not let a man die

**ADAM.** You're right honey
I should have told him to stay alive

**NICOLE.** That is so funny sweetheart
Thank you for making jokes about the man who died at my wedding

**ADAM.** It's my wedding too
I know it must be hard to remember when everything is about you

**NICOLE.** I'm the bride

**ADAM.** I'm the groom

**NICOLE.** I'm the bride

**ADAM.** I'm the groom

**NICOLE.** I'm the bride
I'm the bride

**ADAM.** I'm the groom

**NICOLE.** I'M THE BRIDE

**ADAM.** I would have liked to pick one thing

**NICOLE.** You chose the band

**ADAM.** Big difference that makes now

**NICOLE.** The band is huge
Music is huge

**ADAM.** (I would have done a better job with the rabbi)

**NICOLE.** What?

**ADAM.** Thank you for the music
For giving it to me

**NICOLE.** Do not quote ABBA in a time of crisis

**ADAM.** I can quote whoever I want

**NICOLE.** You're right honey
Quote away

**ADAM.** "Welcome, welcome, I'm so freaking old I'm pretty much dead already so why would anyone hire me to do anything but sleep and eat pudding"

**NICOLE.** I DID NOT CHOOSE HIM MY PARENTS DID

**ADAM.** YOU ARE AN ADULT

**NICOLE.** POT KETTLE, ASSHOLE

**ADAM.** I'M NOT A POT
I'M AN ADULT

**NICOLE.** YOU DIDN'T *DO* ANYTHING

**ADAM.** MAMMA MIA, HERE WE GO AGAIN

**NICOLE.** IF YOU DO THAT ONE MORE TIME

**ADAM.** WHAT?
WHAT, SUPER TROUPER?

    *Beat*

**NICOLE.** How are you going to react when our five-year-old gets cancer? Or when I get cancer?
How are you going to react when I lose a breast?

**ADAM.** Don't say that

**NICOLE.** Both breasts
And we lose the house
When it burns down in a fire that decimates everything and kills our little girl with leukemia

**ADAM.** Those things aren't going to happen

**NICOLE.** You don't want kids?
Kids come with diseases
All the time
Houses burn down

**ADAM.** You don't have to worry about that stuff

**NICOLE.** So we can be unprepared like today?
I deal with things Adam
When something happens I confront it
I do not watch a man die at my WEDDING

**ADAM.** I think that is what you did

**NICOLE.** I am the bride
I was in shock
I don't know CPR
And you're supposed to be the man

**ADAM.** Is it the 1950s

**NICOLE.** It is when I say it is

**ADAM.** Why do you get to say everything?

**NICOLE.** Because I'm the only one who will!

**ADAM.** Well you could shut up for a change

**NICOLE.** Ex-Cuse me

**ADAM.** It's the 1950s
I can say that

**NICOLE.** It's not anymore

**ADAM.** You can't choose everything!

**NICOLE.** Okay
Choose

**ADAM.** What

**NICOLE.** Anything

**ADAM.** THERE'S NOTHING TO CHOOSE NOW

**NICOLE.** I don't know if I want to be married to you

**ADAM.** Well too bad, 'cuz you are

**NICOLE.** Not really

**ADAM.** I was there
Pretty sure you are

**NICOLE.** I was a paralegal for two years
Pretty sure I'm not

**ADAM.** Can't argue with that resume

**NICOLE.** That whole do you take this person do you take this person I do
I do by the power vested in blah blah blah?

We didn't do that
We may have held hands and let go ten times
But he did not ascertain that we'd come of our own will
We did not say I do
Not married

**ADAM.** On what
A technicality?

**NICOLE.** And technically we're not

**ADAM.** It's symbolic
That doesn't change anything
If we've chosen to commit to one another
And we made that choice right?

**NICOLE.** We committed to a party

*End of Part I*

## PART II

*Out of the darkness, each speaker exists in a separate light*

**DAVE.** To the bride and groom

**MICHELLE.** To you guys

**DAVE.** Someone once told me

**MICHELLE.** As someone once said

**DAVE.** //Love looks not with the eyes
But with the heart

**MICHELLE.** //Love looks not with the eyes
But with the heart
And we can all
See your hearts today

**DAVE.** Your hearts have 20/20 vision

**MICHELLE.** You guys are the perfect couple

**DAVE.** Aren't they a perfect couple?

**MICHELLE.** So perfect

**DAVE.** When you look at them
You think: this is love

**MICHELLE.** That's love

**DAVE.** It is an inspiration to see two people
As in love as you

**MICHELLE.** When I think of love
And inspiration
And meaning in my life
I think of you

**DAVE.** I know what you're all thinking
Now's the time when the best man roasts the groom
Puts him on a skewer
Marinates it
Gets some rub in there

**MICHELLE.** You know
Some people say love
It's like
A river

**DAVE.** But I'm not here to make fun of my buddy
The glasses he wore in high school
The spinelessness with which he lives his entire life
I'm kidding

Can I get some cymbals, please?

**MICHELLE.** Some say love
It's like a razor
Making your soul bleed
In a romantic way

**DAVE.** What I am going to say is
Congratulations
Nicole
You look beautiful
And you look so much better with the weight off
Good for you
I don't know what you see in this guy
Maybe his bank account?
Drum man!

**MICHELLE.** Some say love
It is a hunger
An endless, aching, need
Like

*The sound of an endless aching need*

**DAVE.** And what a lovely ceremony
It was breathtaking
Am I right?
Percussion, keep up!
And isn't marriage its own kind of death anyway?
Where'd the band go?
Adam, you're beautiful
Nicole, you're beautiful—so don't get lax with that diet

**MICHELLE.** I think love is a flower
And you guys are the seediest seeds

**DAVE.** L'Chaim

**MICHELLE.** To lying!
Or however you say it
Tradition!

*Shift*

**SETH.** Hi
Adam, thank you for asking me to speak
Mr. and Mrs....
And Mr. and Mrs.—Dr. and Mrs.—Mr. and Dr....
To all the parents
I am honored to speak about my friend
Marriage is

Not something anyone should enter into lightly
I look at you guys
Ready to start on this new life together
>    *He starts to get choked up*
As a team, a unit
Remember: the strongest twigs are the ones bound together, they don't break
And I hope you guys are strong twigs
One united, bundle of sticks
Is there a word for that?
Oh no um
You should make your own name
Decide what your bundle is going to be
Create your own future out of that bundle of sticks
Make your own beautiful children out of those sticks
And watch those sticks get married
And make their own stick piles, and their own tiny baby sticks
And I hope the two of you never take any of those sticks for granted
Because we all know how rare it is
To find our own stick
That will stick with us
Despite all the other sticks out there
Cheers
>    *Shift*

**EVA.** I met Nicole at summer camp
Lake Winnetocawagabagopinelandingstream
We hit it off instantly
Actually we didn't
Nicole was one of the cool girls
I was the loser in the corner of the cabin
The one where everyone dips her finger in warm water to
It's not important
I was having a hard summer
My dad died
And that was really hard
Seeing a person so full of life become nothing but a pile of bones and flesh
I had never seen a dead—anything before
Let alone a human body losing all signs of life
It was a brain aneurysm
It was sudden
I rode in the ambulance with him
But by then he was already gone
They told me he was sick

But I heard them whisper to my mom
"He's gone"
I heard
Even though they thought I didn't
I did
And I understood
When she vomited all over the body
I didn't think
"Oh no Daddy's Yankees shirt is dirty"
I thought
He'll never wear that shirt again
And he didn't
They don't bury people in what they're wearing when they die
Even if it's their favorite shirt and you tell your mother He'd want to be
buried in that
They don't

      *Beat*

So Nicole was great that summer
She saw that I was having a hard time and she became my friend
In secret, so she wouldn't get kicked out of the popular group
But we were friends, in secret
And we stayed friends
No one else from Lake Winnetocawagabagopinelandingstream is here tonight,
so
I think that says a lot
I am so happy for you
Both of you
Finding someone to share your life with is
'Til Death do you part
And you deserve it
To life

        SETH *is in a hall or foyer*
        *Maybe drinking*
        *Maybe staring into his drink*

        EVA *walks out into the hall and screams*
        *A loud primal scream*

        *She sees* SETH

**EVA.** I'm happy
**SETH.** Me too
I'm happy for them

**EVA.** They're a beautiful couple
**SETH.** They are
**EVA.** Weddings are beautiful
**SETH.** They are
**EVA.** I think my speech was bad
**SETH.** No
**EVA.** I had a better one prepared
It had cue cards and a fun anecdote
**SETH.** I thought you were very honest
**EVA.** I had a good speech planned
And no one will get to hear it
**SETH.** You could say it now
**EVA.** What?
**SETH.** I'll be your audience
**EVA.** I lost my cue cards
That's why I was so
**SETH.** I thought what you said was
Very deep
**EVA.** I cried
**SETH.** Hey
I did too
**EVA.** You seem to really care
About marriage
**SETH.** I'm getting separated
**EVA.** Oh
**SETH.** We're discussing it as a possibility
She's discussing it, and I listen
When she has time to call
She travels a lot for work
It's hard
A relationship is something you have to work at
**EVA.** Sure
**SETH.** You married?
**EVA.** No
I can be controlling
And I tend to over-share or
Overstep
I don't have good boundaries
That's something I'm trying to work on

Controlling my boundaries
Without being controlling
It's hard
**SETH.** Boundaries are tough
Every relationship
You gotta figure them out
Are you gonna be strictly strict about things
And how strict are you going to be
Is friendly drinks okay
Dinners
Hugs
Harmless kisses that only happened one time or
     *Beat*
**EVA.** Did you have a big wedding?
**SETH.** It was a lot like this one
Sort of
Her brother got ordained on the internet
I thought he was
Okay
I grew up going to church but
We thought it was nicer to do a tent outside thing
It's great for pictures so that's what We
The food was okay
I really wanted those fries
With all the dips
**EVA.** I love those
**SETH.** And you can get the craziest kinds
**EVA.** Yes!
**SETH.** Chipotle mayo
Lavender mayo
Other kinds of mayo
I saw someone on *Top Chef* do it once
**EVA.** I love *Top Chef*
**SETH.** Me too
**EVA.** But this season hasn't been the same
**SETH.** I know!
**EVA.** Did you have a nice honeymoon, at least?
**SETH.** No
**EVA.** You're funny
**SETH.** You're kind

*Beat*

**EVA.** You're sweet

**SETH.** You're a good listener

**EVA.** You're a good speaker

**SETH.** I don't know about that, you heard my speech

**EVA.** You're funny

**SETH.** You said that

> *Something between a giggle and a sigh from* EVA

**SETH.** You have a pretty laugh

**EVA.** Ha

**SETH.** You're pretty

**EVA.** No

**SETH.** Yeah

**EVA.** No

**SETH.** You are

**EVA.** I'm not

**SETH.** I think you are

**EVA.** I don't think I am

**SETH.** You really are

**EVA.** I'm really not

**SETH.** Really

**EVA.** Nuh uh

**SETH.** Uh huh

**EVA.** I'm passable but

**SETH.** Agree to disagree?

**EVA.** Fine

**SETH.** So it's settled

**EVA.** I guess

> *They kiss*
> *It's slow*
> *Romantic*
> *Like they've been waiting their whole lives for this*
> *Or the last ten minutes*

**EVA.** My purse!

**SETH.** Oh

Wow

We got swept up the

But I can't

**EVA.** What?

**SETH.** Your purse with the um
(condoms)

**EVA.** Cue cards
For my speech

**SETH.** Oh

**EVA.** Yah

**SETH.** So you don't…

**EVA.** You just…

**SETH.** I did

**EVA.** Great
So now you can hear my speech

**SETH.** Great


MICHELLE
*Back where the toasts were*
*With the microphone*

**MICHELLE.** Is everybody having fun!
It's time for Adam and Nicole's first dance and the band left
But I have my phone
And I found their song on YouTube
My connection isn't great
I have two bars
One second there's a commercial

*Looks out to the room*

Don't go
You have to see the first dance
You can't miss that
It's early
It's only 10

*Looks at her phone*

I have to go

*She runs off*
*Some dead air*
*Eventually,* DAVE *comes up to the mic*

**DAVE.** I am supposed to tell you
The couple is going to have their first dance
And they've been taking lessons
Because that's what happens when you get married

You do pussy shit that you never would have chosen to do in a million years
Like take dance lessons

> *He takes out his phone, holds it up to the microphone*

I have AT&T so
Let's see what I've got on here

> *A definitively non-wedding song plays*
> NICOLE *and* ADAM *start their choreographed wedding dance*
> *They may have a few false starts*
> *Given that this is not the song they rehearsed with*

**NICOLE.** You missed the dip

**ADAM.** I didn't miss it, it's coming

**NICOLE.** You missed it

**ADAM.** Shit

> *Dancing*

**ADAM.** (*Re: the dancing*) Can you not

**NICOLE.** What

**ADAM.** Forget it

> *Dancing*

**NICOLE.** My grandmother had to hear everything Dave said

**ADAM.** You grandmother can't hear anything she says

**NICOLE.** Everyone we know heard it

**ADAM.** Half of them left already

> *Dancing*

**NICOLE.** You could have stopped him

**ADAM.** What was I gonna do
Go up there and tell him to stop in the middle of

**NICOLE.** Yes

**ADAM.** You know he travels to the beat of his own drum

**NICOLE.** It's an offensive beat

**ADAM.** Your friends weren't any better

> *Dancing*

**NICOLE.** The lessons were your idea

**ADAM.** Because you have two left feet

**NICOLE.** And you have one tiny penis

> *The song ends or maybe just cuts out*

> ADAM *and* NICOLE *look out at the guests, at each other*

**ADAM.** I'm gonna

**NICOLE.** *(Fine)* Yeah
> *He kisses her*
> *He dips her*
> *Maybe she's impressed*
> *A little*

**ADAM.** Told you I didn't miss it.

**NICOLE.** Whatever

It's not that tiny

**ADAM.** I know

**NICOLE.** Don't be cocky

**ADAM.** Why not

**NICOLE.** You're lucky my grandmother's deaf

**ADAM.** I am
> *They kiss again*
> *It starts to get kind of heavy*
> *Like in a potentially gross kind of way*

> *The room where the wedding was*
> *A few chairs are still set up*
> *Some flowers*
> *A lot of it was taken down in the commotion*

**EVA.** It's so quiet in here

**SETH.** I know

**EVA.** It creeps me out

**SETH.** I'll protect you

**EVA.** Shhh this is a holy space

**SETH.** I think it's a conference room

**EVA.** It became a holy place
It had religious stuff in it

**SETH.** This?
I'm pretty sure that is a fancy sheet
Attached to some sticks
With some flowers on it
> *Beat*

**EVA.** What do you think he was thinking? Before he

**SETH.** I don't know

**EVA.** I wonder if he knew
I wonder if you consciously know that it's happening

Like when you're falling asleep, and you can feel yourself fading

**SETH.** I don't know

**EVA.** It makes you think about what's important

The people that are important

The lack of people

> SETH *is somewhere else*

Are you okay?

**SETH.** Yah

> *He's not*

**EVA.** Do you want a

> *She hugs him*
> *They separate*
> *But the energy, it's electric (boogie woogie woogie)*

My purse!

> *She runs to look for it*

I know it's here somewhere, because I was going to leave it in the other room, but I remember remembering Nik and Adam had to go there after the ceremony for a Jewish thing, so I thought if I left it…aha!

**SETH.** Cue cards?

**EVA.** Thank goodness

**SETH.** Too bad you already gave your toast

**EVA.** Sit

> *She goes back to the altar*

Are you listening?

> SETH *nods*

Don't laugh too loud

We don't want to get caught

**SETH.** Who's gonna catch us?

**EVA.** You can laugh a little

At the jokes

**SETH.** Okay

**EVA.**

> Good evening. Nicole, thank you for

I talk to her for a bit here

> *Flip*

Then Adam

> *Flip*

Then the parents

When Nicole and I were in the tenth grade, she thought she was pregnant. Her period was late. You could say it had taken a pregnant pause.
(PAUSE FOR LAUGHTER)
When she told me, I had just watched the episode of

Did you ever—
Nevermind

When she told me, I had just watched the episode

A show where one of the characters gets pregnant

**SETH.** Got it

**EVA.**

So in my mind I'm thinking: I know this can happen in real life. Because when you're 16 you think TV shows represent real life!
(PAUSE FOR LAUGHTER)

I told her she had to take a test, but she was scared people would see two teenagers and call our parents. I got the idea that we should dress up like adults.
(PAUSE FOR LAUGHTER. SHAKE HEAD & SMILE)

We put on my mom's blazers and heels, and went to the drugstore. Then, we had the brilliant idea to make it look like a planned pregnancy.
(MINI PFL)

We bought a bunch of baby paraphernalia: diapers, pacifiers, and so forth, along with the pregnancy test. We walked out of there, tottering in our heels, carrying these big bags of baby stuff that had cost us our entire allowance.
(PFL / HEAD SHAKE-SMILE)

Nik, you have always been my partner in crime. As humorous as this anecdote may be, it says something about our friendship. We have always been there for each other. I think back to when we first met at summer camp and we were instantly inseparable. We were the coolest girls in

*She flips past that card*

Seeing you two find happiness gives me all the faith in the world. As they say, "Love looks not with the eyes, but with the heart."

That's it

SETH *kisses her there, under the huppah*

**EVA.** What do you think?

**SETH.** I think you are funny
In a good way
And honest
And pretty
Even though you don't think you are
And I think we have to live while we can

**EVA.** I meant about my speech

> *They kiss some more and it builds*
> *No condoms, but fuck that, they have cue cards*

> *Elsewhere—a hallway, a corner*
> MICHELLE *dials on her cell phone*

**MICHELLE.** Hello?
Hi may I please speak to—

Michelle

No I'm okay

This is an emergency

My heart is breaking
I'm totally kidding
I

Hello

> *She dials again*

Hi can I please speak to Carlos

No it is he works there Carlos the ambulance driver

I'm totally serious

No wait don't hang up please I really think there's a chance he could be the love of my life—you know when you just click with someone?—and I think he's confused about where to meet me and—

Hello

> *Dials again*

Hi

Yes may I please speak to a female operator

I think she'll understand me better

Michelle

I'm at—I don't know the address

Like when I have sex?

Oh I'm safe here, I'm trying to talk to Carlos who I met him on a call earlier today and we had this connection and—

But your job is to help people and—

No I'm not On Something, are you?

> *She looks at the drink in her hand*

I don't know, a few

Well I'm not going to anyway, because you guys are useless and I don't know why I called 9-1-1 for HELP in the first place and maybe you should think about not doing so much false advertising

Hello?

> *A beat*

> *She goes back to dialing*


> DAVE, *back at the microphone*

**DAVE.** I would like to apologize for using a certain word earlier
Apparently the term pussy shit offended some people and I am sorry if the term
Pussy Shit
Was offensive to you
Apparently some of you are a little Traditional
So I will watch what I say
Much like a husband may have to watch what he says
To accommodate his wife's every irrational whim
She may tell him to make his friend apologize for no fucking reason and he will
Because marriage is signing up to surrender your freedom, in favor of doing shit that someone else wants you to do
And we are celebrating a marriage tonight
Which incidentally is an institution
That will include Nicole's pussy
It's funny
A lot of assholes spend a lot of time trying to preserve the pussy as the domain of marriage
In the name of tradition
So if you are here to celebrate a good old-fashioned traditional marriage
You should be celebrating the The Pussy

Because 50% of all this is about Nicole's pussy if you think about it

If it's the word Shit that was offensive to you
Well, then you're shit out of luck

Now Adam and Nicole will eat cake

> NICOLE *and* ADAM *take center stage again*
> *Posing with the cake*
> *Their clothes seem a little askew*

**NICOLE.** Ohmygod I could

> *Talking herself down*

It could be worse
Nobody
Else died
I had sex in a closet and my hair looks fine

**ADAM.** And it was pretty great

**NICOLE.** I haven't had to speak to my mother all night
Silver lining
Silver fucking lining

> *They start to feed each other cake*

**ADAM.** I'm proud of you, hon
You're not letting your emotions get the best of you

**NICOLE.** Mmm hmm

**ADAM.** Just a few more pictures
Then we can get back to that closet and calm you down again

**NICOLE.** Funny

**ADAM.** Are you saying you didn't just need a little

**NICOLE.** Do you hear yourself?
Do you ever stop and listen to what you say

**ADAM.** It's hard when you're always talking over me

**NICOLE.** I talk so much so people won't realize what a douche you are

**ADAM.** And you're such a treat

**NICOLE.** You better watch it

**ADAM.** Earlier, I was ready to take Dave's car and drive it straight to Belize
Eve had to drag me back here and pry the keys out of my hand

**DAVE.** Okay
Who's ready for the garter belt

**ADAM.** I can choose too

**DAVE.** Let's make some noise for Adam!
He's The Man

And marriage is all about the man
And the pussy
But the dick is in charge
Very complicated shit

**NICOLE.** You need to make him stop

**ADAM.** I don't need to do anything

**DAVE.** What they are about to do will symbolize
That Nicole is now Adam's sexual property

**NICOLE.** Make him stop

**DAVE.** Chattel, as they said in biblical times

**NICOLE.** I'm serious

**ADAM.** I am too

**NICOLE.** Shut up Dave

**DAVE.** Babe you're the one who signed up for this

**NICOLE.** Shut the fuck up

**DAVE.** Hey no heckling the MC

**NICOLE.** You are so pathetic, do you know that?
With your 22-year-old girlfriends
And your shitty apartment
What you say is not funny
It is not smart
And you are not special
And if people want to spend their lives together as actual adults in the twenty-first century, let them do it
And don't use that as an excuse to take out all your anger because you have done nothing of worth in your entire adult life
You don't have the balls to do anything, besides criticize everyone else for their choices
At least they're choices
At least we're committing to something
And if we choose to celebrate our love
LET US FUCKING CELEBRATE OUR LOVE

  ADAM *moves toward her*

Don't touch me

  *She exits*


  EVA *and* SETH *are in the room where we left them*
  *But obviously a lot has happened since*
  *They're barely clothed and a little breathless*

**SETH.** That was

**EVA.** Yeah

**SETH.** Did we just

**EVA.** Yeah

**SETH.** I don't usually

**EVA.** Me neither

**SETH.** I think you're
The way you take care of everything
You were on top of those pictures this afternoon
That photographer would have been lost without you

**EVA.** I like you
I don't want that to sound like more than it is but I like you and I know the
timing is complicated but things are always going to be complicated and
maybe sometimes you just have to accept the complication and open yourself
up to the possibility of something
Complicated
Because I like you and we could take things slow

If you wanted

Or if you didn't that's okay too

But if you did

Or didn't

I do

**SETH.** I'm so sorry I—

**EVA.** It's fine

**SETH.** I'm just
This was

**EVA.** Fun
We're drunk
It's a wedding

**SETH.** I have a lot I need to deal with right now
With my
I need to work on things with um

**EVA.** I respect that

**SETH.** You don't have to

**EVA.** You shouldn't have said you like *Top Chef*

**SETH.** I really do

**EVA.** I really do too

**SETH.** It's a great show

**EVA.** It is

*A lingering beat*

Should we

**SETH.** Uh huh

**EVA.** Hey

If it doesn't work out

I'm kidding

I'm not

I don't know what I am

**SETH.** It probably won't so

*He gets a little choked up*

**EVA.** It'll be okay

**SETH.** You think?

**EVA.** People work through these things

**SETH.** Really?

**EVA.** One-time mistakes happen and everyone moves on

No permanent damage done

One time doesn't mean anything

**SETH.** I think it's been the whole time

**EVA.** Oh

**SETH.** Maybe I can ask her to go to counseling

**EVA.** I hear that's helpful

**SETH.** Or

Renew our vows

**EVA.** That's sweet

**SETH.** Have a party

**EVA.** It wouldn't have the fries though

**SETH.** No

What I said before was—

**EVA.** See you in there?

**SETH.** Yup

*He starts to leave*
*Then remembers his pants*

First I should

**EVA.** Me too

*They put on their clothes in silence*
*Then start to leave at the same time*
*But that's awkward*

*So* SETH *waits while she leaves first*
*And then he goes*

*The* FLOWER GIRLS *emerge from their hiding place*
*Perhaps under the altar? Perhaps in a corner nearby?*

**FLOWER GIRL 2.** That was

**FLOWER GIRL 1.** That is not how they

**FLOWER GIRL 2.** That was crazy

FLOWER GIRL 3 *whimpers*

**FLOWER GIRL 1.** I feel sick

**FLOWER GIRL 2.** You're fine

**FLOWER GIRL 1.** That was gross

**FLOWER GIRL 2.** It's natural

**FLOWER GIRL 1.** How are they allowed to do that?

**FLOWER GIRL 2.** I don't know

FLOWER GIRL 3 *whimpers*

**FLOWER GIRL 1.** I want my mom

**FLOWER GIRL 2.** You cannot tell your mom

**FLOWER GIRL 1.** My mom says if—

**FLOWER GIRL 2.** IS YOUR MOM HERE?

**FLOWER GIRL 1.** I'm going

**FLOWER GIRL 2.** There's nowhere to go

**FLOWER GIRL 1.** Someone has to—

**FLOWER GIRL 2.** THERE'S NO ONE

**FLOWER GIRL 1.** But—

**FLOWER GIRL 2.** DO YOU WANT TO DIE?!

**FLOWER GIRL 3.** THERE ARE TOO MANY THINGS!

FLOWER GIRL 3 *sits down, or sort of collapses*


*Back in the foyer*
*At one end,* MICHELLE *looks toward the front doors, holding a full,*
*untouched blue drink*
*At another,* EVA *is halfway through a drink of her own*
NICOLE *enters*

**NICOLE.** What are you
Where have you been?

**EVA.** Sorry

**NICOLE.** Sorry?

**EVA.** What do you need?

**NICOLE.** What do I

I need

I need

I need for

And to

**EVA.** What?

**NICOLE.** I could do anything

**EVA.** Okay

**NICOLE.** Relationships are like

Not everything

We need to focus on ourselves

We need to lean the fuck in

We can take a trip

Some sexy island where no one can hold us down and

We need to go somewhere unsexy

No sex

Like ladies' night but forever

**EVA.** Let's take a breath for a second

**NICOLE.** I don't need to breathe

I need to live

We need to leave

> *She starts to*

But we all took that stupid shuttle bus

Except for Dave

Dave who refuses to do anything I

And Adam said

You have his keys

**EVA.** You have been through a lot today and

**NICOLE.** Eva

We're gonna get away

We don't need men

It's like your dream

You won't be the only single one

> EVA *opens her mouth like she's about to say something*
> *But just pours some booze in it*

**NICOLE.** Alright Michelle it's you and me

Where do you want to go?

**MICHELLE.** I'm kind of waiting for someone

**NICOLE.** Who

**MICHELLE.** My date

**NICOLE.** You don't have a date

**MICHELLE.** Carlos

**NICOLE.** Michelle

You came alone

**MICHELLE.** He's meeting me he's just late

**NICOLE.** You do not have an imaginary date

Okay?

This is the real world

We are not in your fantasyland where everything magically works out

**EVA.** I think you need to talk to Adam and you'll feel better

**NICOLE.** Is that right Eva?

**EVA.** What are you

**NICOLE.** So you didn't have to stop him from leaving

And then lie to me about it

**EVA.** He didn't really want to

**NICOLE.** No?

Please tell me what he wants

**EVA.** That's not what I

**NICOLE.** And tell me what I need

And please tell me what I should do about this joke of a wedding SINCE YOU WEREN'T EVEN THERE

**EVA.** I'm sorry

**NICOLE.** I heard

Can I have the keys

**EVA.** I really think if you

**NICOLE.** Keys

**EVA.** I don't have them

**NICOLE.** Eva

**EVA.** Nik

**NICOLE.** Eva

**EVA.** Nik

**NICOLE.** Eva

Okay you're right

You're right

I'm sorry

Thank you

       NICOLE *opens her arms*

*A tentative beat*
*They hug*
EVA *really needed a hug*
*And*
*Is* NICOLE *groping her?*

**EVA.** What are you—

**NICOLE.** GIVE ME THE GODAMN KEYS

NICOLE *tries to get into* EVA's *pockets*
*She tackles her—or her dress, and* EVA *with it—to the ground*

**EVA.** NO!

EVA *pushes her off and they regain their stances*
EVA *holds the keys*
*And in a weird quick move she somehow stuffs them up her dress, down her…*

**NICOLE.** Did you just

**EVA.** I dunno

*They catch their breath*

**NICOLE.** I was being nice when I asked you to be in my wedding
And you still fucked it up
I just can't tell if you're actually incompetent, or if you're trying to sabotage everything I have
And after everything I
I forgave
I understood
I moved on
I let you be my friend

*To* MICHELLE

And you
You are going to be waiting a long long time

*She starts to leave*

I am going to go find my stupid groom now
Because it is ladies' night somewhere
BUT NOT HERE

*Beat*

Please fix your hair

NICOLE *exits*
MICHELLE *hasn't moved*

**EVA.** You okay?

**MICHELLE.** Uh huh

*The keys fall to the floor*

EVA *leaves*

MICHELLE *screams*

*A loud, primal scream*


FLOWER GIRLS 1 *and 2 where we left them*
FLOWER GIRL 3 *is a mess and the others try to console her*
**FLOWER GIRL 1.** My mom says it's good to express your feelings
**FLOWER GIRL 2.** Your mom is LAME
**FLOWER GIRL 1.** She says if you sing your feelings
It helps
**FLOWER GIRL 2.** She'll be fine
You'll be fine
FLOWER GIRL 3 *is not fine*
FLOWER GIRL 1 *starts singing, to her own tune*
**FLOWER GIRL 1.**
I saw some kind of weird stuff today
All these things happened
Like a guy got sick
**FLOWER GIRL 2.** And died
**FLOWER GIRL 1.**
He didn't die they took him to the hospital my mom said
**FLOWER GIRL 2.** Your mom is an idiot
**FLOWER GIRL 1.**
No she's not
But doesn't singing make you feel better?
         *2 shuts up*
It does
Cuz people have lots of feelings
And it's good to get them out
My mom knows what she's talking about
She went to Yale
That's a really good school

We saw some people doing it that was weird
It was probably the grossest thing I ever saw
**FLOWER GIRL 2.** Like ever
**FLOWER GIRL 1.**
We saw some people doing it that was weird
It was probably the grossest thing I ever saw

**FLOWER GIRL 1 AND 2.**
We saw some people doing it that was weird
It was probably the grossest thing I ever saw

**FLOWER GIRL 1.** And I thought we were gonna die

**FLOWER GIRL 2.** And I thought we were gonna die too

**FLOWER GIRL 1 AND 2.**
Cuz Bloody Mary
Bloody Mary

> *Letting themselves get into the vocals*

Blooooooody Maaaaaryyyyyyyyyyyyyy

*A very silent beat*
*They all realize what they've just done*

**FLOWER GIRL 1.** Maybe it doesn't count if you're singing

**FLOWER GIRL 2.** It counts

**FLOWER GIRL 3.** (*Softly*)
Maybe there is no such thing as Bloody Mary actually

And if there is the other stuff we saw today was way more scary

FLOWER GIRLS 1 *and* 2 *take this in*
*They breathe, almost relieved*
*But not*


EVA *walks outside*
DAVE *is smoking*

**DAVE.** If you leave now there will be no one left at this party

**EVA.** I needed some air
It's getting scary in there

**DAVE.** Tell me about it

*A beat*

**EVA.** Can I

*He hands her the cigarette*
*She smokes*
*Awkwardly*

**DAVE.** Everyone is married

**EVA.** I know

**DAVE.** It's like every few years, there's a memo of what to do next and they all do it
We all must get married
We all must have a house and a yard and a 401K

We all must change who we are
We all must conform
How does that happen

**EVA.** I don't know

**DAVE.** I'll tell you one thing
If I ever do have one of these
Which I won't
It's not going to be so fucking blue

**EVA.** I chose the blue

> *He takes a flask out of his jacket pocket and offers it to her*

**DAVE.** Your toast was

**EVA.** Yah

**DAVE.** It was a lot

**EVA.** I had a lot to drink

**DAVE.** It was pretty intense

**EVA.** Weddings

**DAVE.** Yeah but you seemed
You seem
Pretty messed up
Emotionally

> *She drinks*

Are you the one that Adam

**EVA.** Yup

**DAVE.** You're kind of a home-wrecker, aren't you?

**EVA.** It wasn't...

**DAVE.** No judgment here

> *She drinks*

You're pretty cute

**EVA.** Thanks

**DAVE.** At first I thought you were kind of a nightmare
During pictures this afternoon I thought
That chick needs to get laid
But clearly you do alright
I respect that

> *He drinks*

**EVA.** Okay

**DAVE.** It's a compliment
Take it
And I like a little of that messed up shit

Keeps things interesting
>*He offers her back the flask*

More?
>*She goes to take it, but he pulls it back*

Say please

**EVA.** Please

**DAVE.** You are really fucking cute

**EVA.** And you are kind of a dick

**DAVE.** But one that's available, right?
Or is that not your thing
Do you prefer if there's a girlfriend or wife
Give you some excitement in your sad life as a P.R. girl

**EVA.** H.R.

**DAVE.** Same thing

**EVA.** It's not

**DAVE.** It is

**EVA.** It's actually not

**DAVE.** You don't get it

**EVA.** Try me

**DAVE.** You wouldn't understand

**EVA.** Make me
>*Beat*

**DAVE.** Are you gonna be good?

**EVA.** You tell me
>*A beat*

**DAVE.** Why don't you tell me

**EVA.** Because I want you to tell me
>*Beat*

**DAVE.** Will you do what you're told

**EVA.** Maybe

**DAVE.** I think you mean yes, bitch

**EVA.** Yes

**DAVE.** You're kind of a slut
Aren't you
A home-wrecking slut
Hey I get it
You can't help yourself
You just want some attention

A way to work out your daddy issues

Sorry I didn't mean to
**EVA.** It's fine
**DAVE.** I really didn't
**EVA.** It's totally fine
>        *Beat*
**DAVE.** I don't know what the fuck I'm doing
**EVA.** Neither do I
>        *They stay there, staring out into the parking lot*


>        *The bridal party members are all still onstage as*


>            NICOLE *and* ADAM *approach the microphone*
**NICOLE.** Hello
Excuse me
We'd like to say a few words
>        *She passes the mic to* ADAM
**ADAM.** Yes
>        *She waits for him to say more*
>        *He doesn't*
**NICOLE.** First to our families, we want to thank you so much
>        *She passes the mic to* ADAM
**ADAM.** Yup
>        *Waits for him again*
**NICOLE.** And to our bridal party, thank you for everything you contributed
to this day
>        *She waits for* ADAM *again*
>        *He nods*
We appreciate all of you being here
>        ADAM *leans into the mic*
**ADAM.** And we appreciate how you stayed the whole time and committed
to the party you RSVP'd to
**NICOLE.** And didn't try to leave early
No one had to force you to come back
**ADAM.** Doesn't matter as long as you made it to the party
**NICOLE.** I don't even know what this party is anymore
**ADAM.** Well the party's over now
**NICOLE.** It is

**ADAM.** Goodnight and get home safe

**NICOLE.** (*To* ADAM) I can't do this

I can't I'm sorry

> *She stops*
> *Something in the distance has caught everyone's attention*

> *An elderly woman, dressed in what you might call Sunday best—a hat, pearls,*
> *maybe a cane—makes her way through the audience*

**MRS. GOODMAN.** Excuse me

I'm looking for the party room

They said it was down the hall

They have very long halls here

They're beautiful halls

Long

Everything feels longer when it's late

Some nights my husband will work very late and I don't fall asleep until he
gets home

It feels like forever

I went to bed early tonight even though he was working

I've never done that before

I was so tired

But a few hours later I woke up

I took a bath

I got dressed

And I got back into my bed and waited

I didn't know what to do next, but I knew I should be awake

And then the phone rang

I didn't have my hearing aid in

Because I was in bed

I put it in when I saw the flashing light on the phone

I picked it up and they told me to sit down

And I said I'm in bed

And they said sit up

And I said I am sitting up that's the same as sitting down

And they said Ma'am your husband is sick

And I said how sick

And they said Ma'am, your husband was officiating a wedding at the Oakfield Club when his heart stopped

And I said

Did it start again?

And they said

No Ma'am

And they asked me who should be called
And what are my plans
But all I could think was
A wedding sounds lovely
I haven't been to a wedding in years
And the Oakfield Club
That's something
I'll bet a wedding there is something to see
So I got dressed
I was already dressed, but I put on something nice
And I called a taxicab
I never do that but I thought
It's late
And this is a special occasion
And then in the car I thought
I wonder if the wedding was cancelled
I wonder if they're still having a party
What if I've done all this for nothing
But I had gotten dressed, and called a car, and driven halfway there so I thought
I might as well see for myself
Life is too short not to see for yourself
And here you all are
Celebrating
That's good
Love should be celebrated
Life is very precious and love should be celebrated
My husband's favorite thing in the world is celebrating the love of two people at a wedding
He always says
He says
He says
He said

> *Nobody moves for moment*

> *And then, the lights begin to shift*
> *Perhaps music starts to play*
> *Maybe it starts as one person humming, others joining in*
> *Maybe it begins as the tune of the* FLOWER GIRLS' *song earlier*
> *Maybe they're not all humming the same tune*
> *Eventually it becomes a wedding standard though—an 80s ballad?*
> *Canon in D?*
> *Probably Canon in D*

*Maybe it was that from the start*
*And as the music plays*
*Everyone walks slowly, procession-ally, rhythmically*
*Until the space is clear, as it was in the beginning*
*And* MICHELLE *is left alone onstage in a spotlight*

> *She takes in the audience*

**MICHELLE.** Dear
Everyone who's still here
We are gathered today to join Adam and Nicole in holy matrimony
Again
I know you thought you saw this happen before but it wasn't actually official
Sometimes stuff doesn't work out like you planned
And you don't understand why, but it's all for a reason
Like two years ago I got ordained by the Universal Life Church of Universal Life and Church
In case anyone ever asked me to do their wedding
Which they didn't
Until now
You may think tonight was sort of
Unconventional
But it has only made Nicole and Adam more sure they are meant to be together
Everything happens for a reason
It makes me wonder why Carlos said he was going to come be my date and he didn't
And why wouldn't the 9-1-1 people want to help us be together
And why wouldn't the universe
But there was totally a reason for all that
Carlos probably wasn't The One so it's good he didn't waste my time
I know when I find the one it will be totally right
You have to believe everything will work out and it will
You have to picture it and see it
Like if I close my eyes
It's like

> *She closes her eyes*

Everything is quiet
White
We're in an event space
No, a restaurant
There's music playing
Bach, or Enya

There's the sound of birds chirping
It's from doves flying overhead
Holding white roses in their beaks
I enter the space, alone, dressed nicely but not fancy
The hostess greets me at the door
She says my table is ready before I even say who I am
We walk through the sleek white space slowly
It's almost shiny
It glows with a sort of
Newness
There's candlelight
I hear the doves overhead
One swoops down to rest on my shoulder
I'm wearing a cardigan so I don't mind
After a minute it gets annoying
It's a nice cardigan
Cashmere
J. Crew
J. Crew Collection
So I gently brush the bird away, but it falls and tumbles into one of the candles
The dove is on fire
I can't believe it
The dove is in flames
The hostess quick as knives runs to it and smothers the fire with her hands
The dove is okay
It's going to be fine
Not one of its wings is singed it's like
A miracle
It flies away
The hostess seats me at my table
As I sit down, I look around and realize I am the only customer in the restaurant
At first I wonder if this is a bad sign—like if they have salmonella or a chef from the 80s
But I see the glowing white walls, the candles, the feisty doves brimming with a will to live
And I think: this is a nice place, it has to have nice food
I decide to call the waitress over to order a drink, but she's already standing there, holding a glass of Prosecco, which is my favorite
I ask if I can see a menu
I'll have a little snack while I wait for my boyfriend to meet me

I'm so hungry I haven't eaten all day to fit into my dress
But it was worth it
I've taken my cardigan off by now and my strapless neckline makes me look
like a goddess
Or a *Teen Vogue* intern
The waitress returns with a menu, which is the nicest menu I've ever seen
I open it, like a book too pretty for words and it says
The Reasons I Love You
I look up to tell the waitress: I think you brought the wrong thing, but she's
gone
I look down at the menu and realize it's kind of specific
It says things like
I love the way you play with your hair when you're thinking, and it gets
knotted and stuck around your finger and you have to cut it off with nail
scissors
And
I love how you rescued that ferret and let it sleep in your bed even though
you got rabies and almost died and most people would judge you for it
And right when I start to realize: these things are about me
There he is
My perfect boyfriend
He's in a suit, or something
And he's on his knee, holding out a ring
A princess cut diamond, 2.5 carat, platinum setting, nothing too flashy
It's a good ring
It's not from a wholesaler, or a second tier store
It's from a place like Van Cleef, or Tiffany's and he's paid retail
And I gasp
And I cover my mouth with my hands
And I laugh for a second
And then I cry a few perfect tears
And I say
Of course, a thousand times yes, I'll marry you!
And he says
I didn't ask yet
And we laugh
And kiss
And suddenly there's clapping
A lot of clapping
I can hear it coming from everywhere
I look around and all my friends and family are there
Hundreds of them

I didn't know I knew so many people
And they're all my closest friends
Everyone who means something to me is there
And I realize they were hiding behind the white chiffon curtains the whole time
And my fiancé's friend, who happens to be a *New York Times* photographer is snapping pictures, and we're all laughing, and everyone is looking at my ring, and I smile the biggest smile, my teeth hurt, my lips hurt, my heart hurts
And I'm so embarrassed the next day because all the pictures are online in the Style Section of the *New York Times*
It was so extravagant and amazing it is a must-read story
And we go on *Good Morning America* and I have this powder blue suit and yellow Jimmy Choos (I know it sounds like a weird combination, but it looks great)
And Hoda says to me: That is the nicest ring I've ever seen, I mean really, that man must love you because that is the most beautiful, classiest ring I have ever seen
And Kathy Lee says: Amen, sister!

> *A cell phone ringer goes off somewhere in the audience*

Sorry

Nicole do you take Adam?

Adam do you take Nicole?

And are you both here because you want to and not because anybody made you?

Okay then
Good.

### End of Play

# HOME INVASION
## by Krista Knight

## BIOGRAPHY

Krista Knight's work includes *Kirk at the San Francisco Airport Hyatt* (New York Theatre Workshop's Dartmouth Summer Residency, Vineyard Theatre Reading Series, Playwrights Foundation Rough Reading, Martha's Vineyard Playhouse Monday Night Special), *Primal Play* (New Georges, Playwrights' Center of Minneapolis), the punk rock adaptation of Medusa, *HISSIFIT* (Cradle Theatre), *Salamander Leviathan* (Joe's Pub at The Public Theater, Ars Nova's ANT Fest, Fingerlakes Musical Theatre Festival, Inkwell, KCACTF Musical Theatre Award from the Kennedy Center for best book), *Doomsurfing* (Parkside Lounge), *Selkie* (Williamstown Theatre Festival, Dutch Kills Theater Company), and 17 plays and musicals for young audiences. Commissions include the new musical *Don't Stop Me* with Dave Malloy, the script for a ride at Tokyo Disneyland, The Berkeley Rep School of Theatre, Case Western Reserve University's Biomedical Engineering Department, The Assembly, and Live Girls! Theater.

Knight has been in residence at La Napoule Art Foundation, Tofte Lake Center, The Orchard Project, Atlantic Center for the Arts, Page 73's Summer Residency at Yale, Santa Fe Art Institute, Ucross Foundation, Yaddo, and The MacDowell Colony. She is an alumna of Ensemble Studio Theatre's Youngblood, terraNOVA Collective's Groundbreakers, Page 73's Interstate 73, The Civilians' R&D Group, and The New Georges Jam, and is a current member of Fresh Ground Pepper's PlayGround PlayGroup. She was a Page 73 Playwriting Fellow (2007), MacDowell Fellow (2008), and the Shank Playwriting Fellow at the Vineyard Theatre (2011-2012). Knight holds a B.A. from Brown University, an M.A. in Performance Studies from New York University, and an M.F.A. in Playwriting from the University of California San Diego. She is a current Juilliard School Lila Acheson Wallace American Playwrights Program Fellow. Her play *Home Invasion* won the 2016 Heideman Award at Actors Theatre of Louisville. For more information, visit KristaKnight.com.

## ACKNOWLEDGMENTS

*Home Invasion* premiered at the Humana Festival of New American Plays in April 2017. It was directed by Eric Hoff with the following cast:

| | |
|---|---|
| GHOST ONE | Andrea Syglowski |
| GHOST TWO | Kelly McAndrew |
| KATY | Regan Moro |
| TOM | Sam Breslin Wright |

and the following production staff:

| | |
|---|---|
| Scenic Designer | Justin Hagovsky |
| Costume Designer | Alice Tavener |
| Lighting Designer | Steve O'Shea |
| Sound Designer | Christian Frederickson |
| Fight Director | Ryan Bourque |
| Stage Manager | Stephen Horton |
| Assistant Stage Manager | Lindsay Eberly |
| Dramaturg | Jessica Reese |
| Properties Director | Mark Walston |

Special thanks to New Georges and Serials at The Flea for catalyzing earlier iterations.

## CHARACTERS

GHOST ONE
GHOST TWO
KATY
TOM

## SETTING

A fancy Tribeca loft.

Regan Moro and Kelly McAndrew
in *Home Invasion*

41st Humana Festival of New American Plays
Actors Theatre of Louisville, 2017
Photo by Bill Brymer

# HOME INVASION

*A fancy Tribeca loft.*

*There are jewels and phones placed about.*

*Two* GHOSTS *in white sheets with eye holes in them.*

GHOST TWO *plays a synthy ghost riff on a keyboard.*

**GHOST ONE.** It's not spooky enough.

**GHOST TWO.** Give me a second.

**GHOST ONE.** I'm looking for something "bone-chilling."

**GHOST TWO.** My hair is on end. Your hair isn't on end?

**GHOST ONE.** "Bone-chilling" is the feeling we want to convey, I think.

**GHOST TWO.** Let it soak over you a little.

**GHOST ONE.** How about we add a little—

(GHOST ONE *joins ghost riff—maybe on some bongos.*)

**GHOST TWO.** Oh I like that!

**GHOST ONE.** *(Getting into the "spirit.")* Yeah here we go.

**GHOST TWO.** You're feeling it.

**GHOST ONE.** I'm feeling it.

**GHOST TWO.** You're feeling spooky.

**GHOST ONE.** Very spooky!

**GHOST TWO.** I think we can kill them with fear alone this time.

**GHOST ONE.** Oh I don't know if we're there yet.

**GHOST TWO.** Your heart stops. It's science.

**GHOST ONE.** I don't know.

(GHOST TWO *plays some more on the keyboard.*)

**GHOST TWO.** How about now?

**GHOST ONE.** Oh I like that.

**GHOST TWO.** You like that.

**GHOST ONE.** We're good ghosts.

**GHOST TWO.** We make the heart muscles thicken.

**GHOST ONE.** The blood back up.

**GHOST TWO.** Tissue swell.

**GHOST ONE.** Breath get short.

**GHOST TWO.** Skin clam.

**GHOST ONE.** Lungs fill with fluid.

**GHOSTS ONE & TWO.** Feet fill with fluid!

*(Sound of lock being picked.)*

**GHOST TWO.** Uhoh uhoh someone's here!

(HOME INVADERS *in ski masks enter.*)

**GHOSTS ONE & TWO.** Shhh shhh shhh shhh!

**KATY.** Wow!

**TOM.** Come on.

**KATY.** Look at this place!

**TOM.** "In and out" what happened to in and out!

**KATY.** (*Re: keyboard.*) I used to have one of these.

(KATY *plays some keys.*)

**TOM.** Be quiet—don't—don't *play* it!

**KATY.** There's nobody home. What part of "They're in Miami for the week" don't you understand?

**TOM.** Please don't be rhetorical, it's demeaning—

**KATY.** Yeah okay.

**TOM.** You should respect me enough to not phrase things that way when I tell you I don't like it when you phrase things that way.

**KATY.** You sound just like my ex.

**TOM.** Did you rob houses with your ex? Hey. Hey. Hey. Did you rob houses with your ex? Hey. Which ex?

(GHOST TWO *sneaks up and plays a ghost riff.*)

**TOM.** What was that?

**KATY.** Did you hear an echo?

**TOM.** …Maybe they have on a radio?

**KATY.** Yeah—Okay…

**GHOST TWO.** It's bone chilling—look look look—it's chilling their bones!

**GHOSTS ONE & TWO.** Brrrrrrrrrr!

**GHOST ONE.** Adrenaline is starting to pump.

**GHOST TWO.** Heart rate is going up.

**GHOST ONE.** Blood vessels are dilating.

**GHOST TWO.** Pupils enlarging.

**GHOST ONE.** Breath quickening.

**GHOST TWO.** Muscles tensing.

**GHOST ONE.** Nervous system overstimulating.

**GHOST TWO.** Mania manifesting!!

**GHOST ONE.** We are such good ghosts!

(GHOST ONE *knocks something over or off.*)

**KATY & TOM.** (*Startled.*) Ah!

**GHOST ONE.** Oops—got excited.

**TOM.** (*Re: falling object.*) Geeze be careful!

**KATY.** What—I didn't do anything!

**TOM.** You're knocking things over.

**KATY.** I haven't moved!

**TOM.** You're being reckless!

**KATY.** Who cares what happens to this stuff—we're here to steal it, TOM.

**TOM.** SHUT UP SHUT UP SHUT UP what is wrong with you!? Don't use my name!?

**KATY.** What—they don't have a surveillance camera—I checked—I'M not an idiot—what's wrong with *you?*

**TOM.** Demeaning phrasing, once again! If there's no camera, why are we in ski masks?

**KATY.** Then take it off—

(KATY *goes for* TOM's *mask but he pulls back.*)

**TOM.** No, I like mine! What if they come home early?

**KATY.** They are GONE. GONE. I'll show you on my phone how gone they are.

(KATY *takes out phone.*)

See? Status after status of how they are in Miami until Wednesday.
Tuesday, August 18: "Wow, I can't wait to have fun with Mario and the girls in the South Beach Four Seasons Penthouse."
Friday: "I wish I could take all my jewelry but want to travel light so leaving most of it at home. Yacht emoji sad face."
Sunday: "Oh my god—Mario just bought another iPhone for Deanna—how many expensive electronics can one apt. hold?"
And this morning: "Uber X black Escalade is here! Aug Vaycay 2K17 ALL SYSTEMS GO!"

**TOM.** Does any part of you think that might have been crafted // to attract us?

**KATY.** They're gone!!

**TOM.** You're not FB friends with them, are you?

**KATY.** What no.

**TOM.** Then all those statuses were public?

**KATY.** What I don't know.

**TOM.** Who goes to Miami in August?

**KATY.** Tom!

**TOM.** My name that's my name don't use my name!

**KATY.** (*Wielding a knife hazardously.*) Nobody is here.

**TOM.** Okay, Katy! Then put that away.

**KATY.** The knife is just for safe-zys.

**TOM.** Okay!

**KATY.** Nobody is going to get hurt.

> (GHOST TWO *grabs* TOM's *throat and starts choking him.* KATY *is looking the other way.*)

**GHOST ONE.** Hey, hey! That's cheating.

**GHOST TWO.** Why?

**GHOST ONE.** Because you said we could do this on adrenaline, cortisone, and norepinephrine alone.

**GHOST TWO.** You're right.

**GHOST ONE.** You're a purist.

**GHOST TWO.** I'm a purist.

> (GHOST TWO *releases* TOM *from the choke hold.*)

**TOM.** (*Catching breath.*) Oh my god what was that?!?

**KATY.** Let's just grab as much jewelry and Apple products as we can and get out of here.

**TOM.** HELLO WHAT WAS THAT?

**KATY.** What was what? I don't have any peripheral vision with this mask on. Wait a second.

**TOM.** What?

**KATY.** Why *would* they be so obvious about their status updates?

**TOM.** Something feels like a trap.

**GHOSTS ONE & TWO.** (*Chanting.*) GHOST TRAP
GHOST TRAP
GHOST TRAP

**GHOST TWO.** I can't believe how well this is going.

**GHOST ONE.** I know!

**GHOST TWO.** Airbnb-ing a Tribeca loft is the best, one of the best, ideas you've ever had!

**GHOST ONE.** It would never have worked if you hadn't gotten the Facebook password from the dark web.

**GHOST TWO.** Thank you security bug Heartbleed.

**GHOST ONE.** We're gonna kill so many people!

**GHOST TWO.** Yay!

> (*They high-five.*)

**GHOSTS ONE & TWO.** Ghost trap!

**TOM.** I don't like this at all—

**KATY.** Let's get out of here—

(GHOSTS *touch* KATY.)

AH!

**TOM.** What?

**KATY.** I just felt something.

**TOM.** Good or bad?

**KATY.** BAD! Bad, Tom, Bad!

(GHOSTS *touch* KATY.)

Ah! There it is again.

**TOM.** I don't like this I don't like this I don't like this.

(*One of the* GHOSTS *puts hands over* TOM*'s eyes.*)

I can't see!

**KATY.** What?

**TOM.** I've gone blind—I can't see!

**KATY.** FOLLOW THE SOUND OF MY VOICE!

**GHOST ONE.** Katy…

**KATY.** Did you just say my name?

**TOM.** There's something in my mask—there is something moving my mask!

**KATY.** Oh god.

**TOM.** Oh god.

**KATY.** Oh god. Tom.

**TOM.** Katy.

**KATY.** Tom!

**TOM.** Katy! Am I the only one you've ever robbed with?

**KATY.** God dammit, Tom. Let's get out of here. Open the door.

**TOM.** I'm trying.

**KATY.** Open the door!

**TOM.** It's locked.

**KATY.** It can't be locked. How can it be locked? We picked the lock how is the door locked?

**TOM.** Hello? Hello!? Somebody?

**KATY.** Help!

**TOM.** Help!

**KATY.** Help! We're locked in!? Help!

(KATY *and* TOM *try in vain to pull it open.*
GHOST ONE *&* GHOST TWO *prance around them spookily, perhaps*
*BOOing, perhaps poking.*)

**KATY & TOM.** (*Overlapping, much panic.*) Help! No! No! Let us out! Help!
Help! No! No! NO! Ah! Ah!

**KATY.** I think my heart just stopped.

(KATY *and* TOM *die of fear.*

*Jovial, celebratory laughter from* GHOSTS.
*Big musical sendoff where* GHOSTS *puppet dead bodies of* KATY *and*
TOM *in choreographed dance number.*)

### *End of Play*

# WE'RE GONNA BE OKAY
by Basil Kreimendahl

## ABOUT *WE'RE GONNA BE OKAY*

*This article first ran in the* Limelight Guide to the 41st Humana Festival of New American Plays, *published by Actors Theatre of Louisville, and is based on conversations with the playwright before rehearsals for the Humana Festival production began.*

In the shared yard between their two shotgun houses, Sul and Mag kick back with their neighbors Efran and Leena for a friendly cookout. But Efran is a fast-talker—the kind of guy who holds you hostage with his ideas—and he has a bee in his bonnet. With the Cold War ramping up, Efran is convinced they should pool their resources to build a bomb shelter on their shared property line. And even though these two families don't know each other that well, they do have one thing in common: they all sense that their way of life is on the verge of destruction. The signs are everywhere—in the increasing reports of nuclear bomb tests in the news, in the cultural paradigm shift already happening around them, and most importantly, in the growing sense of dread that sinks like a pit in their stomachs. They can't escape the feeling that something...*something* isn't right.

Playwright Basil Kreimendahl says the frenzy around fallout shelters in the late 1950s and 60s provided plenty of inspiration when writing *We're Gonna Be Okay*. "I found this book at the library about bomb shelters—they were really a hot commodity," they explain. "And there were all these different ways of making them!" The Cold War boom in bomb shelter advertising and production went hand-in-hand with mounting American anxiety about nuclear proliferation. By setting the play during the Cuban Missile Crisis, Kreimendahl is tapping into a period of history that brought existential fear into the foreground of everyday life. "It was the first time we realized that we could destroy ourselves," muses the playwright. "Preparedness" became the watchword of the day, as a cartoon turtle named Bert taught schoolchildren how to "duck and cover" to protect themselves from radioactive blasts.

In retrospect, it's easy to see how woefully inadequate Bert the turtle's instructions are. But for the characters in *We're Gonna Be Okay*, extreme circumstances call for an extreme response. Efran believes it's his duty to preserve the hallmarks of civilization after nuclear apocalypse, so he insists that the shelter accommodate a kitchen table...because table manners are *crucial*. And as Sul and Efran's shelter plans take shape, their respective teenage kids, Jake and Deanna, worry they'll have to repopulate the planet—despite their utter lack of attraction. Even so, the plans to build a bomb shelter are an extreme fix for the wrong problem; not everyone is convinced that nuclear war is the source of their unease.

140

As Kreimendahl points out, "It wasn't just a time of fear, but also a time of social change." Though the play is set against a climate of fear created by international politics, the anxiety in *We're Gonna Be Okay* is also driven by transformation on a much more intimate scale. Jake and Deanna are discovering the shape of their queer sexuality; Leena is realizing that her passion for life needs an outlet; Mag is learning to give voice to her feelings; and Sul is beginning to understand what real strength is. And then there's Efran, whose escalating panic seems to stem from his sense that the world is shifting around him and he's powerless to turn the tide. "It's actually very personal," remarks Kreimendahl. "For things to change, people have to change."

The social anxiety laid bare in *We're Gonna Be Okay* is drawn with compassion and delicacy, and a deeply felt understanding of how tectonic cultural shifts can inspire outsized terror. As is common in Kreimendahl's work, the play also sports a healthy appreciation for everyday absurdities, and a sly sense of humor. In an early scene that has echoes of 60s-era women's liberation and consciousness-raising groups, Leena, Mag, and Deanna macramé on their porch and ponder their unconscious minds. Just when it seems they might be on the verge of transformative insight, they break into a dance party as Deanna plays the Peter, Paul, and Mary song, "If I Had a Hammer," on her guitar. "It's talking about revolution," says Kreimendahl of the song choice, "but the way it's presented—it's pop-y, and there's something kind of happy about it. But meanwhile the lyrics are like, 'Danger! Warning!'" With a mischievous chuckle, they add, "So I thought it would be even better if they were doing the mashed potato."

As the characters in *We're Gonna Be Okay* stand at the precipice of change both societal and deeply personal, we sense that some of them are ready to embrace it and forge ahead into new lives. But in order to move forward, will they have to leave someone behind? One of the many truths the play illuminates is that fear can be a dogged emotion to shake. Though the title has gone through several iterations, Kreimendahl kept returning to the phrase *We're Gonna Be Okay*. "I thought about that title for every character in the play," says the playwright. "And I think it means something different to each of them. Some of them believe it...you know, maybe it's not okay now, but maybe it will be." Commenting on what feels right about the title, Kreimendahl says, "It feels hopeful—and I think the play is hopeful. Or I guess I am. I'm hopeful that people have the courage to change."

—Jenni Page-White

## BIOGRAPHY

Basil Kreimendahl is a resident playwright at New Dramatists. Their plays have won several awards, including the Rella Lossy Playwright Award and a National Science Award at the Kennedy Center American College Theater Festival. Kreimendahl has been commissioned by Oregon Shakespeare Festival's American Revolutions program, and by Actors Theatre of Louisville for *Remix 38* (2014 Humana Festival). Their play *Orange Julius* was developed at the 2012 O'Neill National Playwrights Conference and had its New York premiere at Rattlestick Playwrights Theater, in a co-production with Page 73. Their play *We're Gonna Be Okay* had its world premiere at the 2017 Humana Festival. Kreimendahl's plays have also been produced or developed by New York Theatre Workshop, American Theater Company, Victory Gardens Theater, The Lark, La Jolla Playhouse, and Labyrinth Theater Company. They have been a Jerome Fellow and a McKnight Fellow at the Playwrights' Center in Minneapolis, won an Art Meets Activism grant from the Kentucky Foundation for Women, and are a visiting writer at Williams College. Kreimendahl's work has been published by Dramatists Play Service, Dramatic Publishing, and HowlRound. They received their M.F.A. from the University of Iowa in 2013.

## ACKNOWLEDGMENTS

*We're Gonna Be Okay* premiered at the Humana Festival of New American Plays in March 2017. It was directed by Lisa Peterson with the following cast:

EFRAN .......................................................... Sam Breslin Wright
SUL................................................................... Scott Drummond
LEENA .............................................................. Kelly McAndrew
MAG .................................................................. Annie McNamara
DEANNA................................................... Anne-Marie Trabolsi
JAKE.......................................................... Andrew Cutler

and the following production staff:

Scenic Designer...................................... Dane Laffrey
Costume Designer.................................... Jessica Pabst
Lighting Designer.................................... Brian H. Scott
Sound Designer....................................... Christian Frederickson
Stage Manager ...................................... Stephen Horton
Assistant Stage Manager............................. Jessica Kay Potter
Dramaturg.............................................. Jenni Page-White
Casting................................................ Erica Jensen, Calleri Casting
Music Supervisor...................................... John Grammer
Dialect Coach ......................................... D'Arcy Smith
Dance Supervisor...................................... Ashley Thursby
Fight Supervisor....................................... Eric Frantz
Properties Director.................................... Mark Walston
Directing Assistant ................................... Lila Rachel Becker
Assistant Dramaturg................................... Paige Vehlewald

*We're Gonna Be Okay* was developed with support from the Playwrights' Center's Jerome Fellowship Program, Minneapolis, Minnesota.

# CAST OF CHARACTERS

MAG          A working-class woman in her late 30s, early 40s. Mag is a quiet woman, but she's on the verge of discovering something inside of herself that's louder.

SUL           A working-class guy around the same age as his wife, Mag. Sul's a quiet guy, but an extremely thoughtful one. He sees Efran as the kinda guy he'd like to be, but even when he imitates him, it's never quite right.

DEANNA     Mag and Sul's daughter; she's around 16. She's feminine but a little rock and roll masculine. Like a 60s lesbian Joan Jett. Slightly apathetic appearing, but it's because she sees a lot. She also sees the idiocy of it all.

LEENA       A middle-class woman in her late 30s, early 40s. She's somewhat aware of the changes happening in the country and in thought. She's not actually in the thick of it but desires to be.

EFRAN       A middle-class guy around the same age as his wife, Leena. He's a fast talker. The kind of guy who holds everyone hostage with his talk, and is in real need of being "liked" so he overdoes it.

JAKE         Leena and Efran's son; like Deanna he's also around 16. Less mature than Deanna, but he's got that All-American boy thing going for him. He's energetic and full of vigor, but he's more than he seems at first.

144

**TIME**

1962
During the Cuban Missile Crisis

**PLACE**

Middle America

**NOTE**

There are sound transitions that begin each scene. This is just a thought towards the idea that sound could juxtapose and heighten the internal paranoia and conflict happening within the small family units and group dynamics alongside the growing national fear. These sounds might be from the news, or things like "Duck and Cover," the chaos of the time.

Scott Drummond and Sam Breslin Wright
in *We're Gonna Be Okay*

41st Humana Festival of New American Plays
Actors Theatre of Louisville, 2017
Photo by Bill Brymer

# WE'RE GONNA BE OKAY

## ACT I

### (Oct. 15, 1962)   Chapter One: Heyser Turns A "Brass Knob"

*Sound transition.*

*The façade of two shotgun houses. Two neighbors. It's an Indian summer and the grill's smoking. Two grills, two families, one BBQ.*

**EFRAN.** Sul! Waitta ya get a load a these steaks I got.

**SUL.** Steaks? Efran/that's too expensive

**EFRAN.** Hey. It's no biggie. I got a deal on 'em. This salesman, a steak salesman, comes to the door last week. He says, "I was drivin by the neighborhood on my way north." You know, 'cause *north* that's where people who buy steaks live. "When I saw this porch. Looks like you put some care into this porch." Why yes I did sir, I say. He says, "I thought there is a man who eats steak. There is a man who enjoys a good piece a beef. There is a man who *deserves* a Grade A slab a red meat once in a while. Have I got a deal for you."

I was sold.

Bought a few steaks and Leena froze 'em. We are about to enjoy the first eating of the salesman steaks.

**SUL.** Today is one a those days I'm proud to be your friend.

**EFRAN.** And my neighbor. Don't forget the neighbor part.

**SUL.** Can't.

**EFRAN.** Nope. Today, in this country it's a man's neighbors. To neighbors!

**SUL.** To salesman steak!

**EFRAN.** Salesman steak! Yes, sir.

Can you believe that? Door to door steak sellin?

**SUL.** What's the world comin to?

**EFRAN.** I tell you, Sul. I don't know. I just don't know.

With everything you read—you had a chance to look at all those pamphlets?

**SUL.** Yeah, yeah. Took a look at 'em. Me and the wife. Seems awful expensive.

**EFRAN.** That's why we go into it together.

Make it big enough for both families. You got the know-how. We do it ourselves. Ground up.

I started doin some figurin. The supplies, the supplies aren't what's expensive.

Now those pamphlets they're about a pre-fabricated shelter. But you and I, we'd build it ourselves. Save lives.

I mean when I get to thinkin about this world, and with all that's goin on, it ain't a matter of "if" but a matter of "when." So I been thinkin about what comes after the big event. When everything's gone and man has to start over from scratch. So I think on who do I want to be here? It's you. It's you, your family, me, my family.

Don't you think so? Good people.

**SUL.** Hey, I wanna be here. I do. But it ain't come yet, and we got a mortgage and/

**EFRAN.** You got the know-how. I got the supplies.

**SUL.** Wait now,/you

**EFRAN.** No, no I'm serious.

**SUL.** I don't know.

**EFRAN.** Come on, Sul. We're neighbors.

**SUL.** Yeah, but I can't—well—you know, honestly, I can't put any money towards it.

**EFRAN.** That's what I mean, we go in on it together. You got the know-how, the fix-it guy thing. You know how to build things, Sul. And I get the supplies.

**SUL.** I don't know if I'm comfortable with that.

**EFRAN.** Are you sayin your work's not worth anything? Geez, Sul. Give yourself more credit than that.

**SUL.** Well no, I'm not saying that/exactly.

**EFRAN.** So what's the problem here? I don't see any problem. A man goes to work, it doesn't matter what he does, the man gets paid for it. Am I right?

**SUL.** Sure.

**EFRAN.** Yeah, he gets paid for it. So what's the difference? We live in a free market, Sul. That's the beauty of capitalism. You dig a hole and you damn well can count on getting paid for it, right?

**SUL.** I hear what you're sayin, Efran.

**EFRAN.** You hear me?

**SUL.** Yeah, I do.

**EFRAN.** So you're in?

**SUL.** I didn't say that.

**EFRAN.** Alright, Sul. Level with me here. It's me, Efran, your neighbor, your neighbor. You and I agree that counts for somethin in the world, am I right?

**SUL.** Sure.

**EFRAN.** Right. So come at me.

**SUL.** What?

**EFRAN.** Level with me here. What's the hold up, what's the bottom line? Lay it out on the table. You and me, right here, right now. Lay the cards on the table. Let's see what we're workin with here.

**SUL.** Okay, well/

**EFRAN.** Hit me!

**SUL.** Well, I hear what you're/sayin

**EFRAN.** Come at me!

**SUL.** Okay well yeah so you dig a hole and you get paid for it, but who owns the hole, Efran? The guy who dug it or the guy who paid for it? 'Cause in my experience/it's the guy

**EFRAN.** Okay, okay. Whatta ya take me for huh? What kinda guy do you take me for. Look, look. The beauty of it is I'm not paying you. Look, let me throw somethin back at ya.

(*This is* EFRAN*'s version of "If a tree falls and no one's there to hear it…"*)

If a man digs a hole on his own property, but someone pays him to dig it, does he own the hole? Huh?

**SUL.** I don't know.

**EFRAN.** This is the thing. We build it right down the middle of the property line. You get building supplies on your side and on my side I get building know-how. Win win.

**SUL.** Yeah. I don't know.

**EFRAN.** I won't take no for an answer, Sul.

**SUL.** I'm just not comfortable with it.

**EFRAN.** Ah come on.

**SUL.** I'm sorry, Efran. I can't go in on it with you.

(LEENA *and* MAG *carry corn on the cob and potato salad out from the house.*)

**LEENA.** Poor Sul.

**EFRAN.** Poor Sul?

**LEENA.** Is he on you about the bomb shelter?

**SUL.** What?

**MAG.** I think it's a good idea.

**LEENA.** We're clearly married to the wrong men Mag. We should swap.

**MAG.** There's so much tension in the world.

**LEENA.** He's addicted to crisis, this man.

**EFRAN.** It is my job to protect my family, right Sul?

**SUL.** Sure.

**EFRAN.** That's what I'm doin. If that means buildin a bomb shelter, then I build it.

**LEENA.** Of course you do, honey.

**EFRAN.** I do.

**LEENA.** I know, I know.

**MAG.** I'm all for it. It would make me feel a whole lot better. Lately, I've been waking up with a cold sweat, and panic in my stomach.

**LEENA.** I'm not convinced, but last night I did have a shelter dream.

**EFRAN.** You did?

**LEENA.** Yeah. You two were out there digging and digging, and I was washing the dishes and looking out the window at you. Suddenly this gush of black came rushing out. A geyser in the back yard. You two were covered in black from head to toe, jumping up and down. I raced out to see what you had broken, with the plumber's number in my hand. And lo and behold...it was black gold. A geyser of oil springing out of the lawn!

**EFRAN.** She fell asleep to *The Beverly Hillbillies*.

**LEENA.** I did! I did, didn't I? I hadn't even realized that. We have to stop falling asleep to television. It's going to ruin our brains.

**EFRAN.** I told you, you don't have to worry about that anymore. We got the color television. See here's my theory. The black and white it numbs the brain. Makes like—colorless world. Now we got the color television. I think it's gonna zap that creativity back in you.

**LEENA.** That's true. But I haven't felt creativity zap into me.
I used to make things.

**MAG.** I didn't know that about you.

**LEENA.** It's true.

**EFRAN.** Yeah. She'd make all kinda things. Little things for—things that would—I mean, unbelievable things—you could/

**LEENA.** Anything with my hands. Honestly, I have to say there's something revolutionary about making things. You know? Women creating together. There's a whole counterculture. I want to call them something but basically it's just crafts, I suppose.

**EFRAN.** Hey! There ain't nothin wrong with crafts.

**LEENA.** I know.

**EFRAN.** She thinks it's not real art, 'cause it doesn't go in a frame.

**SUL.** It could.

**EFRAN.** It could! Sure it could.
Sul, always usin his thinker.

**SUL.** I might have the thinker, but you got the steaks.

**EFRAN.** And they are ready! Oh boy. Wait'll ya get a load a these juicy babies between your gnashers.

**MAG.** Maybe we could have a craft night?

**EFRAN.** There's an idea!

**LEENA.** Do you make things?

**MAG.** I'd like to.

**EFRAN.** Leena here can teach you everything you need to know 'bout makin things.

**MAG.** Maybe I can get Deanna to come.

**EFRAN.** That sounds like a great idea.

**SUL.** It'd be good for her.

**MAG.** Yeah.

**EFRAN.** What's the matter, she goin through that teenage girl stuff?

**MAG.** It's normal.

**EFRAN.** I ain't sayin it's abnormal—Holy God! You taste that steak?

**SUL.** It's good.

**EFRAN.** It's good! Right?

**SUL.** It's good.

**LEENA.** I have a whole closet of supplies.

**EFRAN.** A whole freakin closet!


### (Oct. 16, 1962)   Chapter Two: EXCOMM

*Sound transition.*

LEENA *and* MAG *on* LEENA's *porch. There are bags full of things like yarn and construction paper.*

**MAG.** Wow Leena, you are really hip to the times.

**LEENA.** I can mash potato to just about anything.
We both have teenagers. You know, you pick stuff up.

(MAG *doesn't know.*)

Hand me that blue paper, yeah. I'm gonna make a blue bird.

(*Silence.*)

**MAG.** Ahm.
Hmm.

**LEENA.** What?

**MAG.** I don't know what I want to make.

**LEENA.** That's normal. All those magazines over there have ideas in them. Options.

I thought Deanna was comin.

**MAG.** She is.

**LEENA.** Okay.

**MAG.** (*Defensive.*) She is.

(*Beat.*)

**LEENA.** Mag? I don't want to butt in, but can I make a suggestion to you?

**MAG.** Yeah?

**LEENA.** Macramé. Macramé.

**MAG.** Macramé?

**LEENA.** Yes. Look. This book is all macramé.

**MAG.** (*Of the book.*) Oh.

**LEENA.** I told you.

**MAG.** Oh!/

**LEENA.** Start simple, a plant hanger or something.

**MAG.** This one?

**LEENA.** Why not? This is your song, Mag. Sing it however you want. The red bag has everything in it.

(*Beat. MAG's whole body relaxes, euphoria sets in.*)

**MAG.** Very relaxing.

**LEENA.** I always tell Efran, if all those kids would just macramé they wouldn't need to smoke marijuana. That's what I say.

**MAG.** Maybe you could go into the schools. Teach macramé over marijuana.

**LEENA.** I thought about it.

**MAG.** You should. You really should.

**LEENA.** I thought it through though. What if they all just end up making bags to keep their drugs in? I couldn't live with myself. It's like Robert Frost said, you shoot an arrow, but you don't know where the wind's gonna take it.

**MAG.** The wind blows your arrows. That's for sure.

**LEENA.** All over the place.

**MAG.** I mean one bad wind and…well, one bad wind and you could lose everything. Your house blows over, your windows blow out and what are you left with, really? You could lose everything. Just like that. All it takes is one bad wind.

(*Beat.*)

**LEENA.** Mag, I didn't know you had such a fear of wind storms.

**MAG.** No. I don't, it's just. It could be anything, really. Just like that. All the

things you worked hard for, all the people you love. Gone.
I'm sorry. I'm sorry I'm being such a downer. Ugh. Sorry.

**LEENA.** You know what, Mag. These are heavy times.

**MAG.** Heavy times, right?
There was a map right there in the. A map. And everyone is…well. Right there in the paper. All these little dots/and everyone is

**LEENA.** Mag.

**MAG.** Testing bombs, bombing things.

**LEENA.** You can't let it get you down.

**MAG.** Every time Deanna goes to school and I say goodbye I think I might not ever see you again.

**LEENA.** Okay Mag, let me share something with you that really gets me through the hard times.

**MAG.** Okay.

**LEENA.** We wake up with a choice.

**MAG.** We do?

**LEENA.** We can live our lives like we're terrified something's gonna come along and ruin it, or we can live our lives like everyday we live is a gift. One way is living in joy and gratitude and the other…well.

**MAG.** No, I know you're right, but if you know, you know in your gut that something is brewing out there, shouldn't you do something about it? Shouldn't you just do whatever you can about it?

**LEENA.** I suppose so. You shouldn't just let your world fall apart, if there's something you can do about it.

**MAG.** Yeah.

**LEENA.** But there's things we can't know. I mean for instance, aneurysm. Any time you could just collapse dead. Heart attack, Sul could just collapse dead./You can't prepare for that.

**MAG.** Oh my God.

**LEENA.** You can't follow him around waiting to give him CPR. Can you make him eat a lot of onions? Sure. Can you urge him to go for walks? Sure. That's all.

**MAG.** Right. You can prepare, try to save something, even if it's just a couple of years.

**LEENA.** I think so.

**MAG.** That's why I think Efran is really on to something.

**LEENA.** The bomb shelter?

**MAG.** Yes. Don't you think so?

**LEENA.** I suppose so. But, Mag, honestly, sometimes I wonder if I'd even want to live. If I'd even want to survive that kinda thing. I mean can you imagine?

**MAG.** I don't know.

**LEENA.** Don't worry so much. Sul is a good man.

**MAG.** Yeah.

**LEENA.** I'm sure he'll come around.

**MAG.** I don't know.

**LEENA.** Well, you've got to tell him. That's all.

**MAG.** (*This seems like an impossible task.*) Sure.
I just wish he'd stop being so, so…

**LEENA.** Fatalistic?

**MAG.** Wow, Leena that is some word.

**LEENA.** Putting my degree to use.

**MAG.** You have a degree?

**LEENA.** Biology, but I don't really have any use for it.

**MAG.** Whatta you mean? You could do all kinds of things. Like teach.

**LEENA.** I don't know.

**MAG.** You should really think about it.

**LEENA.** Maybe.

(*Beat.*)

**MAG.** Whatta you think about chickens, ya know havin fresh eggs in the bomb shelter?
Chickens also eat ticks. You never know what's gonna seek shelter.

**LEENA.** Okay, Mag. Listen to me. Are you listening?
My family had chickens. They're like flying rodents. They poo everywhere and it all smells like ammonia. Now imagine, being in a hole in the ground, with one pipe for ventilation, suffocating on ammonia, chicken feathers in our throats. That's the kinda thing that turns people violent.
I'm just sayin. Worse than ticks. Think about it.

(DEANNA *comes out on* MAG's *porch with her guitar.*)

**MAG.** Deanna.
Look. I'm macramé-ing.

**DEANNA.** Geez Mom, that's actually kinda hip.

**LEENA.** Told you.

Deanna, do you wanna come over here and make something? I have lots of stuff, construction paper, yarn. I'm makin a blue bird.

**DEANNA.** I was just gonna hang here.

**MAG.** It's good to be social?

**DEANNA.** I'd rather just hang out here.

**MAG.** Alright.

**LEENA.** Look at us, it's ladies' night!

(*Beat.*)

**MAG.** Leena, what're you gonna do with the bird?

**LEENA.** Oh. Well, I had this kinda crazy idea. Don't laugh at me. I thought I'd make paper animals for all the ones we'd miss being down in a bomb shelter.

So what animal would you miss the most? I'll make it.

**MAG.** That's a hard one.

**LEENA.** Don't be shy. I have lots of paper.

**MAG.** Ahm. A horse?

**LEENA.** Do you ride horses, Mag?

**MAG.** No. I mean I haven't, ever. No.

**LEENA.** So a horse?

**MAG.** I think?

**LEENA.** It's up to you, Mag.

**MAG.** A horse then.

**LEENA.** Horse it is! Deanna?

**DEANNA.** Dolphins. They're really important.

**LEENA.** Oooh, that's exotic. What color is a dolphin, exactly? Gray? Blue?

**DEANNA.** You could make it a white skeleton of a dolphin.

**LEENA.** That's morbid. These paper animals are supposed to brighten up our lives.

**MAG.** I say, gray.

**LEENA.** I'm learning so much about you.

**MAG.** You are?

**LEENA.** Colors and animals say so much. You know that Indians have a spirit animal. It's true. So maybe the horse is your spirit animal. Makes sense to me, there's somethin inside of you Mag.

**MAG.** Oh no no no. There's not.

**LEENA.** You're not foolin me.

**MAG.** What's the spirit animal do?

**LEENA.** Well.

They are just with you, in spirit. I just wanna say, I'm glad we decided on the fixer-upper. That we moved in next to you. Here we are on my porch havin a ladies' craft night. Talkin about our unconscious.

(DEANNA *plucks a string.*)

Are you gonna play us a song?

**MAG.** Yeah, play us a song. I haven't heard you play in so long.

**DEANNA.** Ah, sure. I guess.

　　*(She starts to play, something like "If I Had a Hammer.")*

**LEENA.** I love this song.

It's Peter Paul and Mary.

**MAG.** Oh?

　　*(DEANNA sings a few verses. She continues to sing throughout the following
　　dialogue:)*

**LEENA.** She's really good, Mag.

**MAG.** Yeah.

Can you mash potato to this song?

**LEENA.** Can I? Why, yes, I can.

　　*(LEENA gets up and does the Mashed Potato.)*

Come on Mag/it's

**MAG.** Oh no.

**LEENA.** It's easy, come on, come on. I'm gonna show you.

**MAG.** No, no. I just wanna/watch

**LEENA.** Yes, yes. Tonight we say "yes" to everything.

　　*(She pulls MAG up.)*

There you go. You're doin it.

Then you do both feet at the same time.

You got it.

Dance Party here we come!

**MAG.** I'm doin it! I'm doin it!

**LEENA.** This is just the beginning Mag! Life is just waiting to be grabbed
by the horns.

　　*(MAG and LEENA continue to mash potato through the end of the song. It
　　becomes a Mashed Potato march. There's intensity and purpose to this march.
　　LEENA leads it and she sings the final verse with DEANNA.)*


### (Oct. 17, 1962)　　Chapter Three: SS 5 Nuclear Missiles

*Sound transition.*

SUL *sits on his porch.* EFRAN *comes out onto his porch.*

**EFRAN.** Sul.

**SUL.** Efran.

**EFRAN.** Gettin a little porch time in, huh?

**SUL.** Yup.

**EFRAN.** Yeah.

(*Silence.*)

It's quiet out here, ya know? Peaceful.

**SUL.** Yeah.

**EFRAN.** I like to sit out here myself sometimes. I like to sit out here and just look out at the neighborhood, ya know?

Everyone's just finished dinner about now. They're settling in. Quiet. Jesus. It's like somethin out of a magazine ya know? Like an advertisement sellin me a new suit. Ya know what I'm talkin about Sul? There's a husband comin home from work in a new suit. Wife standin by ready to receive him. They got a kid ya know, a little boy who's all dressed up like an astronaut. That little boy, Sul, he's dreamin 'bout bein an astronaut and becoming president once he's planted the American Flag up on Mars. That's the age we live in.

**SUL.** Yeah.

**EFRAN.** Let me tell ya somethin, Sul. There's a dark side out there. There's a seething underbelly. Sure, sure it doesn't look like it, but even in our neighborhood. There's a whole world out there hidden to us. We don't know about it because we're not involved in that kinda thing. 'Cause we're good people. We don't have eyes trained to see it, that's all.

**SUL.** I suppose that's probably true.

**EFRAN.** Sure it is.

**SUL.** I tend to not dwell on that sorta thing.

**EFRAN.** Sure, sure I hear ya. Who the hell wants to think about that sorta thing? Right?

**SUL.** Not/me

**EFRAN.** Who wants to think about what sordid affairs are happenin right under our noses.

**SUL.** There's nothin to be done about it.

**EFRAN.** Nothin to be done about it.

**SUL.** Nope.

**EFRAN.** I'm an American, Sul. You know that right?

**SUL.** Yeah?

**EFRAN.** I'm an American and I love—love this country. My country. I respect my president, I mean I get that little twinge inside me when they sing "The Star Spangled Banner," honest to God, I can't help it. That's the kinda guy I am.

**SUL.** I know what you mean.

**EFRAN.** You get that too? That little twinge?

**SUL.** Of course.

**EFRAN.** That's why I like you Sul. You know my dad was a workin man, like you. Built things with his hands. Automobiles. A Ford would drive by and my dad would look over at me and say, "Son, these hands built that car." These hands. You know I never worked a job like that. I never learned to build things. Regret that sometimes.

**SUL.** It ain't all it's cracked up to be.

**EFRAN.** What're you talkin about? Sure there's something in that to be proud of. There really is. I never learned to build things but I'll tell ya what, I took my own life, Sul, I took my destiny, and I wrestled it to the ground. These hands. I shaped my life into somethin I could be proud of.

**SUL.** I admire that about you. Guys like you. I really do.

**EFRAN.** Well, we're two guys mutually admiring each other—look Sul, I'm sayin all this to ya for a reason. As much as I'm an Amercan, I gotta tell ya, I'm not feelin too confident these days.

**SUL.** Whatta ya mean?

**EFRAN.** Well, there's things goin on, like I said, an underbelly. You read the paper, gangs of youth runnin around kickin people with heavy shoes. Things are goin on, and frankly. I hate to say this but it's true. I'm startin to think the people runnin things don't give a damn about you and me and our families. I mean Kennedy can't even get them to pass Medicare or money for the colleges, but what did they pass? They passed money for foreign trade. With everything that's goin on, we're left behind. We're left behind. That means we've got to fend for ourselves.

**SUL.** Doesn't sound like anything new to me.

**EFRAN.** Sure, sure we've always fended for ourselves that's one a the things that make Americans great. We do that, we fend for ourselves. That's why we've got to do somethin.

**SUL.** Efran, I'm not a bomb shelter kinda guy, and besides I don't think there's as much to worry about/as you do

**EFRAN.** All I'm askin, Sul is that you think about it. Okay?

**SUL.** Okay.

**EFRAN.** Because they don't have a plan. You think they're stockpilin food for the masses? Hell no they aren't. They got bigger things to worry about. When it comes to us they just wanna keep us subdued so they don't have a mass panic on their hands. Look, I'm just askin that you REALLY think about it.

**SUL.** Okay, Efran. I'll think about it.

**EFRAN.** You're good man, Sul.

(EFRAN *goes inside of his house.* MAG *comes out to hang a plant in her macramé plant hanger on the porch.*)

**SUL.** You want me to give you a hand with that?

**MAG.** Nope. I got it.

**SUL.** Okay.

If you hold the hammer from/the bottom

**MAG.** I said, I got it.

**SUL.** Okay.

Mag, take the nail/with your

**MAG.** I got it, Sul.

**SUL.** Okay.

**MAG.** Whatta you think?

**SUL.** I think it's nice. Where'd ya get it?

**MAG.** I made it.

**SUL.** You grew that plant? How did I miss that?

**MAG.** The hanger. I made the hanger. Macramé.

**SUL.** Oh God. Wow, Mag. That's. That's really great. You made that?

**MAG.** Yeah.

**SUL.** It's nice.

**MAG.** You look tired.

**SUL.** Just work. And Efran, well it's just.

**MAG.** Have you thought about it?

**SUL.** About what?

**MAG.** The bomb shelter? Efran?

**SUL.** Mag. No. If we're gonna have a bomb shelter it'll be because. I mean. We don't even know them that well.

**MAG.** We know them.

(*Silence.*)

**SUL.** It's been a heat wave, don't you think?

**MAG.** It's been hot.

**SUL.** Yeah.

**MAG.** Sul, have you ever heard of a spirit animal?

**SUL.** No.

**MAG.** I hadn't either. But I have one, and it's a horse.

**SUL.** You have a spirit horse?

**MAG.** Yeah.

**SUL.** What's it do?

**MAG.** It's with you in spirit.

**SUL.** So in the world, you are ridin round on a spirit horse? I don't know, Mag.

**MAG.** Maybe I am?

**SUL.** I don't think so.

**MAG.** Why not?

**SUL.** That just doesn't seem like you. Have you ever ridden on a horse? That doesn't sound like you.

> (*Beat.*)

**MAG.** If there was a nuclear bomb, which animal would you miss the most?

**SUL.** Oh, that's a hard one.

I don't know.

**MAG.** Come on, pick one.

**SUL.** Well, let's see. Ah, maybe a—well. Hmm. Fish. I'd say fish, since I like to go fishin.

**MAG.** Hmm, fish? Really?

**SUL.** What?

**MAG.** I wonder what that says about you.

**SUL.** That I like to fish.

**MAG.** That means that a fish is your spirit animal.

**SUL.** Christ. I don't have a spirit animal and neither do you. Where'd you get this stuff?

**MAG.** Leena. And I kinda think you do and it's a fish, and I don't really know what I think about that. All this time I've known you and you've had a spirit fish.

**SUL.** That's crazy talk.

**MAG.** And I've had a horse, and we've not known this about each other.

**SUL.** We've not known it, because it isn't real.

**MAG.** I think it is, and maybe I even like it. Maybe I like having a spirit horse.

**SUL.** That's it. No more macramé for you. This is crazy talk.

**MAG.** When I think about my horse, I like it. I feel good.

**SUL.** Mag.

**MAG.** No really, Sul.

**SUL.** This is/

**MAG.** Why don't you try it?

**SUL.** Try what?

**MAG.** Thinkin 'bout your fish, just try it.

**SUL.** Oh God.

**MAG.** Come on, please?

**SUL.** I can't think about a spirit fish, that's crazy.

**MAG.** Please?

**SUL.** No. Absolutely not. No.

**MAG.** Okay.

    *(Silence.)*

**SUL.** What?

**MAG.** Nothin.

**SUL.** No, what is it? You mad at me now?

**MAG.** No.

**SUL.** What is it?

**MAG.** I just, I don't know, I thought you had more imagination, I guess.

**SUL.** Oh, come on. 'Cause I won't imagine a stupid fish?

**MAG.** Yeah.

**SUL.** Mag.

    *(Beat.)*

I'm not a boring guy. I know you think/I'm boring

**MAG.** I don't think/that

**SUL.** Oh yes you do!

**MAG.** Sul, I really don't.

**SUL.** Some of us are just quiet people Mag. Okay? Not all of us are talkers. We're not all like Efran and Leena. Some of us are quiet people.

**MAG.** Quiet people don't have to live quiet lives.

**SUL.** What do you mean?

**MAG.** Just that. Our lives don't have to be quiet.

**SUL.** What's wrong with a quiet life?

**MAG.** Nothin's wrong with it. I guess.

**SUL.** You think I'm boring?

**MAG.** Sul, I don't think you're boring.

**SUL.** You think our life is boring?

**MAG.** I don't know. Do you?

**SUL.** Well, I don't know!

**MAG.** I mean, you won't even imagine with me.

**SUL.** Oh God.

**MAG.** I mean this is why.

**SUL.** What?

**MAG.** Nothin. Nothin.

**SUL.** No, come on tell me, what?

**MAG.** It's just. I mean I understand.

**SUL.** You understand what?

**MAG.** Sul, nothing I just. I understand, that's all. I won't push you, if you're not ready.

**SUL.** What are you talkin about?

**MAG.** Sul, come on.

>          (*Beat.*)

It wasn't just me. We both/lost

**SUL.** Mag! I don't wanna talk about this.

**MAG.** Of course/you don't

**SUL.** Now I really mean it!

**MAG.** Okay, okay.

>          (*Silence.*)

**SUL.** God.

Alright, you want me to imagine a stupid fish?

**MAG.** Yeah, I do.

**SUL.** Fine, fine. Here. I'm imaginin a stupid fish, okay?

**MAG.** You have to close your eyes.

**SUL.** Oh God. Here, I'm closin my eyes.

**MAG.** Sul. Really do it.

**SUL.** Fine.

>          (DEANNA *comes outside.*)

**DEANNA.** Mom, have you/seen my

**MAG.** Shh.

**SUL.** No, no. I'm not doin it now.

**DEANNA.** Doin what.

**SUL.** Nothin.

**MAG.** No. Your dad was tryin to imagine his spirit animal. Do it, Sul.

**SUL.** No, no. Your mother she's got/this

**DEANNA.** Why won't you do it, Dad?

**SUL.** The whole thing is crazy.

**MAG.** No, it's not                    **DEANNA.** It's not crazy.

**MAG.** See?

**DEANNA.** Don't be such a square, Dad.

**SUL.** I am not a square. I have a motorcycle.

**DEANNA.** Which you never ride.

**SUL.** People now-a-days drive like lunatics.

**DEANNA.** Square.

**SUL.** Alright, I'm startin to feel ganged up on, by the women.

**MAG.** Why don't we all do it together?

**DEANNA.** You mean like a real family?

(*Beat.*)

**MAG.** Deanna has a dolphin.

**SUL.** A dolphin? Really? You've never even seen a dolphin.

**DEANNA.** So?

**SUL.** I don't know. Just curious is all. A dolphin? Why?

**DEANNA.** I think they're spiritual.

**SUL.** But you've never met one.

**DEANNA.** It's just a feeling.

**MAG.** Maybe we could all close our eyes for a minute?

**SUL.** Oh God.

**DEANNA.** Come on Dad

**SUL.** Alright. Let's do it. On a three count. 1—2—3

(*They all close their eyes and imagine their spirit animals.*)

**MAG.** I want you to build the bomb shelter/

**SUL.** Mag/

**MAG.** Before Efran finds someone else to help him, and we lose out/

**SUL.** Look/I

**MAG.** And I want us to be safe, I wanna be safe. I don't want us to mutate into something horrible. 'Cause that's what will happen.


**(Oct. 18, 1962) Chapter Four: Defensive Capabilities**

*Sound transition.*

*The backyard.* EFRAN *rests on his shovel topside of the hole in the ground. He's practically sparkling white clean.* SUL *is inside the hole deep enough that we can't see him. Just the shovel full of dirt he throws up out of the hole.*

**EFRAN.** You like science fiction, Sul?

**SUL.** (*He can't hear him.*) Huh?

**EFRAN.** Science fiction, ya know? It's like our future. Geez, it blows me away I tell ya.

**SUL.** I don't know, Efran.

**EFRAN.** No, I'm serious, Sul. I've been thinkin on this book I'm readin J.G. Ballard *The Drowned World* and let me tell ya it's blowin my mind. It really is. It's the end of the world and man can't help but revert back into bein cavemen.

**SUL.** I really don't know.

**EFRAN.** Just think about it. I think it could really happen. It makes sense to me. I mean why wouldn't we just lose all sense of civilization, right?

**SUL.** I don't think our hole's big enough.

**EFRAN.** What? Whose hole?

**SUL.** The bomb shelter. Geez.

**EFRAN.** It's plenty big enough.

**SUL.** You think so? The way it is now, we're gonna be layin on top of each other.

**EFRAN.** Oh come on now, I like you and all, and sure Mag's a beautiful woman. A beautiful woman. Not sayin she's not. But neither one of us are the "key party" type.

I don't think you are, anyway. Are you?

**SUL.** What?

**EFRAN.** Are you and Mag swingers?

**SUL.** God, no. I'm just sayin, some of us, take up a lotta room. If I have to live down here, I wanna feel like I can breathe.

**EFRAN.** Well yeah, I mean we could be in there for weeks. Maybe a month. That's a long time to not stretch your legs or get a little alone time.

**SUL.** What?

**EFRAN.** Huh? Look, I hear ya. Me and Leena are gonna want some alone time. Things could get tense, otherwise. Very tense, believe me. It ain't me, it's her. I tell ya, Sul. I tell ya.

**SUL.** What?

(SUL *throws up his shovel and climbs out of the hole. He's covered in dirt.*)

Alright, it's your turn.

**EFRAN.** Need a few more minutes, I'm just catchin my second wind, you know? Hey, you wanna beer?

**SUL.** Sure.

**EFRAN.** Don't look so down in the mouth. What's goin on? Down mouth, sad frown. Geez, Sul.

**SUL.** It's nothin. Where's Jake at?

**EFRAN.** What's nothin between two neighbors. Hey. Hey. To neighbors. Right, right?

**SUL.** To neighbors.

**EFRAN.** There you go. Now what's got you frownin? Trouble in paradise?

**SUL.** God, no. Mag and I are fine. I'm just beat.

**EFRAN.** Take a break, pal. You been workin like a dog out here.
Hey, Sul. Look. I wanna talk to ya 'bout somethin serious for a minute here.

**SUL.** Yeah, what is it?

**EFRAN.** I wanna talk about civilization.

**SUL.** Okay.

**EFRAN.** I'm startin to get concerned. I'm startin to really get concerned.

**SUL.** What's this about?

**EFRAN.** I'm just thinkin, what we built here, well it's kinda like a cave. Am I right? We'll be livin in a cave.

**SUL.** Sure.

**EFRAN.** Does this worry you at all?

**SUL.** Well/

**EFRAN.** I just don't want us to forget who we are. You know? I tell ya. We could just forget everything about who we are. Geez. That'd really be terrible, Sul. I'm just sayin, I'm concerned we're gonna go right back to bein primitive man.

**SUL.** Well/

**EFRAN.** I'm talkin about culture here. Now we've got to plan ahead. We've got to make sure we have some semblance of civilization. Got to keep the culture goin.

**SUL.** Okay. So what/do you

**EFRAN.** Now Sul. I'm thinkin we've got to preserve some things. We have to, I don't know.
We need a dining room table.

**SUL.** Efran, I don't think we've got room/for

**EFRAN.** We have to make the room, that's what I'm sayin. Otherwise imagine this, we're all sittin around in our dirty hole, dirt caked on our skin, eatin food out of a can with our fingers. Just sittin wherever. Sittin on the ground maybe!

**SUL.** I'm sure we can make room for plates. You know knives, forks, spoons.

**EFRAN.** And where are we gonna sit? I mean our kids could forget that people used to sit at the dinner table with each other. Used to say, "Pass the peas," and "Sit up straight."
Christ, we could start bein hunched over.

**SUL.** I don't think we gotta really worry about that.

**EFRAN.** Hunched over, Sul. With a can, eatin sweet corn out of a can, with our forks.

**SUL.** We can put the corn in a bowl.

**EFRAN.** Look. I have an idea.

You know those campers, got everything, got beds, kitchen, kitchen table? Got everything all in there.

**SUL.** Yeah.

**EFRAN.** We can have a kitchen table that folds into the wall.

**SUL.** Like a murphy bed?

**EFRAN.** Right! Exactly. Folds into the wall. We just fold it out when it's dinner time.

**SUL.** We could each have our own private room. Off to each side.

**EFRAN.** Wait a minute now. Hold on. Two more holes?

**SUL.** Just a little one, two little ones. I don't think that's too much to ask.

**EFRAN.** A dinner table is one thing but two more holes?

**SUL.** Yeah. I mean for privacy.

**EFRAN.** Okay, okay. Now Sul, is this a deal breaker for you?

**SUL.** Well/I mean it could be

**EFRAN.** Just enough room for a full-size mattress? Maybe a little side table, put your book on, your glass a water.

**SUL.** It would be better.

**EFRAN.** It's not really what I planned, ya know. I had an idea of it in my head.

**SUL.** Things change.

**EFRAN.** I know, geez I know. What's goin on? You've been ridin my ass all afternoon.

**SUL.** If I'm gonna help build this thing, I wanna make sure we all have what we need, that's all.

**EFRAN.** Oh I see.

**SUL.** Yeah.

**EFRAN.** Leverage.

**SUL.** What?

**EFRAN.** You've got leverage here and you're gonna use it. Okay Sul, okay I'm on to you.

**SUL.** Efran it's really not like that.

**EFRAN.** Okay. Sure. Sure. Well my hands are tied here. For now my hands are tied. You want two more holes. Fine! Fine. Two more it is.

(*Silence.*)

**SUL.** We should get some help.

What's Jake doin? Why isn't he out here helpin us dig?

**EFRAN.** You know these kids. He just turned 16, I mean two years ago I couldn't get him to take off his cowboy outfit and now. Now. Academics, track team, baseball practice. I don't know where he is half the time.

**SUL.** Sure.

**EFRAN.** I'll get him out here though. Why should he reap the benefits without puttin in a little sweat time, right? What kinda lesson would that be?

**SUL.** I don't know.

**EFRAN.** Right? It's up to us, we gotta teach these kids that you don't get somethin for nothin. This ain't Russia.

**SUL.** It sure ain't.

**EFRAN.** No, sir. That's the thing.

No, we have to teach these—Jake! Jake! Hey, Jake!

**JAKE.** (*Offstage.*)Yeah?

**EFRAN.** Get out here! Put your shoes on!

**JAKE.** (*Offstage.*)What's goin on?

**EFRAN.** And grab a shovel from the basement!

**JAKE.** (*Offstage.*)What?

**EFRAN.** You heard me. Shoes and a shovel!

**SUL.** I can admire you Efran. I really can.

You're in charge, you know? You're really in charge.

**EFRAN.** It ain't always easy, I tell ya what. I tell ya.

**SUL.** Nah, nah. You got the life.

**EFRAN.** Sure, sure I do. I do. Castle and all that.

**JAKE.** What's goin on?

**EFRAN.** Democracy, that's what's goin on. Get down in that hole and do some diggin. Everyone's got to pull their weight around here.

**JAKE.** Dad, I just got home/from baseball practice

**EFRAN.** No whinin. Sul and I been out here breakin our backs all day to provide you shelter in the wake of a nuclear attack. Don't you think you should put in a little work?

**JAKE.** Yeah, but/I just finished

**EFRAN.** No buts, ifs, ands or whats. Only yesses. Now go on, get down there.

**JAKE.** Dad/I

**EFRAN.** Jake.

**JAKE.** Dad!

(*Beat.*)

You can't make me/dig

**EFRAN.** What? What'd you say? I can't MAKE you? You are my son, if I tell you to get down in that hole and dig you better just get down in that hole and dig. Don't give me that face. You aren't too big to bend you over my knee and spank your ass.

**SUL.** Ef/ran

**EFRAN.** You want Sul to see that? Huh?

(JAKE *gets down in the hole.*)

**JAKE.** How long do I have to dig for?

**EFRAN.** We'll tell you when.

Sul, *this* is what democracy looks like.

**JAKE.** How deep?

**EFRAN.** We'll tell you "when."


**(Oct. 19, 1962)   Chapter Five: The Campaign Must Go On**

*Sound transition.*

JAKE *and* DEANNA *in the backyard looking down into the hole.*

**DEANNA.** It's big.

**JAKE.** Apparently it ain't big enough.

**DEANNA.** You did this?

**JAKE.** Most of it. Say they want two more holes off to the side.

**DEANNA.** You better get diggin.

**JAKE.** It's bullshit.

**DEANNA.** You gonna tell your dad that?

**JAKE.** I might. I just might.

Said he wants me to skip baseball practice today to help dig.

**DEANNA.** Poor you.

**JAKE.** You don't get it. Baseball. Baseball is the American pastime. It's the foundation of this country. Where would we be without baseball?

**DEANNA.** Is that a real question?

**JAKE.** Yeah. Baseball is like the glue. It brings this country together—we say the damn Pledge of Allegiance and sing "The Star Spangled Banner."

**DEANNA.** Right.

**JAKE.** I'm just sayin.

**DEANNA.** Okay. Well, see you from afar in the cafeteria.

**JAKE.** You goin to school this early?

**DEANNA.** What's it to you?

**JAKE.** I don't know. Just, why?

**DEANNA.** Better than standin around, I guess.

**JAKE.** Standin around at school is better than standin around with me?

**DEANNA.** I don't mean that.

Felt like the end of our conversation. Baseball is America, the end.

**JAKE.** I'm not just a pitcher. I mean, I have other interests besides baseball.

**DEANNA.** Okay?

**JAKE.** I do.

**DEANNA.** I believe you.

**JAKE.** You don't. I can tell.

**DEANNA.** Look, I'll see you around.

**JAKE.** Wait.

    *(Beat.)*

My mom said you play the guitar.

**DEANNA.** Yeah.

**JAKE.** What kinda music do you like?

**DEANNA.** What's happening here? I mean, what is this?

**JAKE.** Whatta you mean?

**DEANNA.** You've lived here for half the school year without saying a single word to me. What's the sudden interest?

**JAKE.** You see this hole right here?

**DEANNA.** Yeah?

**JAKE.** You and I are gonna be livin in it. Bunk beds. Right about here.

**DEANNA.** Okay, if IF there is a nuclear war. And if we all even make it into the shelter.

**JAKE.** The chances of it happenin are pretty good.

**DEANNA.** Let's say it happens. Then you and I will be living in this hole together, in our bunk beds, we'll tell each other all of our secrets and *then* we'll become best friends. We don't have to do it in the reverse order, okay?

**JAKE.** Okay, I guess. What if we're the last two people left on the planet? And we have to, ya know, procreate, repopulate the whole planet.

**DEANNA.** Sorry, I guess you'll just have to procreate all alone, ya know, like you usually do.

**JAKE.** Okay, look look, I'm not sayin I'm happy about it either. But if it came down to it, I just thought maybe we could *at least try* to be friends first. Since unfortunately, you might be birthin my children and all.

**DEANNA.** Okay, so yes. Yes, it is better to stand around at school than stand around with you.

**JAKE.** That came out all wrong.
I guess it's all just really weird.

**DEANNA.** Yeah, it's weird.

**JAKE.** It's like an arranged marriage or something.

**DEANNA.** What?

**JAKE.** Yeah, don't you think so?

**DEANNA.** I think you're goin far out with this, man.

**JAKE.** No, really. Think about it. It's like our parents have decided our fate.

**DEANNA.** I bet I can guess who you'd bring down in the shelter.

**JAKE.** What? What is that supposed to mean?

**DEANNA.** Nothing.

> (*Beat.*)

Cool out. It's not gonna happen, okay?

**JAKE.** How can you say that?
I mean, really? How can you be so sure?

**DEANNA.** I'm not sayin somethin horrible isn't gonna happen. I'm just sayin maybe I won't even be around here for it.

**JAKE.** You have to.

**DEANNA.** No, I don't.

**JAKE.** Yeah you do.

**DEANNA.** Maybe I'll just leave.

**JAKE.** Why?

**DEANNA.** 'Cause, maybe I wanna live my life, okay?

**JAKE.** What life?

**DEANNA.** Whatever life there is. I don't know!

**JAKE.** That doesn't make sense, if you wanna live why wouldn't you stay here and go in the bomb shelter?

**DEANNA.** I said I wanna live a life, not a half-life. That bomb shelter, this town. I mean what's the difference? It's all just. Nothing.

**JAKE.** At least you'd survive?

**DEANNA.** Yeah and that's about it.

**JAKE.** Isn't that enough?

**DEANNA.** Maybe for some people.
I don't know. Look, I gotta go. I'll see ya.

**JAKE.** You wouldn't really run away, would you?

**DEANNA.** Just forget I even said anything.

**JAKE.** I mean you could end up. Well. And what the hell? We might really have the responsibility, I mean to repopulate the planet.

**DEANNA.** I said to forget I even said anything. And you know what, maybe I can't even have any kids, ever think about that?

**JAKE.** Is that true?

**DEANNA.** I don't know. But maybe.

**JAKE.** Oh God, just like. Here we are, the human race depending on us to repopulate and lo and behold, *I'm* stuck down in the shelter with the last woman on earth who doesn't even work.

**DEANNA.** I'm goin to school.

**JAKE.** Wait.

**DEANNA.** You clearly don't know anything about women.

**JAKE.** What do you know.

**DEANNA.** I know more than you think.

**JAKE.** I don't know what you're getting at.

**DEANNA.** Just that I get it, okay? It takes one to know one.

**JAKE.** You should just go to school 'cause you're not even making any sense to me.

**DEANNA.** Sorry.

**JAKE.** Why?

**DEANNA.** Didn't mean to freak you out. I've just seen you around at school and I thought you know you do all the stuff you're supposed to but you're kinda different.

**JAKE.** What's that supposed to mean?

**DEANNA.** Come on Jake! You like boys.

**JAKE.** What?! What?

**DEANNA.** Hey, I'm cool/about it.

(*Silence.*)

**JAKE.** Look, I gotta go. I'll see ya.


**(Oct. 21, 1962)   Chapter Six: The Element of Surprise**

*The backyard.* EFRAN *and* SUL *are grilling side by side in front of the shelter hole.*

**EFRAN.** She's lookin right-sized now. Big.

**SUL.** Yup, yup. Got the holes dug, got the reinforced support beams in.

**EFRAN.** To us!

**SUL.** To neighbors!

**EFRAN.** To neighbors.

**SUL.** Steaks?

**EFRAN.** Hey, hey Sul, Sul. Of course. Right? This is me here. We're celebratin, got the salesman steaks.

(LEENA *and* MAG *come outside, carrying food in bowls with Saran Wrap.*)

**LEENA.** Potato salad.

**MAG.** And pasta salad.

**EFRAN.** Oh boy, oh boy. Oh geez, you got the bacon in there and everything. Sul, you ever had the potato salad with the bacon in it?

**SUL.** Nope, I/haven't

**EFRAN.** You ain't lived yet. Let me tell ya.

**LEENA.** Mag made an amazing pasta salad.

**MAG.** It's nothin.

**SUL.** (*Trying to imitate* EFRAN.) Whatta you mean? Efran, wait 'till you taste this pasta salad. It's my favorite.

**EFRAN.** I bet. Hey, hey we're eatin good. This is a celebration. A shelter celebration. Mag, get a good look down there. Sul and I got a few more ideas too. Make the place more civilized.

**MAG.** Wow.

**EFRAN.** Pullin out all the stops. Nothin's too good for our families. Right, Sul?

**SUL.** You. Are. Right.

**EFRAN.** Yes, sir.

(JAKE *and* DEANNA *come outside with plates and utensils.*)

**LEENA.** Right over here with those.

**MAG.** Did you get the servers?

**DEANNA.** Yes, Mom.                    **JAKE.** It's so hot out here.

**EFRAN.** Hey, hey it's an Indian summer. It's hot in an Indian summer. I'll tell ya what'll make ya feel better though, a heapin pile a beef. Grade A beef.

**SUL.** Iron.

**EFRAN.** Iron!

Iron in the blood, that's right. Mag, I tell ya, this husband a yours, he knows things. He really does.

**SUL.** Come on now.

**EFRAN.** No, no. You do. You know things, Sul.

**MAG.** Sul, I didn't tell you but I found out Leena has a degree.

**SUL.** Is that right?

**EFRAN.** Oh yeah, Leena here is smart and beautiful.

**LEENA.** I've actually been thinking, Jake's getting older and you know maybe with my degree/

**EFRAN.** Your brain is one a the things I love about you.

**LEENA.** Maybe I should use it.

(*Beat.*)

**EFRAN.** You use it! Come on. Hey, let me tell you, she uses it.

**JAKE.** She does.

**LEENA.** I mean really, like teach or something.

**EFRAN.** You don't need to do that. I make enough money.

**LEENA.** It's not about that.

**EFRAN.** Come on now. I have a handle on things, and we need you here.

**LEENA.** I'm serious, Efran. I think it'd be good for me.

**EFRAN.** Who's gonna do all the work that has to be done around here? Right?

(SUL *and* MAG *stay out of it.*)

**LEENA.** Jake's getting older, there's really not gonna be as much work/to do.

**EFRAN.** There's always gonna be work at home that has to happen. I mean come on.

(*Silence.* LEENA *drops it for now.*)

**LEENA.** Did I tell you about my craft project?

**EFRAN.** No! What is it?

**LEENA.** I'm makin all of the animals we'll miss outta construction paper.

**EFRAN.** Holy God.

**LEENA.** That way we can take them with us into the bomb shelter.

**EFRAN.** That's a hell of an idea, Leena. Hell of an idea. It's a freakin Noah's Ark, we got.

**JAKE.** *They* had to repopulate the whole planet.

**DEANNA.** Pass the pasta salad.

**EFRAN.** "*Pass the pasta salad*," you hear that, Sul?

**SUL.** I sure did.

**EFRAN.** We can't lose that. Can't let that happen.

**MAG.** What's that?

**EFRAN.** Mag, Mag we're talkin 'bout civilization, how to keep it goin. You know? I mean we've got to make sure that man doesn't de-evolve, am I right?

**MAG.** I hadn't thought about that.

**EFRAN.** This is the thing. It could happen.

**LEENA.** Only if we let it.

**EFRAN.** Let me throw somethin at everyone. In this book I'm readin, the glaciers melt, the world drowns and then man can't help but naturally subvert back into primitive man. No matter how hard they try, they just start bein like cavemen. They lose the sense a civilization. You think that could happen?

**MAG.** Oh.

**LEENA.** That sounds really negative. *The Drowned World.* This is why you're addicted to crisis, Efran. You invite fear into your subconscious.

**EFRAN.** Okay, now. Look, this book is literature. I'm readin literature, which as we know, expands your mind. This book is way deep, Leena. Way deep.

**LEENA.** But is it makin you feel anxious?

**EFRAN.** Well, expandin your mind, sometimes, that expansion first comes with a little bit of anxiety.

**LEENA.** I told you. I always tell him.

**EFRAN.** Wait a second now. Hold on. Hold it right there. Are you tryin to tell me I shouldn't expand my knowledge, because I might get a little scared?

**LEENA.** I don't know, maybe.

**EFRAN.** That's not right. I can't believe you're sayin that. Ignorance is bliss? No, come on now.

**LEENA.** It's not ignorance. It's about how you think about the new information you're gettin.

**EFRAN.** Okay, Leena. Geez.

>    (*Beat.*)

I'm serious here. I'm seriously askin everyone as an intellectual conversation. You think that could happen? Things are happenin. I gotta say I feel like we could totally lose control.

**LEENA.** Listen. This is what you do. You just pretend you are the captain of a ship.

**EFRAN.** What/

**LEENA.** Just listen. You're the captain. You run this ship and you speak in an authoritative voice, and you say, "Hey! Stop it! I'm in charge here. The glaciers are not gonna melt! The world is not gonna drown!" Then your subconscious mind stops makin it a reality.

**EFRAN.** Okay, look/

**LEENA.** It's true, Efran. I read a story about this famous opera singer. Right before he was about to go on one night, he got stricken with a terrible stage fright. His throat closed up, and he just started screamin out, hollerin out backstage, "The little me doesn't want to sing, but the big me does! Stop it! The big me wants to sing! The big me wants to sing! The big me *is going to* sing!"

(*Beat.*)

**EFRAN.** Okay. I know the world ain't gonna drown, tomorrow. I just wanna know if you think man would revert to cavemen in the event of a disaster?

**SUL.** I guess so.

**DEANNA.** Of course.

**EFRAN.** That we'd revert?

**MAG.** Yeah, I guess it makes sense.

**EFRAN.** You know what. I think so too. I really do. I think it's true. That's exactly what would happen. We'd all become Neanderthals.

**JAKE.** Maybe bein a caveman wouldn't be so bad?

**DEANNA.** Yeah, maybe they played baseball with their clubs.

**JAKE.** I bet they did.

**EFRAN.** Wait a second now, baseball, well I consider baseball to be a civilized pastime. I never heard a no caveman playin baseball. I think, for you Jake. Keep baseball alive.

**LEENA.** I just wanna say, why isn't anyone talkin about Halloween? It's right around the corner.

**DEANNA.** Ten days away.

**LEENA.** Deanna, do you love Halloween as much as me?

**DEANNA.** It's the/best holiday.

**LEENA.** Best holiday, right? I know, it is. With all this bomb shelter, we haven't thought at all about Halloween.

**EFRAN.** There might not be a Halloween.

**LEENA.** Efran!

**EFRAN.** I'm just sayin. What if there wasn't a Halloween? We'd all feel pretty stupid for even thinkin 'bout it.

**LEENA.** Are you callin it stupid?

**EFRAN.** No. No. I'm just sayin, is all.

**DEANNA.** At least we could say, "Remember what we planned to do for Halloween?" We could have that.

**JAKE.** We could all dress up as cavemen.

**EFRAN.** Okay, that's not funny. That's not funny at all. No one is allowed to dress up as a caveman. That's just that.

**JAKE.** Maybe that's what I want!

**EFRAN.** Why would you want somethin like that?

**MAG.** Maybe we could do a joint Halloween?/All of us?

**JAKE.** What's wrong with cavemen?

**EFRAN.** I'll tell ya what's wrong with 'em, first off they/grunted at each other

**LEENA.** Okay, Efran really?

**EFRAN.** What?

**LEENA.** Not now, please.

**JAKE.** It's just Halloween.

**MAG.** Like all pirates, or something?

**SUL.** Mag.

**EFRAN.** It's not just Halloween, that's how it starts.

**LEENA.** Okay, really.

**EFRAN.** I'm makin a point here.

**LEENA.** You're embarrassing me.

**EFRAN.** Oh come on. We're all friends here. Neighbors, right? And I mean if we're all gonna be down in the shelter together, let's be ourselves. There's nothin wrong with that. Don't you think so, Sul?

**SUL.** I suppose not.

**EFRAN.** Right, so come on, everything's out on the table.

(*Silence.*)

**SUL.** That crazy woman escaped from the mental hospital again, thought they saw her in North Dakota.

**EFRAN.** Sul. I'm serious here.

**LEENA.** Efran, really?

**EFRAN.** Come on, what's everyone so bunched up about? All I'm askin is that we get down to somethin here. I wanna know if there's anything we need to worry about.

**MAG.** What do you mean?

**EFRAN.** Well Mag, honestly, can we be honest here? We have to be honest.

**MAG.** Of course.

**EFRAN.** Well, I guess I just don't want any unexpected surprises. If we can know then we can be prepared. Okay look, I wanna know about any loose cannons. Ya know? Do we have any loose cannons here?

**LEENA.** You're goin down a road here.

**EFRAN.** Well it's a road I wanna go down. Now for instance, okay I'll start, I am not a morning person. I need an hour before I can handle anyone even talkin to me. See? This is what I'm talkin about.

Come on, somebody. Jake? Jake. Okay. Let me level with you Jake's a growin boy, hormones and all that/and sometimes he

**JAKE.** Dad!              **LEENA.** Efran?

**EFRAN.** I'm just sayin you stink. Sometimes you stink,/but that's just normal.

**JAKE.** I can't believe you!

    (JAKE *storms off.*)

**EFRAN.** Jake! Come on it's normal! Hey come on you, you didn't even finish your potato salad.

**LEENA.** Leave him/alone.

**EFRAN.** Ah come on. I don't understand what the problem is here, I really don't.

**SUL.** I guess maybe we're all a little private.

**EFRAN.** Maybe so, Sul, but privacy is gonna be a hot commodity down in the shelter. So let's get prepared/for that.

**LEENA.** We can cross that bridge when/we get there.

**EFRAN.** When we get there? Leena, I think that'll be too late.

**LEENA.** Efran, really.

**EFRAN.** I mean we're putting two teenagers, a boy and girl down in a hole together. I mean we/could end up

**DEANNA.** Can I be excused?

**MAG.** Deanna?

**DEANNA.** Can I?

**MAG.** Why?             **SUL.** Sure.

**DEANNA.** Thanks, Dad.

    (DEANNA *leaves.*)

**MAG.** Sul?

**SUL.** What?

    (*Beat.*)

**EFRAN.** Well I'm just gonna say it. We have to be honest here. I mean, that's the kinda thing I'm talkin about.

**MAG.** What?

**EFRAN.** Well, Deanna.

**SUL.** What about her?

**EFRAN.** She seems like she could be a loose cannon.

**MAG.** No.             **LEENA.** Efran, please.

**EFRAN.** A little down, a little unsocial. Let's lay it on the table.

**SUL.** There's nothin to lay on the table.

**EFRAN.** There's somethin.

**MAG.** No, she just. I mean we've been through/a lot

**SUL.** There's nothin.

**LEENA.** Okay, Efran this is the kinda thing I've been talking about. You need to stop.

**EFRAN.** Okay, wait, now I know that teenage girls/are different

**SUL.** There's nothin wrong/with Deanna

**EFRAN.** Sul, I'm not sayin there's anything/wrong just that

**SUL.** Then leave it!

**EFRAN.** Okay, clearly I'm touchin/on somethin

**LEENA.** Stop! Please. Would you please just stop?

**MAG.** It's just that we've been through a hard/time

**SUL.** Mag!

**EFRAN.** It's alright/we're neighbors

**SUL.** It's not anything.

**MAG.** It's not anything?

**SUL.** I just/mean

**MAG.** It's not anything? Really, Sul?

**SUL.** Mag, I just/don't wanna

**MAG.** If it's nothing then what's the big deal? Huh? It's no big deal. Efran really, it's not a big deal/it's just

**SUL.** Mag.

**MAG.** It's all my fault right?

**SUL.** Stop.

**MAG.** I'm the one whose fault it is right? I lost the baby, that's/what you think isn't it?

**SUL.** Jesus Christ!

**MAG.** Just admit it.

**SUL.** How could you Mag. Jesus Christ! How could/you

**MAG.** How could I what?

**SUL.** It's none of their business! Our business is not their business.

**MAG.** It's not our business either/

**EFRAN.** Hey now/look it's

**SUL.** Efran! I don't think you/wanna

**LEENA.** Okay, okay.

**SUL.** God Mag! Goddamn it.

(SUL *leaves.*)

**EFRAN.** Sul, come on now.

**LEENA.** I can't believe you. I told you! I asked you to stop.

**EFRAN.** Hey/come on. I didn't know.

**LEENA.** You just can't stop can you. Mag, I'm sorry. I'm so sorry.

**MAG.** Yeah.

We're all sorry. Everyone's sorry.

(*Silence.*)


## (Oct. 22, 1962)   Chapter Seven: DEFCON 3, Part One

*The front of both shotgun houses. It's just starting to get dark, 7 p.m. The lights are on in both houses. It's so quiet you can hear nature. We see the families' movement.* EFRAN *and* LEENA *have the TV on.* SUL *and* MAG *have a radio on. We hear both sounds playing at exactly the same time. President Kennedy addresses the nation.*

**KENNEDY.** Good evening my fellow citizens. This government, as promised, has maintained the closest surveillance of the Soviet military build-up on the island of Cuba. Within the past week, unmistakable evidence has established the fact that a series of offensive missile sites is now in preparation on that imprisoned island.

The purpose of these bases can be none other than to provide a nuclear strike capability against the Western Hemisphere.

The characteristics of these new missile sites indicate two distinct types of installations. Several of them include medium range ballistic missiles capable of carrying a nuclear warhead for a distance of more than 1,000 nautical miles. Each of these missiles, in short, is capable of striking Washington, D.C., the Panama Canal, Cape Canaveral, Mexico City or any other city in the southeastern part of the United States. Additional sites appear to be designed for intermediate range ballistic missiles capable of traveling more than twice as far and thus capable of striking most of the major cities in the Western Hemisphere. In addition, jet bombers capable of carrying nuclear weapons are now being uncrated and assembled in Cuba. This urgent transformation of Cuba into an important strategic base by the presence of these large, long-range and clearly offensive weapons of sudden mass destruction constitutes an explicit threat to the peace and security of all the Americas.

Now further action is required, and is underway, and these actions may only be the beginning. We will not prematurely or unnecessarily risk the costs of worldwide nuclear war in the which even the fruits of victory would be ashes in our mouth, but neither will we shrink from that risk at any time it must be faced.

Let no one doubt that this is a difficult and dangerous effort on which we have set out. No one can foresee precisely what course it will take or what costs or casualties will be incurred. But the greatest danger of all would be to do nothing.

(*Blackout.*)

*End of Act I*

## ACT II

### (Oct. 22, 1962)   Chapter Eight: DEFCON 3, Part Two

*Inside the bomb shelter. Everyone has their blanket and pillows, as if this is a slumber party. The shelter is lit by candles and/or lanterns. It's unfinished and half-assed.*

**EFRAN.** Okay, okay. Now I know you're all scared.

**LEENA.** Well/let's not

**EFRAN.** Maybe, maybe some of you are frightened. We all just heard the President. The shit has hit the fan. The shit has really hit the fan. But, we're prepared. We are prepared. Sul and I. Sul. Come on over here with me, stand here with me. Sul and I are confident that what we have built here is a damn fine bomb shelter. Ain't that right, Sul?

**SUL.** Yeah. Yes.

**EFRAN.** Yes. So, so all of you should, rest easy. You're safe now. As Roosevelt told us, the only thing we have to fear is fear itself. So let's not.

**LEENA.** So now we should fear fear?

**EFRAN.** Leena. Jesus I'm/tryin here.

**LEENA.** I'm just repeating back to you so you can hear yourself.

**EFRAN.** Is this really the time? I don't think it is. I don't think this is the time. This is the moment we come together. 'Cause, look, people, really, we're stuck here. Together. In this hole.

Not that there's anything to worry about. It's just, ya know, where we find ourselves. But look. We might not have as many provisions as we would've liked, but no one's going hungry. Sul and I put these, what's it Sul?

**SUL.** Reinforced/support

**EFRAN.** Reinforced support beams. Sturdy. Okay? Now there's a few things we didn't get to yet. The kitchen table, the bunk beds, but look, there's a few pieces of extra plywood, and we're all creative people, okay? Nothin to worry about. We've got everything we need. Each other, human ingenuity. We might be stuck here, really stuck here. Together. Trapped even, but that doesn't mean we have to live like animals. We don't have to live like animals 'cause we have. A filthy. A filthy hole in the ground. But it's okay 'cause we have things like. Like. Oh Christ!

Oh Christ, did anyone remember a-a-a broom, a dustpan? Anyone? No?

No, of course not. Where the hell would we put it anyway. The dirt. The dust. You'd sweep it up but where would you dump it? There isn't a goddamn place to dump it! Oh Christ!

**LEENA.** Okay, okay. Efran. I/think you should

**EFRAN.** Leena. Leena. Leena, listen to me. Listen. We didn't think about it. It won't be long before we are covered in filth. Okay? There isn't anywhere to dump it. Leena, I'm serious here.

**LEENA.** We'll make a pile.

**EFRAN.** A pile?

**LEENA.** In the corner. A pile.

**EFRAN.** A fucking pile?

**LEENA.** Okay, Efran. Don't talk like that to me. Go to bed. I think you should go to bed.

**EFRAN.** Look, all/I'm sayin is

**LEENA.** Go. Efran, go.
This is my serious face.

(EFRAN *goes to bed.*)

I'm sorry.

**SUL.** No. It's a serious time.     **MAG.** Don't be.

**LEENA.** I'm really sorry this is

**SUL.** We're all tired.     **MAG.** Leena, it's really okay.

**LEENA.** Alright, okay. I'll see all of you in the morning. Jake?

**JAKE.** Yeah, Mom. I'm fine.

(LEENA *goes to bed.*)

**SUL.** It's late. We should all go to bed.

**MAG.** Deanna/

**DEANNA.** I'm fine.

**MAG.** If you need/anything.

**DEANNA.** Goodnight.

(MAG *and* SUL *go to bed.*)

Wow.

**JAKE.** What?

**DEANNA.** Just your dad. He really flipped out, man.

**JAKE.** Yeah.

**DEANNA.** Went to freaky town.

**JAKE.** Yup.

**DEANNA.** Got on a rocket to planet weird.

**JAKE.** Okay. I got it.

**DEANNA.** He has a point though.

**JAKE.** What?

**DEANNA.** Where does all the garbage go?

**JAKE.** I don't know.

Down the toilet hole, I guess.

I dug it myself. It's pretty deep.

**DEANNA.** Is there ventilation?

**JAKE.** I don't know, geez.

**DEANNA.** Is it just gonna stink like shit down here?

**JAKE.** Yeah, it's gonna stink like… That's nature's way.

**DEANNA.** Oh man.

**JAKE.** Hey, at least there's a hole, okay? At least you're not…on the floor.

**DEANNA.** Yeah.

>  (*Beat.*)

**JAKE.** You know it might not be that bad down here.

**DEANNA.** Yeah, it's everything I ever dreamed about.

**JAKE.** Thought you weren't comin down here anyway?

**DEANNA.** I guess you can't fight instinct.

**JAKE.** What?

**DEANNA.** You know basic stuff, like when faced with death you run towards life.

Do you think we'll feel it? The bombs.

**JAKE.** Look, I don't know!

**DEANNA.** Alright alright man, relax.

**JAKE.** Quit with the bull. None of us know anything.

>  (*Silence.*)

**DEANNA.** Your mom said "see you in the morning" but how will we know? Since it's always night down here.

**JAKE.** When we wake up! Geez.

**DEANNA.** You got a temper.

**JAKE.** It's because I'm an athlete.

I'm serious. I have to move my body, exert myself, or else all that athleticism just turns to angry.

**DEANNA.** That's ridiculous.

**JAKE.** You don't know.

**DEANNA.** You're just an asshole.

**JAKE.** I didn't wanna be down here with you anyway!

**DEANNA.** You think I wanna be here with/you?

**JAKE.** You could do worse.

**DEANNA.** What the hell?

**JAKE.** All I'm sayin is, you aren't who I wanted to spend the rest of my life with!

(JAKE *blows out the last candle.*)

**DEANNA.** Hey! I was gonna read.

**JAKE.** Now you're not.

**DEANNA.** There's no way I would ever procreate with you.

**JAKE.** Fine with me! I've already realized that there's someone out there in some other bomb shelter who's right for me.

**DEANNA.** He wouldn't want you either.

**JAKE.** Just shut up about that stuff.

**DEANNA.** I said I didn't care!

**JAKE.** Nothing's…! I'm all… Just…keep your mouth shut about it.

**DEANNA.** Okay.

**JAKE.** Promise?

**DEANNA.** Shut up and go to bed.

(MAG *gasps from their bedroom. She sits up in the darkness.* SUL *lights a lantern.*)

**SUL.** Mag, Mag what's—are you?

**MAG.** I'm fine.

**SUL.** You sure? You scared me to death.

**MAG.** I had a nightmare.

**SUL.** That's understandable considering we're about to get—you know.

**MAG.** Sul!

**SUL.** Well. Just being/realistic.

**MAG.** My spirit horse kicked me off of its back.

**SUL.** Mag, enough with the spirit/horse.

**MAG.** It was beautiful. The wind whipping my face. Leather in my hands. All that power between my legs.

**SUL.** Mag.

**MAG.** It was amazing and I was happy. I was really fucking happy, Sul. Actually, happy.

**SUL.** What're you trying to say?

**MAG.** We were going, pounding the earth. It started rearing. Raising up, bucking until it threw me off its back. I hit the ground and the wind knocked out of me and I woke up, but before I did I saw it kick dirt at me. Intentionally. Why would it do that?

**SUL.** It was a dream.

**MAG.** Why would it do that?

**SUL.** Maybe it was sick of being rode hard.

**MAG.** That's not it. We were like one.

**SUL.** You asked, I answered.

**MAG.** I'm not going to be able to sleep now.

**SUL.** Mag, it was just a dream. Okay? You have to sleep. I'm turning the light out

(SUL *turns the light out and the light goes up in* LEENA *and* EFRAN*'s room.* EFRAN *is pacing.*)

| | |
|---|---|
| **SUL.** Just close your eyes. | **LEENA.** Just close your eyes. |
| Go to sleep. | Go to sleep. |

**EFRAN.** Leena, I have some serious thinkin to do.

**LEENA.** You'd think better with rest. Come over here and lie down with me.

**EFRAN.** No. Look, I've been thinking about it. I don't know if there's anyone we can really trust anymore, ya know?

**LEENA.** Efran, what're you talking about?

**EFRAN.** Think about it Leena, what if somethin goes wrong, what if someone flips out down here? That could happen, it could really happen. Then what? There's gotta be some thought put into this. There's things that hold a society together, and that's what we are now. We're society.

**LEENA.** We're all good people.

**EFRAN.** Yeah, right that's what we think, but you can damn well be sure that there's things we just don't know about. Things that show themselves suddenly, let tonight be a bigger lesson to us. The world gets flipped upside down in a second, and what's our plan?

**LEENA.** Efran, I'm too tired for this. I'm really just…tired. I need you to stop. We both need rest. Can we just try and rest now?

**EFRAN.** Okay, sure, sure. You go on and rest.

**LEENA.** Come here.

(EFRAN *gets into bed with her. She touches him under the sheets.*)

**EFRAN.** Leena, geez. Everyone's right out there.

**LEENA.** I know. It's like being back in the dorm.

**EFRAN.** You were wild.

**LEENA.** I still am.

**EFRAN.** Believe me, I know.

(*Beat.*)

**LEENA.** But I'm not really am I?

**EFRAN.** Of course you are. Leena, why would you say that? Take it from me, you are, you are.

**LEENA.** What's so wild about me now?

**EFRAN.** Where is this comin from, geez. We're down here in a hole in the ground. I mean, I think we have real things to worry about, don't you? My mind is racing. I need you, Leena.

**LEENA.** I know.

**EFRAN.** I always have.

**LEENA.** That's not true, Efran.

**EFRAN.** Come on.

**LEENA.** No, really, you always had big ideas, and exciting plans and you were fearless. I always thought you were fearless.

**EFRAN.** Well, I mean that was before we had anything to lose. We have a lot, Leena. There's a lot to lose, and sure, yeah, we did good, you and I, we did good. We really did, but now, now we have a lot to lose.

**LEENA.** And things we've already lost.

**EFRAN.** No, that's not gonna happen. I won't let it.

(EFRAN *curls up into a fetal position, nearly forcing* LEENA *to hold him.*)
Don't worry about anything, I am on this.

**LEENA.** Okay.

**EFRAN.** Okay.


(Oct. 23, 1962)   **Chapter Nine: Proclamation 3504, Quarantine**

*Sound transition.*

*In the shelter.* LEENA *is hanging paper animals. The others are in their own worlds.* MAG *is clearly the most lost.*

**LEENA.** This is a good spot, don't you think so? Mag?

**MAG.** I'm sorry, what?

**LEENA.** For your horse? See? I made one for you a few nights ago. I wanna hang it here, I think.

**MAG.** Can I hold that?

**LEENA.** The horse?

**MAG.** Yeah.

**LEENA.** Of course. Sure.
I'll hang the rest first. Everything alright? I wasn't sure what color, so I/just

**MAG.** No, it's perfect actually.

**LEENA.** Okay.

**SUL.** She had a nightmare last night.

**MAG.** I didn't sleep.

**SUL.** The horse. Kicked her/or something

**MAG.** It didn't *kick* me, Sul. Okay?

**SUL.** Well/whatever it

**MAG.** It kicked dirt in my face. It didn't *kick* me that's not what happened.

**SUL.** Alright!

**LEENA.** I'm sure it didn't mean to.

**MAG.** No, it did. Intentionally. It kicked dirt in my face after it threw me to the ground.

**EFRAN.** Okay look, look we're all just sitting around here getting stupider by the second.

**LEENA.** Efran.

**EFRAN.** Leena, I'm serious here. I'm not kidding. We're getting dumber. Just listen to us. Our brains are drying up. This is how it starts. Next thing you know, we're talking in monosyllables. Can't let that happen. I won't let it happen. That's not who we are.

**LEENA.** It's been one day. We're not turning into cavemen.

**EFRAN.** I'm keeping an eye on it.

**LEENA.** You do that, honey.

**EFRAN.** I was up half the night and I think I've figured it out. Sul, Sul you're a rational guy, am I right? You're the idea guy. You and Mag with all your ideas.

**SUL.** I mean I'd like to/think that I

**EFRAN.** Sure you are! So I'm thinking back, right? Back to before, before when people didn't have all the modern technology that we have, and I mean I'm talking aristocrats, real educated thinkers, philosophers, if you will. I'm thinkin 'bout all of them and what did they do. What did they do to keep civilized. These people, I mean, they were, well probably more civilized than you and I, right?

**SUL.** I'd say so. I mean they started the whole thing.

**EFRAN.** Right, right? So what'd they do? Well, let me tell ya. I'll tell ya what they did. They did things like read books out loud, play mind games, put on little theatre things for each other.

**JAKE.** I don't wanna play any games except baseball.

**EFRAN.** Well Jake, son, you're in a hole in the ground. Can't play baseball.

**JAKE.** You said we were gonna keep baseball alive.

**EFRAN.** That was before.

**JAKE.** Before what?

**EFRAN.** Before the commies got sneaky, okay? Before they pulled the wool over our eyes. Had we had more time to plan, then maybe.

**JAKE.** You're so full of it.

**LEENA.** Jake! Don't talk/that way to

**EFRAN.** No, Leena. This has been a long time coming.

**LEENA.** What're you talking about?

**EFRAN.** There comes a day when every son has to challenge his father. Don't worry, I've been waiting for it.
Come on.

**JAKE.** What?

**EFRAN.** Ya wanna hit me don't ya?

**JAKE.** Well yeah/I do

**EFRAN.** I knew this was comin.

**JAKE.** You don't know anything about me.

**EFRAN.** Come on, let's go let's get this over with

**JAKE.** Dad?                              **LEENA.** Efran/really

**EFRAN.** No. Order has/to be

**SUL.** Okay, look. This is a small space. I know we're all getting a little tense/ but really we shouldn't

**EFRAN.** Sul, you wouldn't understand, you have a daughter.

**DEANNA.** And what, am I supposed to challenge my mother? Jesus.

**EFRAN.** Yes. For your father's affection.

**DEANNA.** What the hell?

**EFRAN.** Don't get all bunched up. This is Freud. I'm talking about Freud here. It's just a fact. You're not aware of it because it's all subconscious.

**LEENA.** Okay honey, remember, you're the captain/of your own

**EFRAN.** That's right Leena, I'm the captain. I'm the fucking captain of this ship. The whole goddamn ship.

**LEENA.** That's not exactly what/it means.

**EFRAN.** And the captain of this ship says we're gonna play civilized games. Mag, Mag, Mag, Mag put the horse down. Pick up a book for Christ's sake.

**SUL.** Okay, Efran you're crossin a line here.

**EFRAN.** I'm crossing a line?

**SUL.** Yes, that's my wife you're talkin to.

**EFRAN.** Fine keep the horse. Sul, why don't you read us something. I think we could all use it. For all our sakes, Sul. Read somethin to us. Soothe our savage beasts—Or Deanna! You got that guitar. Why don't you play us a song.

**DEANNA.** I'm not a dancing monkey.

**EFRAN.** No, and if you were/we'd all be

**SUL.** Okay Efran, okay. What? What do you want me to read, huh?

**EFRAN.** Finally! Someone who is willing to step up to the plate. Sul, you're a real winner. You got a winner here, Mag. Let me tell ya, this guy is the hero type. I'm serious, Sul.

Let's imagine a not too distant future. Apocalypse, a nuclear holocaust. There are gangs of cruel bandits laying waste. Pillaging and raping. Roving all over the topside. And they come to our place. Tryna get inside our hole. Well, Sul, it's you I'd wanna give a gun to. You're the kinda guy I'd want havin a gun. You know what I mean? You're *that* guy to me.

**SUL.** Okay, Efran. Thanks.

**EFRAN.** I mean it. I really mean it.

**LEENA.** Okay, I've had it. I've had enough. I don't want to hear anymore about guns or pillaging and raping. I've had enough. I've just had enough.

**EFRAN.** This is important, Leena.

**LEENA.** I've had it. I've just had it.

**EFRAN.** I'm thinking about our future here.

**LEENA.** You're thinking in fear.

**EFRAN.** I'm not thinking about right now or tomorrow. I'm talking about our future. I'm thinking about the future of the human race. This is important.

**LEENA.** I said I've had enough! I've had enough! Enough! Enough!

**EFRAN.** Leena. Come on/now.

**LEENA.** You're a bully, Efran. You're being a bully.

**EFRAN.** What?

**LEENA.** You heard me. A bully.

(*Long silence.*)

**EFRAN.** I see.

Let me tell ya, I'm startin to get a real clear picture. It's startin to all come together now.

There's a mutiny happenin on this ship. It's a goddamn mutiny. Geez.

**LEENA.** Your ship is sinking! It's fucking sinking.

**EFRAN.** Leena!

**LEENA.** You're goddamn right there's a mutiny! Someone has to save the sinking ship before you drag us all down to the bottom of the ocean with you.

(*Silence.*)

**SUL.** Okay, look maybe we could all just try and/take a

**LEENA.** Mag! I'm sleeping with you tonight! I'm sorry Sul, you'll figure something out.

**EFRAN.** Aw Leena, come on now. We haven't slept apart since we got married.

**LEENA.** That's how serious I am right now.

**EFRAN.** What about that-that-that-that book, you remember? That book? You said we're not supposed to ever go to bed mad at each other, you/ remember?

**LEENA.** Fuck that book. Fuck all the books, what the hell do they know about anything. We oughta use all the self-help books of the world for firewood.

**EFRAN.** Geez, now you wanna burn all the books? What's going on/here?

**LEENA.** I wanna burn something!

>   (*Beat.*)

**DEANNA.** You could burn your bra?

**LEENA.** I *could* burn my bra! I could!

**EFRAN.** Oh come on now!

**LEENA.** You got a problem with that, Efran?

**EFRAN.** Well geez. I mean come on now. Sul, help me out here.

**SUL.** Sorry.

**EFRAN.** Well I mean come on.

**LEENA.** What? What?

**EFRAN.** Alright alright, I'm just gonna say it. I'm gonna say what we're all thinking but apparently I'm the only one with enough guts to say it.

**LEENA.** Please do.

**EFRAN.** You can't burn your bra.

**LEENA.** Why not?

**EFRAN.** Because. Because, because you guys need those things. I mean really, you can't just be all flappin around willy nilly in the wind. I mean Sul and I ain't flappin around. You want that? You want Sul and I willy nilly in the wind? You want that?

**LEENA.** (*Skillfully taking off her bra under her shirt.*) I dare you.

>   (DEANNA *tosses her a lighter [or a match].*)

**SUL.** Deanna! Stay/out of it.

**EFRAN.** Okay, okay if that's what you want.

>   (EFRAN *starts to undo his pants.*)

Don't do it Leena. Don't burn that bra.

**LEENA.** Or what?

**EFRAN.** Don't burn that/bra.

**LEENA.** Or what, Efran, or what?

**EFRAN.** Don't burn that bra.

> (LEENA *burns her bra. She drops it with intention to the ground.*)

Ah Jesus.

> (*He furiously stomps the fire out.*)

This is it! I tell ya this is really it.

**LEENA.** Come on Mag. We're goin to bed.

Come on.

You can take the horse with you.

> (LEENA *leads* MAG *into her bedroom.*)

**JAKE.** Jesus, Dad!

> (*He covers his head with his blanket.*)

**EFRAN.** For Christ's sake! What is goin on around here. Let me tell ya, this is really it!

> (*He storms off into* SUL*'s bedroom.*)

It's the end of the fucking world!

> (*Silence.* DEANNA *and* JAKE *look to* SUL. *Who just looks back.*)

**SUL.** Well.

> (*Silence.*)

Goodnight.

> (SUL *goes into his bedroom.*)

**DEANNA.** Wow.

**JAKE.** Here we go.

**DEANNA.** Your mom is bad ass! Wow.

**JAKE.** I guess.

**DEANNA.** You guess? That was the most amazing thing I've ever seen.

**JAKE.** I don't know.

**DEANNA.** Your mom has fire and passion. I mean she could freakin—I don't know.

**JAKE.** Christ. It smells like burnt. Bra.

**DEANNA.** That's the smell of the fight, your mom's a revolutionary, man.

**JAKE.** Quiet about it, already. She's not a revolutionary. She's just my mom.

**DEANNA.** (*Blows out the candle.*) And she's amazing. Really amazing.

**(Oct. 24, 1962)   Chapter Ten: "It Looks Really Mean, Doesn't It?"**

*Sound transition.*

*After midnight. The lantern is on in* LEENA*'s room.* LEENA *is brushing her own hair.* MAG *is still distant.*

**LEENA.** There are things goin on, Mag. I mean you read the paper. There's things goin on out there. Amazing things. There's people out there. There's people risking…everything! For something bigger. I mean that's really living. I think that's really living.

(LEENA *starts to brush* MAG*'s hair.*)

If after all this, there's still a world out there. I swear, Mag, I'm gonna fight for it. I'm gonna really live. You should do it with me. We don't have to be alone.

(*Beat.*)

Mag?

**MAG.** Mmm?

**LEENA.** What's goin on with you, Mag? I mean I burned my bra in our hole and you didn't even blink an eye. You're worryin me.

**MAG.** I'm sorry, Leena. I'm just. I'm trying to understand.

**LEENA.** Understand what?

**MAG.** My nightmare.

**LEENA.** Okay.

Tell me.

I'm really good at interpreting dreams.

**MAG.** Really?

**LEENA.** Yeah, I'm a crack.

**MAG.** Okay, well, I was on the back of my horse. No saddle, just me and the horse.

**LEENA.** Bareback.

**MAG.** Yes. The wind whippin my face. Leather reins in my hands. All that power between my legs. It was amazing and I was actually, happy. We were pounding! Pounding the earth. Everything was wild and wonderful. Then, suddenly, it started rearing. Raisin up, buckin. It threw me off its back. I hit the ground and the wind knocked out of me and I woke up, but before I did I saw it kick dirt at me. Intentionally. Why would it do that?

(LEENA *starts laughing.*)

What?

**LEENA.** I'm sorry.

**MAG.** Why are you laughing? Leena, this is really/serious.

**LEENA.** I'm sorry but, really Mag?

**MAG.** What?

**LEENA.** How long has it been?

**MAG.** What, how long has what been?

**LEENA.** Since you and Sul, ya know?

**MAG.** What?

**LEENA.** Ya know. Ya know.

**MAG.** Oh! Leena. Geez, I mean that's—really private.

**LEENA.** Oh come on, it's just us.

**MAG.** What does that have to do with why my horse kicked dirt in my face?

**LEENA.** No, no you're right. It's just that the beginning of the dream sounded like—

Okay, alright, kicked dirt in your face. Well.

**MAG.** Everything was going so well. I was so happy and I know the horse was happy too, and I just don't understand what happened. We were just goin along. Why did it have to come to such an end?

**LEENA.** Horses in dreams are all about power and endurance, strength and sex. And the way you were riding it all bareback is—wild freedom, self-abandonment.

**MAG.** Yeah?

**LEENA.** And it was wearing a harness, right?

**MAG.** Yeah.

**LEENA.** You had the reins in your hand and you were driving it forward.

**MAG.** Yeah?

**LEENA.** Isn't it obvious?

**MAG.** No, tell me?

**LEENA.** Then it kicked you off its back. Mag, your inner wild horse is trying to tell you something.

**MAG.** What's it saying?

**LEENA.** It's saying, stop trying to control me! It's saying, let go of the reins!

**MAG.** Why did it kick dirt in my face?

**LEENA.** That's just a punctuation. Like "Let go of the reins…you idiot!"

**MAG.** Wow.

**LEENA.** Yeah, your inner wild horse is serious.

**MAG.** I was holding onto the reins for dear life but we were going so fast.

**LEENA.** You gotta let go of those reins, Mag.

**MAG.** I think you're right.

**LEENA.** Of course I'm right.

(LEENA *turns the lantern off and the lantern in* SUL*'s room goes on.*)

**EFRAN.** I can't sleep. How are you sleepin? Sul? Sul? SUL?

**SUL.** What?!

**EFRAN.** How the hell are you sleepin?

**SUL.** I'm not.

**EFRAN.** You were.

**SUL.** I was, yeah. Now I'm not.

**EFRAN.** How can you sleep right now?

**SUL.** I'm tired.

**EFRAN.** Shit's goin on, Sul. There's shit going on.

**SUL.** And it'll be goin on tomorrow.

**EFRAN.** We gotta come up with a plan. I mean that's what I've been doin. My head is racing trying to find a goddamn plan. Are you?

**SUL.** No/not really

**EFRAN.** Sul. I need you now. You're the idea guy. I need you now, on my side, figuring this out. We've got to figure this out.

**SUL.** Efran, maybe there's nothin to figure out. You ever think about that?

(*Beat.*)

**EFRAN.** Whatta you mean?

**SUL.** I just mean…maybe there is no plan. Nothin to figure out.

**EFRAN.** So the plan is we do nothin?

**SUL.** I guess so.

**EFRAN.** I think you might be on to somethin here.

**SUL.** We get a good night's sleep. I haven't slept since we've been down here. Last night Mag had a nightmare/that kept us both up

**EFRAN.** You might really be on to somethin here. I mean who comes up with the plans? It's me. You and I. We came up with the bomb shelter. We had a goddamn plan. We come up with the plans. Maybe we should just NOT. Just not find the solution. See what happens. Just keep our fat mouths shut for once.

**SUL.** Starting right now.

(SUL *turns the light out.*)

**EFRAN.** This is a swell idea, Sul. A swell idea. Geez. Let me tell ya, I'm really glad that we're pals. Aren't you? Sul? Are you glad we're pals?

**SUL.** Sure.

(*Beat.*)

**EFRAN.** Sul.

Somethin ain't right. I got a bad feelin.

**SUL.** Everything's gonna be fine.

**EFRAN.** Nah. It ain't. I got a bad feelin.

**SUL.** You're just tired.

**EFRAN.** Sul.

It really is the end of the world.

**SUL.** Maybe.

**EFRAN.** Even if there's no bombs, no radiation. I'm feelin somethin terrible.

**SUL.** Efran, you're the. I mean you're not that kinda guy. Everything works out for you. You know? I see you, you're this guy who makes everything right. But you can't always make things right. Not by talkin. That's all. I mean you should be. I'm the guy who. I mean I'm the guy. I'm the guy who shit happens to. Not you.

**EFRAN.** I liked my life. I mean everything was just right, ya know? I don't want anything else.

**SUL.** You still got your life. I mean yeah, things are... Things are/gonna be

**EFRAN.** Fucked. Things are fucked.

**SUL.** Look, even terrible things don't last forever.

There's things that feel like. Seems like they won't ever change. Like you're just stuck. But you don't know how to get unstuck. I don't know. I'm just thinking maybe. Even if you don't believe you can you gotta keep tryin. It'll all just catch up to you, and you'll look around and realize everything's changed now. That things are better.

(*Beat.*)

**EFRAN.** I can count on you, can't I Sul?

**SUL.** Yeah, we all wanna be okay.

**EFRAN.** That's the thing, Sul. Everything's slipping away. I mean I'm tryin. I'm really tryin to hold onto to it, but there's forces out there. I'm startin to think whatever it is is stronger than me.

**SUL.** Maybe you oughta stop tryna wrestle everything to the ground.

**EFRAN.** Maybe. I don't know. Maybe.

Jesus. I'm havin a real heart to heart with you right now.

**SUL.** Yeah.

(*Beat.*)

**EFRAN.** What do you think?

**SUL.** About what?

**EFRAN.** My heart?

(*Beat.*)

**(Oct. 25, 1962)   Chapter Eleven: "I Regret Very Much That You Still Do Not Appear to Understand What it is That Has Moved Us in This Matter..."**

> *Sound transition.*
>
> JAKE *is tossing a baseball back and forth from hand to glove.* SUL *is reading a book, and* EFRAN *is nearby him stubbornly doing nothing.* MAG *is thinking very hard about letting go of the reins.* DEANNA *is sitting across from* LEENA, *staring at her.*

**DEANNA.** I wanna know you.

**LEENA.** Deanna, we know each other.

**DEANNA.** No but I mean really know you. Ya know?

**LEENA.** I think so.

**DEANNA.** So.

**LEENA.** Well, what do you want to know?

**DEANNA.** Everything.

**LEENA.** Oh gosh. That's a lot.

**DEANNA.** What do you like? What do you love? What gets your heart racing and your blood pumping?

**LEENA.** Oh geez. Well. Geez, no one's ever asked me—I've never had to.

**DEANNA.** Yesterday, when you burned your bra/I just

**LEENA.** That was your idea.

**DEANNA.** Yeah but you did it. You actually did it.

**LEENA.** I was in a mood.

**DEANNA.** No, it was—I felt somethin.

**LEENA.** You did?

**DEANNA.** Yeah! I don't know what it was but it was wonderful.

**LEENA.** You know what?

**DEANNA.** What?

**LEENA.** I felt somethin too.

**DEANNA.** Yeah?

**LEENA.** Yeah. I felt on top a the world/or somethin.

**DEANNA.** You were, you were on top a the world.

**LEENA.** Oh gosh.

**DEANNA.** I could feel that.

**LEENA.** Maybe you were experiencing sisterhood.

(DEANNA *kisses* LEENA.)

Deanna, ahm.

**DEANNA.** Oh, I mean. Blah. Haha. What? I didn't mean that. Oh God. I don't know why I did that. You're right, I'm experiencing sisterhood. It's confusing.

>   (*Beat.*)

**LEENA.** What women have between each other is very intense.

**DEANNA.** Yeah.

**LEENA.** Yup.

>   (MAG *lets out a scream that comes from her depth. It goes on for a long time. Then awkward silence, until…*)

**MAG.** Deanna! Play us a song.

**DEANNA.** What? Mom, what?

**MAG.** You're both bein so quiet over there. Come on. I feel like dancin. Goddamn it!

**SUL.** Mag, is/everything…?

**MAG.** I'm fine, Sul. I've never been better. Deanna? Play us somethin.

**DEANNA.** Aw Mom. I don't really feel like it.

**MAG.** Come on, I wanna dance.

**DEANNA.** I don't feel like playin a dance song.

**MAG.** Play whatever you feel. Just play some music. Please, I wanna tap my foot to somethin.

**LEENA.** Go on.

**DEANNA.** Alright. Alright.

>   (DEANNA *gets her guitar and plays something like Brenda Lee's "Break It To Me Gently." She sings.*
>
>   *Silence.* JAKE *and* EFRAN *wipe their eyes in a way that they think is unnoticeable.*)

**EFRAN.** Goddamn/it.


**(Oct. 25, 1962)   Chapter Twelve: Invasion Is Imminent, You Turkey**


>   LEENA *and* EFRAN *are in their room and* MAG *and* SUL *are in theirs.* JAKE *and* DEANNA *sit together.* DEANNA *is tuning her guitar.*

**JAKE.** You're actually pretty good.

**DEANNA.** Thanks?

**JAKE.** That song you sang. It kinda hit me.

>   (*Beat.*)

Hey, can I tell you somethin?

**DEANNA.** Yeah.

**JAKE.** I never kissed anyone, that's why. The song. I mean that's why it hit me 'cause I was thinkin about how I'm not gonna ever. Ya know?

**DEANNA.** Look, it's/really not

**JAKE.** We're never gettin outta here.

**DEANNA.** And you think that's gonna make me kiss you?

**JAKE.** I think maybe there's somethin weird about you.

**DEANNA.** We're all weird.

**JAKE.** Ya know I was thinkin 'bout baseball—this stupid game. Cared so much about it. There were other things goin on. God! I'm such an idiot!

**DEANNA.** Don't be so hard on yourself.

**JAKE.** You could try to like me, couldn't ya?

>    (*Beat.*)

Geez!

**DEANNA.** I don't know!

>    (*Beat.*)

Look, I understand.

**JAKE.** Yeah?

**DEANNA.** I look around sometimes and I think, what the hell?

**JAKE.** Yeah.

**DEANNA.** 'Cause I look. I look and I never see me out there. I don't know if that even means anything, if it means that I don't fit anywhere. So, maybe, I kinda envy you, with your baseball.

**JAKE.** I'm not really that.

**DEANNA.** I know. But at least you tried to fit.

**JAKE.** All that's gone now. Right? I mean here, down here. We could make this work, be whatever. I could try to like you and I think you're supposed to like me, right?

**DEANNA.** What?

**JAKE.** There's nothin wrong with that, that's normal. Isn't it?

**DEANNA.** Who cares about normal.

**SUL.** Mag, talk to me. What's goin on?

>    (*Beat.*)

Tell me what's goin on?

**MAG.** I wanna be somebody different.

**SUL.** I like who you are.

**MAG.** It's like I feel like there's someone else inside here.

**SUL.** Whatta you mean?

**MAG.** There's more inside here. There's more and I never let it out.
And I don't really know how.

**SUL.** You and I, Mag, we're.

**MAG.** What?

**SUL.** I'm worried we could become those kinda people. Live our whole lives
and have things we never say.

**MAG.** I don't wanna be that anymore.

**SUL.** We can be whatever we wanna be down here. And I mean, if the world
as we knew it ended, we could be whatever we wanna be out there.

**MAG.** I can feel sometimes I'm movin my body with my head, but it's not
how it wants to move. You ever feel like that?

**SUL.** Nah. But sometimes I wanna talk so loud. Sometimes I wanna be the
loudest voice.

**MAG.** Yeah.

**SUL.** Maybe that's just not who we are, but maybe. I'm, I'm willing to try, Mag.

**EFRAN.** Leena, I really liked our life. Don't you? Don't you like our life?
Didn't ya?

**LEENA.** It was a nice life, Efran.

**EFRAN.** Was.

**LEENA.** Things are different now.

**EFRAN.** Yeah.
The world ended while we were down here.

**LEENA.** There'll be somethin new, that's all.

**EFRAN.** I feel somethin terrible.

**LEENA.** I know.

**EFRAN.** I mean, what am I supposed to do now? Geez, Leena, I don't know.
I think the world went some place and I got left behind.

**LEENA.** Run like hell, Efran. That's what you do, run like hell.

**EFRAN.** You want me to leave?

**LEENA.** No, I want you to run like hell, to me, to catch up to me.

    (*Silence.*)

Say somethin.

**EFRAN.** The thing is. I'm the kinda man I always wanted to be.
So where do I go, Leena? This is what I'm asking myself.

**LEENA.** Are you actually happy?

**EFRAN.** No. But I was! I mean I think I was, I think there was a time,
right? When I was?

**LEENA.** I don't know, but there are things in this world that make my heart race and my blood pump. But if someone asked me, I wouldn't be able to tell 'em what they are. And I want to find out.

**EFRAN.** It was when the guy I am made you happy.

**LEENA.** What was?

**EFRAN.** When I was happy.

>  (*Beat.*)

**JAKE.** Where are we gonna bury our parents? You know, if we're down here for a long time.

**DEANNA.** We'll probably have to eat them.

**JAKE.** What the hell?

**DEANNA.** You wanna starve to death?

**JAKE.** What're we tryin so hard to live for?

**DEANNA.** What do you want?

**JAKE.** I want to at least try to be normal.

**DEANNA.** Fine. You want to try to be normal? Let's be normal.

>  (DEANNA *straddles* JAKE *on his sleeping bag and kisses him.*)

**JAKE.** That was… I don't/know

**DEANNA.** You know you look like your mom.

**JAKE.** What?

**DEANNA.** Yeah, you have her eyes, I think.

**JAKE.** Shut up/

>  (DEANNA *kisses* JAKE *again.*)

**DEANNA.** No. You don't

>  (DEANNA *stands.*)

**JAKE.** Keep trying.

>  (JAKE *maneuvers* DEANNA *into a Humphrey Bogart-style backbend kiss.*)

**DEANNA.** Gross.

**JAKE.** Come on. Please?

**DEANNA.** Fine.

>  (*They take off their shoes and shirts.* DEANNA *straddles* JAKE.)

**JAKE.** I guess this is normal?
It's good right?

**DEANNA.** Not really.

>  (*They touch each other, then* JAKE *crosses to pick up* LEENA*'s discarded, burnt bra.*
>  *He starts to put on the bra.*)

**JAKE.** Can you?

**DEANNA.** (*Helping him attach the bra.*) This is kinda… Come here.

(DEANNA *pushes* JAKE *onto the toolbox and grabs him from behind.*)

**LEENA.** Is everything alright?

**JAKE.** Yeah.

(*To* DEANNA.)

That's not it. Do this.

(*They knock over boxes and supplies.*)

**EFRAN.** What's goin on out/there? Jake?

**JAKE.** Nothin!

**SUL.** What's going on?

**DEANNA.** Nothing!

**LEENA.** Jake?

**JAKE.** Nothin.

**SUL.** Deanna, what's/going on?

**EFRAN.** Hey,/hey!

**LEENA.** Okay, okay/you two

**SUL.** Alright, alright!

**MAG.** What's happening?

**DEANNA.** Everybody cool out!

**JAKE.** You were right, down here, who cares about normal.

**EFRAN.** Jake? Somebody better start makin sense.

**JAKE.** Exactly. You know what, I'm just weird, I'm weird.

(*There's a loud bang from above ground/ thunder/ siren? Everyone drops to the ground in silent terror.*

*Silence.*)

**SUL.** (*Calmly, soothing.*) It's okay.

**JAKE.** It's okay.

**SUL.** We're alright.

(*There's another bang. Everyone gathers together.*)

We're all gonna be okay.

(*The trap door in the ceiling of the shelter opens. Light spills in. It's so bright it blinds them. The light grows and grows until it's so bright we can hardly stand it. Sharp blackout.*)

### *End of Play*

# AIRNESS
## by Chelsea Marcantel

## ABOUT *AIRNESS*

*This article first ran in the* Limelight Guide to the 41ˢᵗ Humana Festival of New American Plays, *published by Actors Theatre of Louisville, and is based on conversations with the playwright before rehearsals for the Humana Festival production began.*

When Nina walks into a Staten Island dive bar for her first air guitar competition, she thinks winning will be easy. After all, she plays the actual guitar in a *real band*, so how hard can getting up on stage and shredding on an *imaginary* instrument possibly be? But when her debut performance isn't the success she'd counted on, she realizes that if she wants to qualify for the National Championship, she's got a lot to learn. Following Nina's journey from skeptical newcomer to air guitar goddess in the making, Chelsea Marcantel's music-filled comedy, *Airness*, is a tribute to good friends, killer rock classics, and the raw joy of letting go.

After her initial defeat, Nina's determined to hone her air guitar skills in any way she can. She spends the next few months traveling across the country from competition to competition, studying other performers' routines. (One of the delights of the play is that it features a variety of live air guitar performances, from triumphant wins to hilarious epic failures.) Nina finds a mentor in Shreddy Eddy, an experienced figure on the circuit. "He's like the ambassador of the sport," Marcantel says of Shreddy. "The world of air guitar, in real life, is a very inclusive, welcoming community, and he represents that communal spirit." Nina quickly gets to know Shreddy Eddy's cohorts as well, each of whom have something important to teach her. There's Golden Thunder, renowned for the fierce originality of his choreography. There's Facebender, who suffuses every song he "plays" with the utmost feeling. There's Cannibal Queen, who slays with her flawless technique. And then there's D Vicious, the reigning national champion—whom Nina has her own secret reasons for wanting to beat.

Observing what works for friends and competitors isn't enough to guarantee Nina total air guitar domination, however. Every contest involves a "freestyle round," in which each player performs 60 seconds of a rock song of their choosing—but this can't just be any song. Throughout the play, Nina struggles to find the one track that, above all others, will enable her to shed her inhibitions and express herself in an unfiltered way. "It's about how you feel when you're up there," Shreddy tells her. "It's the pure joy of jumping around naked in your bedroom, but in front of screaming fans." Because at its highest level, air guitar is about moving beyond mere imitation and transcending everyday reality to become a rock star in your own right.

According to Marcantel, "Nina discovers that what she actually has to do— not just to win at air guitar, but to live her best life—is dismantle the walls she's built around herself and set herself free."

Although Marcantel has never tried her hand at air guitar, she does have a personal connection to the art form. "I once dated someone who got into air guitar," she recalls, "and this dovetailed neatly with the end of our relationship. I couldn't understand why anyone would give up their real time and their real relationship to do this imaginary thing. I filed that away as a thing I didn't get." Years later, watching a documentary on air guitar and its eclectic subculture of enthusiasts sparked the playwright's newfound interest in this world. Marcantel elaborates: "In all my plays, I'm interested in humans as small-group primates. I'm fascinated by the idea that when we find our tribe, the rules and values of that tribe become more important to us than the rules of greater society. The world of competitive air guitar seemed like a perfect tribe to explore. Because I realize now that for the guy I was with, it wasn't just air guitar that he loved, I don't think—it was the fact that he'd finally found his tribe."

In that spirit, while each character in *Airness* dreams of achieving the ultimate in individual glory—representing the U.S. at the World Championships in Finland—they're also crazy about the sport because of the close bonds it allows them to forge, with audiences and fellow contestants alike. "The whole thing is about the connection between audience and performer," says Marcantel. "You get to wear leather pants and jump off speakers, and if you're really good at it, you have the audience in the palm of your hand. It's about paying homage to the gods of rock guitar, drinking a lot, traveling a lot, and hanging out with people who love these same things." In Marcantel's play, we get to share in that excitement; as Nina becomes increasingly immersed in this colorful world, so do we.

But *Airness* isn't just about learning how to break hearts and melt faces in 60 seconds. At its core, it's also about embracing the endless possibilities that lie in who we are, and who we could become. As Marcantel puts it: "People find out that air guitar exists and they're like, 'Holy crap, you can do that?' It's a fun reminder that humans are endlessly inventive." And, most crucial of all: "It's a reminder that you become the best version of yourself with the help of those around you. This play is about people who build each other up instead of tearing each other down, and I think that's really important."

—Hannah Rae Montgomery

## BIOGRAPHY

Chelsea Marcantel is a New York City-based writer, director, and collaborator. Reared by Cajuns in southwest Louisiana, she has lived and made theatre among the tribes of the Midwest, Appalachia, and now the Mid-Atlantic, where she completed a Lila Acheson Wallace American Playwrights Fellowship at The Juilliard School. Marcantel's plays include *Everything Is Wonderful, Airness, Ladyish, Devour,* and *Tiny Houses.* They have been produced all around the United States and Canada. She has been entrusted with young minds at Virginia Intermont College and Emory & Henry College, and loved every minute of it. As a writer, Marcantel is extremely interested in humans as small-group primates, and what happens when the rules and value systems of our chosen groups cease to serve us. She reads a lot of books, watches a lot of documentaries, and listens to a lot of podcasts. She is an avid self-producer, and an enthusiastic member of the Writers Guild of America and the Dramatists Guild. More information can be found at ChelseaMarcantel.com.

## ACKNOWLEDGMENTS

*Airness* premiered at the Humana Festival of New American Plays in March 2017. It was directed by Meredith McDonough with the following cast:

THE NINA .....................................................Marinda Anderson
ANNOUNCER........................................................ Matt Burns
CANNIBAL QUEEN ..........................Angelina Impellizzeri
SHREDDY EDDY.................................................... Nate Miller
FACEBENDER.....................................................Lucas Papaelias
GOLDEN THUNDER...........................................Marc Pierre
D VICIOUS........................................................Brian Quijada

and the following production staff:

Scenic Designer................................................... Deb O
Costume Designer ..................................... Alison Siple
Lighting Designer.......................................Paul Toben
Sound Designer..................................... Lindsay Jones
Movement Director...............................Jenny Koons
Stage Manager ............................... Bekah Wachenfeld
Dramaturg........................................Hannah Rae Montgomery
Casting.............................Paul Davis, Calleri Casting
Air Guitar Consultant.............................. Matt Burns
Properties Master.............................. Carrie Mossman
Production Assistant ...................................Codey Leroy Butler
Directing Assistant ...................................... Lila Rachel Becker
Assistant Dramaturg..............................................Bryan Howard

*Airness* owes a developmental debt of gratitude to The Juilliard School.

## THE CHARACTERS

Each character represents one of the pillars of Air Guitar. This pillar is reflected in performance, song choice, approach to the competition, and personal interactions with others while in character. Mostly, the characters go by their stage names. Except for NINA and D VICIOUS where indicated, they are always wearing the exaggerated costumes of their onstage personas.

All characters are in their 20s or 30s; any part can be played by an actor of any race, except: GOLDEN THUNDER, who should be an actor of color, and FACEBENDER, who should be white. FACEBENDER should also be older than the rest of the group by a few years.

> Ed "SHREDDY EDDY" Leary: artistic merit
>
> Gabe "GOLDEN THUNDER" Partridge: originality
>
> Mark "FACEBENDER" Lender: feeling
>
> Astrid "CANNIBAL QUEEN" Anderson: technical ability
>
> Nina "THE NINA" O'Neal: airness
>
> David "D VICIOUS" Cooper: charisma/stage presence
>
> ANNOUNCER/SPRITE EXEC/HOODED FIGURE: These parts are played by the same male actor; sometimes his voice may be heard, without the actor being onstage.

## THE SETTING

All scenes take place in dirty, dingy bars in urban areas across the U.S.— some small, some very large.

Each bar has the same setup: a bar with bar stools serving drinks, a stage, and a backstage/green room area with chairs and couches.

The only exceptions are: the Second Vignette, which takes place on a sound stage (that can be made to look like a dirty, dingy bar if desired) and the Third Vignette, which takes place in the Dark Horse World, which can be as non-realistic as desired (and as close to the "Total Eclipse of the Heart" video as possible).

## THE SCENES

Performances are 60 seconds long, completely choreographed, and astonishingly awesome. They are not half-assed, and they are not jokes. They reveal as much about their performers as the dialogue.

### Scene 1 :: Staten Island, New York – Qualifier
- NINA plays "Don't Stop Believin'"
- GOLDEN THUNDER plays "The Supercut of Unity"

### First Vignette :: Competition Videos
- GOLDEN THUNDER plays "Rebel Yell"
- FACEBENDER plays "Hotel California"
- GOLDEN THUNDER, FACEBENDER, and CANNIBAL QUEEN play "Take It Off"

### Scene 2 :: San Diego, CA – Western Conference Finals
- FACEBENDER plays "Somebody To Love"

### Scene 3 :: Boston, MA – Mid-Atlantic Conference Finals
- CANNIBAL QUEEN plays "Arpeggios From Hell"

### Second Vignette :: D Vicious's Commercial
- D VICIOUS plays "Crowd Chant"

### Scene 4 :: Chicago, IL – Central Conference Finals
- SHREDDY EDDY plays "I Don't Wanna Grow Up"

### Scene 5 :: New York, NY – Eastern Conference Finals
- NINA plays one line of "I Hate Myself for Loving You" in Round One
- NINA plays "99 Problems" in Round Two

### Scene 6 :: New York, NY – After the Loss / Invite to the Dark Horse
- We hear but don't see "Sweet Child of Mine"

### Third Vignette :: The Dark Horse Competition
- NINA plays "Shadows of the Night"

### Scene 7 :: Los Angeles, CA – The National Championship
- D VICIOUS plays "Crazy Train"
- Everyone plays a riff from their song
- Everyone plays "Crazy On You"

## OFFICIAL RULES OF COMPETITION

*(Source: usairguitar.com/rules-2/)*

U.S. Air Guitar obeys the rules set forth by the Air Guitar World Championships:

- Each performance is played to 1 minute (60 seconds) of a song.
- The 60 seconds can start anywhere in the song.
- The instrument must be invisible & be a guitar.
- A competitor does not have to live in a city to compete in a qualifier held there.

### Rounds

**Round 1** (freestyle): each competitor performs to a song of their choice

**Round 2** (compulsory): top competitors from round 1 perform surprise song

### Judging Criteria

All performances are scored on a scale from 4.0 to 6.0—6.0 being the highest possible. A single score is given to each air guitarist based on their overall performance in that round. The scores from BOTH ROUNDS are added to determine the contestants' final scores. The score reflects the quality of the performance based on three key criteria:

- **Technical merit**
You don't have to know what notes you're playing, but the more your invisible fretwork corresponds to the music that's playing, the better the performance.

- **Stage presence**
Anyone can do it in the privacy of their bedroom. Few have what it takes to rock a crowd of hundreds or even thousands—all without an instrument.

- **"Airness"**
The last criterion is the most difficult to define yet often the most decisive of all. Airness is defined as the extent to which a performance transcends the imitation of a real guitar and becomes an art form in and of itself.

In music, as in everything, the disappearing moment of experience
is the firmest reality.

—Benjamin Boretz

You don't choose air guitar. Air guitar chooses you.

—C-Diddy, 2003 World Air Guitar Champion

Marinda Anderson and Lucas Papaelias
in *Airness*

41st Humana Festival of New American Plays
Actors Theatre of Louisville, 2017
Photo by Bill Brymer

# AIRNESS

## Scene 1 :: Staten Island, New York – Qualifier

*Lights up on a small, dingy bar in Staten Island, New York. It is late afternoon, and there are no patrons here yet, but a few of tonight's competitors have come early to start drinking and get the lay of the land. They are all young, but they are old-timers. They have done this dozens of times before, in a dozen cities and towns.*
SHREDDY, GOLDEN, *and* D VICIOUS *sit at the sticky bar, drinking beers.* SHREDDY *and* GOLDEN *are in full persona mode.* D VICIOUS *is not playing along.*

**VICIOUS.** Worst idea you've ever had, man.

**SHREDDY.** Somebody does crucified Jesus every year. Don't be that guy.

**GOLDEN.** "Agent of Unity" is getting me nowhere, dude. I didn't even make the finals in Nashville.

**VICIOUS.** Nobody gets that you're an "agent of unity." It's like a joke—if you have to explain it, it doesn't work.

**GOLDEN.** How does it not work? I'm playing an Earth-shattering supercut of songs with overt and covert political themes, that tracks the history of "otherized" peoples in America, and ends with the embracement of differences. It's sonic coherence on every level. How are people not putting it together?

**SHREDDY.** It's a killer supercut, man. But it's maybe just a little bit too much. That's a lot of threads to weave into sixty seconds.

**VICIOUS.** You don't need to change it, you need to streamline it. That's the danger of a supercut, man—your song is complicated, so your performance needs to be simple.

**GOLDEN.** But I'm not like you. I start with my message, and then—

**VICIOUS.** *(Interrupting.)* It's a rock show, not a lecture, dude.

**GOLDEN.** The whole impetus of air guitar is world peace, Vicious. If we lose sight of that, what are we even doing here?

**SHREDDY.** I saw a naked guy play his dick in Des Moines this year.

**GOLDEN.** Aw, come on!

**VICIOUS.** That happens every year, too, Golden. *(Short pause.)* Did he place?

**SHREDDY.** Disqualified for having an instrument onstage.

**VICIOUS.** Right.

**GOLDEN.** Is that what this sport is coming to? Surely there are still judges out there with some integrity. I am out here trying to heal the motherfuckin' world and the world refuses to be healed! (*Short pause.*) If I don't place here tonight, I'm out. I don't have a hometown qualifier like you, Shreddy, or a free ride to Nationals like his highness over here. If I can't get my message across tonight, I'm out for the season.

**VICIOUS.** And this will be, what, the fourth year you don't qualify for Nationals?

**SHREDDY.** Come on, dude.

**VICIOUS.** What, is that not a fact? Am I not allowed to bring up the actual fact that neither one of you have ever qualified for the National Championships?

(*To* GOLDEN.)

Originality only gets you points if the judges can figure out what the hell you're doing.

**SHREDDY.** Don't listen to this guy. It's our year, Golden. We're both going to the finals, for sure.

(*To* D VICIOUS.)

We're comin' for you, Champ.

**VICIOUS.** I'm fuckin' terrified over here.

**SHREDDY.** What? Last year was your first year at Nationals, and you won the whole thing. One of us could pull that off. Plus, this season, my song is untouchable. Which you would know, if you'd been to any of the qualifiers.

**VICIOUS.** You've always got the perfect song, Shreddy. That's never your problem. Your "angry record store dude" persona's got his head so far up his ass, that you're not giving anything to the crowd. It doesn't matter how superior your taste is, if you can't put on a show.

(*A tense pause.*)

**SHREDDY.** Dude, that Sprite commercial really inflated your ego.

**GOLDEN.** Shit went straight to your head.

**VICIOUS.** Aw, shut up.

**GOLDEN.** You aren't even dressed to play the halftime show.

**VICIOUS.** I've got plenty of time to figure that out.

**SHREDDY.** What are you playing?

**VICIOUS.** Got plenty of time to figure that out, too. I'll probably just throw something together in the green room during Round One.

**SHREDDY.** You're not even going to watch us play?

**VICIOUS.** No offense, my dudes, but I have a lot on my plate right now. I'm only here to play halftime because it's my home turf and I'm doing the organizers a favor. I'm actually thinking of hiring a manager soon. I got lots to get done.

**SHREDDY.** Like what?

(FACEBENDER *walks into the bar. He pretends to take a guitar case off his back and set it on the stage. He then walks over to* SHREDDY, D VICIOUS, *and* GOLDEN.

GOLDEN *holds out his hand to* FACEBENDER, *but* FACEBENDER *bypasses the hand and pulls him into a bear hug.*)

**GOLDEN.** Facebender! Good to see you, man!

**FACEBENDER.** Golden Thunder. My dear friend. I hope your journey to New York was pleasant.

**GOLDEN.** It was all right.

(SHREDDY *doesn't offer* FACEBENDER *his hand, but* FACE-BENDER *pulls him into a warm embrace anyway.*)

**FACEBENDER.** Shreddy Eddy, it fills my heart to the brim to see you hale and hearty.

**SHREDDY.** Happy to have you in the room, buddy.

**FACEBENDER.** Happy to be here, friend.

(FACEBENDER *turns to* D VICIOUS *and does an exaggerated, sweeping bow [but he does not hug* VICIOUS*].*)

My liege.

**VICIOUS.** (*Enjoying this a little more than he should.*) Come on, Bender.

(FACEBENDER *looks around for a bartender, and not seeing one, walks behind the bar, finds a glass, and helps himself to a pint.*)

**GOLDEN.** We haven't seen the bartender in like half an hour.

**FACEBENDER.** I'll keep track of my own tab. I trust myself.

**GOLDEN.** (*Pause.*) Did you catch my song in Nashville, Bender? My super-cut of ultimate unity?

**FACEBENDER.** Indeed I did. I saw the video online.

**GOLDEN.** What did you think?

**FACEBENDER.** I thought it was astonishing. Gorgeous, and heartbreak-ing, and a balm for these troubled times.

**GOLDEN.** Yeah, see? He gets it. Judges only gave me a 5.1.

**FACEBENDER.** Egregious!

**SHREDDY.** The judges at some of these small qualifiers, I mean, who are they? What qualifies them to judge competitive air guitar on our level, you know?

**VICIOUS.** (*Trying to refocus the group's attention on himself.*) Most of them wouldn't know a real moment of airness if it smacked them across the face.

**GOLDEN.** Exactly. And this is the truest art form. The only pure art form left.

**FACEBENDER.** Incorruptible.

**GOLDEN.** Un-commercializable.

**SHREDDY.** Totally democratic.

**VICIOUS.** And we look fuckin' cool doin' it.

(*They clink their beer glasses.*)

**SHREDDY.** But do these new judges understand that? No. They do not. These qualifiers used to be judged by rock gods, real legends. But now there are so many of them, it's washed-up promoters and satellite radio DJs.

**VICIOUS.** Not at Nationals.

**SHREDDY.** No, no, you're right. If we can get to Nationals, we'll be rocking for people who actually appreciate what they're looking at.

**FACEBENDER.** So let us focus our powers, gentlemen. The hour of triumph is nigh.

(CANNIBAL QUEEN *enters. She looks around, sees* D VICIOUS, *gets a little pissed [he's not where he should be right now] and addresses the guys at the bar.*)

**CANNIBAL QUEEN.** Hey, Shreddy. Golden. Facebender.

**SHREDDY.** Hey, CQ.

**CANNIBAL QUEEN.** (*Emphatically.*) Cannibal Queen.

**FACEBENDER.** Care to join us for a pregame libation?

**CANNIBAL QUEEN.** I'm good. Vicious? I thought we were going to get dinner before the show?

(CANNIBAL QUEEN *exits.* FACEBENDER, SHREDDY, *and* GOLDEN *make "ooooh, you're in trouble" noises.*)

**VICIOUS.** (*With great dignity.*) Later, Bad News Bears.

(D VICIOUS *exits following* CANNIBAL QUEEN.)

**FACEBENDER.** She is enchanting.

**GOLDEN.** That's not the word I'd use.

**FACEBENDER.** As skilled as she is mysterious. The Aphrodite of air guitar.

**SHREDDY.** That's excessive, but I will admit, Cannibal Queen's got the best technique in the game right now.
There's nothing the judges can pull out in the second round that she can't nail.

**FACEBENDER.** And yet, she remains as cruelly cast aside as the three of us. Hopes dashed at every qualifier throughout the Midwest, watching her chances of Nationals disappear like ashes in the wind.

**GOLDEN.** CQ is cold onstage. Low on charisma. She nails it technically, but the crowd comes to have a good time. This isn't Carnegie Hall—

**SHREDDY.** (*Interrupting.*) Technical points win championships—

**GOLDEN.** (*Interrupting.*) But air guitar's appeal is audience-based. Its whole existence is its effect on the audience, tell me that's not true. Dispute it, if you can, Shreddy. You can't!

**SHREDDY.** Don't dismiss your technical scores, is all I'm saying. You might be able to fudge your left-hand placement here, in small qualifiers, but on the national stage? The international stage? That just doesn't wash. That's not gonna wash in Finland. Air guitar is not a joke to anyone in Finland.

> (*The air is getting tense.*
> NINA *enters the bar. She looks around. The men stare at her.*)

**FACEBENDER.** Good evening. Are you lost, miss?

**NINA.** I... uh. I think I'm just really early.

**FACEBENDER.** For the Air Guitar qualifier? I regret to inform you that the show doesn't start for a few more hours.

**NINA.** Oh, um, yes. That's it, that's what I'm here for.

**SHREDDY.** I think they open the doors at 9. There's a place with good tacos up the street, if you need to kill time.

**NINA.** I'm actually, uh, registered to compete. Tonight. Here. In air guitar.

**GOLDEN.** Really?

**SHREDDY.** Fresh meat!

**FACEBENDER.** Delightful.

**SHREDDY.** I'm Ed Leary. "Shreddy Eddy."

**GOLDEN.** Gabe Partridge. "Golden Thunder."

**FACEBENDER.** And I'm Mark Lender. "Facebender."

**NINA.** Ed, Gabe, Mark.

**GOLDEN.** Shreddy Eddy, Golden Thunder, and Facebender.

**NINA.** Those are your stage names?

**SHREDDY.** They're our personas.

**NINA.** But you're not onstage.

**GOLDEN.** We're in the venue, though.

**FACEBENDER.** We are in the arena. Among its denizens. It has already begun, you see.

**NINA.** I guess.

**SHREDDY.** When we're among competitors, we go by our personas.

> (*She stares at them. They stare at her, waiting for her to introduce her persona.*)

**NINA.** (*After a beat.*) I'm Nina.

**SHREDDY.** What do you go by onstage?

**NINA.** Well, uh, I didn't know stage names were, like, mandatory.

**SHREDDY.** (*Disappointed.*) They're not. But, like, you gotta have a persona. To protect yourself.

**NINA.** From what?

**SHREDDY.** From everything outside the music.

**NINA.** (*Rolling her eyes.*) Oh my god.

**SHREDDY.** When you get up there tonight, you won't be a girl onstage at a shitty bar in Staten Island, doing a mime routine. You'll be a rock goddess, playing Wembley Stadium. Madison Square Garden. The International Space Station. Melting faces and breaking hearts for sixty seconds. That rock goddess needs a name.

**GOLDEN.** So if you start to doubt that you can do it, you remember that she can.

**NINA.** I'm in a real band. I actually play the real guitar. So I'm not, you know, *super* worried about this. You guys seem like *really* invested, but how talented could anybody here tonight *really* be?

(*They silently turn away from her and back to their beers.*)

Oh, come on, don't be like that. Do you guys really take yourselves this seriously?

**FACEBENDER.** Ourselves, rarely. Air guitar, inevitably.

**NINA.** Well, shit. We got off on the wrong foot. I didn't mean to insult anyone.

**SHREDDY.** (*Not turning around.*) We're not insulted. We just don't want to talk to you anymore.

(NINA *stands awkwardly for a moment, unsure whether to stay or go. Normally being too cool and "over it" works for her.*)

**NINA.** This thing doesn't start for like three hours. That's a long time.

**GOLDEN.** It will be for you.

**NINA.** (*Exasperated.*) Look, I'm sorry, okay? You big babies. (*Pause.*) Instead of shutting me out, you could educate me, you know? Show me the error of my ways. (*Short pause.*) Unless you think I'm a threat.

**FACEBENDER.** (*The first to turn to her.*) Miss Nina. This is not a community built upon competition, but camaraderie.

**SHREDDY.** There are a few dicks in the mix, but for the most part, everyone's chill.

**NINA.** I can be chill.

**FACEBENDER.** Do you swear it?

**NINA.** Swear.

**SHREDDY.** Okay then. Let's just see. What song are you performing?

**NINA.** Oh. Um, I thought I'd do "Don't Stop Believin'."

(SHREDDY, GOLDEN, *and* FACEBENDER *all groan in unison.*)

**SHREDDY.** Are you serious right now?

**NINA.** What? It's an iconic song.

**GOLDEN.** Doesn't mean we want to hear it. *Again.*

**SHREDDY.** Not to mention the fact that the song doesn't exactly melt faces.

**GOLDEN.** Or deliver any kind of social impact or crucial message.

**NINA.** Neal Schon is a guitar prodigy! He played with Santana at fifteen!

**SHREDDY.** But, the *song.* It just doesn't shred. And it doesn't have anything to do with you, unless you consider yourself just a small-town girl livin' in a lonely world. Journey is for stepmoms and frat boys. You have to play something that blasts *your soul,* Nina.

**NINA.** (*Dismissive.*) Look, I prepared the Journey song, I don't have another song, I can't come up with a whole new thing in three hours. I don't have time to rehearse.

**GOLDEN.** If you picked the wrong song, rehearsal is kind of irrelevant, anyway.

**NINA.** (*Annoyed.*) Oh, that's helpful. Thanks.

**SHREDDY.** A boring, overplayed, trite-ass song only works if your cut is subversive.

**NINA.** (*Confused.*) My... cut?

(SHREDDY, FACEBENDER, *and* GOLDEN *groan.*)

**SHREDDY.** (*Interrupting.*) If you bomb up there, it's gonna bring down the quality of the show as a whole. I have like fifty different song cuts on my phone. Do you want to use one?

**NINA.** I'm good, thanks.

(*They shake their heads sadly.*)

**FACEBENDER.** (*Trying to find some hope for her.*) Freestyle is merely the first round of competition. An exemplary score in the second round might be enough to propel you to victory.

**GOLDEN.** And since you're local, you get two shots at Nationals. If you lose tonight, you can try again at the Eastern Conference Finals in a few months.

**NINA.** (*Something occurs to her.*) Wait, wait, you guys aren't from here?

**FACEBENDER.** San Diego.

**SHREDDY.** Chicago.

**GOLDEN.** Big Sky, Montana.

**NINA.** Y'all came from *out of state?* To *Staten Island?* For *fucking air guitar?*

(*There is a hostile silence.*

*The door opens, and* CANNIBAL QUEEN *walks back in.* NINA *gasps and puts her hand over her mouth.* CANNIBAL QUEEN *looks at her confused; she doesn't know who* NINA *is.*)

**CANNIBAL QUEEN.** (*Pissed.*) So Vicious has decided he can't be bothered to play the halftime show tonight. Has anybody seen an organizer?

**FACEBENDER.** Maybe in the green room?

**SHREDDY.** What a dick-lick.

**GOLDEN.** Great. The crowd will be pissed off before I even get up there.

(CANNIBAL QUEEN *exits to the green room.*)

**NINA.** (*A little panicky.*) He's still competing tonight, right? D Vicious?

**SHREDDY.** No. He was never gonna compete tonight.

**NINA.** But his name is on the poster!

**SHREDDY.** As the halftime entertainment. Vicious is the reigning champ. You're gonna have to make it all the way to Nationals if you wanna face off against him.

(NINA *is rethinking every decision that brought her to this moment. The lights shift into show-mode.*)

**ANNOUNCER.** Ladies and germs, welcome to your Staten Island Air Guitar qualifier! Since this is the home turf of our reigning National Champion, D Vicious, the Gods of Air have deigned to let us send tonight's winner all the way to Nationals! This is the last shot for those of you without a hometown semi-final, so I hope you're fuckin' hungry!

(*A bright, garish spotlight comes up onstage;* NINA *nervously moves into the light.*)

**NINA.** (*Spiraling.*) What am I doing here? Okay, hold the guitar. Fake guitar. Not-guitar. You can play it. You can play anything. You look like a fucking idiot and your parents would die of shame if they were in this bar right now, but you can play it. Breathe. Just play it, Nina.

****** NINA'S FIRST PERFORMANCE ******

(NINA *stands onstage, ready. Nothing happens.* FACEBENDER *cues her from the audience to extend her arm and point her finger.*

*The intro of "Don't Stop Believin'" plays, which is entirely piano.*)

**NINA.** (*Yelling at the sound guy from the stage.*) No, don't start it at the beginning, you gotta start it—hey, start it over! Start later, at—aw, shit.

(*To herself.*)

Come on, Nina. You know the song. Just play the song. Don't freeze up. Play the song.

(*For an uncomfortable amount of time,* NINA *doesn't do anything to the music.*

*Then she recovers, slightly, as we hear the crowd start to boo, bored. Finally, the*
*guitar drops in. She plays the song as if she had a guitar in her hand, and it's*
*accurate, but she seems miserable and she's not even looking at the crowd. Almost*
*as soon as the guitar starts, the song is cut off. Finally, the sixty seconds are over.*
*The small crowd boos, not even really engaged in this.)*

**FACEBENDER.** *(From the bar.)* Merciful God, is it over?

**CANNIBAL QUEEN.** *(From the bar.)* Woof.

**NINA.** *(Mortified.)* Kill me. Somebody kill me.

(NINA *freezes onstage, mortified.*
GOLDEN THUNDER *approaches her and nudges her off the stage.)*

**GOLDEN.** Please move aside. This crowd needs healing more than ever.

**\*\*\*\*\*\* GOLDEN THUNDER'S PERFORMANCE \*\*\*\*\*\***

*(The Supercut of Unity begins to play—it is an epic mashup of three Michael*
*Jackson songs [maybe "They Don't Really Care About Us"/"Black or*
*White"/"Man in the Mirror"]. Whatever this supercut is, the performance*
*should include at least one costume change/reveal.*

GOLDEN *gives an amazing air guitar performance. What he lacks in guitar-*
*playing accuracy, he makes up in originality and interpretive glory. And he is*
*the winner. Having to defend his art form to* NINA *has brought out a deeper*
*level of artistry than he thought he had inside himself. His final costume change*
*reveals a t-shirt that says "Make Air Not War," maybe in sequins.)*

**ANNOUNCER.** All right, party people, the scores from both rounds are
in! Taking first place here tonight in the Staten Island Qualifier, moving
on to the National Finals, the man who puts the "art" in "farting around":
Golden Thunder!

*(Everyone onstage except* NINA *rallies around* GOLDEN *and cheers.*
NINA *sees this, sees the power of this tribe, and it speaks to her.*
*Lights dim on the bar in Staten Island.)*

### First Vignette :: Competition Videos

*A small light comes up on* NINA *and* SHREDDY, *hunched over a laptop on*
*the side of the stage. It is a few weeks later. They are watching old competition*
*videos on the internet.* NINA *has a pen and a notepad.* SHREDDY *is*
*holding out to her a single printed piece of paper.*

**SHREDDY.** I'm just going to need your John Hancock on this.

**NINA.** Oh come on. I told you I would buy all of your drinks—

**SHREDDY.** *(Interrupting.)* From now till Nationals.

**NINA.** From now till Nationals. And my word is good. We do not need a contract.

**SHREDDY.** Well, considering that you showed up in Staten Island outta nowhere, acted like a complete jerk to everybody, and then got up onstage and thoroughly annihilated yourself, you'll understand why I can't perform these services for you on the honor system. I'mma need you to sign this.

**NINA.** (*Taking it from him and signing.*) Fine. Whatever.

> (*He takes the contract from her, takes a picture of the paper with his phone, then folds it up, and puts it in his pocket.*)

**SHREDDY.** I'll email you a copy.

**NINA.** I'm good, thanks.

**SHREDDY.** Suit yourself. Let's begin.

**NINA.** Teach me. I have a notebook.

**SHREDDY.** We'll start with the foundation. You did the reading I sent you, yes?

**NINA.** Yes.

**SHREDDY.** Pop quiz! First round is—?

**NINA.** A sixty second cut of a song I choose.

**SHREDDY.** Second round is—?

**NINA.** Sixty seconds of a song chosen by the judges.

**SHREDDY.** Points are given—?

**NINA.** On a scale of 4.0 to 6.0.

**SHREDDY.** Exactly like—?

**NINA.** Figure skating.

**SHREDDY.** Optimum number of beers before a performance is—?

**NINA.** Two?

**SHREDDY.** (*Makes a buzzer noise.*) Eghnt! Three. This is known as the Monro Rule, discovered by and named after British champion slash air guitar god Zac Monro. Three beers.

**NINA.** Got it. Making a note.

**SHREDDY.** Now tell me: what are the six pillars of air guitar?

**NINA.** (*Reading from her notebook.*) Artistic merit, originality, feeling, technical ability, charisma, and airness.

**SHREDDY.** Great. Excellent. Memorize them. Internalize them. Metabolize them.

**NINA.** I don't know what any of that means.

**SHREDDY.** And *that* is why God invented YouTube.

> (*He types something into the computer.*)

Okay, okay, so this is the Portland qualifier, two years ago. This is a great place to start. It was a pretty small house, but everybody really tore it up that night.

(*Three small squares of light come up in the middle of the stage.* FACE-BENDER, CANNIBAL QUEEN, *and* GOLDEN *step into the boxes of light. They are in the videos. We watch them, and we see what* NINA *and* SHREDDY *are seeing.* NINA *and* SHREDDY *have the power to start and stop the videos, and the bodies of* FACEBENDER, CANNIBAL QUEEN, *and* GOLDEN *must respond accordingly.*)

Okay, so here's our pal Golden Thunder. His highest marks are always in originality, as you saw in Staten Island, where he slayed.

**NINA.** Yeah. His whole unification theme was great.

**SHREDDY.** You picked up on that, huh?

**NINA.** He was wailing to an amazing supercut of songs with overt and covert political themes. What moron wouldn't put that together?

**SHREDDY.** He approached airness that night. There is no denying it. (*Short pause.*) We'll cover airness. Eventually.

**NINA.** One thing at a time.

**SHREDDY.** Obviously. So. As you'll see:

(*He presses "play" and* GOLDEN *comes to life.*
*Billy Idol's "Rebel Yell" plays.* GOLDEN *rocks out for a few seconds.*
SHREDDY *presses "pause," and* GOLDEN *freezes.*)

Golden's gift is that he can take a song that the judges have heard a hundred times, in this case "Rebel Yell," and make it totally his own, a brand new thing.

**NINA.** Looks pretty standard to me.

**SHREDDY.** Wait for it.

(SHREDDY *presses "play" again, and* GOLDEN *returns to rocking. [No matter the cut, we should clearly hear the words "rebel yell."] After a few seconds,* GOLDEN *drops his pants, revealing boxer shorts he has created himself, that are half Confederate Flag, half Union Flag.* NINA *hits "pause."*)

**NINA.** Oh no.

**SHREDDY.** It's not over.

(SHREDDY *hits "play."* GOLDEN *rocks. After a moment, he fires a cannon and then plays guitar while writing. Fires another cannon. Shakes hands with himself. Finally, he drops his boxers and reveals a pair of American Flag briefs.* SHREDDY *hits "pause."*)

**NINA.** Was he writing the Emancipation Proclamation in the middle there?

**SHREDDY.** Exactly. And firing cannons. And surrendering at Appomattox.

**NINA.** Amazing.

**SHREDDY.** Absolutely. Originality—you've got the idea.

**NINA.** Good stuff.

**SHREDDY.** Moving on! Facebender. What did I tell you in my email?

**NINA.** (*Read from her notebook.*) His highest marks are always for feeling.

**SHREDDY.** Exactly. In a lineup full of ego and testosterone and dudes grabbing their balls, Facebender is a bright spot of actual heart. He sends out his energy in a glorious wash over the crowd.

> (SHREDDY *hits "play," and* FACEBENDER *comes to life. We hear "Hotel California" by the Eagles.* FACEBENDER *plays, he feels, he doesn't move his hands much, but his face is a mask of emotion. He begins to cry, softly. It is so beautiful. It is also totally rock-n-roll.* NINA *hits "pause."* FACE-BENDER *freezes.*)

**NINA.** Is he crying?

**SHREDDY.** He is.

**NINA.** It's… it's so beautiful.

**SHREDDY.** That dude uses air guitar to swim against a tide of real sadness. The judges see that. And they fucking respect it.

**NINA.** You can't fake that kind of heart.

**SHREDDY.** Exactly. You have to earn it. (*Short pause.*) Now, Cannibal Queen—

> (CANNIBAL QUEEN *activates in her block of light, sensing her turn is next.*)

**NINA.** (*Interrupting.*) Nope. I don't want to watch her video.

> (CANNIBAL QUEEN *looks annoyed and disappointed.*)

**SHREDDY.** You can't just get up there and play whatever. It's not a dance routine. CQ is a classically trained guitarist, 100% about the music. Accuracy, specificity, and timing.

> (CANNIBAL QUEEN *gets ready to play.*)

**NINA.** I know how to play guitar. That's the one thing I don't need coaching on.

> (CANNIBAL QUEEN *deflates again.*)

**SHREDDY.** You asked for my help, and I'm telling you—

> (CANNIBAL QUEEN *is ready!*)

**NINA.** (*Interrupting.*) Can we move on to the second round? My compulsory performance was almost as bad as my freestyle.

> (CANNIBAL QUEEN *deactivates, really annoyed now.*)

**SHREDDY.** Worse.

**NINA.** Hey!

**SHREDDY.** I'm your mentor, not your boyfriend.

(*Then quickly.*)

Now, your scores from Round One will be averaged with your scores from Round Two. For Round Two, as you experienced, it's harder to prepare. Every finalist performs sixty seconds of a song picked by the judges. No one knows what the song will be ahead of time, so you have to be prepared for them to get really creative.

**NINA.** Creative how?

**SHREDDY.** Sometimes they pick a song nobody's ever heard. Sometimes it's so cliché that you have to overcome your own snobbery.

**NINA.** For instance?

**SHREDDY.** For instance, Des Moines, three years ago.

(CANNIBAL QUEEN, FACEBENDER, *and* GOLDEN *change places.*)

The judges pulled out "Take It Off" by The Donnas.

(SHREDDY *hits* "*play.*" *We hear* "*Take It Off.*" CANNIBAL QUEEN, FACEBENDER, *and* GOLDEN *all begin to play.* FACEBENDER *is having a rough time. After a few seconds,* SHREDDY *hits* "*pause.*")

You see how lost Facebender looks?

**NINA.** He's all over the place. That is in no way the shape or size of an actual guitar.

**SHREDDY.** Exactly. That was his first year. He had the heart and the drive, but he didn't have the mechanics. He totally tanked it. Plus, he had to go first. You want to go as late as you can, so you can hear the song a bunch of times. But, the later you go, the more original you have to be. Which is why Golden Thunder did better in this round.

**NINA.** Oh I can't wait.

(SHREDDY *presses* "*play.*" *We hear* "*Take It Off.*" GOLDEN THUN-DER *immediately takes his shirt off.* SHREDDY *presses* "*pause.*")

**NINA.** Really?

**SHREDDY.** I said he did better. I didn't say he did great. But Cannibal Queen—

(SHREDDY *hits* "*play.*" *We hear* "*Take It Off,*" *and* CANNIBAL QUEEN *slays. The sixty seconds finish.* NINA *hits* "*pause*" *and* GOLDEN, FACEBENDER, *and* CANNIBAL QUEEN *freeze.* CANNIBAL QUEEN *has a huge grin on her face.*)

Cannibal Queen takes it all.

**NINA.** (*Darkly.*) Yes. Yes she does.

(SHREDDY *looks her and raises his eyebrows.*)

**NINA.** (*Avoiding a question she senses is coming.*) Hey… in Staten Island. You're right, I was rude. I was… Anyway, I'm sorry if I offended you.

(*NOTE: If* SHREDDY *is played by an actor of color, omit the word "white" from the following line.*)

**SHREDDY.** (*Shrugging.*) Hey. I'm a straight white dude from the Midwest who doesn't believe in religion. It's kind of hard to offend me.

**NINA.** (*Pause.*) Han shot second.

**SHREDDY.** (*With gusto.*) DIE IN A FIRE!

(*Lights dim on the Vignette.*)


### Scene 2 :: San Diego, CA – Western Conference Finals

*Lights up on a larger, still dingy, bar in San Diego. It is two months after Staten Island. It is late afternoon, and there are no patrons here yet.* GOLDEN *and* NINA *sit in the green room, drinking beers.* GOLDEN *is not quite ready to let her into the tribe.*

**NINA.** So we could all still make it to Nationals this year?

**GOLDEN.** If the Gods of Air are willing. Facebender's from San Diego, so he's got a good shot at the Western Conference title here tonight. Shreddy's hometown in Chicago, CQ's hometown in Boston, and I gloriously qualified in Staten Island, as you witnessed. Thankfully, because qualifiers are thin on the ground in Montana.

**NINA.** You guys hang out a lot?

**GOLDEN.** Nah. We're so spread out, we only see each other at competitions.

**NINA.** Bummer.

**GOLDEN.** But the group text is *fire.*

**NINA.** I'm sure.

**GOLDEN.** You're just here for moral support as well?

**NINA.** Uh, no. I'm doing recon.

**GOLDEN.** You don't need to do more recon. You need to put down the notebook and get back onstage. Air guitar is about the audience. The only way to really get better is to perform.

**NINA.** I know about audiences. What I don't know about, really, is air guitar.

**GOLDEN.** You went down in flames in Staten Island. I know that had to sting like a motherfucker. But the longer you put off your comeback, the harder it's going to be to get back on that horse.

(NINA *is quiet.*)

**NINA.** I got lower scores than the guy who performed as resurrected Jesus.

**GOLDEN.** (*Defensive.*) To be fair, Pearl Jam's "Alive" was a strong artistic choice. If Jesus hadn't been drunk out of his mind, he might have swept the whole thing. (*Pause.*) So what are you working on for your comeback?

**NINA.** Got a couple things in the hopper. Tell me what you think.

**GOLDEN.** Okay.

> (SHREDDY *enters behind them, unseen.*)

**NINA.** "Two Princes" by the Spin Doctors.

**GOLDEN.** Baby stuff.

**NINA.** The rhythm guitar part in that song is fucking irresistible! Everybody loves that song!

**GOLDEN.** What else?

**NINA.** "Smells Like Teen Spirit."

**GOLDEN.** Okay, yeah, Nirvana is always a solid choice.

**NINA.** But?

**GOLDEN.** But what else you got, that's a little more original? That sends a message to the <u>crowd</u>, instead of being just fun for <u>you</u>?

**NINA.** Last but not least, I've been working on some choreography for "American Girl." Tom Petty.

> (*There are two possibilities for the following exchange. The second can be used if the actors playing* NINA *and* GOLDEN *are both actors of color, as they were in the original production.*)
>
> (*Option 1:*)

**GOLDEN.** (*Unenthusiastic.*) I get it.

**NINA.** Because I'm… I'm an American girl. I guess.

**GOLDEN.** No, no, it makes sense.

> (*Option 2:*)

**GOLDEN.** Were you raised by white people?

**NINA.** Hey!

**GOLDEN.** No, no, I get it.

**NINA.** But?

**SHREDDY.** (*Piping up.*) But, why are you the *only* person who could perform "American Girl"? Or "Smells Like Teen Spirit"? Or "Two Princes"? How is sixty seconds of one of those songs an extension of your soul, and <u>only your</u> soul?

**NINA.** Dude, how is "I Don't Want to Grow Up" by The Ramones an extension of YOUR soul?

**SHREDDY.** Nina, that song is *my entire life.*

**NINA.** Yeah, yeah, yeah. How?

**SHREDDY.** You got bigger things to worry about than why I play what I play. What about your persona? Been working on that?

**NINA.** Oh yeah.

**SHREDDY.** And?

**NINA.** What do you think of
> (*Putting on a British accent.*)

"Kate Middle Finger"?

**SHREDDY.** Who is she?

**NINA.** (*British accent.*) My persona!
> (*She drops the accent.*)

It's like a play on the royal family.

**SHREDDY.** No one in the royal family plays rock guitar.

**NINA.** Okay, what about "Ruth Slayer Ginsburg." Get it? It's a pun!

**SHREDDY.** Is it?

**GOLDEN.** This is not the roller derby. You don't get points for puns.

**NINA.** Oh shut up. I think it's harder for girls. Who are my role models?

**SHREDDY.** Cannibal Queen.

**NINA.** I hate that cunt.

**SHREDDY / GOLDEN.** (*In unison.*) Whoa!

**SHREDDY.** What is that *language* about? Did CQ do something to you?

**NINA.** Fuck off.

**GOLDEN.** Well, fine, because now that Shreddy's here, I have some gossip for the group. Guess what I heard. Guess.

**SHREDDY.** Um…

**GOLDEN.** You won't guess.
> (*Dramatic pause.*)

Facebender's kid is coming tonight!

**SHREDDY.** Facebender has a KID?

**GOLDEN.** Yeah, a daughter, he had her when he was like sixteen. And he always invites her to the San Diego finals, and she never comes. Until *tonight*, you guys.

**NINA.** Whoa.

**GOLDEN.** Yeah. Whoa. So we gotta do everything we can to pump up the crowd. His charisma marks have to be off the charts.

(SHREDDY *points to* NINA *to prompt her to recite a lesson he has taught her about charisma.*)

**NINA.** (*Proud of herself.*) Oooh! It doesn't matter if the crowd loves you or hates you, as long as they're making a lot of noise. Like TV wrestling!

**SHREDDY.** (*Proud of* NINA.) Exactly, Grasshopper.

**GOLDEN.** Charisma marks are always high for villians. Cannibal Queen, for one—

**SHREDDY.** (*Interrupting, to* NINA.) Your fave gal. We're gonna come back to that, by the way.

**GOLDEN.** (*Continuing.*) And D Vicious, who won the National Championship last year. He does this thing where he makes the crowd love him, then hate him, then love him again. In sixty seconds. Surely you've seen his routine?

**NINA.** Oh. I've seen it. Up close.

**GOLDEN.** But Facebender's not a villain. He's like... your sad uncle...

**SHREDDY.** ...from another century, or a story... or...

**NINA.** He's Don Quixote. A man out of time.

**SHREDDY.** (*Nodding in agreement.*) Huh.

**NINA.** He dreams the impossible dream.

**GOLDEN.** Don't we all, sweetheart.

**NINA.** Is he gonna play "Free Bird" for the freestyle round again?

**GOLDEN.** He's been playing it all season.

**NINA.** That's why he hasn't qualified yet.

(SHREDDY *and* GOLDEN *look at her sideways, affronted on their friend's behalf.*)

He's Don Quixote, playing, like, a Huckleberry Finn song.

**SHREDDY.** (*A realization.*) She's right.

(FACEBENDER *enters. Very nervous.*)

**GOLDEN.** Facebender Lender! Don't be nervous! This is your night, my dude!

**FACEBENDER.** You are a true and loyal friend, Golden Thunder. I wish I shared your optimism.

**SHREDDY.** We heard about your daughter, man.

**GOLDEN.** I told them. Hope it wasn't a secret.

**FACEBENDER.** A secret? Indeed no. My... my Sophia. She's never seen me play before. I haven't always been... the ideal patriarch. Of our little kingdom.

**GOLDEN.** And you're gonna melt her face off!

(*They all look at him sideways.*)

Nope. Weird to say about a man's daughter. Now I say it, I hear it.

**SHREDDY.** She's gonna love it. How old is she? Doesn't matter. She's gonna love it.

**FACEBENDER.** (*Dropping the façade for a moment.*) I can't fuck this up in front of my kid. The only way this is anything at all is if I'm good at it. If it's not balls-out amazing, I'm… I'm just… I've already let her down a thousand times.

**GOLDEN.** Hey? Hey, Facebender? What are you always telling me?

**FACEBENDER.** To take the threat of alcohol poisoning more seriously.

**GOLDEN.** No. Yes. No. What are you always telling me when I start to doubt my badassitude? Huh, buddy? What's the greatest thing about air guitar?

**NINA.** Oh, I wanna know this.

**GOLDEN.** What does air guitar teach? (*Pause.*) "Everything we need to rock, is already inside us."

> (SHREDDY *and* FACEBENDER *nod sagely.* NINA *is moved, unexpectedly.*)

**FACEBENDER.** (*Recovering his persona somewhat.*) The greatest truth of this, our chosen art form. Sage of you to remind me, Golden Thunder. But… I have a dread in my bones.

**NINA.** A dread?

**FACEBENDER.** A real dread. That the ode I have selected for my freestyle contribution, will do me no favors. It has won me no accolades thus far. Why should I expect it to triumph this night?

**NINA.** You think the song will fail you?

**FACEBENDER.** Or I, the song. And my Sophia.

> (CANNIBAL QUEEN *enters. She has the worst timing. She looks at their anxious faces.*)

**CANNIBAL QUEEN.** Ugh. Who died in here?

**FACEBENDER.** Cannibal Queen, even your lovely disposition cannot retrieve me from the funk into which I have fallen. But thank you for trying.

**CANNIBAL QUEEN.** Yeah sure. My pleasure.

> (*Looking around.*)

Has anyone seen Vicious?

> (NINA *inhales sharply.*)

**SHREDDY.** He coming tonight?

**CANNIBAL QUEEN.** Maybe. He said he might.

**GOLDEN.** (*Teasing.*) Aw, you need your bf to hold your hand? Since you haven't qualified yet?

**CANNIBAL QUEEN.** Next week. Boston. Home turf. Mark my fucking words, I'm going home with first. And Vicious is not my bf. I'm married, for Chrissake. He's just, we're just, whatever.

**NINA.** You're married?!

**CANNIBAL QUEEN.** Who are you, again? I'm usually the only vagina in the room.

**NINA.** I'm... um...

**SHREDDY.** She's still working on a persona.

**NINA.** The...

**SHREDDY.** She's not competing again until NYC, so she has some time.

**NINA.** Nina!

**CANNIBAL QUEEN.** The Nina? Are you backed by the Pinta and the Santa Maria?

**NINA.** The Nina.

**GOLDEN.** Righteous. I love that.

**CANNIBAL QUEEN.** It has... a ring. I guess. Cool. Anyways, if any of youse see D Vicious, tell him I'm looking for his ass.

**SHREDDY.** Your "not-boyfriend."

**GOLDEN.** With whom you "just whatever."

**CANNIBAL QUEEN.** Exactly.

> (CANNIBAL QUEEN *exits.* NINA *looks at* SHREDDY, *almost frantically.*)

**NINA.** He's not really going to be here tonight, is he? David Cooper?

**GOLDEN.** She knows his *full* name.

**SHREDDY.** Let me guess, you saw his Sprite commercial.

**NINA.** No. I mean, yes, I saw it, I just... do you really think he'll be here?

> (FACEBENDER *slowly and sadly begins to remove his wig.*)

**SHREDDY.** Probably not. He hasn't come to a single qualifier this year, and he bailed on that Staten Island half-time show. That dude used to be a friend, but now he's just...

**NINA.** The competition?

**SHREDDY.** (*Bitterly.*) Yeah.

**GOLDEN.** (*Looking over at* FACEBENDER.) Aw, Facebender, man, put your wig back on!

**FACEBENDER.** (*Teetering on the edge.*) What is the point, my friends? Shall I disgrace myself and dishonor Lynyrd Skynyrd on the same night, in front of my only progeny?

**SHREDDY.** (*Sighing.*) What?

**GOLDEN.** He's still conflicted about "Free Bird."

**NINA.** (*Taking charge.*) Okay, Facebender, look me in the eyes. Take a deep breath in, now hold it, now a deep breath out. Good. Now another deep breath in, hold it, aaaand out. You're doing great.

**SHREDDY.** What are you, like a first responder?

**NINA.** Nope. I'm a web developer. And I'm about to troubleshoot the shit outta this situation.

**FACEBENDER.** I put myself entirely in your hands, The Nina.

**NINA.** We have four hours till the show. Plenty of time for you to choreograph a performance for a new song, IF it's the right song. And IF we all contribute.

**SHREDDY.** I'm in.

**GOLDEN.** Whatever I can do to help, Bender Buddy.

(NINA *begins to pace, thinking on her feet. They all watch her.*)

**NINA.** Okay. First let's consider our audience. What do West Coast people like?

**FACEBENDER.** Sunshine!

**SHREDDY.** Driving with the top down and the music blasting!

**GOLDEN.** Almonds!

(*Off their looks.*)

What? They do! They all eat organic food and drink green juice and almonds are like, part of that.

**NINA.** Okay, so what we're circling around here, is a culture of people, including you, Bender, who like the sun, and wind in their hair, and who want to live forever.

**FACEBENDER.** Yes. Yes!

**NINA.** And then, there's a special person in the room. There's a specific, special person in the audience that you want to reach, even more than the judges, isn't there? How do you reach her? What is the song that feels like sunshine, that speaks directly from you to her?

**SHREDDY.** We find that song, and it'll play right to your strengths.

**GOLDEN.** Oh, this is some voodoo.

**NINA.** No. It's targeted advertising.

**GOLDEN.** She's right, Bender. If you can grab Sophia by the soul, the judges will have no fucking choice but to go along for the ride.

**NINA.** You're her father. What's the sound?

**FACEBENDER.** (*He finds the song inside himself.*) Oh! OH, my comrades. There is a song. I know it. And it slays.

## ****** FACEBENDER'S PERFORMANCE ******

(*Lights shift quickly and* GOLDEN, SHREDDY, CANNIBAL QUEEN, FACEBENDER, *and* NINA *appear, lined up across the bar's stage, under the bright lights of the show. We hear a sound cue of a medium-sized, but enthusiastic, cheering crowd.*

FACEBENDER *steps out in front of the other characters as sixty seconds of Queen's "Somebody to Love" begin to play, including the amazing guitar solo that starts at 2:09.*

FACEBENDER *is the perfect combination of bombastic and vulnerable. He is laying it all on the line. He's found the perfect song to convey how much he loves his daughter [did he used to sing this to her as a baby?] and how hard he rocks at the same time. He's a luminous success, basking in how hard he's feeling it, and the judges can't deny the power of that.*)

**ANNOUNCER.** People, I am thrilled to announce, in first place here tonight at the Western Conference Finals, moving on to the National Championship, the man who ain't ashamed to rock with his heart on his sleeve: FACEBENDER!

**NINA.** (*To* SHREDDY.) What do you get if you win the World Championships, anyway?

**SHREDDY.** Limited-edition custom Flying Finn electric guitar.

**NINA.** A REAL GUITAR?? A real guitar is the grand prize??

**SHREDDY.** (*Shrugging.*) What?

(*Lights dim on the bar in San Diego.*)

### Scene 3 :: Boston, MA – Mid-Atlantic Conference Finals

*Lights up on a medium-sized, still dingy, bar in Boston. It is the next week. It is late afternoon, and there are no patrons here yet.*

NINA *sits in the green room, drinking a beer and working on her computer. This goes on in silence for a moment, until* CANNIBAL QUEEN *enters.*

**CANNIBAL QUEEN.** Oh, good, you're here. The Nina, right? I wanna talk to you.

**NINA.** (*A little panicky.*) What? Why? Can't you see I'm working?

(*Genuinely curious,* CANNIBAL QUEEN *gets momentarily derailed from her original purpose.*)

**CANNIBAL QUEEN.** What kind of work can you do from the back of a shitty bar?

**NINA.** (*Hostile.*) I build websites. I'm self-employed. I can do it from anywhere.

**CANNIBAL QUEEN.** Oh. Cool. You don't have to quit your job for the season.

**NINA.** People quit their jobs to play air guitar?

**CANNIBAL QUEEN.** Oh, yeah. That's half the fun. We travel around, go to all the qualifiers, pretend to be rock stars, try to get to Finland. We have a shit-ton of fun.

**NINA.** But then everybody has to go back to reality at some point. And they don't have a place to work.

**CANNIBAL QUEEN.** There's always another bartending job. Or an Uber to drive. No one's leaving their job at the Pentagon or anything.

**NINA.** And what job did you quit to be here tonight?

**CANNIBAL QUEEN.** I've got a Masters in classical guitar. So, I mean, I guess I'll teach eventually, when I'm like fifty. Mostly right now, I just do air guitar. And I'm married.

**NINA.** So it's _his_ money that keeps you in leather pants and hair extensions?

**CANNIBAL QUEEN.** Okay, number one, this is my real hair. Number two, yes, it's his money, and he doesn't care what I do with it as long as I'm happy. He's older, he works sixty hours a week, air guitar keeps me out of his way. (_Refocusing._) And number three—I want to talk to you, woman-to-woman. I can really help you, you know. If more of us, who are competent, join the circuit, eventually they'll have to let one of us win.

**NINA.** I don't want your help.

**CANNIBAL QUEEN.** Look, I'm not an idiot. I can tell you have some fucking problem with me, and I've said maybe five words to you. You one-a those bitches who can't be friends with other girls?

**NINA.** I'm friends with plenty of girls.

**CANNIBAL QUEEN.** Good. So let's get down to business. I don't know what the scarecrow, the tin man, and the lion have been telling you, but it's different for us. You have to be really careful not to give the crowd everything.

**NINA.** What does that even mean?

**CANNIBAL QUEEN.** Don't let them use you as entertainment.

**NINA.** Entertainment?

**CANNIBAL QUEEN.** Okay, so like, costume for one thing. You'll see girls who do the whole short skirt, pigtails, fuck-me boots thing—they never win. The organizers _love_ when they enter, because they give the crowd something to drool over. But they never place. They'll tell you to smile, jump around, flash your tits, but don't listen to that bullshit. I wear black pants, black v-neck top, every time. Like a classical musician. I don't give them anything but the music. You have to fight for every second of stage time, and that starts with not dressing like a prostitute.

(NINA *is silent.* CANNIBAL QUEEN *decides to continue being helpful, in her own special way.*)

**CANNIBAL QUEEN.** And you need a better song. Your freestyle round in Staten Island was shit.

**NINA.** I'm working on something new.

**CANNIBAL QUEEN.** What?

**NINA.** Heart.

**CANNIBAL QUEEN.** Heart?! Oh, barf. Come on, it's so cliché. What are you working on, "Crazy on You" or something?

(*That is the song she's been working on.*)

**NINA.** Um, NO. "Barracuda." And Nancy Wilson's guitar playing basically defined the sound of the 70s and 80s.

**CANNIBAL QUEEN.** Jesus. You don't have to do a Heart song just because you're a girl. If you want to play with the boys, think like the boys.

**NINA.** Or, you know, think for yourself.

**CANNIBAL QUEEN.** Yeah, don't give them any excuse to write you off, is all I'm saying. If you're gonna do this, actually <u>do</u> it. The right way.

(NINA *takes this in.*)

**NINA.** Why are you lecturing me?

**CANNIBAL QUEEN.** This is how mean people make friends—we instruct.

**NINA.** You and I are not gonna be friends.

**CANNIBAL QUEEN.** What is your damage?

**NINA.** You're married! You're married, and you're fucking Da— D Vicious. Aren't you?

**CANNIBAL QUEEN.** Ooooooh. Are you a fangirl? Are you a little D Vicious fangirl?

**NINA.** No. I'm his fiancée.

**CANNIBAL QUEEN.** WHAT?!

**NINA.** Or. I was.

**CANNIBAL QUEEN.** Oh, shit. Fuck me. When were you dating him?

**NINA.** We broke up about eight months ago. So you can take your friendly advice and shove it up your ass.

**CANNIBAL QUEEN.** Hey! I didn't know he had a fiancée! He never told me.

(NINA *is not expecting to hear this, and it throws her for a moment.*)

**NINA.** Would you have cared if he had told you?

**CANNIBAL QUEEN.** Yes. YES. I don't poach.

**NINA.** You cheat on your husband.

**CANNIBAL QUEEN.** Not that it's any of your business, but that's an *established* part of our marriage. It doesn't mean I go around scamming on other girls' dudes.

**NINA.** Well. You scammed on mine. And you still are, aren't you? You're still dating him.

**CANNIBAL QUEEN.** Hey, I'm sorry a shitty thing happened to you, but it actually wasn't my fault. This bad blood is between you and Vicious. Leave me out of it.

(*The door to the green room opens, and* D VICIOUS *enters.*)

Oh, Christ.

(VICIOUS *moves to* CANNIBAL QUEEN *first, not looking at* NINA. *He tries to kiss her on the cheek.*)

**VICIOUS.** Hey, gorgeous.

**CANNIBAL QUEEN.** (*Pulling away, nodding her head at* NINA.) Nope.

**VICIOUS.** (*Seeing* NINA.) Fucking HELL. Nina?

**NINA.** It's The Nina now.

**VICIOUS.** What? What the fuck are you doing here?

**CANNIBAL QUEEN.** And that's my cue to find another place to be.

(CANNIBAL QUEEN *exits.*)

**VICIOUS.** (*Calling after her.*) Astrid? ASTRID?!

(*Wheeling around to* NINA.)

What is this, some kind of fucking ambush?

**NINA.** Oh, calm down. It's not an ambush. I didn't even know you'd be in Boston.

**VICIOUS.** I'm the reigning National Champion. I could be anywhere.

**NINA.** I haven't seen you at any of the other qualifiers.

**VICIOUS.** How many of these competitions have you been to?

**NINA.** Five or six. All over. Facebender's victory in San Diego last week? I was there. I helped him pick his new song. We're *friends* now.

**VICIOUS.** Stop. Stop talking. You made fun of me, you bitched at me, for a *solid year* for playing air guitar. And now you're suddenly on the circuit?

**NINA.** My persona is "The Nina."

**VICIOUS.** THAT'S THE STUPIDEST NAME I'VE EVER HEARD.

**NINA.** Get used to hearing it. All the cities I've been to, I haven't been competing. I've been plotting. When I get back to New York for the Eastern Conference Finals, I'll be unstoppable.

**VICIOUS.** Are you—are you trying to get me back?

**NINA.** No.

**VICIOUS.** This is about my Sprite commercial, isn't it?

**NINA.** NO! That stupid commercial was only online, anyway! And nobody likes Sprite!

**VICIOUS.** People fucking LOVE Sprite!

**NINA.** You didn't win the goddamn Nobel Prize!

**VICIOUS.** And yet, you're following me. You never wanted me to do this, you made fun of me to your friends, your parents, anyone who would listen, you NEVER came to a SINGLE show, but now that I'm the champion, oh, suddenly, here you are. Now you care, and you're at every qualifier. I'm suspicious, I gotta tell you. But, fuck it, I shouldn't be. You can't just be supportive, you always know better.

**NINA.** Oh, I have problems with being supportive? Says the guy who bailed out of nowhere.

**VICIOUS.** Oh, yeah. We had a perfect relationship and no problems and I just bolted. Sure, you go ahead and tell yourself that.

**NINA.** When you started to get really good at air guitar, you checked out of our relationship.

**VICIOUS.** Maybe I did, Nina. Because I suddenly remembered what it was like to be around people who *wanted to be around me.*

**NINA.** I loved you! I loved our band and our apartment and our life. I loved you.

**VICIOUS.** It was impossible to feel that.

**NINA.** (*Discovering this.*) Oh, this is your *favorite.* This moment when I feel stupid and say idiotic things and you have all the power. You *love* this.

**VICIOUS.** Oh, that is so typically your shit. You act like you don't need help from anybody, but blame everyone else when you fail. Well guess what? I don't have time for you anymore. I have things to do that don't involve trying to constantly reassure you that you're an okay human being. Go ahead and hate yourself. I gave up. I don't want that life, and I don't want you. You're fucking awful.

**NINA.** (*Pause.*) I'm not doing this to get you back.

**VICIOUS.** Then why are you here, Nina??

**NINA.** Because. When someone breaks your heart, you find out what they love most in the whole world. Then you take it from them.

**VICIOUS.** You are very dark inside.

(*Unseen by* NINA, GOLDEN, FACEBENDER, *and* SHREDDY *enter the green room. As soon as they see what's happening they stop short, and quietly eavesdrop.*)

**NINA.** You're goddamn right I am. And whose fault is that?

**VICIOUS.** Your terrible parents?

**NINA.** You broke up our REAL band, you broke up our REAL relationship, for what? To fuck somebody else's wife and spend every night in shitty bars with people who think you're cool because you're the best at IMAGINARY GUITAR? To play PRETEND with a gaggle of second-rate UNFUCKABLE LOSERS who couldn't be contributing members of society if they tried? THIS is your kingdom? THIS is where you're god? You ruined my REAL LIFE, and you get to be happy in PRETEND LAND? FUCK THAT, and FUCK YOU. It may be shitty, it may be imaginary, but I'm here to take it from you.

(VICIOUS *nods his head in the direction of the new arrivals. No one says anything.* NINA *is mortified;* SHREDDY, GOLDEN, *and* FACE-BENDER *are crestfallen.*)

**VICIOUS.** Yeah. Good luck with that. (*Short pause.*) See you at the finals.

(VICIOUS *exits.* NINA *turns to her friends, desperate to apologize.*)

**NINA.** Guys! GUYS! I didn't mean that stuff, I didn't! He gets into my head. Please!

(*They brush past her and take positions at the front of the stage.*)

**SHREDDY.** (*Without looking at her.*) Whatever, Nina.

### ****** CANNIBAL QUEEN'S PERFORMANCE ******

(*Lights shift quickly.* GOLDEN, SHREDDY, FACEBENDER, *and* NINA *appear, lined up across the bar's stage, under the bright lights of the show. They are joined downstage by* CANNIBAL QUEEN *and* VICIOUS. *We hear a sound cue of a medium-sized, but enthusiastic, cheering crowd. There is also a fair amount of boo-ing in the mix, but that's okay;* CANNIBAL QUEEN'*s persona is a villain.*)

**ANNOUNCER.** Well, well, well! Ladies and gentlemen, chalk one up for the Women's Movement! Taking home the gold tonight here in Boston, and repping the Mid-Atlantic region at Nationals next month, your hometown heroine, the lady we all hate to love: CANNIBAL QUEEN!

(*The crowd cheers.*)

What's that? What's that?? Hey Cannibal Queen, your subjects want a fuckin' encore!

(CANNIBAL QUEEN *steps out in front of the other characters and absolutely shreds Yngwie Malmsteen's "Arpeggios From Hell."*

CANNIBAL QUEEN *is technically flawless, with the concentration of a surgeon. She isn't flashy. She gives the audience nothing but the music; but the music, and her facility with it, is astonishing. It is by far the most technically difficult song of the competition, and she doesn't miss a single note. She also doesn't smile. When she's done, she takes a brisk, curt bow, like a concert pianist, then stands up straight and flips off the audience with both middle fingers. They go wild with boos.*

VICIOUS *walks up to* CANNIBAL QUEEN *and plants a huge kiss on her lips.* GOLDEN, SHREDDY, *and* FACEBENDER *gather around* CANNIBAL QUEEN *to congratulate her. Everyone except* NINA *exits together, celebrating.* NINA *is alone onstage, looking miserable.*

*Lights dim on the bar in Boston.*)


### Second Vignette :: D Vicious's Sprite Commercial


*A small light comes up on* NINA, *hunched over a laptop or her phone on the side of the stage. It is a few days later. She is watching the outtakes of* D VICIOUS's *Sprite commercial on the internet.*

*Over the course of this Vignette, we will see how* D VICIOUS *went from an enthusiastic lover of the sport of air guitar, to the jaded buzzkill he is today. The outtakes of this commercial are a microcosm of his past year. In the first take, he is ten times happier than we've seen him. In the final take, he's the man we now know.*

VICIOUS *enters; he is in his full persona and costume for the first time.*

*We hear Joe Satriani's "Crowd Chant" played, and* VICIOUS *runs around the stage performing. He's exuberant. He works the song's built-in call-and-response like a master. After 30-45 seconds, the song cuts off abruptly.*

*We hear the* SPRITE EXEC's *voice (but we don't see him), which seems to come from everywhere.*

**SPRITE EXEC.** So what am I watching here?

**VICIOUS.** This is something new I'm working on. "Crowd Chant." Joe Satriani? I have a few other cuts on my phone, too, if you want to see something different.

**SPRITE EXEC.** "Crazy Train." That's what we want to see.

**VICIOUS.** But, I won Nationals with "Crazy Train."

**SPRITE EXEC.** Exactly. And that's why we hired you.

**VICIOUS.** But everyone's already seen me do that song.

**SPRITE EXEC.** Look, if it works, work it. Don't mess with success, kid.

**VICIOUS.** But—

**SPRITE EXEC.** And stay in your box.

**VICIOUS.** My box?

(*A small square of light comes up in the middle of the stage.*)

**SPRITE EXEC.** Your mark. Stay on your mark, genius. Look down.

(VICIOUS *looks down at the little box of light on the floor.*)

**VICIOUS.** Oh. Um, okay.

**SPRITE EXEC.** Let's take it from the line. We'll just dub "Crazy Train" over whatever he just did.

**VICIOUS.** Hey, I can—!

**SPRITE EXEC.** (*Interrupting.*) David Cooper Sprite commercial, take two.

(VICIOUS *centers himself and regains most of his enthusiasm. He takes a big sip from an imaginary can of Sprite.*)

**VICIOUS.** (*Holding an imaginary can.*) Take it from me, D Vicious: Sprite will *slay* your thirst!

(VICIOUS *does a mean air guitar lick, and looks deliriously happy to be here.*)

**SPRITE EXEC.** Okay, lose the air drinking.

**VICIOUS.** But it's funny!

**SPRITE EXEC.** Is it?

**VICIOUS.** Because I'm an air guitar champion.

**SPRITE EXEC.** Stick to the script, please.

(VICIOUS *looks annoyed. He resets.*)

David Cooper Sprite commercial, take ten.

**VICIOUS.** Take it from me, D Vicious: Sprite will *slay* your thirst!

(VICIOUS *does a sick power slide across the stage. Stands up. Looks defiant and pleased.*)

**SPRITE EXEC.** Don't do that.

**VICIOUS.** Come on, man! The power slide is my signature move.

**SPRITE EXEC.** You slid right out of frame.

**VICIOUS.** Well, follow me!

**SPRITE EXEC.** Stick to your blocking. This is not hard, here, "champ."

**VICIOUS.** (*Crestfallen.*) Whatever.

(VICIOUS *is chastised. He resets.*)

**SPRITE EXEC.** David Cooper Sprite commercial, take fourteen.

**VICIOUS.** Take it from me, D Vicious: Sprite will *slay* your thirst!

(VICIOUS *does a sweet double crane kick.*)

**SPRITE EXEC.** (*Weary.*) No power slides. No karate. No finger guns. No twirling. No death drops. No air guitar. Just say the line and look at the camera. Got it?

**VICIOUS.** COME ON!

**SPRITE EXEC.** Reset!

(VICIOUS *is livid. He resets.*)

**SPRITE EXEC.** (*Wearier still.*) David Cooper Sprite commercial, take twenty-five.

**VICIOUS.** (*Grumpily.*) Take it from me, D Vicious:

(*He steps halfway out of his box of light.*)

Sprite will—

**SPRITE EXEC.** (*Interrupting.*) You're off your mark.

**VICIOUS.** (*Stepping back into the light, flipping up both middle fingers.*) Go fuck yourself!

(VICIOUS *storms off.* NINA *closes the laptop. She's actually feeling bad for* VICIOUS, *and she doesn't want to.*)

**NINA.** Damn. Damn it.

(NINA *exits.*
*Lights dim on the Vignette.*)

## Scene 4 :: Chicago, IL – Central Conference Finals

*Lights up on a large, but still dingy, bar in Chicago. Somewhere like The Metro. It is the next week. It is late afternoon, and there are no patrons here yet.*

NINA *sits alone at the bar, nursing a beer. She got here very, very early. She wanted to catch people coming in the door. She waits. Eventually,* FACEBENDER *walks in.*

**NINA.** Bender! Facebender! Over here!

**FACEBENDER.** Ah. The Nina. (*Pause, he turns to go.*) If you'll excuse me.

(NINA *stands and blocks his way.*)

**NINA.** Please! Stay. I want to apologize. Did you get my messages?

**FACEBENDER.** I did. Thank you so much for your remorseful sentiments. (*Pause.*) I must to the green room now.

**NINA.** I apologized! Now forgive me!

**FACEBENDER.** (*Dropping his façade.*) You called us "second-rate unfuckable losers."

**NINA.** I was out of my mind.

**FACEBENDER.** When we come to these competitions, it's OUR space, get it? It might smell like old sweat and stale beer in here, but it's supposed to be safe.

**NINA.** I didn't mean all that stuff you heard me say to David. That wasn't the real me! He… he turns me into a rage monster. It's really gnarly. It's like I took a time machine right back to our breakup. But I'm not that person anymore, I promise. I'm a million times sorry, okay?

>(FACEBENDER *is unconvinced.*)

Hey, remember San Diego? Remember when I calmed you down, and we all worked as, like, a kickass squad, and then you absolutely *slayed?* And then you added me to the group text? That's the real me. That's The Nina.

>(FACEBENDER *regards her for a moment, then relents. His demeanor softens. His façade is still dropped.*)

**FACEBENDER.** Do you want to know how I got into air guitar?

**NINA.** I would love to know.

>(*During this speech,* FACEBENDER *walks behind the bar and grabs himself a beer, before joining* NINA *in front of the bar again.*)

**FACEBENDER.** I work for the County of San Diego.

**NINA.** What do you do? None of you ever talk about your jobs.

**FACEBENDER.** Because when we're here, everything outside is irrelevant. Except for right now, when I'm telling you this story.

**NINA.** Got it.

**FACEBENDER.** Do you know what a Public Guardian is?

**NINA.** Like… Batman?

**FACEBENDER.** (*Laughing.*) No. Nothing like Batman. If a person, usually a poor person, dies, and there's no family or friends or will that can be located, somebody still has to clean out their apartment, and bury their body, and tie up their loose ends. That's my job. The apartment-cleaning bit.

**NINA.** Whoa. How do you get a job like that?

>(*During the following monologue, it's important that* FACEBENDER *does not feel sorry for himself at all. These are the facts of his reality, and communicating them to* NINA *will make her understand why air guitar is vital. He is not sharing a sob story or looking for pity from her or the audience.*)

**FACEBENDER.** Well, it was a match made in heaven. Nobody wants that job, and at the time, nobody wanted me. I was bumming around, couldn't find anything steady. Had run up some sizeable debts. I heard about this job from a buddy, and it sounded easy enough, so I applied. And I got it. You basically just have to be willing to walk into disgusting apartments. Sometimes we have to wear hazmat suits and booties. These people can be dead for weeks, or months, before anyone finds them. Before anyone cares. Sometimes there are flies, or roaches, or mice. Lots of times, people's apartments are just full of wall-to-wall junk. This one lady last year, died standing up and stayed that way. There wasn't room in her place to fall over. We work in pairs, to keep us from stealing. It's weird, seeing what strangers kept in their closets, what they ate, what movies they watched, what kind of toilet paper they used. We go through everything, looking for signs of relationships. Is there an address book? A business card? A computer? Who are the people in these photographs? Are they still alive, would they care that this person is dead? It's the most depressing kind of archeology, but somebody has to do it. And that somebody in San Diego County has been me, for the last few years. I've been through a lot of partners. But I'll tell you one thing.

**NINA.** (*Rapt.*) What?

**FACEBENDER.** When I die, somebody is gonna know. Right away. Lots of people. I used to go through my life like I was gonna live forever, but now I know. It could be any day. But I won't go out anonymous. No stranger is going to have to pick through my stuff, wondering if there's anybody out in the world who'd care to inherit the $300 in my bank account. Before I started playing air guitar, I hadn't seen my daughter, or her mother, in like six years. I felt like too much time had passed, and I was embarrassed to reach out to them. Now, we hang out at least once a month. It's awkward as fuck, but it's happening. It's getting there.

(*Unseen by* NINA *and* FACEBENDER, GOLDEN *and* SHREDDY *enter the bar.*)

My list of friends gets longer and longer. I text them every day. I hug them every time I see them. When I die, there are gonna be so many broken-hearted motherfuckers, playing sad, sad air guitar solos at my funeral. I put it in my will.

**NINA.** That's amazing.

**FACEBENDER.** I look death in its nasty face every day. And then at night, I come here, and I get up onstage and *live* like there's no tomorrow. Because there isn't. There really isn't. It's silly and it's fun and it's absurd, but life is a slow march off a cliff into nothingness, so why not be as silly as you want?

**GOLDEN.** I'm gonna play "Stairway to Heaven" at your funeral. All eight minutes and three seconds. Got my routine all worked out.

**SHREDDY.** I was thinking Weezer's "Say It Ain't So." Some strong power chords to carry you into the next life.

**FACEBENDER.** (*Resuming his persona.*) Gentlemen, Miss The Nina is heartily sorry for her offenses in Boston. I move that we unanimously accept her sincere apology.

**NINA.** I'm so, so, SO, SO SORRY. I'm the worst. I know.

**SHREDDY.** Lots of people want to fuck us, actually.

**GOLDEN.** And we ARE contributing members of society. This all might be pretend, but it's serious pretend.

**NINA.** I get it. Can I please get back on the group text? PLEASE?

(GOLDEN, FACEBENDER, *and* SHREDDY *exchange looks.*)

**SHREDDY.** What do you say, guys?

**GOLDEN.** (*Shrugging.*) Ah, hell.

**FACEBENDER.** I believe the standard ritual of reconciliation will serve as a suitable penance.

(*The three men turn to look at* NINA.)

**NINA.** Which is?

(*The three men walk over to* NINA *and, one by one, very specifically, they "lean" their air guitars against the bar in front of her.*)

**SHREDDY.** Tune our guitars.

**NINA.** Oh, COME ON!

**GOLDEN.** Tune them! That shows us you're truly sorry!

**FACEBENDER.** It is the traditional mode.

**NINA.** (*Grumbling.*) Fine.

**SHREDDY.** Do mine first, since I'm competing.

(NINA *"picks up" the "guitar" that* SHREDDY *put down, and begins to tune it as she would a real guitar. He watches her to make sure she's really doing it.*)

Much obliged.

(NINA *tunes the air guitars until they are all ready, however long that takes.*)

**NINA.** (*Grumbling good-naturedly.*) This is a bit much, y'all.

**GOLDEN.** Ah-ah-ah! You'll never win if you're not totally committed. If you think you're too good to be here, the judges can smell it a mile away. Mockery is the enemy of airness.

**FACEBENDER.** Sir, have you just created that glorious motto in this moment?

**GOLDEN.** Sure did.

**FACEBENDER.** Extraordinary!

**GOLDEN.** I thank you.

**NINA.** Okay, how many of these things do I have to watch before I understand what airness is?

**GOLDEN.** One never understands airness. One ACHIEVES airness.

**SHREDDY.** It can't be coached. It almost can't be explained.

**NINA.** Oh, that clears it up.

**SHREDDY.** I'll tell you what airness is NOT. Airness is NOT taking notes on what everyone is doing, but never getting up onstage to try anything yourself.

**GOLDEN.** VERY true.

**FACEBENDER.** In our world, Miss The Nina, the life of the spectator and the life of the performer are two halves of the same whole. You cannot fully appreciate one without the other.

**NINA.** I'll get there, okay? Next month? New York? I'll be so ready.

**GOLDEN.** New York is a huge venue and the competition will be fierce as hell.

**NINA.** (*Slightly annoyed.*) I'll know when I'm ready. Trust me.

**SHREDDY.** (*Doubtful.*) Okay. It's just way more fucking fun if you actually play.

(*They all nod. NINA looks uncomfortable. The door opens, and CANNIBAL QUEEN sticks her head in. Seeing who's in the room, she scurries as fast as she can through the bar and exits to the green room, without saying a word to anyone.*)

**FACEBENDER.** (*Softly, to himself, but GOLDEN overhears.*) Why does she run from me?

**GOLDEN.** Dude, that was most definitely not about you.

**NINA.** (*To distract them all from CANNIBAL QUEEN's entrance.*) So, Shreddy! Chicago is your home turf. Gonna do "I Don't Wanna Grow Up" again tonight?

**SHREDDY.** Indeed. Johnny Ramone and I are in this together.

(NINA *gives him a look.*)

What??

**NINA.** I mean, so many Ramones songs objectively rock harder.

**GOLDEN.** (*Groaning.*) Oh, come on!

**FACEBENDER.** An arbitrary pronouncement.

**SHREDDY.** Were that true, WERE that true, and I'm not saying it is, how hard a song rocks or how technically impressive it is, is NOT the only thing to consider when choosing a song. Everything about "I Don't Wanna Grow Up" makes it perfect for air guitar, for me, and for the Central Conference Finals.

**NINA.** (*Exaggerated.*) Gooooo ooooooon.

**SHREDDY.** The Ramones are from Forest Hills, Queens. I am from the South Side of Chicago. We are in Chicago now. This is all urban kismet.

**NINA.** "I Wanna Be Sedated" is better-known.

**SHREDDY.** Grraaah! Have you learned nothing? Am I, Shreddy Eddy, a man who wants to be sedated??

**NINA.** Well, it's just—

**SHREDDY.** (*Interrupting.*) You are the music and the music is you! You think I just picked my song off a jukebox? "I Don't Wanna Grow Up" was written by Tom Waits for the Bone Machine album, and he wrote that song for EXACTLY ME.

**NINA.** Exactly you?

**SHREDDY.** (*Getting really worked up.*) EXACTLY. It's about a young man, a few years into adulthood, looking at his parents, looking at his society, and stating firmly, "This is fucked, and I opt out." He doesn't want the car, or the mortgage, or the soul-sucking job, or to be bald and filled with doubt. He doesn't have an alternative solution, because he's running on fear, he's frantic, he's not thinking logically. The rhythm of it, the speed of the recording, the repetition—it's a tantrum. He's trying to stay a child, he's running as fast as he can in the opposite direction, even though there's NOTHING THERE. It's fucked up and it's inevitable. You can't not grow up. (*Pause.*) That's what Tom Waits knew. That's what the Ramones recorded. That's what I bring to the stage.

**NINA.** Wow.

**GOLDEN.** Shreddy Eddy's highest marks are always for artistic merit.

**SHREDDY.** Air guitar is hard work, The Nina. Here (*He smacks his head.*) and here (*He smacks his heart.*).

　　　(*Almost angry.*)

You don't waltz into a qualifier with Journey because you're mad at your ex-boyfriend. Some of us here want to win this because we believe it's special. You want to qualify in New York next month? You want to be an air guitar champion? You need to risk everything, because you're gonna have to take it over my dead body. I'm your friend at the bar, I'm your friend in the green room, but for those sixty seconds onstage, I'm your competition. And I bleed this.

### ****** SHREDDY EDDY'S PERFORMANCE ******

(*Lights shift quickly.* GOLDEN, SHREDDY, FACEBENDER, NINA, *and* CANNIBAL QUEEN *appear, lined up across the bar's stage, under the bright lights of the show. We hear a sound cue of a large, enthusiastic, cheering crowd.*

SHREDDY EDDY *steps out in front of the other characters and slays the Ramones' recording of "I Don't Wanna Grow Up."*

SHREDDY EDDY's *anger and fear and doubt are perfectly channeled by this song. He is right—it was written for him. It's almost impossible, for sixty seconds, to believe that he didn't write and record this. His performance isn't flashy, it isn't overly emotive, but it is in earnest. This is the best match of man and music that the judges have seen in a long time. He lives inside it. He gets closer to airness than anyone we've seen yet.*

NINA *stares at him, his performance fanning the flames of a massive, massive crush that's been growing inside her for a while now.*)

**ANNOUNCER.** And in first place... was there a doubt in anyone's mind? Your hometown hero, Proud Son of the South Side, angry young man with loins burning to represent the Central Conference at the finals next month— SHREDDY EDDY!!

(*Lights dim on the bar in Chicago.*)

### Scene 5 :: New York – Eastern Conference Finals

*Lights up on a large, but still dingy, bar in New York City. Somewhere like The Bowery Ballroom. It is the next month. It is late afternoon, and there are no patrons here yet.*

CANNIBAL QUEEN *and* VICIOUS *are sitting at the bar, drinking. They came here together tonight, but the conversation has turned tense.*

**CANNIBAL QUEEN.** Come on, just fucking admit it, Vicious.

**VICIOUS.** I live in New York.

**CANNIBAL QUEEN.** You're came tonight for one reason. To psych her out.

**VICIOUS.** False.

**CANNIBAL QUEEN.** I'm judging you.

**VICIOUS.** This is why I don't tell you shit.

**CANNIBAL QUEEN.** Oh, like the fact that you had a fiancée?

**VICIOUS.** You have a husband!

**CANNIBAL QUEEN.** Which I told you!

**VICIOUS.** Fuck off. I'm not having this fight with you again, Astrid.

**CANNIBAL QUEEN.** You're mean when you're scared.

**VICIOUS.** (*Pause.*) Scared? What on earth do I have to be scared of?

**CANNIBAL QUEEN.** Well, Nina, clearly.

**VICIOUS.** Nina is not a threat to me in any way, especially air guitar.

**CANNIBAL QUEEN.** Then why are you here trying to intimidate her?

**VICIOUS.** I'm a guest of the organizers. They asked me to pick the Round Two song.

**CANNIBAL QUEEN.** You could've done that over email.

**VICIOUS.** I'm here in person to support my friends.

**CANNIBAL QUEEN.** Bullshit. You haven't given a crap about any of these people, including me, since your Sprite commercial hit YouTube.

(*Softer.*)

You used to be the most fun guy on the whole circuit, Vicious. The absolute most fun guy to be around backstage, or in the green room, or at the hotel. It didn't matter how you did onstage on a particular night, you were always excited to be in the room. That's the guy I want to be around. That's the guy we all want to be around. And I don't know if he even exists anymore.

**VICIOUS.** Well, it's real easy to be the "fun guy" when you don't have anything to lose. You guys have nowhere to go but up. I have a legacy to protect.

**CANNIBAL QUEEN.** Well if your "legacy" is all you care about anymore, then you should be scared of Nina. You've got the charisma on lock, Vicious, but Nina's a better guitarist than you. I've seen it. I watched your old band videos online.

**VICIOUS.** You did what?

**CANNIBAL QUEEN.** Come on, they're on YouTube. It's not like I hacked your computer.

**VICIOUS.** That's still fucking weird.

**CANNIBAL QUEEN.** She hasn't played since Staten Island, how else am I supposed to know what I'm up against? Nina's got terrible stage presence, and she's totally in her head, but she's got good musicality. And she's been at a dozen shows in the last few months, studying up. I've seen that girl literally everywhere. If she shows up here tonight and pounds it out enough to qualify, she's gonna come at us hard in the championship.

**VICIOUS.** Nina's a decent guitarist. I don't know that she's better than me, I don't know why you would say that, except to piss me off, but she's decent. She doesn't really want to be here, though. This is all a vendetta thing for her. She doesn't have the heart. And, fuck, she's never gonna win Nationals. For fuckssake, she's...

**CANNIBAL QUEEN.** Yes?

**VICIOUS.** (*Covering.*) Nothing.

**CANNIBAL QUEEN.** She's a girl? She'll never sweep Nationals because she's a girl?

**VICIOUS.** You're putting words in my mouth.

**CANNIBAL QUEEN.** Then deny that's what you thought.

**VICIOUS.** FINE. I thought it. But I didn't say it.

**CANNIBAL QUEEN.** That's bad enough.

(*Pause, a realization.*)

You don't lose a moment's sleep over me.

**VICIOUS.** (*Flirty.*) I lose plenty of sleep over you, babe.

**CANNIBAL QUEEN.** Shut up. You never, for a single moment, thought that I had any chance at beating you. Did you?

**VICIOUS.** (*Losing it.*) You don't!

**CANNIBAL QUEEN.** Prick!

**VICIOUS.** You don't! What, like that's big news? I shred harder, I work the crowd better... you... You give the audience something to look at between real competitors.

**CANNIBAL QUEEN.** Fuck off and die.

**VICIOUS.** I have to be twice as good as you, because I don't get to flash my panties and bat my eyelashes. Instead of whining and crying about how girls never win, I don't know, Astrid, why don't you *fucking work harder*, huh? You have every advantage that I do, plus more, so don't point your finger at me and say I'm keeping you down. You have no idea what it's like, as a dude, to work and sweat and rehearse for weeks, cut together the perfect song, drive for hours to compete, and then get upstaged by a pair of tits that just showed up to have fun.

**CANNIBAL QUEEN.** Is that honestly what you think I am? You think I don't take this as seriously as you do?

**VICIOUS.** You don't have to when you start on third base. But you know what? You can't touch me. I'm channeling the rage and glory of my forefathers. That's why I'm not scared of you, OR Nina. You're a sideshow around here. I'm the main event.

**CANNIBAL QUEEN.** I see you. Holy shit, I see you for real. And you're a moron.

(*They are both furious. A beat of silence.*

*The door to the bar opens, and* NINA *is standing there.* NINA *is dressed, for the first time, like an air guitar goddess. She sees the two of them, feels the tension in the air, but before she can speak,* CANNIBAL QUEEN *grabs her hand and drags her into the green room. Lights dim on the bar, and* D VICIOUS.

*Lights up on the green room.* GOLDEN, FACEBENDER, *and* SHREDDY *are sitting on the couches. They look toward the door as* CANNIBAL QUEEN *blows in like a hurricane, dragging* NINA *behind her.*)

**GOLDEN.** Hey! Wha—what is happening?

**CANNIBAL QUEEN.** (*To* NINA, *ignoring everyone else.*) What song are you doing tonight?

**NINA.** I—I don't—

**CANNIBAL QUEEN.** Vicious is here to knock you off your game. I hope you found a killer song, and you're prepared to throw down, because the biggest mindfuck you can give that dickbag is to absolutely slay tonight.

    (*Pause, she evaluates* NINA's *outfit for the first time.*)

Congrats on not dressing like a baby prostitute. At least that point got through.

**FACEBENDER.** What a fierce and beautiful partnership! The Nina and Cannibal Queen. Truly the most formidable female force in New York City this night!

**GOLDEN.** Hold on. CQ, did you and Vicious break up?

**CANNIBAL QUEEN.** (*Icily.*) I have ended our arrangement.

    (*Unseen by* CANNIBAL QUEEN, FACEBENDER *straightens his wig and takes a hopeful step toward her.*)

That is in no way any kind of invitation to anyone in this room.

    (FACEBENDER *is crestfallen. He takes a step back.* CANNIBAL QUEEN *notices nothing. Maybe no one else in the room does, either.*)

**SHREDDY.** What song ARE you doing for freestyle tonight, The Nina?

**NINA.** Guys, I— I really— I don't know if I can do this.

**SHREDDY.** What?!

**CANNIBAL QUEEN.** Oh fuck, he got to you.

**NINA.** On the way over here, I was thinking about it, and I was like, what am I doing? I've been flying all over the country, spending hundreds of dollars and hundreds of hours trying to figure out how to give a sixty-second performance. I have pages and pages of notes and I've watched every video, and I've rehearsed for hours, but I'm fucking terrified I'm going to get up there and shut down again. I'm gonna fuck it up.

**CANNIBAL QUEEN.** Like you did at the Hungry Brain two years ago?

**NINA.** How do you—? You watched our band videos?

**CANNIBAL QUEEN.** They are *on the internet.* Why is everyone so shocked?

**NINA.** But why—

**CANNIBAL QUEEN.** (*Interrupting.*) Do you know what your problem is?

**NINA.** (*Sarcastically.*) Please tell me.

**CANNIBAL QUEEN.** You can't stop looking at yourself.

    (NINA *says nothing.*)

Air guitar, "there" guitar, it's the same thing. I know that look. You're not inside the music, you're not onstage, you're in the audience, judging yourself. That's something that rehearsal is not gonna fix. You gotta get up onstage and work through that shit.

(NINA *says nothing. This is an old issue for her, and* CANNIBAL QUEEN *has hit the nail on the head.*)

You wanna know why I show up in these shitty bars month after month and *pretend* to do a thing I can *actually* do better than just about anyone in the world?

**FACEBENDER.** Yes.

**CANNIBAL QUEEN.** Because there is a shield that I have to carry, all around myself, all day, every day, just to be safe and move through the world. All the parts of myself that are freaky or loud or ugly or dangerous have to stay tucked inside, so I don't feel what dudes shout at me on the street, or say about me in the goddamn halls of Congress. But when I get onstage, sister, I can put that shield down and let all my darkness come rushing out.

**NINA.** Wow.

**CANNIBAL QUEEN.** When's the last time you felt that free, The Nina?

**NINA.** Um. Before puberty?

**CANNIBAL QUEEN.** Let it go, girl. Just take a breath, tell that voice in your head to go fuck itself, and raise hell.

**NINA.** But why would anyone want to see me up there, when they could see you?

**GOLDEN.** Air guitar is not about "or." It's about "and."

**FACEBENDER.** Another glorious truism.

**GOLDEN.** (*Shrugging.*) It's a gift.

**SHREDDY.** He's right, Nina. It's not about whether the world *needs* another badass air guitarist. It's about how *you feel* when you're up there. It's the pure joy of jumping around naked in your bedroom, but in front of screaming fans.

**GOLDEN.** So get your head outta your notes and your ass up onstage. Otherwise, what has all of this been for, The Nina?

**NINA.** (*Pause, she decides.*) You're right. I have to do this. It's been months since Staten Island. I'm basically a new person now.

**CANNIBAL QUEEN.** And what is this new person's song?

**NINA.** (*Proudly.*) "I Hate Myself For Loving You." Joan Jett.

(*The entire group falls silent.*)

What? What?! Joan Jett! She's an icon! And Mick Taylor from the Rolling Stones plays the solo. It kills!

(*She turns to* SHREDDY.)

Shreddy, you know that track kills.

(SHREDDY *just shrugs at her.* CANNIBAL QUEEN *shakes her head.*)

**CANNIBAL QUEEN.** Oh, girl.

**NINA.** What?!

**FACEBENDER.** (*Delicately.*) Miss The Nina, is it possible that you are not playing this song for yourself, or for the crowd, but… as a thinly veiled commentary upon one particular person in the crowd?

**NINA.** What? No. What does that even mean?

**CANNIBAL QUEEN.** Oh, come on. That song is a huge "fuck you" to Vicious. Just admit it.

**NINA.** Joan Jett!

**GOLDEN.** Denial!

**NINA.** Joan Jett made me want to play guitar.

**GOLDEN.** (*Helpfully.*) So play "Dirty Deeds." Or "Little Liar." Hell, even "Love Hurts" would be more subtle.

**NINA.** Why are you so upset?

**GOLDEN.** Because you are trying to take air guitar and weaponize it! It's basically sacrilegious.

**CANNIBAL QUEEN.** Also, bad strategy. Vicious gets to pick the Round Two song tonight. And he can change it at any time.

**NINA.** So?

**CANNIBAL QUEEN.** So do you really want to provoke him? I'm sure he knows your musical weaknesses better than any of us.

**NINA.** I don't care what Vicious thinks.

**GOLDEN.** Uh, clearly you do.

**NINA.** Joan Jett. Mick Taylor. "I Hate Myself For Loving You." It's gonna slay. I'm gonna win. End of discussion.

(NINA *exits, confident and excited.*)

**SHREDDY.** How, after all these months, is it still about him?

****** NINA'S SECOND PERFORMANCE ******

(*Lights shift quickly.* NINA *takes the stage in New York.*

*We see* NINA *play the last line of her cut of "I Hate Myself for Loving You" [which should be the title lyric]. She seems very pleased, and the crowd is cheering loudly. We know she's done pretty well in the first round.*)

**ANNOUNCER.** All right! Let's hear it for The Nina! Okay, folks, we are moving into to Round Two here in New York!

(D VICIOUS *walks out onstage in front of the other competitors. The crowd goes nuts.*)

Your champ, D Vicious, has selected our compulsory track tonight, and actually just pulled a little switcheroo on us a few minutes ago, but I gotta say, I think that the choice is pretty bitchin. Hit it!

*(The opening lyrics of Jay Z's "99 Problems" fill the stage. This is 100% directed at* NINA. VICIOUS *smirks as the song plays, taunting her. After we get the picture, the song fades down so we can hear the following dialogue.)*

**CANNIBAL QUEEN.** Holy shit, son.

**GOLDEN.** The clapback on this just reached epic level.

**NINA.** There are like two chords in this song! How is this the song?! What am I supposed to do with this?

**FACEBENDER.** Ruthless.

**GOLDEN.** Genius.

**SHREDDY.** Shameless.

**NINA.** Hopeless.

> *(The cut of "99 Problems" fades back up and* NINA *begins to play. She's okay at it, not the best, and definitely thrown off.*
>
> *She finishes the round on an okay note. We hear some applause.*
>
> *But it won't be good enough.)*


### Scene 6 :: New York – After the Loss / Invite to the Dark Horse

*Lights up on the green room of the previous scene's bar in New York. It is an hour or so after the Eastern Conference Finals.* NINA *is sadly packing up her stuff or changing into street clothes. It's over for her.*

**SHREDDY.** *(Reassuring.)* It was your first year. And you showed up in a big way. You weren't bad out there tonight, you just...

**NINA.** Weren't good enough?

**SHREDDY.** Well, yeah. *(Short pause.)* No. No, you know what, fuck it, you slayed. Your first round was so solid. None of us could have predicted Vicious would pull out Jay Z in Round Two.

**NINA.** But I should have been ready, no matter what the song. That's what you trained me for. And I could have done it, if I'd been focused instead of trying to hurt Vicious. I thought I HAD it. But you knew I didn't. Y'all tried to tell me. I'm such a fucking idiot.

> (SHREDDY *makes a decision. He takes out his phone and types something into it. He hands it to* NINA.)

**SHREDDY.** I want to show you something.

**NINA.** *(Wearily.)* What?

**SHREDDY.** *(Referring to the video on his phone.)* This is my first-ever competition. Chicago, four years ago. I warn you, it's pretty brutal.

**NINA.** It can't be worse than my first qualifier.

(NINA *hits "play." We hear the opening chords of "Sweet Child of Mine" coming from the phone. They watch for a moment.*)

I stand corrected. This is pretty upsetting. (*Short pause.*) WHOA!

**SHREDDY.** YEAH. Some douche-canoe took off his shoe and chucked it at me.

**NINA.** I see that.

**SHREDDY.** And I completely sucked.

**NINA.** I see that, too.

**SHREDDY.** So, why would a guy who shit the bed that hard his first time out, ever EVER, want to play air guitar again?

**NINA.** I think I have an idea.

**SHREDDY.** I went back to the green room that first night, in absolute shame, trying to sneak out the back door. But before I could make my escape, Golden was there. And Cannibal Queen. Facebender. Satan's Sidekick. Mazel Tov Cocktail. Captain Air-Merica. They bought me shots. We laughed together. They didn't mock me. They didn't kick me out because I'd failed. (*Short pause.*) I found my tribe that night.

**NINA.** (*Quietly.*) Yeah.

**SHREDDY.** And I think we're your tribe, too.

**NINA.** I think you're right.

**SHREDDY.** (*A little hesitant.*) And… even though the season's almost over… If I wanted to keep spending time with you. Just one-on-one? Would you be into that?

**NINA.** Yeah. I would. I would be really into that.

(*They both smile. NINA looks back at SHREDDY's phone.*)

You dodged that shoe like a ninja.

**SHREDDY.** You're going to watch it again?

**NINA.** Not right now. Later, for sure. Like, a buuuuunch of times.

(SHREDDY *snatches his phone from* NINA. *She grins at him. He grins back. Suddenly, without warning, a* HOODED FIGURE *[by which I mean he is wearing a hoodie and the hood is up] enters, carrying a large black envelope. There is ominous, gothic music coming from his pocket [playing on his phone or a small Bluetooth speaker]. Something like the intro to "Time Stands Still" by* Release the Archers.

*The* HOODED FIGURE *proceeds directly to* NINA *and hands her the envelope.* GOLDEN THUNDER, CANNIBAL QUEEN, *and* FACEBENDER *are silently following him into the room, eyes wide.*)

**HOODED FIGURE.** Prepare yourself, The Nina. The Dark Horse competition begins in two hours.

(*The* HOODED FIGURE *exits.* NINA *is confused. Everyone else is stunned.*)

**GOLDEN.** Holy mother of god, is that what I think it is?

**CANNIBAL QUEEN.** I... I've never seen one in real life.

**FACEBENDER.** We saw the Hooded Figure moving through the arena and were compelled to follow. But who could have foreseen that his destination was The Nina?

**NINA.** Um, what am I holding?

**GOLDEN.** The Nina. That is a motherfucking invitation to the mother-fucking Dark Horse Round.

**NINA.** I need more information.

**FACEBENDER.** That is your ticket to glory, M'Lady.

**SHREDDY.** When all the qualifiers are over, the Air Guitar organizers hold a Dark Horse competition. It's one round, sudden death, invitation-only. And the winner gets to go to Nationals.

**NINA.** Really?! Why am I only hearing about this now?

**SHREDDY.** (*This is obvious.*) You can't plan on a Dark Horse! We never know when it will be, or where, or who the organizers will invite.

**CANNIBAL QUEEN.** They're giving you another shot. They see something in you.

**NINA.** Like what?

**ALL EXCEPT NINA.** (*In unison.*) Airness.

**CANNIBAL QUEEN.** And if you expect to win, that's what you're gonna have to give them.

**NINA.** Great. To go to Nationals, I have to give the judges a thing that none of you can even explain to me.

**SHREDDY.** (*Parsing it out.*) Airness is like... like, okay, we're here, we're like, miming, some of the greatest guitar licks ever played, right? We're paying homage to those songs, those guitarists. It's like what little kids do, they hear this music, it gets inside them, and then they have to spaz out about it. That's where air guitar comes from, from a time before you cared about looking cool. You're just trying to get inside the thing.

**GOLDEN.** Airness is when you actually do get inside the thing.

(NINA *sighs in exasperation.*)

**SHREDDY.** Airness is when you're not paying homage anymore. You're the creator.

**FACEBENDER.** You've... transcended.

**NINA.** Transcended not having an actual guitar in my hands?

**CANNIBAL QUEEN.** Exactly.

**SHREDDY.** You're expressing something as true and as free and as powerful as Hendrix or Page or Malmsteen or Nancy Wilson, but you're doing it without an instrument.

**CANNIBAL QUEEN.** Did you throw Nancy Wilson in there because she's a girl?

**SHREDDY.** Nancy Wilson's guitar basically defined the sound of the 70s and 80s. Tell me you don't get shivers between your shoulder blades when the electric guitar drops in on "Crazy on You."

**NINA.** THANK YOU. EVERY time.

**SHREDDY.** Airness isn't unattainable. It's just that hardly anyone ever gets there.

**GOLDEN.** And those who do, sweep the whole shebang.

*(They all silently contemplate the ineffable essence of airness for a moment.)*

**CANNIBAL QUEEN.** You've got airness inside you, waiting to get out. But first, we gotta know: WHAT'S. YOUR. SONG? You need a completely new tactic for the Dark Horse.

**NINA.** How am I supposed to pick the perfect song under this kind of pressure?!

**SHREDDY.** Hive mind—activate!

*(SHREDDY spins around to each of them, in turn. They build on each other's suggestions, interrupting each other and finishing other's thoughts, creating a swirling atmosphere of collaboration and inspiration.)*

Golden Thunder! What should our girl play and why?

**GOLDEN.** Um… "Cherry Bomb." In male drag.

**SHREDDY.** Okay, great stuff, but—

**GOLDEN.** *(Interrupting.)* Listen! Forty-five seconds in, she explodes out of the man costume like a cherry bomb, and she's wearing a sequined mini-dress. Crowd goes ballistic.

**CANNIBAL QUEEN.** *(Interrupting.)* Ha!

**GOLDEN.** It's a slam-dunk! It's—

**CANNIBAL QUEEN.** *(Interrupting.)* Not a slam-dunk! The Runaways are a punk band, that's a punk song, it's vocal-driven. Think bigger!

**SHREDDY.** What's your suggestion?

**CANNIBAL QUEEN.** Nina. You're not on my level, technically, but I think you could handle Joe Sat—

**CANNIBAL QUEEN/FACEBENDER.** *(In unison.)*—riani!

**FACEBENDER.** Joe Satriani! Capital!

**GOLDEN.** Nice!

**CANNIBAL QUEEN.** I'm thinking "Surfing with the Alien" from Surfing with the—

**FACEBENDER.** (*Interrupting.*) But Lady Cannibal, there are no lyrics to "Surfing with the Alien."

**CANNIBAL QUEEN.** She doesn't need lyrics. She's an air guitarist.

**GOLDEN.** Yes, but she's gotta sell the intention of the song. Her connection to the audience depends on her connection to the so—

**CANNIBAL QUEEN.** (*Interrupting.*) "Surfing with the Alien" is a technical masterpiece!

**SHREDDY.** But that's what you do, Cannibal Queen. You can't both be the one with the flawless technique.

**CANNIBAL QUEEN.** (*She knows he's right.*) Shit.

**SHREDDY.** Sir Facebender! You are our only hope! Save us, aged one!

**FACEBENDER.** (*Dropping his façade.*) Dude, what have I told you about the age jokes?

**SHREDDY.** (*Sincerely.*) Sorry.

**FACEBENDER.** (*Resuming his façade.*) Nevertheless, I am prepared to come to your rescue, fair The Nina. I submit "I Believe in a Thing Called Love."

**GOLDEN.** (*Simultaneously.*) Great song!

**CANNIBAL QUEEN.** (*Simultaneously.*) Crowdbait.

**GOLDEN.** (*To CANNIBAL QUEEN.*) And what is wrong with giving the people what they want?

**CANNIBAL QUEEN.** It's fluff! It's showmanship and mushy shtick. You—

**GOLDEN.** (*Interrupting.*) That song has AMAZING costume opportunities. The leotards and wigs, alone, are—

**FACEBENDER.** (*Interrupting, in earnest.*) It is an ode to romantic yearning! Have you never had your hopes set on someone who stretched your heart beyond its limits?

> (*A short pause. Will CANNIBAL QUEEN finally realize that she is his Dulcinea?*)

**CANNIBAL QUEEN.** If you've totally forfeited your taste, why not just play some Sammy Hagar Van Halen and be done with it?

> (FACEBENDER, SHREDDY, *and* GOLDEN *groan.* FACE-BENDER *is hit especially hard.*)

**NINA.** (*Over their groans.*) I love The Darkness. But that song doesn't feel like my... guts.

**FACEBENDER.** (*Sighing.*) Fair enough.

**CANNIBAL QUEEN.** I assume you have a suggestion, Shreddy?

**SHREDDY.** Of course I do. And it's a hands-down winner. (*Short dramatic pause.*) "Everlong." Foo Fighters.

**FACEBENDER.** (*Simultaneously.*) Alas!

**GOLDEN.** (*Simultaneously.*) No! Shreddy. You know she'll have to play whatever she plays tonight again at Nationals.

**SHREDDY.** Someone already qualified with "Everlong"?

**FACEBENDER.** (*Simultaneously.*) Satan's Sidekick.

**GOLDEN.** (*Simultaneously.*) This late in the game, all the obvious bands are gonna be taken.                                    ·

**SHREDDY.** Motörhead? Hendrix? Vaughn?

**GOLDEN.** (*Simultaneously.*) Taken, taken, taken.

**FACEBENDER.** (*Simultaneously.*) Alas, alas, alas.

> (NINA *has been thinking hard, getting inspired, finally grasping the concept of airness.*)

**GOLDEN.** Okay, how does everyone feel about Swedish Death Metal, it's a—

**NINA.** (*Interrupting.*) Wait, wait, everybody shut up. Shreddy, what was that thing you said about airness? … That… air guitar comes from a time before you cared about looking cool?

**SHREDDY.** Yeah. Like when you were a kid, and you'd just spaz out.

**NINA.** Right. That's where my song lives! In my kidhood, jumping around at slumber parties, knocking the other girls over because I couldn't control my arms. It's maybe not cool, or difficult, or flashy, but it's in my bones. That's where I'm gonna find my airness.

**SHREDDY.** What's that song, The Nina? Do you have it?

**NINA.** (*Pause, discovering.*) Yeah. Yeah, I have it.

**CANNIBAL QUEEN.** Fantastic. We have two hours until the Dark Horse.

> (GOLDEN THUNDER *holds up a glue gun and a fistful of sequins or feathers that he has conjured from seemingly nowhere.*)

**GOLDEN.** Let's get to work.

> (*Lights dim on the green room.*)

### Third Vignette :: The Dark Horse Competition

*There is a scenic transition into a very different world than any we've been in. It feels like we've landed in a dark air guitar skulls/fight club world that reminds us a little of the "Total Eclipse of the Heart" music video.*

NINA *enters and a box of light appears in the center of the stage. She walks into it.* SHREDDY, CANNIBAL QUEEN, FACEBENDER, *and* GOLDEN *are following her. They stand to the side and watch, expectant and nervous.*

**ANNOUNCER.** (*Booming voice, very ominous reverb, seems to be coming from everywhere.*) Gentlemen of the Jury, your next Dark Horse competitor—THE NINA.

#### \*\*\*\*\*\* NINA'S DARK HORSE PERFORMANCE \*\*\*\*\*\*

(*The music begins, and* NINA *loses her mind to Pat Benatar's "Shadows of the Night."*

*She is overflowing with joy. She hasn't felt this free since before puberty. She is exuberant, she is fun embodied. Not self-conscious, not mocking, not afraid of anything. She and Pat Benatar are taking on the world together. We can see her as a young girl, jumping on her bed and screaming this song. The judges see it, too.*)

**ANNOUNCER.** (*Booming voice, very ominous reverb, seems to be coming from everywhere.*) Gentlemen, I believe we have our Dark Horse champion. We will see you at the National Championship, The Nina.

(NINA's *friends crowd around her, ecstatic.*
*Lights dim on the Dark Horse competition.*)

#### Scene 7 :: Los Angeles – The National Championship

*Lights up on an extremely large, very glam stage in Los Angeles. Should technically be an outdoor concert arena, somewhere like The Greek, but if that's not possible, it's a cavernous, glitzy bar where famous bands have played for decades.*

D VICIOUS *is onstage, giving an interview to* THE ANNOUNCER, *who is an air guitar organizer in this scene. They speak into microphones. This is being recorded for a later broadcast.*

*There might be roadies and other people milling around, setting up for the concert. There might even be a video camera set up, recording the interview.*

**ANNOUNCER.** Okay, okay, okay, L.A. I'm here with our reigning National Air Guitar champ, D Vicious, to talk shop about tonight's National Finals competition. How are you feeling today, Champ?

**VICIOUS.** Feelin' good! Loose. Ready to slay. I've spent the last year as the National Champ, and it's been a wild ride, but I want another shot at Oulu.

**ANNOUNCER.** Wow, already focused on the World Finals, huh? Aren't you worried about tonight?

**VICIOUS.** No. I'm not worried.

**ANNOUNCER.** Bold words, bold words! Not to put you on the spot, big guy, but we haven't seen you at many qualifiers this year. Maybe you don't really have the lay of the land anymore.

**VICIOUS.** My greatest competition has always been, and will always be, myself. And right now, we're pretty in sync with each other.

**ANNOUNCER.** Spoken like a true villain, Vicious! All right, I'll take the bait, let's talk about you. What was your championship year like? You win Nationals, there's so much buzz, but then it's the off-season. What's February like for D Vicious?

**VICIOUS.** (*At a loss.*) I mean, it's Black History Month.

**ANNOUNCER.** Okay, true, true, but like, what have you been *working on* this year? I mean your "Crazy Train" performance is the stuff of legend. But we haven't seen you play so much as a halftime show in an entire year. Can you give us a hint about what you're gonna throw down tonight?

**VICIOUS.** Let me ask you a better question—why mess with success?

**ANNOUNCER.** Well, I mean, you're not gonna play "Crazy Train" again, so...?

**VICIOUS.** If it works, work it, man.

**ANNOUNCER.** (*Very surprised, dropping his persona.*) Dude, you can't be serious.

**VICIOUS.** If there's anything I've learned this year, it's that you gotta give the people what they want.

**ANNOUNCER.** Um... sure...

(*Refocusing the interview.*)

One last question before we go. It's been said by some of the greats that air guitar is the only true abstract art form left, because it can't be corrupted or commercialized. You faced some backlash from fans last year, when you starred in an online commercial for a soft drink. Tell us about how you reconcile your performance side with your commercial side?

**VICIOUS.** (*Annoyed.*) Well, I mean, if those fans who are upset about my "corruption" of their "pure" "art form" want to send me checks to cover my bills, they're more than welcome to. You can only do something for the love of it up to a certain level, you know? After a while, the things you've paid into need to start paying you back.

(*The* ANNOUNCER *realizes he better wrap this up real quick before* VICIOUS *says something even more alienating to the fans.*)

**ANNOUNCER.** Well that's just about all the time we have for today. Come out and see D Vicious and the rest of our bitchin' finalists at the Air Guitar National Championships, happening to-fuckin'-night!

**VICIOUS.** Come out and watch us slay tonight, L.A. I promise to melt your faces.

> (*The* ANNOUNCER *gathers his recording equipment, shakes* VICIOUS'*s hand, and exits.* VICIOUS *exits a separate way.*
>
> NINA *and* SHREDDY *are revealed on the side of the stage. They've been watching this whole thing.*)

**NINA.** I didn't know him at all, did I?

**SHREDDY.** Hey, don't feel bad. Everybody's a whole lot of people, right?

**NINA.** Hey, have you ever watched the outtakes of his Sprite commercial? Almost makes you feel sorry for him.

**SHREDDY.** Yeah. Almost.

> (*Envious.*)

He's gonna have the most advantageous spot in the lineup tonight.

**NINA.** But we have something he's lost.

**SHREDDY.** Raw fucking joy?

**NINA.** Raw fucking joy.

> (*They beam at each other. There's excitement about the competition and the fact that they're together.*
>
> GOLDEN, FACEBENDER, *and* CANNIBAL QUEEN *join them onstage, hugging and high-fiving. They are all totally amped.*
>
> LIGHTS COME UP IN A BIG WAY. *Suddenly, they're actual rock stars. We hear a screaming crowd, dimly, in the distance. It's* MOTHER-FUCKING EPIC. *The audience is like, "Holy Shit. This is for real." Electricity in the air!*)

**NINA.** This is amazing!!

**SHREDDY.** It truly is. Every time.

**NINA.** (*Looking at him with wonder.*) This is where you've been the whole time. In your mind. Even back in Staten Island, you were here. You've always been here.

**SHREDDY.** (*Tapping her heart and his heart.*) This is where true legends are born, The Nina.

> (*Looking around.*)

But the lights are a really rad bonus.

> (*His face lights up, he stares at her, she stares at him. Goo-goo-eyed.*)

**\*\*\*\*\*\* D VICIOUS'S PERFORMANCE \*\*\*\*\*\***

> (D VICIOUS *takes center stage.*)

**ANNOUNCER.** And here he is, folks! Our current reigning American Air Guitar Champ, back to defend his title, his honor, NAY his glory! Put your filthy hands together for: D! VICIOUS!

(VICIOUS *raises his hands over his head. We hear the crowd cheer. He brings his hands in front of him and begins to play, and we hear the first few notes of "Crazy Train." But then the track slows down into a weird, slo-mo warped version.* VICIOUS *looks ridiculous. Exactly as ridiculous as a man playing slo-mo air guitar to a distorted track. It's a rote performance, crafted and rehearsed, but devoid of heart.*

*The music fades down, but not out. The others watch* VICIOUS, *and comment during his bizarre song.*)

**NINA.** Incredible.

**GOLDEN.** He fucking *hates* this.

**SHREDDY.** More than hates it. It's a joke to him. He's gotten so good that he's actually come *back around* to mockery.

**GOLDEN.** Mockery is the enemy of airness.

**NINA.** (*To* GOLDEN.) And if you pick the wrong song, rehearsal is kind of irrelevant.

**GOLDEN.** Exactly.

**FACEBENDER.** He resembles a tortured monkey, forced to perform for loathéd masters.

**CANNIBAL QUEEN.** This is some sad, sad shit.

**SHREDDY.** Who does the same song two years in a row? That's not just unwise—it's fucking unfun.

**NINA.** People. We worked our asses off to get here, and the Old Guard has fallen. Let's storm this motherfucking castle.

(GOLDEN *puts his hand out, like they're going to circle up in a sports movie.*)

**GOLDEN.** "Airness" on three! (*Pause.*) "Airness" on three, guys!

**CANNIBAL QUEEN.** Nope. We're not doing that.

**GOLDEN.** (*Unfazed.*) Okay. But just know *I'm* doing it.

(*He taps his heart.*)

In here.

(VICIOUS *finishes his slo-mo song.*

*Lights shift quickly.* GOLDEN, SHREDDY, FACEBENDER, NINA, *and* CANNIBAL QUEEN *line up across the bar's stage, joining* VICIOUS. NINA *in the middle. We hear a sound cue of a HUGE, enthusiastic, cheering crowd. Thousands of people. Drunk, happy, losing their damn minds.*

*As the* ANNOUNCER *says their names, each character steps forward, and plays a short, five-second riff of their freestyle song.*)

**ANNOUNCER.** Okay, people, here we are at ROUND TWO! You know what comes next for our National Championship finalists!

From the East Coast, GOLDEN THUNDER!

(GOLDEN *plays a riff from "The Supercut of Ultimate Unity."*)

Repping the Western Conference, FACEBENDER LENDER!

(FACEBENDER *plays a riff from "Somebody to Love."*)

Your Mid-Atlantic champ, CANNIBAL QUEEN!

(CANNIBAL QUEEN *plays a riff from "Arpeggios from Hell."*)

Central Conference Victor, SHREDDY EDDY!

(SHREDDY *plays a riff from "I Don't Wanna Grow Up."*)

Your Dark Horse Heroine—THE NINA!

(NINA *plays a riff from "Shadows of the Night."*)

And reigning champion D VICIOUS!

(VICIOUS *steps forward and plays a riff, then flips the crowd off.*)

And now, without any ado, here is the song the judges have selected for Round Two of tonight's National Championship.

(*The competitors stand very still to catch the first strains of the music. A beat of silence; even the crowd's cheering falls away. WHAT SONG WILL IT BE? We hear the first few notes of Heart's "Crazy on You." NINA punches the air.*)

**NINA.** Nancy! Fucking! WILSON!!

(*The finalists begin playing, one by one, down the line. [In reality, they would be taking turns, but for our purposes, we will just stagger their starts.] Everyone is rocking hard.*

*D VICIOUS plays, but his heart is obviously not in this. He hates Heart. A female guitarist, in Round Two of the finals? Fucking really?*

*And finally, NINA plays. She's been longing to play Heart all along. She's inside the music. She's exploding with rapturous joy. She's a child, she's a woman, she's having the time of her life. She's also, still, a fantastic guitarist. She's not paying homage, she's not pretending to do anything, she has transcended. SHE'S FOUND THE AIRNESS. The others stop playing, one by one, and watch her in awe. Even VICIOUS can't compete, and just stares at her.*

*NINA finishes playing the song [not the whole song, it's like a five-minute song] just as the ANNOUNCER enters.*)

**ANNOUNCER.** It was a close one out here tonight, folks, but the judges have made their decision. This year's Air Guitar National Champion, who'll be repping Uncle Sam at the World Championships in Oulu, Finland, is: "THE NINA"!!

(*VICIOUS stomps offstage. The others crowd around NINA, sharing in her glory.*)

**SHREDDY.** (*Very excited for her.*) Fuck you!

**NINA.** (*Grabbing him.*) Come here.

(NINA *grabs* SHREDDY *and kisses him.*)

**GOLDEN.** That was some airness, people. True airness. I'm just glad I got to see it in my lifetime.

**CANNIBAL QUEEN.** Me too, Golden. Me too.

(FACEBENDER *looks at* SHREDDY *and* NINA *kissing, and he sighs.* GOLDEN *turns and sees them.*)

**GOLDEN.** Aw, look at this!

**FACEBENDER.** (*Earnestly.*) I just love love stories. Don't you?

(CANNIBAL QUEEN *turns to* FACEBENDER, *as though she's really seeing him for the first time.*)

**CANNIBAL QUEEN.** (*Sincerely.*) Yeah. I really fucking do.

(*Blackout.*)

### End of Play

# CRY IT OUT
a new play
about new parents
## by Molly Smith Metzler

# ABOUT *CRY IT OUT*

*This article first ran in the* Limelight Guide to the 41$^{st}$ Humana Festival of New American Plays, *published by Actors Theatre of Louisville, and is based on conversations with the playwright before rehearsals for the Humana Festival production began.*

A long winter is winding to an end when Jessie and Lina start meeting for coffee in Jessie's backyard. Both on maternity leave, cooped up with their "little larval creatures" (as Lina puts it), they're starved for conversation—and Jessie is elated to meet the funny and forthright renter in the duplex next door. Their friendship becomes a lifeline for them both as they laugh about their strange new existence, dictated by naptimes and nursing, and worry about going back to work. But as much as they need each other, their vastly different finances don't put them on a level playing field. And when they learn that they're being watched from the mansion on the cliff above their neighborhood, it seems that worlds are about to collide. In Molly Smith Metzler's *Cry it Out*, a rich blend of dark humor and raw honesty opens up questions about how privilege impacts the kind of parents (and friends) we're able to be.

Metzler's take on the trials and absurdities of being a new parent was inspired by her own experience living with her baby daughter in Port Washington, the economically diverse area of Long Island where *Cry it Out* is set. The playwright recalls that after an intense period of focus on her career, her life shifted radically when her pregnancy and her husband's new job moved them away from Brooklyn. "Suddenly I was in this sleepy oceanside town, and I went from being very busy, on airplanes and in rehearsal, to being trapped at home, completely alone in this new place with a baby," Metzler explains. "I didn't realize it at the time, but I was doing intense research for this play. The experience was so isolating, so shocking in its newness, that I wrote everything down." Several years later, when her daughter was a toddler and Metzler's writing career had begun pulling her toward an eventual move to Los Angeles, she reopened her journals. She remembers, "I was able to go back to those writings and say: I want to talk about some of the questions I had, and that I think a lot of new parents have."

Given the level of uncertainty that comes with this new role, finding other parents to connect with—even complete strangers—becomes essential. In *Cry it Out*, the lively rapport between Jessie and Lina stems from exactly such a need. "I think of them as lighthouses for each other; they both sleep better knowing the other is there, and they keep one another afloat," says Metzler, who observes that new moms will often bond despite very different backgrounds. "If you both have newborns, you suddenly have more in common than with *any* friend you've ever had," she laughs.

But as the end of maternity leave looms, Jessie's successful law career and upward mobility force a difficult decision about whether to return to work, while working-class Lina's means of survival are much more tenuous. By placing their predicaments side-by-side, Metzler sharply illuminates how massive the dilemmas around balancing work, childcare, and finances can be—assuming one even has the luxury of weighing choices. And then there's dealing with what everybody *thinks* you should be doing, in a culture that still expects women to be caregivers but denies adequate parental leave. "I hope the play challenges our tendency to judge each other in these very personal decisions that all parents have to make," Metzler says.

Adding more fuel to these complicated dynamics is the entrance of another pair of struggling new parents, Adrienne and Mitchell—who live in wealthy Sands Point, in a swanky estate overlooking Jessie's little yard. (The two neighborhoods, as in real life, are separated only by a steep cliff.) Though this couple seems to have it all, they're hardly immune from the tug of war between their old identities and new responsibilities. "I wanted to make sure the questions are hard no matter where the characters fall economically," notes Metzler. But while Mitchell and Adrienne are having a rough time, money does give them options. "It seems so unfair that we don't all start at the same place as parents," the playwright contends. "Privilege allows you more choices."

*Cry it Out* is Metzler's second play to premiere in the Humana Festival, following the success of her class-conscious hit comedy, *Elemeno Pea*, in 2011. An Actors Theatre commission, *Cry it Out* was written specifically for the Bingham Theatre. "Social economics, and who's above who, is an important element in the play, and the height of the Bingham makes that detail literal and visual," she explains. "I wrote towards the voyeuristic quality of the space, the intimacy. The idea that the audience is in the yard with these characters, who are vulnerable and unaware they are being spied on, is exciting to me." Drawing us into Jessie's backyard allows Metzler to beautifully capture the texture of parenthood's early days, which are life-changing and urgently difficult—but seldom depicted onstage. "Much like babies are put down in their cribs and forced to cry themselves to sleep," she says, "new parents get thrust into this position, and you have to figure it out on your own. I hope the play can create a space of empathy to think about that."

—Amy Wegener

# BIOGRAPHY

Molly Smith Metzler is the author of *Cry it Out, Elemeno Pea, The May Queen, Carve, Close Up Space,* and *Training Wisteria.* Her regional credits include: Actors Theatre of Louisville/Humana Festival, South Coast Repertory, Northlight Theatre, Boston Playwrights' Theatre, Chautauqua Theater Company, City Theatre, PlayMakers Repertory Company, Geva Theatre Center, and more. In New York: Manhattan Theatre Club (MTC). Metzler's awards include the Lecomte du Nouy Prize from Lincoln Center, the National Student Playwriting Award from The Kennedy Center, the Association for Theatre in Higher Education's David Mark Cohen Award, the Mark Twain Comedy Prize, and a finalist nod for the Susan Smith Blackburn Prize. She is a proud alumna of the Ars Nova Play Group, the Dorothy Strelsin New American Writers Group at Primary Stages, and the Cherry Lane Mentor Project. She has written plays for Actors Theatre of Louisville and Chautauqua Theater Company, and is currently under commission at MTC and South Coast Repertory. In television, Metzler has written for *Casual* (Hulu), *Orange Is the New Black* (Netflix), *Codes of Conduct* (HBO), and is currently a writer/producer on *Shameless* (Showtime). She is also a screenwriter, currently adapting Ali Benjamin's award-winning novel *The Thing About Jellyfish* into a film for Oddlot/Pacific Standard (Reese Witherspoon's company). Metzler was educated at SUNY Geneseo, Boston University, New York University's Tisch School for the Arts, and The Juilliard School. She lives in Los Angeles but spends a ton of time in her hometown: Kingston, New York.

## ACKNOWLEDGMENTS

*Cry it Out* premiered at the Humana Festival of New American Plays in March 2017. It was directed by Davis McCallum with the following cast:

| | |
|---|---|
| JESSIE | Jessica Dickey |
| LINA | Andrea Syglowski |
| MITCHELL | Jeff Biehl |
| ADRIENNE | Liv Rooth |

and the following production staff:

| | |
|---|---|
| Scenic Designer | William Boles |
| Costume Designer | Kathleen Geldard |
| Lighting Designer | Tyler Micoleau |
| Sound Designer | Stowe Nelson |
| Stage Manager | Lori Doyle |
| Dramaturg | Amy Wegener |
| Casting | Erica Jensen, Calleri Casting |
| Properties Master | Carrie Mossman |
| Production Assistant | Abbie Betts |
| Directing Assistant | Lexy Leuszler |
| Assistant Dramaturg | Paige Vehlewald |

*Cry it Out* was commissioned by Actors Theatre of Louisville.

# CHARACTERS

JESSIE (mid-30s): Married to a North Shore native; recently relocated to Port (from Manhattan) to raise her family. Educated, articulate, lovely, warm. From the Midwest and has that Midwestern ready-smile. Beloved by every teacher she's ever had. Always gives the perfect toast; always organizes the group gift. But in private, Jessie bends towards anxiety. She doesn't like empty days on calendars, or being alone. Works 90-hour weeks in the city as a corporate lawyer—or did, until Allie was born. Now she's in yoga pants.

LINA (late 20s/early 30s): From Long Beach (on South Shore of Long Island) and you can tell immediately—she is *very* South Shore: acrylic neon nails, big hoops, velour track suits, Mets trucker hats—and a *huge* Italian family. Lina failed out of community college, curses too much, and blasts Kanye too loudly in the car. But she is also fantastically winning. She's fun, funny and refreshingly genuine. Knows how to change a tire. Works at St. Francis Hospital.

MITCHELL (late 30s/early 40s or slightly older): Adrienne's husband, works in investment capital. A math nerd who is amazing with numbers, not people. Serious, shrewd, sensitive. The kid who ate lunch in the library because he was so shy. Mitchell grew up in a tough house in the toughest part of Utica and scholarshipped his way to where he is now. Grades, status, and success are his currency. But becoming a father has changed him. He makes goofy faces now, stares out windows during meetings. His sentences end in question marks.

ADRIENNE (mid/late 30s): Mitchell's wife. Elegant, powerful, aloof, and slightly rock 'n' roll. Has eyes that are cat-like and assessing. The kind of woman you see climbing out of a dark sedan at JFK heading somewhere cool. Adrienne grew up on Central Park West, attended posh boarding schools, studied art abroad, and could give you the best-ever guided tour of MoMA. She has never signed an e-mail with an x or an o, but she is loyal and ferocious. A jewelry designer.

## PLACE

We are in suburban Long Island, in the city of Port Washington.

Port Washington is an affluent, sleepy city with excellent public schools. Commuters are at Penn Station in just 35 minutes on the LIRR, so it's a very popular destination for New Yorkers who have families and want to rent/buy bigger homes.

Port Washington is comprised of many small villages.

This play takes place in the village of Manorhaven, which is directly on the ocean, heavily populated, and, depending on the block, either middle-class or quite rundown.

This block is somewhere in between.

The streets of Manorhaven are crammed with two-family duplexes, some brand new and flashy, some old and decrepit. The new ones have mostly Manhattan transplants living in them; the decrepit ones mostly have "Lifers" living in them—people who have been renting for generations (sometimes under Section 8 housing codes.) Accordingly, there's a lot of socioeconomic diversity here.

Manorhaven also abuts one of the wealthiest neighborhoods in the whole country, Sands Point, which is up on a cliff literally looking down over Manorhaven. A bunch of NY Yankees have houses up there, and it's the model for West Egg in *The Great Gatsby*. Just crazy huge wealth.

Interestingly, the same school bus takes the Manorhaven kids and the Sands Point kids to the same excellent public school in September.

## SET

This play takes place in Jessie's backyard in Manorhaven.

It's been a long, horrible winter. There's no grass, no landscaping, nothing to sit on.

We could see a fence, or the back of Jessie's house, or the side of a neighbor's house…but really, there's no set for this play. Just a patch of dead, sludgy earth where two yards meet.

## TIME

Almost spring, but not yet. This year.

Andrea Syglowski and Jessica Dickey
in *Cry it Out*

41st Humana Festival of New American Plays
Actors Theatre of Louisville, 2017
Photo by Bill Brymer

272

# CRY IT OUT

## 1.

JESSIE's *yard. It's been raining. Puddles. Sludge. A wet, newly-assembled plastic play set sits off to the side, waiting patiently for spring.*

*First, we just hear two voices. Then* LINA *&* JESSIE *enter from their respective homes, baby monitors in hand.* JESSIE *has two mugs of steaming coffee.*

**LINA.** OH MY GOD THIS WAS SUCH A GREAT IDEA!!!!!

**JESSIE.** SHHHH!—sorry— / the window—

**LINA.** Oh shit I'm sorry—

*(Pointing to the window.)*

Where is she—right up there?

**JESSIE.** On the second floor yeah, so—

**LINA.** So I need to shut my big mouth is what you're saying! Sorry.

*(Whispers.)*

*Oh my god, hiiiiii.*

**JESSIE.** *(Whispers.) Hi!*

*(Worried.)*

I didn't interrupt you, did I?

**LINA.** *Are you kidding?!* I leapt for joy when I got your text. I was talking to my breast-pump in there. Like he's Wilson in *Castaway.*

**JESSIE.** *I know,* me too.

*(Handing* LINA *her coffee.)*

Here. Two sugars, one milk, right?—

**LINA.** Fuck yes.

**JESSIE.** *(Re:* LINA's *video monitor.)* So what do you think? Can your monitor stretch up here to my patio?

**LINA.** I don't know, let's see......

*(LINA starts advancing towards JESSIE's house, eyeing her baby video monitor. She moves slowly across the yard.)*

OK I can see the baby...

*(Beat.)*

still see him......

*(Beat.)*

Still see him.............................nope—can't go past here.

**JESSIE.** Ok—let's go to your yard—

**LINA.** No, there's tons of dog shit back there.

**JESSIE.** (*Pulling monitor out of her pocket.*) Don't be silly—let's see how far mine can stretch.....

It's supposed to go 65 feet...

   (*Then:*)

...........no, I lose my signal here.

**LINA.** Alright then, x marks the spot. We can just stand here awkwardly??

**JESSIE.** I'm sorry we don't have patio furniture—we haven't gotten around to it yet.

   (*Noticing.*)

What if I dragged that play set over? We could sit on that—

**LINA.** *Great* idea—here, gimme your coffee.

   (JESSIE *dumps the rain out of the play set and starts dragging it into monitor*
   *range.*)

Oh my God, this is *great* coffee. You are an *amazing coffee maker* and I could make love to you with my mouth right now.

**JESSIE.** ...Thank you.

   (*Play set in place.*)

Yay! Cheers!

**LINA.** To Napping Babies.

**JESSIE.** May they NAP LONG AND PROSPER!

   (*Beat.*)

Sorry, that was a weird thing to say; I got like twenty minutes of sleep last night.

**LINA.** Puh-lease, gurl. I was right there with you.

   (*They both take a seat on the play set; one on the slide, one on top. Two adult*
   *women on a tiny play set.*)

This play set *rocks*. How do you already have an assembled play set?! You have a 12-week-old.

**JESSIE.** Oh my husband. Nate. Assembling things gives him a sense of purpose. You should see our nursery. He installed every single baby-safety gadget on the market, to the point that: I kid you not, Lina—I *cannot access* the room. It's like, booby-trapped with baby lasers.

**LINA.** Well, better that than a guy who doesn't do jack, right? I mean, John is pretty good: he does the middle of the night diaper change. But a lot of my friends back home are with *such dbags.*

**JESSIE.** Where's home?

**LINA.** South Shore. Long Beach. You been?

**JESSIE.** I think so.....there's a boardwalk, right?

**LINA.** Right. And all those loud people eating cotton candy on the boardwalk? I'm related to *every single one of them*. Try it: call out the name Bustamante—every head turns.

    *(Beat.)*

What about you? Where are you from?

**JESSIE.** ...Outside Chicago.

**LINA.** Oh shit, tell me you're not a Cubs fan.

**JESSIE.** What?

**LINA.** Cubs. You a Cubs fan?

**JESSIE.** Is that baseball?

**LINA.** Okay, we can be friends.

**JESSIE.** Oh, good. Because I *really* want to be friends, Lina.

    *(Beat.)*

Sorry.

    *(Beat.)*

I... shouldn't have said that out loud. Now you must think I'm desperate or crazy or something.

**LINA.** *No.*

**JESSIE.** But I have just had *the hardest* time meeting other moms out here. And you're so cooped up in your house all day with the baby—all these hours when babies are sleeping and husbands are working. Where are all the moms??

**LINA.** This is *North Shore*, honey. Nanny Central. The Moms are at SoulCycle or getting raindrop facials at Bliss.

    *(Beat.)*

Speaking of... my ass is extremely wet right now. Is your ass wet?

**JESSIE.** *(Laughs.)* Yes. I'll go get us a towel—

**LINA.** No no no—I was just checking you were wet, too. After being pregnant, I honestly can't tell when I've peed myself. That's just my life now.

**JESSIE.** *That is so true.* Disgusting and very very true.

    *(Beat. They smile at each other. This is going \*well.\*)*

So you didn't think I was a freak, coming up to you in Stop n' Shop yesterday?

**LINA.** Are you kidding?! *I was a pig in shit.* I'd seen you around the nabe too—but it's not like you can run out into the snow to say hi when you have a baby on your boob.

**JESSIE.** Which is why I hurdle-jumped over the cantaloupe to introduce myself.

**LINA.** Well, I'm real glad you did.

**JESSIE.** *Me, too.*

> (*Beat.*)

Truly, it's impossible. Meeting people in Port. And Nate doesn't get home until almost 8 most nights, and I don't like driving with the baby in the car unless the conditions are perfect....so it's a lot of me and her alone in Room.

> (*Beat.*)

Do you know that novel, *Room*? It won the Booker Prize?

> (*Off her blank expression.*)

Anyway, it's a *beautiful* story about a woman who's held captive for years in a gardening shed with her child.

**LINA.** Oh, *Room.* The movie!

**JESSIE.** Exactly. And I keep telling my Mom: that's what this is. It's Room. It's winter in Long Island, and I'm home with a newborn, and it's Room. I'm *in* Room.

**LINA.** That's why I thank God everyday for Stop n' Shop. Sometimes it's the only time I get out in a 48-hour period, I / swear to God.

**JESSIE.** I know! Me too!

**LINA.** And you'd think I'm going to the prom—I do like full face makeup, shave my legs. And usually I don't even need anything. I'll just go stand in the vitamin aisle being like: *oooooo vitamins.*

**JESSIE.** I know—me too, with shampoo and conditioner.

> (*Beat.*)

Oh! You'll appreciate this......guess what *my husband* did the other day? *He* went to Stop n' Shop on his way home from the train.

**LINA.** *No.*

**JESSIE.** Without checking with me. Just "thought he'd be nice" and stop for diapers and milk. And he took his time, too, Lina. Like *checked the ingredients of stuff.*

**LINA.** That son of a bitch. Did you go ape shit?

**JESSIE.** I did. Honestly, I think I was pretty scary. He came in with the bags and I went down to my knees sobbing—just a *puddle on the floor.* And poor Nate is standing there *staring* at me, saying You Usually Like It When I Get Groceries Jess, What's Wrong?? and I'm like YOU ARE IN THE CITY ALL DAY, YOU DON'T GET STOP N' SHOP!!!! *I GET STOP N' SHOP!!! I* GET TO GO TO STOP N' SHOP YOU MOTHERFUCKER!!

**LINA.** Shhhhh, your baby.

**JESSIE.** Sorry.

> (*Beat.*)

I didn't call him a motherfucker, by the way. I don't curse in real life. But I *wanted* to is my point.

**LINA.** Of course you did.

**JESSIE.** They don't get it.

**LINA.** Of course they don't. *They* get to go interact with humans all day and go to *Hale & Hearty* for lunch and eat chopped salads made by someone *whose job it is* to chop salad. I mean. What would you do for a fucking chopped salad right now??

**JESSIE.** I would murder someone.

**LINA.** *I know you would.* But we don't get chopped salad anymore.

**JESSIE.** Nope.

**LINA.** Because we're held hostage all day in dirty yoga pants by little larval creatures who would literally *die* if we checked our e-mail or took a leisurely dump.

**JESSIE.** Though my girlfriends who don't have kids don't get it, either. A couple of them came out to meet the baby a few weeks ago, and it was like Aliens got off the train.

**LINA.** Really?

**JESSIE.** They showed up at 8:45 p.m. *To meet a baby.* And they brought stuff to make cosmos and asked questions like, "So are you *sooooo* eager to get back to work?"

**LINA.** Bitches.

**JESSIE.** Yeah. I don't think I like my city friends anymore. I don't really like anyone anymore.

(*Max makes a peep and they both \*jump\* to check their monitors. He squawks for a second, moans, then quiets.*)

Wow—you've got a good sleeper there, huh. That he self-soothes.

**LINA.** Yeah. We've got napping down. But once the sun goes down?

(*Re: boobs.*)

He just wants to hit the buffet.

**JESSIE.** Oh I know, us too. We're up every three hours still.

(*Carefully, as this is a touchy question.*)

Does Max sleep in a crib, or?

**LINA.** No, Max sleeps between my tits.

**JESSIE.** Oh, that must be *so nice.* I really wanted to co-sleep, but Nate's six-foot-two, so. He couldn't relax with her in the bed.

(*Another touchy question.*)

Are you planning to sleep-train Max?

**LINA.** Is that the thing when you let them Cry it Out?

**JESSIE.** Yes.

**LINA.** *No.* I am *not* doing that shit.

(*Beat.*)

Why, are you?

**JESSIE.** (*Yes.*) .....we might. I mean. I don't know yet. We're still discussing.

**LINA.** Well, you do you, girl. No judgment here. I'm just not into Cry it Out, myself.

(*Beat.*)

**JESSIE.** Why not? I mean. May I ask?

**LINA.** Sure. Because *I don't hate babies.*

(JESSIE *laughs.*)

Well, I'm sorry but that's what sleep-training is: it's barbaric. You put your baby down in a dark crib and *let them scream and scream* until *they learn no one's coming for them?* I mean, are we Vikings? Are we gonna put fucking Viking hats on and club them, too?

**JESSIE.** Wow, you have strong / feelings about—

**LINA.** I think you're *supposed to cry* when you're all alone in a dark room. That's what I think.

And I think your mom or dad—or someone who loves you—is *supposed to come help you.*

**JESSIE.** I know. You're right, you *are* right.

(*But:*)

I just wish *our doctor* said that.

**LINA.** Is your doctor a woman or man?

**JESSIE.** Man.

**LINA.** Then he needs to shut his fucking mouth. This is *our* rodeo. The vaginas are in charge now, and *we vaginas* know what to do.

**JESSIE.** ....yeah we do.

(*But* JESSIE'*s not convinced. She listens to doctors. And Nate. And finds vagina talk a little scandalous.*)

So is Max a "Max" or a "Maximus"?

**LINA.** Max. Max Giuseppe Vanera. Though Boom Boom Pow is what I call him. For some reason.

**JESSIE.** Oh. *Max Vanera.*

(*True.*)

I really like that.

**LINA.** You do? Oh good. My mother said it sounded like a rare STD. As in,

"We're sorry, sir, very sorry, but you have an advanced stage of Maxvanera in your janky penis."

(JESSIE *laughs.*)

She's a beast. My mother. You'll meet her. And you'll agree: she is a beast. She was my "live-in nurse" after the birth and I think I'm fine, never seeing her again.

(JESSIE *laughs.*)

What about you—Allison?

**JESSIE.** Jensen-Gelb. Allison Catherine Jensen-Gelb. Hyphenated. Nate's Jensen; I'm Gelb.

**LINA.** (*Hates it.*) Oh. Very nice. Lots of sounds.

**JESSIE.** Yeah, I like it, too. Not that I can take any credit. Nate named her all by himself.

**LINA.** Where were you? Barbados?

**JESSIE.** No, I uh... wasn't cogent. At the time.

**LINA.** You weren't cogent?

**JESSIE.** No. I uh...

(*Still hard to talk about.*)

...I actually had a crash C-section? A "splash and slash" they call it. It's when it's such an emergency you're not even prepped for surgery; they just Splash you with iodine and Slash you until they get the baby out. I was completely under. General anaesthesia.

**LINA.** *Jesus.* What happened?

**JESSIE.** Uh I'm still not sure, honestly? I think the umbilical cord was cutting off her oxygen and her heart stopped completely? I don't know. All I know is one minute Nate and I were doing our ice chips, the next minute people were screaming Code Blue.

**LINA.** *Fuck.*

**JESSIE.** Nate's face. That's what I remember. The crash team was pulling my gurney down the hall and Nate was getting farther and farther away, at the other end of the hall... and then I saw him just go *boneless* with fear, you know? Down on the floor.

(*Beat.*)

But! Allison was totally and completely fine the moment they resuscitated her.

**LINA.** Well thank God. Those stories go the other way sometimes. I work in a hospital, I hear things. Birthdays are the worst days for a lot of people.

**JESSIE.** I know. We are *very* lucky.

(LINA's *monitor chirps again, and she dives for it.*)

**LINA.** Oh shit, he lost his binky...

> (LINA *stands and watches in suspense; she might have to bolt. Beat. Finally, Max finds his binky and falls silent.*)

Phew. False alarm.

> (*Beat.*)

So you guys were in the city. Before here?

**JESSIE.** Yeah. A charming one bed on 63$^{rd}$ and Lex. I loved it, but it wasn't practical for a baby. There wasn't a washer-dryer, and it was a fourth floor walk-up / which—

**LINA.** Aw hell no.

**JESSIE.** Exactly. So we thought....well? 35 minutes to Penn Station? And we can live right on the ocean?—let's give Long Island a try.

**LINA.** I heard there was a *crazy* bidding war over your place.

**JESSIE.** I know, who would've thought. A little two-family duplex. But we basically had to make a cash offer in the driveway and go 10% over the ask.

> (*Beat.*)

Nate said it was a good investment property—we can rent both sides out, down the line.

**LINA.** He's absolutely right. The rental market out here is *insane*, especially for the newer models like yours. It's because we're so close to Sands Point. Have you driven around up there? (*Pointing up.*) Those houses *start* at 10 mill. And our kids get to go to the same excellent public school those entitled shits do.

**JESSIE.** Yeah, I know.

> (*Carefully.*)

...Nate's parents live out here. Not in Sands Point. They aren't that rich. But: Plandome?

**LINA.** *Your in-laws live in Plandome?* Where?

**JESSIE.** Plandome Road?

**LINA.** *You go to dinner at a house on Plandome Road.*

**JESSIE.** I do. Long and stressful and horrible dinners, but yes.

**LINA.** What number?

**JESSIE.** 1251?

**LINA.** With the lion statue??

**JESSIE.** No that's next door. 1251 is a bit more modest—up on the hill with the white brick?

**LINA.** Oh yeah, okay. That's super "modest."

**JESSIE.** I think it's a little over the top, too. But Ken's worked his ass off in investment banking for the last forty years, so who am I to call it tacky. (Even though I do think it's tacky. I think it's very very tacky.)

**LINA.** So wait—did your husband grow up here? In Port?

**JESSIE.** Yeah. In that house.

**LINA.** So he went to Schrieber?

**JESSIE.** Yeah, class of 94.

**LINA.** Oh my God you have to ask him if he knows John Vanera! John went there too. He's a little younger, class of 97, I think.

**JESSIE.** Oh, how wild! They must know each other!

**LINA.** Did Nate play sports?

**JESSIE.** Tennis.

**LINA.** Maybe they know each other from lunch?

**JESSIE.** They must! Oh how funny! Our husbands totally broke bread!

**LINA.** *So funny.* But John's not my husband. Just. FYI.

**JESSIE.** ....I'm sorry. / Oh, God—

**LINA.** *Don't be.* I mean we'll probably get married. Or not. *Let's get out of his mother's house first*—then we can talk.

**JESSIE.** (*Pointing to her place.*) Oh. That's? You're living with?—

**LINA.** Yolanda Vanera. Yes. Not that she owns it; she rents. For 37 years now, just been paying someone else's mortgage—and now *we* get the privilege of doing the same. But she's only charging us six hundred a month so we're saving up a lot for our own place, which I'm really grateful for. But it's hard, living with another woman, you know? Sometimes she says stuff like Lina, *YOU LOOK SOOO TIRED chica, GIVE ME THAT BABY AND GO TAKE A NAP.* And I'm like BACK THE FUCK OFFA ME, GRANDMA, BEFORE SHIT GETS REAL RIGHT NOW.

**JESSIE.** Shhh.

**LINA.** (*Diarrhea of mouth.*) Sorry. And Also? She's cheap. (I'm sorry—now you've opened the floodgates, I'm going to just let it rip!)—she's *so* cheap. If she's cooking us dinner, she'll make exactly three chicken cutlets. Like little tiny chicken cutlets. And I'm breastfeeding you know? I'm STARVING. I want 19 chicken cutlets. And if I ask for more, she gives me a look, like Oh, You Want More? You're that Kind Of Woman?

**JESSIE.** I think you deserve more chicken.

**LINA.** I do! And I'm sorry but she also drinks a whole box of wine every two days. And she's supposed to be sober—she pretends to go to meetings, but we know she doesn't—and it's the big box she's drinking, too—the Peter Vella White Zin? She doesn't do it in front of us, which is respectful—me and John are sober; six years for him, four years for me—well, eight years for me, but I kept up cocaine in secret for four years, but four years of complete sobriety for me now. Sorry is this TMI?

**JESSIE.** (*A little...*) No. No, good for you. That you kicked it.

**LINA.** You don't kick it. All you do is come to accept that you want it and choose to want something else more.

**JESSIE.** ....huh. Yeah.

**LINA.** But anyway, me and John *cannot* figure out what she does with the wine boxes. There's no evidence! The box is not in the trash, not in the recycling; it's like she incinerates them.

**JESSIE.** The case of the Missing Wine Box.

**LINA.** Exactly but like I said, she's helping us out a lot letting us stay here. And she's changing her schedule at Bed Bath & Beyond so she can be home with Max when I go back to work, which is great because the prices these babysitters are quoting me?—

**JESSIE.** (*Slight alarm.*) Wait, you're going back to work? When?

**LINA.** Uh.... 24 days from today.

**JESSIE.** Oh God, that's so soon.

**LINA.** I know. I can't talk about it, I'll start crying. And I put my good mascara on so you'd think I was pretty, so. I'm not doing it.

(*Beat.*)

**JESSIE.** (*Carefully.*) ....do you *have* to go back? I mean. Is it an option not to?

**LINA.** I love him, but John doesn't make squat. He works at a halfway house in Queens—which is God's work, *it is*—and when I met him he was working in a pizza place in Merrick and this is *way better for him*—making the world a better place—and you can't put a price-tag on that shit. Except you *can* actually and it's zero. After taxes, about zero. Plus I have some credit problems from back when I was high and defaulted on stuff so unless I want to raise Max in Yolanda's House of Denial and Shame, I need to buck up in 24 days, yes I do.

(*Beat.*)

What about you? When you going back?

**JESSIE.** I....don't think I'm going back. I mean, I'm supposed to. On May 15th. And I took my suits to the dry cleaners and reserved a spot for Allie at North Shore, but—

**LINA.** (*Very expensive and excellent.*) Whoa. You got into North Shore Day?

**JESSIE.** My mother-in-law knew someone who knew someone. And paid for it.

**LINA.** *Damn.*

**JESSIE.** I know. We're very lucky.

(*Beat.*)

But anyway I hope she *doesn't* go there because as I was saying, ever since we almost lost Allie, I kind of... *don't* care about protecting the legal interests of a bunch of corporations anymore.

(*Beat.*)

Not that I've figured out how to tell Nate all this.

He's a planner—his business brain, I think—and he has us on a ten-year plan that depends on us being double-income. He comes from a home where his mother didn't really *raise* the four children—there was a Baby Nurse, then there was a Nanny, then there was a Family Assistant, so he's not going to understand, why I would want to do it myself.

(*Beat.*)

He actually... he actually tried to take me to Tulum Mexico a few weeks ago. He came in all gallant, with a lingerie box, saying Pack Your Bags Baby, it's time for us to Get Back to Our Marriage. And he looked at me like I had two heads when I said *there is no way I'm leaving this baby.* But that's what he knows. His father did that for his Mom after each baby—a month in Provence while the baby nurse settled things. So he doesn't understand.

(*Beat.*)

It's just been hard though. He told me this morning he misses me. But not in the *I don't see you, I miss you so much* way—in that *other* way. The way that's kind of an insult, you know? The "I miss you *because you've changed*—I miss the *old* you" way. And I just wanted to punch him in his face and say I *haven't* changed, THIS *IS* ME! THIS *IS* ME, THIS HAS ALWAYS BEEN ME, THIS WILL ALWAYS BE ME—AND YOU CAN'T TAKE ME TO TULUM MEXICO! I DON'T WANT TO GO HAVE SEX IN TULUM MEXICO WHEN WE ALMOST LOST OUR BABY, YOU MOTHER-FUCKER!!!!!

(*Beat.*
*Upset.*)

Sorry. My doctor thinks I should go on antidepressants. I don't mean to be like this....

**LINA.** It's okay. We all cry sometimes.

(*Tenderly.*)

I don't have a tissue. You want a breast pad? I've got two moist ones right here.

(JESSIE *laughs. Loves her new friend.*)

**JESSIE.** Lina, can I ask you something?

**LINA.** Sure.

**JESSIE.** Do you think I'm doing a good job?

**LINA.** What do you mean?

**JESSIE.** With Allie. I mean... I don't have anyone else to ask. And you saw me in Stop n' Shop with her....do you think I'm....good with her?

**LINA.** *Yes.* Absolutely.

**JESSIE.** You do?

(*Tearfully.*)

You think she seems happy and okay?

**LINA.** *Yes.* I think she seems a-mazing. She was alert, and smiley, looking all around.

**JESSIE.** Yeah?

**LINA.** Definitely. And look at you: you have jeans on right now! Girl you are Killing This.

**JESSIE.** THEY'RE MATERNITY JEANS THEY'RE NOT REAL JEANS.

**LINA.** But it's denim. It's real denim—look at this: I'm in jeggings, here, ok? These are leggins made to look like jeans. You are Dead Sexy right now.

**JESSIE.** No.

**LINA.** Allie is *lucky.* I could see that immediately in the grocery store. That's a lucky little girl.

**JESSIE.** (*Reaching in for a hug.*) Can I? I'm sorry—I just, I really need to do this...

(*She hugs her tight.*)

**LINA.** Of course you can. What are friends for.

(*Lights.*)

### 2.

*Lights up on the yard. Three weeks later.*

*A little wrought-iron patio table and three chairs are where the play set was. There might be a little potted plant of something springy on the table, too.*

LINA *enters with her monitor, waves up towards the house. A moment later* JESSIE *enters, monitor in hand, with their coffees.*

**LINA.** Oh my God, you're not going to believe what I did this morning.

**JESSIE.** What.

**LINA.** OK, so—I was nursing Max—as per usge—and the FedEx guy rang our bell, right? And it scared the shit out of me and I went running to answer the door, and Jessie? My tit was still out. I had a whole conversation with him, too, about like... the weather... and did I need to sign this thing or that thing? And the whole time my Tit was Out.

**JESSIE.** (*Laughing.*) No.

**LINA.** Who am I, that I don't even know my Tit is out???

**JESSIE.** I think your house just became the most popular one on the FedEx delivery list.

**LINA.** I know. Seriously. This is all getting serious now. I need supervision I think.

(*Beat.*)

Anyway—how was your weekend? You guys were on the go, huh?

**JESSIE.** *Yes*—sorry we couldn't make it over Saturday. It was so nice of you to invite us.

**LINA.** Eh, it was probably for the best. The Mets won, so everyone got polluted drunk, and then my sister and her stepson came over with his new girlfriend J'Mae. (Not Jamie, J'Mae). And of course J'Mae is a stripper and broke the glass coffee table with her big stripper *foot*, so I gotta vacuum shards of glass out of Yolanda's carpet until 3 a.m.

**JESSIE.** Oh man.

**LINA.** YUP.

**JESSIE.** Still. We were touched you invited us. I wanted Nate and John to meet at last! I know he'll recognize him when he sees him in the flesh.

**LINA.** Hey, people forget people. Just cuz John remembers him vividly from high school doesn't mean Nate has to remember him. / It's no biggie.

**JESSIE.** *Ugh,* / so embarrassing.

**LINA.** I'm kidding. So what's in Montauk, anyway? Little cold for a beach weekend.

**JESSIE.** Oh, Lina.

(*Beat.*)

It was such a terrible weekend.

**LINA.** *Why?*

**JESSIE.** Just. Nate.

**LINA.** *Oh shit.* Did you tell him you're not going back to work?

**JESSIE.** No. I haven't done that yet.

(*Beat.*)

This was just... ugh, *it was so annoying* is what it was. He comes in Saturday morning when I'm getting dressed and says we have to go to Montauk for the day. And I'm like *No. Allie's just getting over a cold, what are you talking about?* And he says that his parents called and said we need to drop everything and come out to their place for the day (they have a beach house in Montauk).

And again I was like *No, I'm not moving the baby today, she's still getting better.* And he starts saying how his parents are *getting older now,* and *they do so much for us /* and can't we do this one little thing—

**LINA.** *Oh God,* come on, man.

**JESSIE.** So we pack the car up, get the sick baby in it, and drive all the way out there, and guess why, Lina. *Guess why Judy and Ken summoned us.*

　　(*Beat.*)

Because the cottage next door to theirs went on the market.

And *a team* of people were waiting for us. A broker. An inspector. An architect.

**LINA.** No. No no no no no. What'd you say?

**JESSIE.** I said Nate, we need to speak about this privately, at home. We need to look at our finances—*(and potential changes to our household income)*—before we meet with *any* of these people. And then I got back in the car, in front of everyone.

**LINA.** YES. Good for you!

**JESSIE.** No, because I really embarrassed him? I guess? He was hurt, and didn't talk the whole way home. And he apparently *loves* that cottage? Which he's *never* mentioned before but all of a sudden it's his lifelong dream, to own the cottage next to his parents'??

**LINA.** Oh Fuck. Come on, dude.

**JESSIE.** Yeah. It was hard.

**LINA.** You need to tell him you're not going back to work. Before he buys that shit.

**JESSIE.** I know I do.

　　(*Forced bright.*)

Anyway! At least Allie's feeling better. That was the silver lining—the stupid trip gave her five extra hours of quality car napping, which, together with the vapor bath, cleared her right up. Thanks again for the tip!

**LINA.** Right? The vapor shit works.

**JESSIE.** Oh and you know what else I tried? The NoseFrida! Do you know about this thing?

**LINA.** Is that the tube you use to suck the snot out of a baby's face?

**JESSIE.** Yes! It's a miracle! Do you have one?

**LINA.** No. I was going to get one, but then I found out it's a *tube you use to suck snot out of a baby's face.*

**JESSIE.** Yeah but it's not like you *taste* the snot. There's a filter / that catches the snot before—

**LINA.** Hard Pass. Passing Hard.

**JESSIE.** Okay but I'm telling you: the first time Max has a serious cold you'll be texting me at 3 a.m. saying Help! Where can I get a NoseFrida?? And the answer is Whole Foods.

**LINA.** Whole Foods! The nightmare is complete.

**JESSIE.** (*Laughing.*) Alright Fine. Fine!

(*Beat.*)

OK! SO! I have a present for you. I could barely contain myself—I wanted to bring it over to you yesterday—but I made myself wait. Are you ready?

(JESSIE *goes into the house; returns with a wrapped present. It's the shape of a record, for a record player.*)

**JESSIE.** Open it!

**LINA.** Is it... a record?

**JESSIE.** Nope.

**LINA.** What is it?

**JESSIE.** *Open it.*

(LINA *unwraps the gift: it's a flattened-out box. For Peter Vella White Zinfandel.*)

**LINA.** Oh my God....

**JESSIE.** *I saw her do it, Lina!* With the wine box. I was out running early yesterday morning, and I saw Yolanda pull into Manorhaven Park, double-park the car, and throw it away in the park dumpster. She throws the wine boxes away in the park dumpster!

**LINA.** *Oh my God,* that is so sad.

(*Somber.*)

This is So Crazy Sad......

(*Beat.*

*Beat.*

*Beat.*)

**JESSIE.** ....I'm so sorry. I thought you would rejoice and laugh that the mystery's been solved.

**LINA.** (*Not laughing.*) No, I am. I'm Laughing. Thank You.

(*Re: the box.*)

It's just potentially the saddest thing I've ever seen....and this woman, who does this, is going to watch my baby next week?

**JESSIE.** ...I'm so sorry, Lina. I didn't mean to upset you...

(*Beat.* JESSIE'*s eager to fix this:*)

Hey, did you see that article? There was an article! In the *Times* Saturday, did you see it?

(LINA *doesn't read the Times.*)

All about how good it is for them. Separation from mom at an early age. How there are *huge developmental advantages.* How they gain leadership skills! And confidence!

**LINA.** ......it didn't say that.

**JESSIE.** *It did*—the article went into the whole science behind it. Max is basically going to be Mark Zuckerberg because you're going back to work now.

(*No giggle.*

*No answer.*)

And you know I'm going to be right over here, right? If Yolanda needs help with Max she can call me anytime. I want you to give her my number.

**LINA.** I'm not doing that to you.

**JESSIE.** *Doing what to me?* I'm just *holding a baby all day,* watching Food Network. She can call me anytime.

**LINA.** ....really?

**JESSIE.** Absolutely. I'll come running right over if / she needs anything at all—

(*There's a sound of a car pulling in and parking. Then the clicking BEEP BEEP of a lock.*)

**LINA.** Is that Nate?

**JESSIE.** It can't be... I don't know who it could be...

**LINA.** Maybe FedEx heard I have a friend next door?...

(JESSIE *hands* LINA *her monitor, and stands, as if to exit, but* MITCHELL *enters. Dressed sharply for work.*

*He jangles his keys in his hand, nervously.*)

**MITCHELL.** I'm sorry, excuse me, ladies, I don't mean to interrupt... I'm late for work but I... I'm Mitchell.

**JESSIE.** Can I help you, Mitchell?

**MITCHELL.** I'm your neighbor. Well, sort of, I live up there, in Sands Point—(*Pointing up.*)—we're that house, we look down on you. Sorry— forgive me for barging in on you like this, you must think I'm crazy. I'm not... I just... turned in here. Why did I turn in here?

(*Beat.*)

**LINA.** Is there something we can do for you?

**MITCHELL.** I've seen you two out walking with your babies and I've seen you drinking your coffee together, and I turned into your driveway, I don't know why.

(*To* JESSIE.)

.....you live here, correct?

**JESSIE.** Yes. Please state your business.

**MITCHELL.** Sorry. I...

> (*Beat.*)

This was a bad idea. I'm sorry. I'll go.

> (*He exits.*)

**LINA.** (*To* JESSIE.) What the hell was that?

**JESSIE.** I don't know. I think he was drunk.

**LINA.** No, that's not a drunk man. Here, hold my monitor—

> (LINA *hands* JESSIE *the monitor, goes around the side of the house, to watch him.*)

Now he's just sitting in his car in your driveway.

**JESSIE.** *What?*

**LINA.** I can't tell what he's doing—he's just sitting there in his Cayenne, staring at me.

**JESSIE.** (*Getting her phone out.*) Oh my God, I'm calling Nate.

**LINA.** Wait—he's coming back—shhh!—Now he's coming back.

**JESSIE.** I'm texting Nate.

> (MITCHELL *enters, a surge of confidence.*)

**MITCHELL.** I'm sorry—that's not how I wanted to go about this, let me start again.

Hi, I'm Mitchell. Danow. I live on Middle Neck Road. That house up there. I can see you—from our veranda. I see you out here with your babies, going for walks together, having your coffee together. You look happy.

And long story short: I wondered if it would be possible for my wife to join you today.

> (*Beat.*)

We have a baby too, and my wife—Adrienne—she's..... having a hard time. I think it would do her a lot of good to get out and talk to some moms like you.

> (*Beat.*)

Would that be okay? If she came down when you do your second coffee meeting at 2:30?

**JESSIE.** ....Uh.

**MITCHELL.** I'll have some food and drinks delivered. Anything, really. I could have anything delivered. You name it.

> (*Beat. No one knows what to say.*)

**LINA.** Look, Mitchell. I'm sure your wife's a very nice lady, but Jessie and me are neighbors. Our husbands were friends in high school. So, there's a real intimacy here. A trust.

**MITCHELL.** Well, we're your neighbors, too, right? If we weren't up on the cliff, we'd practically live in your back yard.

(*Beat.*)

Look, we have a telescope—not for watching you, for bird-watching, but she watches you, my wife does. She doesn't think I see her do it, but I do. I know she wants... what you two have.

(*Beat.*)

If I could just call her before I get on the train and tell her she's been invited to coffee at 2:30, I would really appreciate it. Otherwise I am going to have to call out sick, and truly: I can't call out sick again.

(*Beat.*)

Please.

(*Beat.*)

**JESSIE.** Well......I guess that would be okay.

**LINA.** What?

**JESSIE.** Yes, I think that would be fine, Mitchell. Why don't you tell her to come down at 2:30.

**MITCHELL.** *Thank you.* I'm sorry, your names are?

**JESSIE.** Jessie. Gelb.

**LINA.** ...Lina.

**MITCHELL.** Jessie and Lina.

(*Beat.*)

Thank you so much.

(*Handing* JESSIE *his card.*)

Uh—this is where I can be reached at all times. My cell, my office numbers are here. And our assistant Elaine's number—she'll be the one who drives Adrienne down.

(*Carefully.*)

If it's not too much to ask, do you think you could text me a confirmation that she came?

**JESSIE.** Okay.

**MITCHELL.** Thank you very much, ladies. Thank you. I'm sorry I have to catch a train. Thank you.

(MITCHELL *exits.*)

**LINA.** Oh my God, what's wrong with you???? You're gonna let a complete stranger come down here to your house, where you have a *newborn*???

**JESSIE.** It's one cup of coffee. How bad could it be?

**LINA.** Our organs on eBay. That's how bad. Our freshly cut organs on eBay.

**JESSIE.** Oh come on—they live right there. We drink the same bad Nassau County water.

**LINA.** Yeah but you don't know these Sands Point bitches, like I do, Jessie. I see them in the hospital, all crazy and ghoulish after their face-lifts and I'm telling you: she's gonna show up here in a *Silence of the Lambs* van.

**JESSIE.** Would you stop—I felt *sorry* for him. Didn't you feel sorry for that poor man?

**LINA.** She's gonna tell us to put the lotion in the basket.

**JESSIE.** He was scared. Didn't you see that? That was a man who was Scared. Like Nate, back in the hospital.

**LINA.** "Put the lotion in the basket!!!"

**JESSIE.** Shut up. I'm being serious now. You really don't think we should help a neighbor in need?

**LINA.** No, I don't. But you're generally a much nicer person than me, so okay. I will stand by you. But I'm not bringing Blair Witch in my house. If she has to pee, she's *going in yours.*

(*Monitor sounds; it's Max. He's up.*)

Shit. OK bye.

**JESSIE.** See you at 2:30 though, right?

**LINA.** You fucking owe me for this.

**JESSIE.** YAY! THANKS Lina!

(*LINA exits. Beat. JESSIE looks up, to Sands Point. Squints at the house. Lights.*)

### 3.

*The same day. 2:30.*

*The tiny table has a freshly delivered tray of sliced fruit, charcuterie, and cheese from a fancy place. It's not over the top, but it's way more than three women could enjoy.*

*Seated in the chair usually occupied by LINA is ADRIENNE.*

*She doesn't look like she's had a baby recently. She looks less tired, less puffy, more shiny-haired and more fit than the others. She is dressed down, and is completely engrossed in her iPad. (It is also never commented upon in this scene, and may not even be noticeable, but ADRIENNE wears a wrist brace on her right hand; the kind that stabilizes the thumb.)*

*After a few beats, JESSIE sticks her head out. She wears nicer clothes than we've seen her in—something feminine from her office wardrobe, maybe. And her hair's combed.*

*Allie is asleep in the sling across* JESSIE's *chest.*

**JESSIE.** (*Whispers.*) Adrienne.

(*Louder.*)

*Adrienne.*

**ADRIENNE.** (*Looking up.*) Yes. I'm Adrienne.

**JESSIE.** Hi! How are you? I'm Jessie. This is my house. Thanks so much for coming down.

**ADRIENNE.** I'm so terribly sorry about this.

**JESSIE.** You're sorry?? For what?

**ADRIENNE.** For being here. You and your little buddy have a whole routine—one I'm surely imposing upon—because I have a husband who's a bullheaded prick.

**JESSIE.** No! No, you're not imposing! We thought it was a great idea, to meet a new friend, from the nabe! You're not imposing at all.

(*Beat.*)

I saw your assistant outside in the car? Did you want me to invite her / in to join—

**ADRIENNE.** *No.* Thank you.

**JESSIE.** Okay. Well... ...do you think you could you make yourself at home for a second?—

(*Pointing down to the sling she is wearing.*)

She's asleep in here, and I just / have to transfer...

**ADRIENNE.** (*Like it's a snake.*) Your baby's *in there?*

**JESSIE.** Yeah. She loves being in the sling. You don't have one of these? They're fabulous.

(ADRIENNE *is back on her iPad, done with this.*)

**JESSIE.** Anyway.... I just have to transfer her to the crib, but I'll be back out in two seconds?

(*Beat.*)

Ok?

**ADRIENNE.** (*Eyes on iPad.*) Yep, fine.

**JESSIE.** It'll just take two seconds. And um... Lina will be right over; so why don't you have some of the lovely charcuterie your husband / sent over—

**ADRIENNE.** (*Eyes on iPad.*) He knows I don't eat that garbage.

**JESSIE.** Okey-doke. Be right back...

(JESSIE *exits.*

*Beat.*

*Beat.*

*Beat.*

*Beat.* ADRIENNE *on her iPad.*

*Beat.*

*Beat.*

*Beat.*

LINA *enters.* LINA *has not changed, is still wearing her dirty clothes from this morning.)*

**LINA.** Hey there. I'm Lina.

**ADRIENNE.** Adrienne.

**LINA.** How's it going?

**ADRIENNE.** Good. Fine.

(*Beat.*)

You?

**LINA.** Yeah. Good. Real good. Nice day. Baby went down easily. Boom.

(*Beat.*)

Where's Jess? Putting Allie down?

**ADRIENNE.** Yes, she said she's just transferring her to the nursery and then she'll be out.

**LINA.** Ok, cool. Excellent.

(LINA *crosses to the table, sets up her monitor.)*

Oh my shit, is all this for us?

**ADRIENNE.** Yes. Please help yourself. Mitchell has very good taste, I'm sure the cheese is artisanal.

**LINA.** Well yeah, it better be, lady. It better be fucking *highly* artisanal.

**ADRIENNE.** Excuse me?

**LINA.** I'm kidding. I'm a kidder. I honestly don't even know what artisanal means. I don't think anybody does. I think waiters just add it to their spiel so things sound nicer. "Your Chilean sea bass, madame, prepared with an artisanal blah blah artisanal artisanal."

**ADRIENNE.** It means made by artisans.

(*Beat.*

*Beat.*

*Beat.*

LINA *picks up a piece of mango with her fingers, puts it in her mouth, starts chewing it.)*

**ADRIENNE.** .....there are some little plates over there if / you'd like to have table manners...

**LINA.** Nah I'm good.

> (*Beat.*
>
> *Beat.*
>
> LINA *takes some cantaloupe now, chewing.*
>
> *Beat.*
>
> *Beat.*)

**LINA.** So, have you lived in Port Washington for very long, Adrienne?

**ADRIENNE.** No.

**LINA.** (*Mouth full.*) Me either. We moved out here when I was pregnant. About to pop.

It's one of the things we have in common. Me & Jessie. She moved out here pregnant, too.

> (*Beat.*)

Do you have a son or a daughter?

**ADRIENNE.** Daughter.

**LINA.** Oh, great. Jessie has a daughter, too. What's yours named?

**ADRIENNE.** Livia.

**LINA.** Olivia?

**ADRIENNE.** No, Livia. With an L.

**LINA.** Oh that's nice. Livia. I haven't heard that before. Very unique.

**ADRIENNE.** It's a family name.

> (*Beat.*
>
> *Beat.*)

**LINA.** Whatcha reading over there that's so interesting?

**ADRIENNE.** My e-mail.

> (*Beat.*
>
> *Beat.*
>
> *Beat.*)

**LINA.** Well I have a son named Max and I'm from South Shore. Long Beach. You been?

**ADRIENNE.** No.

**LINA.** It's loud and salty and all about the ocean. Just like me.

> (*Beat.*)

Yep. I love it there.

> (*Beat.*)

What about you, where are you from?

>   (*Snapping her finger.*)

*Adrienne.*

**ADRIENNE.** (*Suddenly very irritated.*) *What?*

**LINA.** I asked you where you're from—

**ADRIENNE.** (*Bites her.*) The city—look, could this other lady hurry up??
Can you go get her, your "bud," and tell her to get out here already? Because
I need to get back but I've got a *babysitter* outside making sure I do this
nonsense, so if we could Get The Show on the Road here, I'd really appreciate
it. I mean, what is taking so long???? She's just *moving a baby.*

>   (*Beat.*
>
>   LINA *leaves her monitor on the table and heads to the back of* JESSIE*'s
>   house.*)

**LINA.** (*Off, into the house.*) Hey Jess? How we doing in here, bud?

>   (*Seeing her.*)

O good, she / finally go down?—

**JESSIE.** (*Entering.*) Ugh sorry about that. She is giving me *a run for my money
today.*

>   (*To both of them now.*)

I had her down, but when I turned the Sleep Sheep on it was on full volume
for some reason? I must've knocked it? So we had to do the whole rocking
rocking rocking again—

>   (*To* ADRIENNE.)

Sorry! What did I miss? Did you show pictures?—

**LINA.** Adrienne is sorta eager to get going, I think.

**JESSIE.** Oh no, really?

**ADRIENNE.** (*Affirmative.*) If you could just text Mitchell that I was here.

**JESSIE.** Okay, sure. I can do that.

>   (*Beat.*)

But—*may I?* See a picture of your baby first? I'd really like to. Unless you
don't...

**ADRIENNE.** Of course I have one.

>   (ADRIENNE *opens an app on her iPad, hands it to* JESSIE.)

**JESSIE.** Oh!..... what a beauty. *What an absolutely scrumptious love muffin.* What's
her name?

**ADRIENNE.** Livia.

**JESSIE.** Olivia?

**ADRIENNE.** No, Livia. With an L. L-i-v-i-a.

**JESSIE.** Oh, well she is Just Lovely. How old?

**ADRIENNE.** Seven weeks.

**JESSIE.** *Seven weeks!* My God! How do you look so good? At seven weeks, I was still in those sexy hospital-issue underpants, squirting breast milk on everyone.

**ADRIENNE.** Well, we don't do that. She didn't latch, so we don't do that.

**JESSIE.** (*Eager to make her feel better.*) *Oh I know.* These babies, right?! They have such little minds of their own when it comes to breast-feeding.

(*To LINA, not true but trying to normalize:*)

Weren't you just telling me the other day that Max gave you a hard time at first?

**LINA.** Nope. He latched like a champ.

**JESSIE.** Well, *someone* was just telling me how much trouble they were having, Adrienne—and the fact is, it's a conspiracy, these La Leche books. They make it all sound So Easy and So Natural but breast-feeding *is hard.* Apparently when I was a baby I *refused* to nurse on the left side and my poor mother walked around engorged for months—

**ADRIENNE.** Sorry—are you done with my iPad?

**JESSIE.** ........oh can't I scroll through just a few more? Please?

**ADRIENNE.** (*Resolved.*) Of course, be my guest.

(JESSIE *goes back to scrolling, genuinely enjoying the pics.*)

**JESSIE.** Oh look at this—Lina, look at those little *stinker toes!* Remember this? When their toes were all wrinkly like old man toes?....Oh, I can't stand it, she's got herself a little hair bow?... My uterus is contracting just looking at this!

(*Scrolling.*
*Scrolling.*
*Then:*)

What's all this jewelry?

**ADRIENNE.** ....I design jewelry.

**JESSIE.** *Oh really?* Like bracelets and earrings?

**ADRIENNE.** (*This is getting tedious.*) Yep, that's it.

**JESSIE.** Wow, cool. Where do you sell your stuff, on Etsy?

**LINA.** (*To* JESSIE.) I fucking *love* Etsy.

**ADRIENNE.** (*Not mean, neutral.*) I'm in The Clay Pot in Brooklyn, Helmut Lang in Tokyo, and Fred Segal in L.A. But as of next month, I'll be nationwide in Barney's.

**JESSIE.** Oh wow so you're... what's the name of your line?

**ADRIENNE.** Adrienne Marra.

**JESSIE.** *Oh my God,* I totally know your name! I think my friend Betsey has an Adrienne Marra wedding band—do you do bridal?

**ADRIENNE.** Some.

**JESSIE.** Yes! Of course! She got it at The Clay Pot, *this makes total sense— wow!!* I feel like I should ask for your autograph / or something.

**ADRIENNE.** No. I don't—that's not something I want to do.

**JESSIE.** Okay. Sure. Wow. Good for you. That's so cool.

> (*Beat.*
> *Trying to keep the ball in the air.*)

We work, too. *Lina's* in hospital administration, at St. Francis in Manhasset. What's your title again, Leen?

**LINA.** "Entry-Level."

**JESSIE.** With room for growth! And I'm an attorney, Acquisitions mostly. At Winston & Strawn, on 45ᵗʰ and Park?

**LINA.** You *were* an attorney, you mean.

> (*To* ADRIENNE.)

Jessie's hoping to rock Mom Jeans full-time.

**ADRIENNE.** Why?

> (*They are both very surprised she has asked a question.*
> *Her "why" just sits there, with a thunk, in the air.*)

**JESSIE.** Uh... because—(and this is still in a very theoretical stage because I haven't spoken to my husband about it yet)—but I think I'd rather be home with the baby.

**ADRIENNE.** How long have you been at your firm?

**JESSIE.** ...since 2005? Which is a long time. It is. I know that. But you have to listen to your gut about things sometimes. You know?

> (ADRIENNE *is silent. It's awkward how silent she is.*)

**LINA.** (*To the rescue.*) Hey, Jess, look at this......... isn't this story-time?

> (LINA *shows her the picture on* ADRIENNE's *iPad.*)

**JESSIE.** (*Looking.*) ....Oh my god, yes, it is... there's Miss Leslie with the Bongo puppet.

> (*To* ADRIENNE.)

Does Livia go to story-time at the library?

**ADRIENNE.** I don't know. The nanny took that picture.

**LINA.** Is this / your nanny?

**JESSIE.** Your nanny's *Justine?!*

> (*Off* ADRIENNE's *slight nod.*)

*We totally know Justine!* We sit right behind her at story-time.

**LINA.** We sure do.

**JESSIE.** OH HOW WILD! I thought she was calling her *Olivia* this whole time, didn't you?

**LINA.** (*At* ADRIENNE.) Yeah, Olivia. With an O.

**JESSIE.** But she was saying *Livia.* How funny! *We already know your daughter.* And what a sweet little dreamboat she is. So curious? And alert? With those bright eyes?

And Justine is great with her. Never on her phone, just totally—

(*Suddenly* JESSIE'*s monitor flares up, full blast. Allie is screaming, wide awake. Demand demand demand.*)

Oh, *come on, Allie, honey!* Give Mommy a break!!! I'm sorry guys—I don't know what is with her today! I'll be / right back.

**ADRIENNE.** (*Wants her iPad.*) Wait, can I have my—

(JESSIE'*s gone, still holding* ADRIENNE'*s iPad.*

*Beat.*

ADRIENNE *sighs.*

*She gets up, goes to her bag, gets her phone out, and starts checking her e-mail, without even glancing at* LINA.

*Beat.*

*Beat.*

LINA *retaliates by pulling out her iPhone and playing Candy Crush on maximum volume.*

*Beat.*

*Beat.*

*Beat. Candy Crush and e-mail checking.*

*Beat.*

*Beat.*

JESSIE *returns, wearing the sling again. Allie is in there, crying.*)

**JESSIE.** Screw it, I'm just gonna bring her out!

(*To Allie.*)

Because you want to be out here, don't you girlfriend? You want to be out here where all the *action is, yes you do.* Say hi to Aunt Lina. *Hi, Aunt Lina!*

**LINA.** Hiiiiiiiii Petunia poops! Hi hi hi hi hi.

**JESSIE.** (*To Allie.*) And this is our new friend, Adrienne. Can we say hi Adrienne? *Can we say Hi, Adrienne?*

(*The baby fusses.*

*To Allie.*)

Ok ok ok ok, Hey hey hey hey hey—ok do we want Boom Dynamite?

**LINA.** *Yes!* We want Boom Dynamite.

**JESSIE.** Shut up, Lina.

> (*Back to Allie.*)

Okay, Al, here we go, here we go...

> (*Like a cheerleader:*)

Ready? OK!

> (JESSIE *&* LINA *start singing "Boom Dynamite." It's a famous cheer they both know from high school.*)

**JESSIE & LINA.** (*Softly, to Allie.*)
We're boom dynamite! [clap clap]
Boom-boom dynamite! [clap clap]
We're dynamite, we're dynamite, we're tick tick tick tick tick tick tick tick
BOOM dynamite [clap clap]
Allie is boom dynamite /
She's dynamite, she's dynamite, she's tick tick tick tick tick tick tick
/ Boom dynamite! [clap clap]

**LINA.** (*Breaking out into dance solo.*) Hold on, Wait a Minute! Put a little Booty in it!

**JESSIE.** (*Laughing.*) Shut up, Lina.

> (*Baby fusses.*)

OK OK... I wasn't stopping, I was just—ok ok we're—

> (*Baby still upset.*)

Ok, we don't want to be Boom Dynamite? Okay...
Should we nurse maybe? Okay, you got it, kid. Yes Get that tit out, Mom. Ok you *got* it, here we go... here we go... you nurse.

> (JESSIE *gets her boob out and gets the baby on her boob—all inside the sling. This is something she is well-practiced at doing.*
>
> *Allison falls immediately, crazily silent.*)

**JESSIE.** (*Whispers.*) Sorry. She's been *so* fussy today. I think she might be teething. I keep feeling little gummy teeth clamping down on my nipple—

**LINA.** Yeah, Max has been gnawing on me like I'm a turkey leg.

**JESSIE.** (*Noticing.*) Adrienne? Where are / you going...?

**ADRIENNE.** (*As she exits.*) For *fucks* sake.

> (*She's gone.*
> *Beat.*)

**JESSIE.** What just happened? What was that?

**LINA.** .....I don't know *what* that was.

**JESSIE.** Do you think I offended her? By breast-feeding?

**LINA.** I think *who cares.* I've dropped farts more pleasant than that woman.

**JESSIE.** I know, the poor thing. I felt so badly for her, didn't you? She was obviously so uncomfortable with us.

(*Adjusting her naked boob.*)

I don't know why.

(*True empathy.*)

And did you see how defensive she got when I asked if she had a picture of Livia? Something must be *really wrong there.*

**LINA.** Hey can I take this gouda home for John?

**JESSIE.** *Lina.*

**LINA.** What?

**JESSIE.** I am *concerned* about that sad woman. You're talking about cheese.

**LINA.** Well, I'm sorry but I'm *not* very concerned about her, Jess. She's got a driver, a housekeeper, an assistant, and a *white* live-in nanny. She's gonna be Just Fine.

**JESSIE.** What does having a white nanny have to do with anything?

**LINA.** It's a thing. Having a white nanny.

**JESSIE.** No it's not—*that's not a thing.*

**LINA.** It's absolutely a thing. What do you think it means when the service says the nanny (who's from Connecticut) has a master's degree in childhood education? It means *white.* Justine's so white she's not even salaried—*she's hourly.* $25 an hour.

**JESSIE.** (*Doubtful.*) How do you know that?

**LINA.** We talk, me & Justine. I told her about a Groupon for keratin treatments at Zing and she talks to me now. And I'll tell you something else, too:

(*Pointing up to ADRIENNE's house.*)

She doesn't think much of Posh Spice up there.

**JESSIE.** Really? What'd she say?

**LINA.** She didn't *say* anything ...she just gave me the eyebrows. You know, that look when you raise your eyebrows while cocking your head to the side, like this?

(*Demonstrating.*)

It's the universal symbol for: *bitch be cray.*

**JESSIE.** Oh come on. You're just being mean now.

**LINA.** Fine. You're not trying to hear me, fine. But I'm telling you, we don't want Home Girl in our band.

(*Back to cheese.*)

Now can I take the gouda or not?

> (*Beat.*)

Jessie.

**JESSIE.** *Yes, take the goddamn cheese.*

**LINA.** *Whoa.* Look who's getting a mouth on her! Getting a lil' mouthy all of a sudden.

I'm going to have to take the whole tray now. Because someone's being Insolent.

> (*Beat.*)

...no? Not even a giggle? Fine—I'm out.

> (*JESSIE's distracted and serious, eyes locked on that house in Sands Point. Lights.*)

## 4.

> *Dim lights up on the yard. Later that day. Evening. Maybe 8:45.*
>
> *The sound of a car parking, beep beep locking of a Cayenne door.*
>
> MITCHELL *enters around the side of the house, looking around, a tad creepily, his phone in hand. He lingers, unsure what to do. He sends a text. Then he disappears around the side of the house.*
>
> Beat.
>
> *After a moment,* JESSIE *enters.*

**JESSIE.** (*Whispers.*) Mitchell?

**MITCHELL.** (*Entering.*) Hi. I'm sorry—I didn't know if I should ring the bell or go to the / back door—

**JESSIE.** (*Warmly.*) No, no, no, it's fine. She's awake. She's doing bath-time with Nate.

**MITCHELL.** Oh no, I interrupted bath-time? What an intrusion. I'm so sorry, / forgive me.

**JESSIE.** Don't be silly. It's good for them to have a little daddy-daughter time.

> (*Turning.*)

Let me just grab it for you, I put it by the front door.

**MITCHELL.** Great, thank you.

> (*Beat.*)

**JESSIE.** Unless..... I'm sorry, would you like to come in? Of course you're welcome to—

**MITCHELL.** *No.* No, no, no. I have imposed on you quite enough for one 24-hour period. I'm fine here.

**JESSIE.** You sure?

**MITCHELL.** Absolutely. Thank you, though. Really.

**JESSIE.** Okay. Be right back.

> (JESSIE *exits.*
>
> *Alone,* MITCHELL *looks around the yard, maybe takes one of those wrought-iron seats.*
>
> *His eyes eventually land on his house. He is expecting to admire it, but instead he's struck by how absolutely dark and cold it looks. He realizes he is dreading going there.*)

**JESSIE.** Here we go. One iPad.

> (*Returning.*)

I tried to protect it from the baby, but I'm afraid there might be a little drool on there.

**MITCHELL.** Occupational hazard.

**JESSIE.** Exactly, yeah.

> (*He takes it from her, and they are physically very close.*)

**MITCHELL.** Thank you.

**JESSIE.** You're very welcome.

> (*Another awkward beat.*)

**MITCHELL.** And... I want to say to you... if I may...

> (*Then:*)

That you should not take my wife personally. She's not herself these days. I'm sure she was a terrible guest.

**JESSIE.** *No,* she was lovely.

**MITCHELL.** (*No she wasn't:*) Elaine said she stomped back to the car like an irate toddler after 8 minutes.

**JESSIE.** Well... she wasn't *super chatty,* no. But who is, at seven weeks? Seven weeks is still a very delicate time for a new mom, you know. I was a total mess at seven weeks.

**MITCHELL.** ....I find that hard to believe.

**JESSIE.** *I was.* Absolutely. You can ask Nate—he almost flew my Mom in from Evanston to deal with me, 911. I kept re-washing baby bottles, just red rum red rum. And I refused to drive? Like, at all. I would start the ignition and have a panic attack. And then stay up all night crying, watching *Hoarders* on TLC.

**MITCHELL.** Why?

**JESSIE.** (*Laughs.*) Why was I watching *Hoarders?* It's actually very addicting.

**MITCHELL.** No, why were you crying?

**JESSIE.** Oh, you know. Normal stuff. Being overwhelmed. Being lonely. Having sore nipples. Standard Baby Blues.

**MITCHELL.** Ah.

(*Shy.*)

Well.....I think what Adrienne is going through is maybe.... less standard.

(*Beat.*

*Beat.*

*Beat.*)

**JESSIE.** Do you think... I mean, it's none of my business... but do you think breast-feeding might have something to do with it? She mentioned that Livia refused to latch?

**MITCHELL.** That's not the problem. And that's not the truth, either. Livia didn't *refuse* the breast, it wasn't offered to her. Adrienne never even tried.

(*Beat.*)

**JESSIE.** You know what, Mitchell? I'm sorry. This is really not my business, and I / should—

**MITCHELL.** She's not *connected* to her. That's the problem.

**JESSIE.** What do you mean "not connected"?

**MITCHELL.** She doesn't play with her. Or hold her.

**JESSIE.** (*Disbelief.*) Of course she holds her.

**MITCHELL.** No.

**JESSIE.** Not at all?

**MITCHELL.** Not at all.

(*Beat.*)

**JESSIE.** How long's this been going on?

(*Carefully.*)

I mean, is she like this every day? Or does it come and go?

**MITCHELL.** I have not seen her *touch* our daughter in five in a half weeks.

**JESSIE.** Oh.

(*Beat.*)

God.

**MITCHELL.** Yeah.

(*Beat.*

*Beat.*

*Beat.*)

The hardest thing is that I really can't gauge how much of this has to do with her work and how much doesn't. Or maybe it was moving out here? I don't know. It's been a big change. (But we built her a studio in the basement?—I thought she'd be thrilled.) And the doctor said it could certainly be all the IVF we did—failed IVF can take a psychological toll on the mother. But I don't think that's what it is—Adrienne was *happy* when she was pregnant. She threw up *every day*, and still she was in good humor. We were just so grateful to finally be pregnant. And she designed the nursery in the new house, in this beautiful giraffe theme? But I don't think she's been in that room since. Like an alien stole my wife.

And I'm trying to be understanding because she's under a lot of professional pressure right now, I know that. She landed a big account at work just before we had Livia—which should be exciting but the whole thing has just made her manic. And she doesn't *need* to be manic; she has a staff in Brooklyn who can handle everything while she's on leave, she's *supposed to be on leave*. But she's locking herself in her studio for days at a time, working on some ear cuff a celebrity wants made for red carpet season or some custom ring for some PR person's wedding. (She's a jewelry designer, that's what she does.) And I keep saying *let your team handle this, Adrienne, that's what they're for. You have a seven-week-old and you are missing her, \*you wanted her and you're missing her\**—and she just slams her studio door and says that if I loved her I'd understand. And maybe that's true? I don't know, I have nothing to compare any of this to. But she forgets to come upstairs and she forgets to eat and she forgets to sleep and she forgets to take Livie to *the one fucking Mommy & Me class* she's supposed to take her to.....I think she forgets we had Livie.

>                (*Beat.*)

**JESSIE.** I'm so sorry, Mitchell. I can't imagine.

**MITCHELL.** I know you can't. *You* spend hours kissing your baby's nose. Whole afternoons.

I've seen you do it.

>                (*Beat.*
>                *Beat.*
>                *Beat.*)

**JESSIE.** Look, why don't you come in. I'll introduce you to Nate and he can make you a drink.

**MITCHELL.** (*Too firm.*) I don't drink.

**JESSIE.** Okay, well we have / club soda and—

**MITCHELL.** I only drank socially before but I quit completely when she was born. My mom was a horrible alcoholic and I didn't want Livia to ever associate that sound with me.

**JESSIE.** Oh. / Okay.

**MITCHELL.** Of ice hitting the glass. When she could've been taking care of me, or engaging me, or holding me. Instead there was *ice*, and I didn't....

*(Getting upset.)*

I didn't want my daughter to know that kind of cruelty was possible.

> *(Beat. There's an action here from* MITCHELL, *and it's strange. Like saying this out loud about his mother has released something in him, and he forgets where he is. As if he's just ran a marathon and is catching his breath.*
>
> *Unsure what to do,* JESSIE *crouches next to him, patiently.)*

**MITCHELL.** Sorry. I don't know what's wrong with me. You're a total stranger and I'm... your crazy neighbor. Oh God. I'm someone's crazy neighbor.

**JESSIE.** *(Laughs.)* It's fine; you're fine... you just.... take a second, ok? Take a breath for / a second.

**MITCHELL.** Okay.

> *(Beat.*
>
> *Beat.*
>
> *Beat.)*

I'm sorry.

**JESSIE.** Stop. Apologizing.

> (MITCHELL *breathes.* JESSIE *waits until it feels okay to ask:)*

Let me ask you something. Are you concerned about the baby's well-being? When you're not home, I mean. Her safety.

**MITCHELL.** Absolutely not. We have a live-in nanny and a weekend nanny. They're always at her side. Both have masters degrees in early childhood education.

**JESSIE.** Okay, good. And she's in therapy? Your wife?

**MITCHELL.** Yes. She goes once a week, in the city, and we go once a week, for couples therapy. We just started doing that in January.

**JESSIE.** Then I think that's kinda all you can do. Postpartum takes time and patience.

**MITCHELL.** *(Respects her opinion.)* Is that what you think this is? Postpartum?

**JESSIE.** Sounds like it, yes. Detachment, lack of interest... those are symptoms they flag, I think.

> *(Beat.* MITCHELL *processes this, looking so underwater.)*

But it does lift. I mean, *it can lift.* I read a lot about postpartum, back before I met Lina, and you're doing *all* the right things.

**MITCHELL.** I am?

**JESSIE.** Encouraging her to get out with other moms, helping her build a community? Getting her into treatment and then *going* to treatment with her? Yes.

> *(Then:)*

I'd *love* to see the look on Nate's face if I ever asked him to go to therapy with me.

> (*This is a slight over-reveal and* JESSIE *knows it immediately. The electricity changes just a touch.*)

Anyway.

> (*Beat.*)

What can I do? Want me to call her and invite her to coffee again?

**MITCHELL.** You would do that?

**JESSIE.** Of course. What are crazy neighbors for.

**MITCHELL.** Uh... restraining orders, usually. Or big electric fences.

> (JESSIE *laughs genuinely.*
>
> *Beat.*)

**JESSIE.** Text me her number and I'll call in the morning.

> (*Beat.*)

I should get back, though. For *Pat the Bunny.*

**MITCHELL.** Of course, yes, sorry. I'm late for *Guess How Much I Love You* myself.

> (*He lingers a moment—perhaps wanting to hug her. He elects not to.*)

Good night, Jessie.

**JESSIE.** You too.

> (*Lights.*)


## 5.


> *Lights up, the following Monday. 10:30 a.m. The sun is out a little.*
>
> LINA *enters, looking the most put together we've seen her. She wears a turtleneck under crisp, blue hospital scrubs, and the tell-tale white Dansko nurse shoes, common in hospitals. She has replaced her big hoops with studs. Her makeup is subdued; her hair is combed back in a pony.*
>
> *She takes her seat at the table, puts her monitor down.*
>
> JESSIE *enters with her monitor.*

**JESSIE.** *Look at you!* Wow wow wow wow WOW.

**LINA.** I figured I should get ready now, while he's sleeping.

> (*Her uniform:*)

It's awful, isn't it?

**JESSIE.** No! *You look positively awesome.*

**LINA.** I look like Kathy Bates in *Misery.*

(JESSIE *laughs.*)

*I do.* She wears this same doinky scrub when she clubs his feet with the mallet.

And look at this—

(*Re: her fingernails.*)

"Sheerest Nude." My girl who does my nails at Eve Nails didn't even charge me. She just wept silently in the corner.

**JESSIE.** Well you do, though, you really look terrific. I would feel like I were in *very good hands* if you were checking me in.

**LINA.** Yeah yeah yeah thank you.

(*Getting a whiff of coffee.*)

Whoa. What's this? It smells like French Vanilla.

**JESSIE.** It is French Vanilla.

**LINA.** But you *hate* French Vanilla.

**JESSIE.** But you love it, and I thought today... you deserved a special treat.

**LINA.** (*Smelling again.*) ..............is this from Dunkin?

**JESSIE.** It is.

**LINA.** *You went to Dunkin for me?*

**JESSIE.** (*Proud.*) I did.

**LINA.** You put the baby in the carseat, drove over there, took the baby out of the carseat, dealt with that fucking janky parking meter, and schlepped the baby into Dunkin for me?

**JESSIE.** I did.

**LINA.** (*Getting emotional.*) Oh come on......... I'm trying *not* to cry today.

**JESSIE.** Well, what can I say? You're worth it.

(*Beat.*)

Plus, I needed something to do with myself this morning. I woke up emotional, too. It's *insane*, Lina. How much I am going to / miss you—

**LINA.** Nope. I can't... we can't.

(*Beat.*)

**JESSIE.** (*Bright.*) So is Yolanda on her way home?

**LINA.** Yeah, she'll be here at 11.

**JESSIE.** Okay. *Good,* right?

**LINA.** Yeah. That way when Max wakes up, she'll be here, and we'll all have lunch together and then I'll go. So the transition will be smooth for him.

**JESSIE.** *Good.* That sounds really good.

**LINA.** Yeah. I think I'm setting her up to win. I mean, I pumped enough milk to take over Häagen-Dazs, and I put all the numbers on the fridge.

Local PD, Local Fire, hospital, Pediatrician, Poison Control, *your cell.* Thanks again for that.

**JESSIE.** No problem.

**LINA.** And John had "the talk" with her last night, too, so I think we're square on all that.

**JESSIE.** *He did?* Wow. What'd he say?

**LINA.** I guess he just said it like real matter-of-factly. Like oh hey Mom, one other thing... you know you can't drink when you're in charge of Max, right?

**JESSIE.** *Wow.*

**LINA.** Yeah.

**JESSIE.** How'd she take it?

**LINA.** Uh. I guess she got super weird and silent and *walked* to church and didn't come home until we were in bed.

**JESSIE.** Oh boy.

**LINA.** But then this morning she pulled John aside and told him *she heard him,* and she will do as he asked, so to please not worry about that being an issue.

**JESSIE.** See? That's great! This is all going to be fine.

**LINA.** ....yeah.

**JESSIE.** It's going to be *great,* Lina. I have a very good feeling about all of this for you. I really do.

**LINA.** (*Wobbly.*) ......yeah, it's gonna be fine.

(LINA *is suddenly looking very sad.*)

**JESSIE.** (*Trying to stay peppy.*) And so... what time do you get back tonight?

**LINA.** Ten-thirty? So.....

(*Voice cracking.*)

John will put him down, which is fine. He's done it a few times before.

**JESSIE.** (*Cheery.*) And you're gonna *see your work friends again!* You must be looking forward to that!!

**LINA.** (*Trying not to cry.*) Yeah—Kim-Ly? My best friend at work? She texted me a picture of my desk, which is all covered with balloons and shit... and I guess they're throwing me a welcome back party? Which she wasn't supposed to tell me...

(*Crying.*)

*But she did.*

**JESSIE.** Oh, Lina.

(*They clasp hands. Squeeze.*)

It's going to go by *so quickly* today. You'll see.

**LINA.** I know.

**JESSIE.** You'll be back home before you know it. And it's going to get easier every day. You just have to get into a new rhythm.

**LINA.** ...yeah.

**JESSIE.** You can do this. I know *you can do this*.

**LINA.** Yeah. *I can.* I can.

> (*Beat.*
> *Shaking it off, pulling herself together.*)

Okay—enough of this! What's going on with you? Distract me.

**JESSIE.** What's going on with me since yesterday?

> (*Thinking, then:*)

Not much.

**LINA.** No?

**JESSIE.** Nope.

> (*Beat.*)

I mean, I finally watched *Silver Linings Playbook?* It's free on HBO now.

**LINA.** (*Excited.*) It is???

**JESSIE.** Yeah and that other one that came out two years ago... the uh... oh god, my brain... based on that astronaut person.

> (*Off* LINA's *blank expression.*)

Anyway Nate and I are watching that one tonight. And I have a pot roast in the slowcooker.

**LINA.** So things are about to get Turnt is what you're saying.

**JESSIE.** Yeah. Super "Turnt."

> (*Beat.*)

Do you even remember evenings anymore? Pre-baby?

**LINA.** What, like date night?

**JESSIE.** Yeah. We were married for six years before we had the baby— that's... six times 365 evenings a year. What did we do? I guess we went out a lot. Went to Inoteca, shared a bottle of malbec?

> (*Dark.*)

God, how embarrassing. *We just drank.*

**LINA.** *Embarrassing* is being banned from Spanky's in Long Beach. You're fine.

**JESSIE.** And then we'd go home and sleep for 10 hours, and wake up and read the entire *New York Times* and make waffles.

> (*More to herself than* LINA.)

I used to collect *lip-gloss*.

I found them in a tin in the back of a drawer yesterday and I felt like an anthropologist, unearthing a relic from another time, you know? *How did I ever have time to think about lip-gloss?* Why did I ever care about anything that dumb?

(*Quite dark.*)

*What a joke I was.*

(*Beat.*)

**LINA.** Hey what's up with you?

(*Beat.*)

You wigging out on me?

**JESSIE.** No.

**LINA.** Yeah you are. You're all *Girl Interrupted* about lip-gloss. What's going on?

**JESSIE.** Nothing.

**LINA.** Is it that I'm going back to work?

**JESSIE.** No. I mean, yes. But I knew it was coming.

**LINA.** Is it Nate?

**JESSIE.** *No.* I've just been having trouble sleeping.

**LINA.** What's going on with Nate?

**JESSIE.** It's not Nate. It's her, okay? That woman. I lie awake for hours at night just.... thinking about her.

(*Pointing.*)

About Adrienne.

**LINA.** The See You Next Tuesday?

**JESSIE.** She wasn't *that bad*, Lina.

**LINA.** Yes she was. Why are you thinking about her?

**JESSIE.** I don't know. Because she's right up there, I guess.

(*Beat.*)

She's up there, and I'm down here, and there's just a skylight between us at night—that skylight over my bed—and *I can feel her looking at me,* I think.

**LINA.** Okay, now you just sound Loco.

**JESSIE.** And I keep thinking maybe she actually *is* me. Or I'm her. We're connected somehow. And then I think....maybe I imagined her completely.

**LINA.** *Yo. Jessie.* Come back to me, crazy.

(*Beat.*)

She was real. She was here. She was rude as shit. And you called her—like you told that dude you would. You called and called last week and she didn't call your ass back.

(*Tough love.*)

And instead of bullshitting me about an imaginary problem, *why don't you get real with me and tell me what's going on with Nate.*

**JESSIE.** ....nothing is.

**LINA.** No?

(*Beat.*)

No big conversations? Happening?

(*Beat.*)

Now that it's the 1st of the month?

**JESSIE.** *Ugh.* Come on, Lina / give me a break—

**LINA.** Hey! I'm just doing what you told me to do. You *told me* to give you shit on the 1st if you hadn't done it by the 1st. And it's the 1st. *Why haven't you told your husband you're not going back to work?*

**JESSIE.** Because I suck. Ok?

(*Fail.*)

I just... fucking suck.

(*Beat.*)

**LINA.** You don't suck, you're just chickening out. And I can't figure out why. I mean he's not perfect—no one is—but Nate *seems to really love and support you.* Doesn't he?

(*No answer.*)

Doesn't he insist you go get a massage every Sunday?

(JESSIE *nods.*)

Didn't he shut down your Mother-in-Law drop-ins with a balls-out e-mail that, truly, he should copyright?

(JESSIE *nods.*)

He has your back and you know it. Rip the Band-Aid.

(JESSIE *nods. She knows.*)

Do you want to practice? Just rolling the words around your tongue?

**JESSIE.** (*Yes.*) ....No. That's ridiculous.

**LINA.** (*Looking at her watch.*) Come on, I've got five minutes. Let's do this.

**JESSIE.** I don't / want to.

**LINA.** (*Vaguely British accent.*) "Yes, Jessie? You said you wanted to speak to me about something? What is it?"

**JESSIE.** Why are you British?

**LINA.** I don't know, I think I was doing Liam Neeson.

**JESSIE.** (*Laughing.*) Yeah, you were. From *Taken.*

**LINA.** *I was totally doing Taken.* "What I have is a very particular set of skills."

*(Getting serious.)*

Ok hang on—I can do Nate. I've met him once, but I can do him, hold on...

*(As Nate.)*

"Yes, Jessie? You said you wanted to talk to me. What's up?"

**JESSIE.** *Wow.*

**LINA.** Thank you.

*(Back in character.)*

"Well? What's going on? Come on, tell me."

*(Beat.)*

"Tell me right now or I'll go wash all your maternity bras in scalding hot water and dry them on high again."

**JESSIE.** Nate. I've been thinking...

*(Beat.)*

This has been such an incredible experience, being home with Allie these last 15 weeks and I have been kicking around the idea that....

*(Beat.)*

Maybe I don't go back to work.

**LINA.** *(As Nate.)* Why wouldn't you go back to work?

**JESSIE.** Because I want to raise Allie myself. I want to be a stay-at-home mother and I've looked at our financial situation, and I think we can do it, and.

*(Beat.)*

This is what I want.

**LINA.** What about your job? You're up for partner this year.

**JESSIE.** ....Well... I don't want to be partner. I want to stay home with Allie.

**LINA.** What about North Shore Day? My parents paid in full already.

**JESSIE.** Well, I spoke to the director of the program, and she is willing to reimburse your parents the full amount (minus deposit) because the wait list is so long.

**LINA.** YOU SPOKE TO THE DAYCARE WITHOUT TALKING TO ME?

**JESSIE.** (He wouldn't yell; he'd just be sullen and judgy.)

**LINA.** *(Sullen and judgy.)* You spoke to daycare without speaking to me?

**JESSIE.** *You let your parents \*pay for daycare\* without speaking to me, Nate.*

**LINA.** You know how hard it is to get into North Shore Day?! It's the best.

**JESSIE.** And I don't like it. *And I'm not taking her there.* And I've crunched the numbers, and we *can* live on your salary. We might need to live a little leaner and supplement with our savings, but that's what *savings are for.*

*(Beat. LINA doesn't have a comeback. Sounds good.)*

**JESSIE.** (Tell me our savings are going towards a house in Sands Point. That's what we decided.)

**LINA.** But the house in Sands Point. That's what we decided our savings / were going—

**JESSIE.** No, actually, that's what *you* decided. I *don't* want Sands Point. I don't want Sands Point, and I don't want Plandome Road, and I don't want Montauk, and I don't want to put Allie in the arms of a stranger all day *so we can afford* all those things I don't want.
*What I want* is to stay in this shitty duplex.

(*Serious now.*)

I want our daughter to be held, fed, loved, burped, and comforted *by her mother.* I want to know if she poops today and what the consistency was, and I want to know what color balloons make her smile at Stop n' Shop, and I want to take her to the park and watch her watch the tide come in and I don't care if we have to eat fucking Ramen to make that happen, that is what is going to happen, because we almost lost her and that "almost" changed everything for me and *I'm not really asking you,* Nate: I'm telling you. *I am not going back to work.*

(*Beat.*)

**LINA.** (*Upset.*) Yeah, really good, Jess. I uh............ I think you got it, girl.

(JESSIE *suddenly realizes:*)

**JESSIE.** Oh God. *Lina.* I'm so sorry.

(*Ashamed.*)

God what was I thinking?? On the day you're going / back to work? Saying all this—

**LINA.** It's okay.

**JESSIE.** No it's not. / *I'm so sorry.*

**LINA.** I mean it. It's okay.

(*Beat.*)

You're gonna do great, Jess. The Ramen stuff? That's good shit. Keep the Ramen.

**JESSIE.** Sorry.

**LINA.** You got this. You're gonna do really good.

**JESSIE.** Okay. Thanks.

(*Beat.*

LINA *looks at her watch. She has to go.*)

**LINA.** ....guess what.

**JESSIE.** *No.* No no no no no.

(*Giving her a big bear hug.*)

Okay, I'm going to text you all day, today, okay? Emojis. Bitmojis. XO's. All day.

**LINA.** Not bitmojis.

**JESSIE.** And I want you to call me if you need *anything.* Breast pump stuff, chocolate, food, change of clothes. I am at your beck and call, okay?

**LINA.** Okay.

(*Pulling away.*)

I'm fucking bad at this. Bye.

(LINA *grabs her monitor and exits quickly.*)

**JESSIE.** Bye, Lina!

(*Beat.*

*Shouting after her.*)

IS IT TOO SOON TO TEXT YOU?

(*We hear* LINA's *laughter, far away. Then it dies out.*

*She's gone.*

*Beat.*

JESSIE, *alone in the yard for the first time.*

*She has a bursting desire to sob, but doesn't.*

*She checks her monitor.*

*She sips her coffee, remembers she hates French Vanilla.*

*She thinks about texting Nate. Doesn't.*

*She feels lonely.*

*This is all we watch for a solid minute.* JESSIE *alone.*

*Finally, she decides she'll just to go back inside. She gets up, gets the mugs and monitor, and heads in.*

*Halfway to her house, <u>an object whizzes by her head and SPLATS a few feet ahead of her.</u>*

*She turns to see* ADRIENNE *coming out of the bushes.*)

**JESSIE.** .....Adrienne?

(ADRIENNE *takes a few steps forward and chucks <u>another egg</u> at* JESSIE's *house. It splats on the patio door, offstage.*)

..........what are / you doing?

**ADRIENNE.** I'm egging your house.

**JESSIE.** ....you're what?

**ADRIENNE.** I'm throwing eggs at your house.

**JESSIE.** Why are you throwing /eggs at my—

**ADRIENNE.** *Did you tell my husband I have postpartum depression?*

(*Beat.*)

**JESSIE.** Uh.

(*Beat.*)

I don't... believe I said / that exactly....

**ADRIENNE.** That's what he said in therapy just now—*and I don't have post-partum depression.*

Not that that's your business, but I don't. I have a psychiatrist who has *not* stamped my file with postpartum. In fact, there aren't any stamps on my file. Of any kind. I don't even need to take a *goddamn multi-vitamin. Don't you know what depression looks like?* My roommate at Brown had depression. She binge-ate pizzas and cut herself. This isn't depression, you moron. / *This isn't depression.*

**JESSIE.** Okay. I—

**ADRIENNE.** This is rage. What I have *is rage.* I am Enraged.

It's 2017, and I make as much money as my husband and I work as hard as my husband and I'm as ambitious as my husband and I daresay those are the very traits he found so *goddamn irresistible* about me that he proposed on our third date. And we have spent fourteen years working side by side, our heads in our laptops side by side, working from morning to dusk side by side.... so I'm having *a little bit of trouble understanding why*—in the name of God—there's something *wrong with me* that I don't suddenly want to close that laptop. That I don't want to sit around here in sweatpants singing Moosha Boom or whatever the fuck, staring at some baby monitor like it's a lava lamp. *Why does that mean there's something wrong with me?* You diagnosed me to my husband with the Big-Term terms, why don't you tell me. With your little Baby Sling and your little dainty Pearl Necklace and your goddamn Pinterest Page. (Yes, I looked you up. I saw your Pinterest Page with its goddamn doilie pinecone craft shits on there.) *My husband thinks you are God's Gift to Maternity.* He watches you out that telescope like some stalker and then complains to our therapist that *I've ruined his life* by not being more like you. That I'm some Cruel Woman just like his mother, because I'm not doing back-flips to wipe baby ass. *Like some alien has taken over his wife's body.* And I just want to punch him in the face because guess what, Mitchell, *an alien did take over my body.* I had to have four fucking IVF miscarriages to get this baby. And if that wasn't enough, when she finally did show up, the goddamn C-section caused the cartilage in my wrist to develop some rare fucking tendon thing called De Quervain's syndrome—also known as "Mommy Thumb"—so now I'm in my studio like a *gimp*, unable to hold my flame straight, and I *can't* hold her. I'm sure he didn't tell you that, did he. I can't hold her. I cannot physically bend my thumb more than 45 degrees. But that doesn't mean I don't touch her. *Of course I touch her.* I take breaks and come up and sing to her, and talk to her, and show her what mommy's working on but I don't do that when Mitchell's home because *Mitchell's home*. And the Old Mitchell *would've understood that*, by the way. The Old Mitchell would've understood that I am trying to manage *the single most demanding professional time* of my life. It's Barney's. If this was Mitchell? If this was Mitchell's deal he was closing, no one would look twice at this. They'd just say—*Oh, he's working, what a big time this is for him, good thing there's an excellent nanny, good thing he'll have that baby's whole life to get to know her*. But because it's me, because I dared to go back to my studio, I'm the Antichrist. *Why are you calling me?* Stop calling me. Stop talking to my husband about me. Stop looking at me—*I can feel you looking at me from down here*. Stop sitting with my nanny at story-time. Stop touching my kid. Stop inviting me to things. Stop nursing your baby out here with your tits out in the open like you're a cow at pasture. *Stop doing what you're doing, lady, because you're making it incredibly hard for women like me to do what we need to do and.... I fucking give up, on women like you.*

> (*In real agony.*)

And now my wrist hurts.

> (ADRIENNE *turns and exits, leaving* JESSIE *standing there, breathing. Lights.*)

6.

> *Lights up on the yard. It's really late. Like 1 or 2 in the morning. The yard is very dark.*
>
> LINA *enters. She is still wearing the scrubs we saw her in earlier today, but she looks like she's been crying—mascara blurry. She paces a little, waiting.*
>
> *After a moment,* JESSIE *enters, some urgency to her step. She wears pajamas and a bathrobe and carries a fireplace lighter, which she hands to* LINA *immediately—*

**JESSIE.** Here.

**LINA.** (*Taking it.*) Thanks.

> (LINA *lights the cigarette in her hand.*
> *She takes a couple of puffs before she can talk.* JESSIE *waits, silently.*
> *Beat.*
> *Beat.*)

**LINA.** There's not a single lighter in that whole fucking house.

**JESSIE.** That's okay. You can keep that one.

(*Beat.*

LINA*'s hands are shaking, she's so upset. She smokes.*)

**JESSIE.** Is Max sleeping?

**LINA.** Yeah.

**JESSIE.** And John is... doing what?

**LINA.** I don't know. Packing.

**JESSIE.** For where? Where are you gonna go?

**LINA.** I don't know, a hotel. I just can't be in that house with her right now. He's gonna text me after the car is packed and Max is in the car seat.

(*Beat.*)

**JESSIE.** Do you... do you want me to go help John pack? / I can.

**LINA.** No, that would be weird.

**JESSIE.** *Don't go to a hotel, Lina*—come to my house. I'll give you our room and the whole upstairs. We'll go down / in the den.

**LINA.** I told you, that's so sweet of you, but your house is too close. I'll get up in the middle of the night and get your chainsaw out of the shed and *go fucking murder her.*

**JESSIE.** Okay.

(*Beat.*)

Is John furious?

**LINA.** I don't know, I'm so mad at John, I wasn't listening to—*I can't believe he didn't call me.* You come home and find a drunk woman holding your screaming child, *you don't call his mother??*

**JESSIE.** How drunk was she? I mean, is there any way he didn't notice? *I didn't hear anything.*

**LINA.** Of course he noticed. *She was drunk.* Fucking drunk.

And she only gave Max *one* bottle today—one bottle in eight hours—so he...

(*Upset.*)

*He was starving,* you know? He nursed for 45 minutes straight when I got home, and the whole time he kept opening his eyes, checking if I'd disappeared and left him in hell again.

**JESSIE.** Oh, Lina.

(*Carefully.*)

It's not your fault, what happened.

**LINA.** (*Very upset.*) *It doesn't matter*—he can't un-learn what he just learned, you know? He *knows that it's possible now.* For him to need me. For him to be alone in hell, and really need me, and have me not come. He cried out for me, and I didn't come.

(JESSIE *holds her.*)

Fuck. *What am I going to do?* I have work tomorrow. John has work tomorrow—

**JESSIE.** Drop Max off here! *I'll watch him.* I can watch him this whole week, this whole / month even—

**LINA.** You already have a baby.

**JESSIE.** Exactly! What's another? I'd be *happy* to watch him.

**LINA.** (*True.*) You can't do that for me and you know it. God. That look on his face.

**JESSIE.** *Oh Lina.* I'm *so* sorry.

(LINA *cries into* JESSIE*'s arms, and she holds her.*
*Lights.*)

## 7.

*Some time later. Maybe a week later. It's sunny. The stage should brighten; time should slow down a little.*

*Lights up on* MITCHELL, *sitting in the seat usually occupied by* LINA. *He wears a tee-shirt, jeans, and sneakers. He looks more relaxed than we've seen him look. His hair is without product.*

*Next to* MITCHELL *is a top-of-the-line infant stroller, in which Livia sleeps. A muslin baby blanket is over top.*

JESSIE *enters, with two mugs of coffee and her monitor.*

**MITCHELL.** She's down *already?*

**JESSIE.** Yep.

**MITCHELL.** You weren't gone ten minutes!

**JESSIE.** Well, it used to take me ten *hours,* believe me. I've just hit the Malcolm Gladwell expert level. Once you've done something 10,000 times?

**MITCHELL.** Ha. Yes.

**JESSIE.** (*Handing him coffee.*) Here. I did have cream.

**MITCHELL.** (*Taking the coffee.*) Oh, terrific. Thank you.

(JESSIE *sits. Sets up her monitor.*
*Beat.*)

So, story-time.

**JESSIE.** Yeah, what did you think?

**MITCHELL.** I thought it was *superb.* What an amazing public service the library is providing Port. They could easily charge for that.

**JESSIE.** That's why it's so well-attended.

**MITCHELL.** And she's *outstanding.* That librarian. Miss?

**JESSIE.** Leslie.

**MITCHELL.** *Leslie,* yes. Those kids were *glued* to her. I thought they were going to have a collective stroke when she got Bongo out.

**JESSIE.** Oh, I know, they *love* that puppet.

(*Beat.*)

Allie can't get enough of him.

(*They sip their coffee.*)

**MITCHELL.** Hey—did you and Lina ever do the walk back from the library? Along Shore Road? It's *beautiful.* And it knocked Livie out.

**JESSIE.** No, we always wanted to but it was never nice enough. This is the first day since October it's been over 65.

**MITCHELL.** *Is it that warm?* I have a hat and gloves on her in there—

(*Panicked.*)

Do you think she looks hot?

**JESSIE.** (*Peeking under the blanket.*) ...No.

**MITCHELL.** I don't know, I think her cheeks are a little flushed. I'm going in.

**JESSIE.** (*Warmly.*) You sure? That's a *very* risky move.

**MITCHELL.** Watch.

(MITCHELL *reaches in, returns with a baby hat. No tears.*)

**MITCHELL.** Pure skill. That's what they call *pure skill.*

**JESSIE.** Bravo.

(*A smile between them.*)

**MITCHELL.** *Anyway,* you guys should do it with me next time. The walk home from the library. You'd love it, all that fresh air.

(*An afterthought.*)

Where *is* Lina today, anyway? Is Max sick?

(*Beat.*)

**JESSIE.** No, he's not sick.

(*Hard to say.*)

Lina's in Long Beach now.

**MITCHELL.** She *moved?*

**JESSIE.** She didn't *move* move. She's staying with her sister in Long Beach, but they'll be back.

**MITCHELL.** Oh, good.

**JESSIE.** Yeah, they'll definitely be back. They want to buy in Port, so Max can go to school here. They just need to get a down payment together.

(*Realizing it's untrue as she says it.*)

Which shouldn't take too long.

(*Beat.*)

But Long Beach is good for them in the meantime. They have a lot of family support there, and their daycare situation didn't exactly pan out here.

**MITCHELL.** Oh no. Which daycare?

**JESSIE.** ...I don't remember. But Lina got a bad vibe.

**MITCHELL.** Ugh. Well you have to listen to your gut on those things. You really do.

**JESSIE.** Yeah.

(*Beat.*)

But anyway, the good / news is—

**MITCHELL.** (*Thinking of it:*) Wait a second. Does Lina need a nanny?

(*Excited to help.*)

Because Justine is looking for hours!—*this could be perfect.*

**JESSIE.** Oh. Lina can't afford Justine.

**MITCHELL.** No no no, Lina could just *have* her. I've already paid Justine in full for May.

**JESSIE.** That's really nice of you, and I'll pass it along, but I think they've decided that *Lina* should be home with Max. That's what they're lining up. The hospital is letting her switch to the graveyard shift, so she can be home during the day, and John's going back to a job he had in Merrick, at a pizza place, so he'll be closer to home.

**MITCHELL.** They should just take Justine.

**JESSIE.** She's happy about this, Mitchell. Really happy.

**MITCHELL.** Okay, well, good, then.

(*Beat.*)

Will you send her my best?

**JESSIE.** I will. I'm gonna see her Saturday.

(*Beat.*)

**MITCHELL.** So *that's* why you looked so sad today at story-time. I saw you before you saw me at the library, and I thought: *There's Jessie, I wonder why she looks sad.* This all makes sense now. You miss your friend.

**JESSIE.** I do miss my friend, but I look sad because I've been fighting with my husband all week.

**MITCHELL.** ....Oh.

(*Beat.*)

I'm sorry to hear that.

(*Beat.*)

Do you want to talk about it? I certainly owe you one.

**JESSIE.** That wouldn't be appropriate.

**MITCHELL.** (*Joke.*) Well, my wife *chucking eggs at your house* wasn't appropriate, either. But I think we can graduate from—

**JESSIE.** (*Sharp.*) *What are you doing here, Mitchell?*

(*Beat.*)

What is it you wanted to stop by to tell me?

(*Beat.*)

**MITCHELL.** Of course. I forgot this is your coveted nap time, of course you have things to do. Sorry.

(*Beat.*)

I uh... just wanted to tell you, myself, that I've taken a leave of absence from my job.

But....perhaps you already guessed that. You don't look surprised.

**JESSIE.** (*Warmly.*) You were at story-time. In a Yankees tee-shirt.

**MITCHELL.** Oh yeah. I guess I was.

(*Beat.*)

Anyway. *Yes.* I am now the official primary caregiver to Livia, and. I don't know.

I... wanted to share that with you.

(*Beat.*)

What do you think?

**JESSIE.** What does your wife think?

**MITCHELL.** Uh. I'm not sure. We haven't had too much of a back and forth recently.

**JESSIE.** You have to tell your wife, Mitchell.

**MITCHELL.** *I told her.* That's not what you asked; you asked me what she thinks. And I have no idea. But she does *know.* I told her in therapy, in front of a trained professional.

**JESSIE.** And she didn't respond?

**MITCHELL.** No, she did. She said thank you. I said, I'm taking a six-month leave so I can be home with the baby full-time, and she said: *thank you, Mitchell.*

**JESSIE.** .....that sounds positive.

**MITCHELL.** Everything that's not about Livie can wait, as far as I'm concerned. But yeah, I guess it was.

(*Beat.*

MITCHELL *checks on Livie in her stroller.*)

**JESSIE.** And your leave is for *six* months?

**MITCHELL.** Six months and then I'll re-assess. That's what I told them. (I own the company, so I get to hold the cards a little, which is nice.)

(*Casual.*)

But yes—the whole thing was pretty undramatic, really. I don't know why I didn't think to do it sooner. You just get into this strange treadmill, at work. Where you think you have to keep running on the program you selected. But you *don't.* You can pull that Red Stop Button and get off. You can leave the gym.

(*Beat.*)

Anyway. I'm boring you.

**JESSIE.** No. (Sorry.)

(*Beat.*)

I think it's good. That you're home with her.

**MITCHELL.** You do?

**JESSIE.** I do. Not that it matters what I think, but I do.

**MITCHELL.** It matters *a lot* to me, what you think.

All these people keep coming up to me at the playground, or at Dolphin Books or Stop n' Shop... complete strangers come up to me and tell me how sweet it is that Livia gets to be with her daddy all day. It's *beautiful,* how welcoming this community is, and *you* were the first person to show me that.

(*Beat.*)

Which leads me to my Big Ask.

I know I'm no Lina, but what do you say? Can I be in your coffee clutch?

(*Beat.*)

**JESSIE.** I'm going back to work Monday.

**MITCHELL.** .....you're what?

**JESSIE.** Going back to work Monday.

(*Contained, professional.*)

Allie is going to North Shore Day from 8 a.m. to 8 p.m., and I'm going to my office in Manhattan.

**MITCHELL.** *This* Monday?

**JESSIE.** This Monday.

(*Beat.*)

**MITCHELL.** But.... we were... *no*. You have a career?

**JESSIE.** Yes, I have a career! I'm an attorney at Winston & Strawn. I went to Columbia Law.

**MITCHELL.** But *this* is what you do. Isn't it?

**JESSIE.** Well. Nate & I have decided that that's no longer practical.

**MITCHELL.** But! You make Allison so happy. She's the happiest baby I've ever seen.

**JESSIE.** (*Trying to contain.*) There are a *lot* of people who can make Allison happy. Certified, professional people.

**MITCHELL.** But *you're* happy. *You're happy here.*

**JESSIE.** (*A burst.*) Well I don't know what the fuck you want me to tell you, okay, Mitchell? I *asked for an extended leave, and I didn't get one.* I asked for six months, four months, two months—*any months unpaid*—and they said no. THEY SAID NO. Because I *\*don't\* own the firm*, Mitchell, so I *\*don't\* hold the cards.* And if I quit, we lose our health insurance, and yes, we *could* go on Nate's, but I didn't realize until he showed me the chart just how prohibitive *his insurance is.* And I want to have more children, and this duplex isn't big enough for that—we need a house. And we need retirement plans. And we need 529s so they can go to great schools. And if I quit now all my sweat equity goes up in flames when I'm *months away* from making partner, and *for what?* So I can be *a resume with big holes in it*, looking to "rejoin" the workforce in ten years, with a husband who resents me because *\*I didn't even try\** to see our vision through? *Is that what you want me to do?*

**MITCHELL.** ...I—

**JESSIE.** I'm sorry *but you're gonna have to drink your coffee by your damn self.*

(*Beat.*

*Beat.*

MITCHELL *looks crestfallen.*

*Beat.*)

**JESSIE.** I didn't mean to speak to you like that.
This has been hard, and I'm not...

(*Sincerely.*)

I'm sorry, Mitchell.

(*Very tenderly.*)

But this also *isn't real.* You know that, right? This time, these coffees. None of it is real.

*It's temporary.*

**MITCHELL.** ....I see.

**JESSIE.** I don't want to fight anymore. I just want to enjoy the time I *do* have with her.

Today, tomorrow, Saturday, and Sunday.

I want it to be okay for me to just *enjoy it*.

**MITCHELL.** Of course it's okay.

> (*Beat.*
>
> *Beat.*
>
> *Beat.*
>
> *Beat.*)

**MITCHELL.** What are you going to do with her? With the time you have.

**JESSIE.** Oh, *nursing,* I think. Her favorite thing. We'll do *lots and lots* of nursing in my bed.

She does this move now where she pulls on and off my breast to smile at me? Just to flirt, really. And I want to let her do that as much as possible. Just. As much as she wants.

> (*Beat.*)

And, we'll go to Home Goods, I'm sure.

She loves touching all the pillows and candles in there.

**MITCHELL.** Oh, I'll have to remember that.

**JESSIE.** Yes! For a cold day or rainy day? Home Goods. Home Goods all the way.

**MITCHELL.** Okay, thanks.

**JESSIE.** (Just don't tell them you're my friend. I always get the stink eye in there because I don't buy anything.)

**MITCHELL.** (*Laughs.*) Okay.

**JESSIE.** And then... we'll stack her rainbow cups and knock them down again. Maybe lie on her jungle mat; make monkey sounds.

> (*Beat.*)

And then we'll probably go up to the preserve. In Sands Point.

I've been facing her out in the Bjorn, so she can see the ocean, and she likes to throw her arms up and tilt her head back in the surf, like she's flying.

> (*Beat.*)

And then we'll sing.

And then we'll read.

And then we'll nurse some more, under the skylight.

> (*Beat.*
>
> *Beat.*)

**MITCHELL.** She's a lucky little girl, Jessie.

(*Beat. A real need beneath this question...*)

**JESSIE.** Is she?

(*Lights.*)

## *End of Play*

# MELTO MAN
# AND LADY MANTIS
## by Eric Pfeffinger

## BIOGRAPHY

Eric Pfeffinger is a member of the Dramatists Guild and the Writers Guild of America, East. His plays have been produced by Actors Theatre of Louisville, the Denver Center for the Performing Arts, Geva Theatre Center, Phoenix Theatre, InterAct Theatre Company, 16th Street Theater, Source Festival, City Theatre of Miami, the One-Minute Play Festival, and elsewhere. He's written new plays on commissions from Signature Theatre, InterAct Theatre Company, Imagination Stage, and the Bloomington Playwrights Project. He's developed new work with PlayPenn, Page 73, The Lark's Playwrights' Week, the Colorado New Play Summit, Orlando Shakespeare Theater's PlayFest, Red Bull Theater, Chicago Dramatists, Rattlestick Playwrights Theater, Write Now, and others. His plays have been published by Dramatic Publishing, *Dramatics* Magazine, Steele Spring, HowlRound, and Indie Theater Now. Pfeffinger's playwriting has received awards from the Ohio Arts Council, the Indiana Arts Commission, and the Midwestern Playwrights Festival. He co-created the web series *#MotherJudger, Mommy Blogger,* and *Sad Dads,* and was a founding member of the comedy troupe Don't Throw Shoes. Pfeffinger has written for *American Theatre* and *National Lampoon* and is the co-author of the novel *The High-Impact Infidelity Diet,* published by Crown and available on finer remainder tables everywhere. Pfeffinger lives in Toledo, Ohio, and enjoys a robust Midwestern humility.

## ACKNOWLEDGMENTS

*Melto Man and Lady Mantis* premiered at the Humana Festival of New American Plays in April 2017. It was directed by Eric Hoff with the following cast:

MELTO MAN ................................................................ Jeff Biehl
LADY MANTIS .......................................... Elia Monte-Brown

and the following production staff:

Scenic Designer .................................................. Justin Hagovsky
Costume Designer .................................................. Alice Tavener
Lighting Designer .................................................. Steve O'Shea
Sound Designer .................................... Christian Frederickson
Fight Director ........................................................ Ryan Bourque
Stage Manager .................................................. Stephen Horton
Assistant Stage Manager .................................... Lindsay Eberly
Dramaturg .............................................................. Jessica Reese

## CHARACTERS

MELTO MAN, suit and tie. A melty man.
LADY MANTIS, dressed presentably. A mantis lady.

## THE TIME

Now.

## THE PLACE

Melto Man's office.

Jeff Biehl and Elia Monte-Brown
in *Melto Man and Lady Mantis*

41st Humana Festival of New American Plays
Actors Theatre of Louisville, 2017
Photo by Bill Brymer

# MELTO MAN AND
# LADY MANTIS

MELTO MAN *at his desk, all business.* LADY MANTIS *seated across from him. Mid-appointment.*

**MELTO MAN.** I actually ran your numbers a couple different ways...let me get this uh...I think you might want to consider whether claiming the home office every year is worth the trouble. It's a lot of record-keeping for

(*Emits an involuntary monstrous bleat.*)

relatively little financial benefit. Nice boots, by the way.

**LADY MANTIS.** What?

**MELTO MAN.** My wife would go nuts for those boots.

**LADY MANTIS.** Thanks.

**MELTO MAN.** Now let me try to show you side by side how these figures...

**LADY MANTIS.** Melto Man, can I ask you something? Non-tax-related?

**MELTO MAN.** Yeah, shoot.

**LADY MANTIS.** So, after you...became...after, y'know, your ah...I'm so embarrassed, I don't recall how exactly, how you, uh—

**MELTO MAN.** Industrial accident. Yeah. In hindsight that is one field trip I wish I had not volunteered to chaperone. Ha-ha.

**LADY MANTIS.** So, I mean, after your—. Transition. Or whatever. At any point did you ever consider...experimenting with being...destructive?

**MELTO MAN.** Sure I did. Of course I did. It's traditional, after all. And I'll admit I still get

(*Emits an involuntary monstrous bleat.*)

urges.

**LADY MANTIS.** But you've never, I don't know, killed some people or burned down a city block or gnawed somebody's head off their ragged neckstem?

**MELTO MAN.** Me, no. But I don't judge. I just...it's just so not *me*, y'know?

**LADY MANTIS.** 'Cause I...find it really hard...not to. Do stuff. Like that.

**MELTO MAN.** Mm-hm. Mm-hm. Mm-hm. Can I ask you a personal question? How about before?

**LADY MANTIS.** Before.

**MELTO MAN.** Like before you—. Before your, I don't know how you—?

**LADY MANTIS.** Industrial accident.

**MELTO MAN.** So, before that, before you were Lady Mantis, back when you were—?

**LADY MANTIS.** —Helen.

**MELTO MAN.** I mean, then: did you—? Want to—?

**LADY MANTIS.** Oh, God, no.

**MELTO MAN.** Yeah?

**LADY MANTIS.** No, no. Why would, I mean—? Anything I—it's because, because of *this*.

**MELTO MAN.** Sure. Yeah, okay. But I mean, I've gone over your previous years' taxes. In preparation. And I'm just saying, I know you haven't always been, uhh, straightforward? Your approach to your obligations as a citizen, at least insofar as your taxes were concerned, seem consistently to have been a little, what should I say, cheaty.

**LADY MANTIS.** Well but I mean—everyone does that.

**MELTO MAN.** Yeah?

(*Beat.*)

Just something to think about. Look. Back when you were Helen, did you ever have violent thoughts?

**LADY MANTIS.** Well. *Those.*

**MELTO MAN.** Ever cruel to people for no reason?

**LADY MANTIS.** There's always a *reason*.

(*Pause.*)

**MELTO MAN.** Y'know, y'know what, why don't we just get back to your—? I've got a three-fifteen and I want to make sure you're completely satisfied with your—

**LADY MANTIS.** This was never my plan, of course. When I was a kid I thought I'd be a teacher or a senator. My guidance counselor said she thought I could be the first woman president. Not that I'd be the first human-insect hybrid to level a military base.

**MELTO MAN.** Yeah, no, of course. Life happens.

**LADY MANTIS.** Just seems like things could have been so different. If it weren't for the lousy hand I've been dealt. Which happens to involve not having actual hands. When I was little, before bedtime, I used to pray—ironic, right?

**MELTO MAN.** Is it? Maybe. I'd have to look it up, "ironic" always gives me trouble. That and

(*Emits an involuntary monstrous bleat.*)

"irregardless."

**LADY MANTIS.** I used to pray to God: let me be successful, let me be famous. Let me be *major.* Never occurred to me to pray: let me be lucky. I had no idea that the worst thing that can happen to you is being unlucky.

**MELTO MAN.** Look, I'm not saying our circumstances, the unique pressures confronting the members of our particular community, don't matter. I mean, look at Ed.

**LADY MANTIS.** I don't know if I…?

**MELTO MAN.** I guess he goes by Behemoth now? Yeah, hard to miss. And I knew him a little, before, and he was always a totally quiet, decent guy…

**LADY MANTIS.** Before—?

**MELTO MAN.** Industrial accident.

**LADY MANTIS.** *Man.*

**MELTO MAN.** Deregulation, am I right? Anyway, I think Ed's choices are limited, insofar as our society isn't really optimally structured to accommodate a fifty-foot-tall ape-man. His job situation's not great, plus he's going through this ugly divorce, I get why he's frustrated. I'm not saying stepping on people and knocking down buildings is his *only* option, just that I wouldn't presume to say what I'd do if I were in his shoes. If he could wear shoes. We're all influenced by our situation. And we need to accept that. I am what I am, y'know, thanks to God and Draco Industries' faulty safety protocols, and I gotta own that and love myself. But circumstances notwithstanding, I don't think that means we're

(*Emits an involuntary monstrous bleat.*)

helpless. You know? We might *feel* like we *want* to cheat on our taxes, but we can *choose* not to. We might feel like we want to—

**LADY MANTIS.** Crush people's faces in our mandibles and lay eggs in their remains.

**MELTO MAN.** —but we don't *have* to. Et cetera and so on.

**LADY MANTIS.** So you're saying I can't blame—this—for what I do.

**MELTO MAN.** *Can't?* Well. I guess—. We can recognize the effects of our situation on our impulses, I think, but no, I believe ultimately we are accountable.

**LADY MANTIS.** You're saying it's not because I'm unlucky. I'm just a bad person.

**MELTO MAN.** Mmmmmm, words in my mouth a little bit, I think.

**LADY MANTIS.** I was basically morally hideous even before the accident, there's something rotten inside me, why even fight it?

**MELTO MAN.** That is extremely not what I am saying.

**LADY MANTIS.** There are abominations in this world who do bad things. Criminals. Sadists. The management and Board of Directors at Draco Industries. And I guess I'm one of those creatures. Difference is: before, I could only do small bad things. But now…now I can finally…be *major.*

**MELTO MAN.** Helen. Helen. These are all the wrong takeaways.

**LADY MANTIS.** Helen's not here right now. Or ever again.

(LADY MANTIS *rears up, sounds a series of threatening clicks.* MELTO MAN *emits a monstrous bleat. They square off.*)

**MELTO MAN.** Denise?

(*Bleat.*)

Reschedule my three-fifteen.

(*Another bleat. A vicious battle. An epic clash of the monstrosities, amidst office furniture.*

*Curtain.*)

**_End of Play_**

# THE MANY DEATHS OF
# NATHAN STUBBLEFIELD
by Jeff Augustin, Sarah DeLappe,
Claire Kiechel, and Ramiz Monsef

All inquiries concerning rights, including amateur rights, should be addressed to:

For Jeff Augustin: William Morris Endeavor Entertainment, 11 Madison Avenue, 18th Floor, New York, NY 10010. ATTN: Michael Finkle, 212-903-1144.
For Sarah DeLappe: ICM Partners, 730 Fifth Avenue, 3rd Floor, New York, NY 10019. ATTN: Di Glazer, 212-556-6820.
For Claire Kiechel: The Gersh Agency, 41 Madison Avenue, 33rd Floor, New York, NY 10010. ATTN: Seth Glewen & Leah Hamos, 212-634-8124.
For Ramiz Monsef: Abrams Artists Agency, 275 Seventh Avenue, 26th Floor, New York, NY 10001. ATTN: Max Grossman, 646-461-9372.

# ABOUT *THE MANY DEATHS OF NATHAN STUBBLEFIELD*

*This article first ran in the* Limelight Guide to the 41st Humana Festival of New American Plays, *published by Actors Theatre of Louisville, and is based on conversations with the creative team before rehearsals for the Humana Festival production began.*

*Innovation.* It's a concept that seems to be everywhere—hailed in some corners as the silver bullet that will fix everything, derided elsewhere as a buzzword so common that it's lost its meaning. The truth about its value probably lies somewhere in the middle. Some of our most pressing problems demand creative solutions, and it's true that a great idea can change the world. But progress, whether technological or social, usually comes at a price. Still, innovation and its twin, invention, are seductive: we can make something from nothing, and with new ideas comes the glittering possibility of fame and fortune. Are all of us just one eureka moment away from hitting the big time? Hope and heartbreak, promise and peril—in *The Many Deaths of Nathan Stubblefield*, Jeff Augustin, Sarah DeLappe, Claire Kiechel, and Ramiz Monsef join forces to write about the slippery nature of innovation, and the myths we tell about it.

In crafting this show, these four playwrights have been inspired in part by stories from Louisville and the state of Kentucky. Although it's perhaps best known for its advances in the realms of bourbon, fried chicken, and bluegrass, Kentucky is also the home of numerous inventions and innovators, and even Thomas Edison passed through and left his mark. His misadventures in Louisville as a young telegraph operator and inventor were an early jumping-off point for this project; it's hard to top his account of getting fired for experimenting on the job and destroying his boss's desk with sulfuric acid in the process. Edison soon left town, but he would find triumph in Louisville later in his career: his installation of thousands of lightbulbs for the city's 1883 Southern Exposition made it the first successful nighttime fair in the United States.

Ultimately, however, it's lesser-known Kentucky innovators who have most fascinated the creative team, which also includes director Eric Hoff and dramaturg Jessica Reese. And so to create *The Many Deaths of Nathan Stubblefield*, they've investigated and drawn from the lives of a wide range of pioneers and dreamers from across the Bluegrass State, including the farmer and self-taught inventor whose mysterious demise gives the show its title. You've probably never heard of him, but depending on how you define it, Nathan Stubblefield invented the mobile phone—and he did it over a century ago. He initially found success as he demonstrated his device across the country; he could transmit sound from over a mile away and earned a patent for his work in 1908. But after a falling-out with investors and other setbacks, a disillusioned Stubblefield spent the end of his life holed up in his workshop, toiling away on his dream of "wireless telephony."

In his lifetime, Stubblefield wound up overlooked, but history has proven him right in some ways; consider, for example, his 1902 prediction that "it will be no more than a matter of time [until] conversation over long distances between the great cities of the country will be carried on daily without wires." *The Many Deaths of Nathan Stubblefield* explores the complex legacies of its namesake and other innovators—their failures and breakthroughs, their curiosity and courage, their inexhaustible drive to forge new paths and reinvent themselves. While working on this project, the writing team challenged themselves to ask: what stories haven't been told yet? What voices are missing from the history of invention, and why? Experimenting with short-form writing and closely collaborating with one another, each playwright has crafted a series of short pieces that examine these questions and many more. Together, their plays form a single theatrical ride that's vivid, imaginative, and thought-provoking.

The final source of inspiration for *The Many Deaths of Nathan Stubblefield* is its cast: the nineteen Acting Apprentices in the 2016–2017 Professional Training Company. During their nine-month apprenticeships, these early-career actors perform in their own season of new work, from solo pieces created by the Apprentices themselves to a trio of one-act plays written for the company. *The Many Deaths of Nathan Stubblefield*, commissioned by Actors Theatre, is a key opportunity for them to continue learning about new play development. In the fall of 2016, the company participated in two workshops for this show here in Louisville; these week-long intensives allowed Augustin, DeLappe, Kiechel, and Monsef to get to know the actors and develop material with them in mind. All in all, it's a unique process: the creative team starts over the summer with just a theme, and they work until the following spring to build a production that showcases the voices of a group of writers and the talent of this season's Acting Apprentices.

Although the archetypal inventor's story centers on someone tinkering away in solitude, it's exciting to bring four playwrights and nineteen actors together and see what they create. *The Many Deaths of Nathan Stubblefield* is the result of months of collaboration, discovery, and experimentation—think of it as an invention unto itself, a splendid contraption, a machine with many moving parts. Eureka!

—Jessica Reese

## BIOGRAPHIES

**Jeff Augustin**'s play *The Last Tiger in Haiti* premiered in a co-production at La Jolla Playhouse and Berkeley Repertory Theatre. Augustin's plays have also been produced at the Roundabout Underground (*Little Children Dream of God*) and Actors Theatre of Louisville (*The Many Deaths of Nathan Stubblefield; Cry Old Kingdom; That High Lonesome Sound*). Augustin's work has been developed at the Eugene O'Neill Theater Center's National Playwrights Conference, The Ground Floor at Berkeley Repertory Theatre, American Conservatory Theater, and Seattle Repertory Theatre. Augustin was the Shank Playwright-in-Residence at Playwrights Horizons and the inaugural Tow Foundation Playwright-in-Residence at Roundabout Theatre Company. He is an alumnus of the New York Theatre Workshop 2050 Fellowship; the Rita Goldberg Playwright's Workshop at the Lark; and The Working Farm at SPACE on Ryder Farm. Augustin is currently under commission from Roundabout Theatre Company, Manhattan Theatre Club, Actors Theatre of Louisville, and La Jolla Playhouse. He's translating part of *Our Town* into Haitian Creole for Miami New Drama's bilingual production. Augustin is a writer for *Claws* on TNT and is developing a new series with AMC. He holds a B.A. from Boston College and an M.F.A. from the University of California San Diego.

**Sarah DeLappe**'s play *The Wolves* (Pulitzer Prize finalist; Lortel, Outer Critics Circle nominations for Best Play/Emerging Playwright; Relentless Award, Sky Cooper New American Play Prize; Susan Smith Blackburn and Yale Drama Series Prize finalist) premiered at The Playwrights Realm, following an engagement with New York Stage and Film, and development with Clubbed Thumb. Subsequent production at Lincoln Center Theater. Fellowships and developmental support include The MacDowell Colony, The Ground Floor, LCT3 Playwright in Residence, Ars Nova Play Group, Page One Fellowship at The Playwrights Realm, SPACE on Ryder Farm, and Sitka Fellows Program. M.F.A.: Brooklyn College.

**Claire Kiechel**'s plays include *Pilgrims* (world premiere at The Gift Theatre in Chicago, The Lark's Playwrights' Week 2016, The Kilroys' The List 2016); *Lulu Is Hungry* with composer Avi Amon at Ars Nova's ANT Fest 2016; and *Some Dark Places of the Earth* at The New School for Drama. Her work has also been presented or developed by the Alley Theatre, Cincinnati Playhouse in the Park, The Civilians' R&D Group, Colt Coeur, Ensemble Studio Theatre, Hangar Theatre, Naked Angels, the Orchard Project, and Pipeline Theatre Company. Kiechel is a 2016 recipient of South Coast Repertory's Elizabeth George Emerging Writers Commission, and has a B.A. from Amherst College and an M.F.A. from The New School for Drama. She was a writer for Netflix's second season of *The OA* and is currently working on the upcoming HBO series *Watchmen*.

**Ramiz Monsef** is the co-author of the musical *The Unfortunates*, which was produced at the Oregon Shakespeare Festival and American Conservatory Theater in San Francisco. His newest play, *3 Farids*, was part of The Bushwick Starr Reading Series and was selected to be in the New Works Festival at TheatreWorks Silicon Valley. Monsef is an actor as well, and has appeared in theatres across the country, including Actors Theatre of Louisville, the Mark Taper Forum, Berkeley Repertory Theatre, Yale Repertory Theatre, American Conservatory Theater, Seattle Repertory Theatre, and seven seasons at the Oregon Shakespeare Festival, as well as Geffen Playhouse, the Kirk Douglas Theatre, Second Stage, Culture Project, and New York Theatre Workshop. He has appeared on television in *NCIS, Law & Order, Training Day*, and *The Watchlist* on Comedy Central.

## ACKNOWLEDGMENTS

*The Many Deaths of Nathan Stubblefield* premiered at the Humana Festival of New American Plays in March 2017. It was directed by Eric Hoff, and was created in collaboration with and performed by the Acting Apprentices of the 2016-2017 Professional Training Company:

Carter Caldwell, Andres Nicolas Chaves, Andrew Cutler, Jenn Geiger, Abby Leigh Huffstetler, Daniel Arthur Johnson, Kelsey Johnson, Elijah Jones, Kevin Kantor, Sam Kotansky, Anna Lentz, Kathiamarice Lopez, Laakan McHardy, Alexandra Milak, Regan Moro, Grace Palmer, Jacob Sabinsky, Anne-Marie Trabolsi and Alice Wu

with casting for specific pieces as follows:

*The Death of Nathan Stubblefield* by Sarah DeLappe
RADIO ANNOUNCER......................................Kevin Kantor
and The Ensemble

*Labor to Be Heard* by Jeff Augustin
COAL MINER.....................................................Andrew Cutler
REPORTERS................ Jenn Geiger, Daniel Arthur Johnson,
Kevin Kantor, Sam Kotansky, Jacob Sabinsky
WHITE GARRETT .........................................Carter Caldwell
AMERICAN MARY...............................................Regan Moro
GARRETT.............................................................. Elijah Jones
BAVARIAN MARY................................................ Anna Lentz
ENSEMBLE ........................................ Andres Nicolas Chaves,
Abby Leigh Huffstetler, Kelsey Johnson,
Kathiamarice Lopez, Laakan McHardy,
Alexandra Milak, Grace Palmer,
Anne-Marie Trabolsi and Alice Wu

*Henriettas* by Sarah DeLappe
HENRIETTA 1.................................................Kelsey Johnson
HENRIETTA 2.......................................Kathiamarice Lopez
HENRIETTA 3.................................Abby Leigh Huffstetler
HENRIETTA 4................................................ Grace Palmer

*Thomas Edison Tries to Write a Play* by Claire Kiechel
LIGHTBULB........................................... Abby Leigh Huffstetler
SCIENTIST 1 ..........................................Kevin Kantor
SCIENTIST 2 .......................................... Jenn Geiger
OLD WOMAN 1 .............................................Alexandra Milak
OLD WOMAN 2 .................................................. Grace Palmer
FILM STUDENT ................................................Sam Kotansky
TELEGRAPH OPERATOR'S
DAUGHTER ............................................ Anne-Marie Trabolsi
EDISON ................................................. Daniel Arthur Johnson
ROBERT.............................................................Jacob Sabinsky

*Final Four* by Ramiz Monsef
ORIGINAL NATHAN ....................................Carter Caldwell
MUTANT NATHAN ........................................Andrew Cutler
BARBARIAN NATHAN ...............................Jacob Sabinsky
HIPSTER NATHAN........................... Andres Nicolas Chaves
OLIVIA................................................................Alexandra Milak

*Batson* by Ramiz Monsef
in collaboration with Elijah Jones
JAMES BATSON..................................................... Elijah Jones
JOE GUTTMAN ................................ Daniel Arthur Johnson
DAVID NIEHAUS/JUROR.............................Andrew Cutler
JURORS ................................................................The Ensemble

*I Will Survive* by Sarah DeLappe
YOLANDA ................................................................. Alice Wu
and The Ensemble

*The Ballad of Nathan Stubblefield* by Claire Kiechel
composer Avi Amon
NATHAN................................................................Jacob Sabinsky
NARRATOR...................................... Daniel Arthur Johnson
CHORUS................................................................ The Ensemble

*House Josephine, Josephine Baker* by Jeff Augustin
ARLAN.................................................................Sam Kotansky
ANA MAY CAKE...................................Laakan McHardy
C...................................................... Andres Nicolas Chaves
LADY DAY................................................ Kathiamarice Lopez

*tina, gena & may* by Claire Kiechel
TINA ................................................................Kelsey Johnson
GENA....................................................................Regan Moro
MAY........................................................ Anne-Marie Trabolsi

*The Death of Kween Nathan Stubblefield* by Jeff Augustin
KWEEN NATHAN
STUBBLEFIELD.........................................Laakan McHardy

and the following production staff:

Scenic Designer......................................................William Boles
Costume Designer ............................................... Alice Tavener
Lighting Designer...............................................Eric Southern
Sound Designer.................................................... Stowe Nelson
Stage Manager ....................................... Olivia Tymon
Dramaturg................................................................Jessica Reese
Movement Supervisor ................................. J. Christopher Age
Dance Supervisor....................................Ashley Thursby
Fight Supervisor...................................................... Eric Frantz
Properties Master...............................................Heather Lindert
Directing Assistant ...............................................Sammy Zeisel
Assistant Dramaturg...........................................Paige Vehlewald

*The Many Deaths of Nathan Stubblefield* was commissioned and developed by Actors Theatre of Louisville.

## A NOTE ABOUT MUSIC

To view or listen to the score for *The Ballad of Nathan Stubblefield*, please visit aviamon.com/nathanstubblefield.

343

Abby Leigh Huffstetler and Anne-Marie Trabolsi
in *The Many Deaths of Nathan Stubblefield*

41ˢᵗ Humana Festival of New American Plays
Actors Theatre of Louisville, 2017
Photo by Bill Brymer

# THE MANY DEATHS OF NATHAN STUBBLEFIELD

### THE DEATH OF NATHAN STUBBLEFIELD
by Sarah DeLappe

**VOICEOVER.** Welcome to *The Many Deaths of Nathan Stubblefield*. Performed by the Actors of the 2016-2017 Professional Training Company, Commissioned by Actors Theatre of Louisville.

*(If we're into it, could include pre-show announcement here.)*

And please, silence or turn off your—

**VOICEOVER.** *(old-timey radio voice)* We interrupt this broadcast to bring you Breaking News, you heard it here first, folks, at WHAS Louisville, coming to you liive from the banks of the miiighty Oohiiiooo, This Just In: "Radio Pioneer Nathan Stubblefield Dies, Poor and Embittered. Ken--tucky Hermit, Stubblefield Had Wireless Phone in 1902 *(an actor walks onstage)* —Predicted Broadcasting."

**NATHAN 1.** I am Nathan Stubblefield.

Murray, KY, April the 23rd, year of our lord 1928— Death, which came several *(another actor walks onstage)* days before his body was found, has ended the dreams of Nathan Stubblefield, who in 1902 had made great strides in what he called "wireless telephony" and which has become radio.

**NATHAN 2.** I am Nathan Stubblefield.

**VOICEOVER.**
Mr. Stubblefield forecast
radio and its ramifications, **NATHAN 3.** I am
including broadcasting, Nathan Stubblefield.
and declared he had solved
the problem of sending the **NATHAN 4.** I Am     (NATHAN 6 *runs on*)
human voice through the Nathan/Stubblefield.
earth, which he said he had
started on before he had **NATHAN 5.** /I Am     **NATHAN 6.** Iamna-
heard of Marconi's efforts. Nathan Stubblefield. -thanstubblefield!

                                                  (*they all look at each other*)

Twenty-six years ago he **NATHAN 7.** I am
took his apparatus to Phil- NAThan STUBble-
-adelphia and there gave a -FIELD     **NATHAN 8.** I AM
successful demonstration, NathAN StuBBLE-
but could not interest -field!!
sufficient capital to market **NATHAN 9.** I am
or further his plans. He Nathan Stubblefield?
became a disappointed and     **NATHAN 10/11.** I.
disillusioned inventor. Am. Nath. An. Stu.
                          Bble. Field.

Mr. Stubblefield, who was **NATHAN 12/13/14.**
65, lived like a hermit in a I AM NATHAN
small house in Calloway STUBBLEFIELD!     **NATHAN 15/16/17.**
County, near here. His wife                      I AM NATHAN
and ten children long ago                        STUBBLEFIELD!
left this section and where **NATHAN 12/13/14.**
they are is not known. He I AM NATHAN
had refused efforts to help STUBBLEFIELD!     **NATHAN 18.** EE
him.                                             BO BUM BEE BA
                                                 BEE BOO!

**ALL NATHANS.** (*not in unison*) I am Nathan Stubblefield
I am Nathan Stubblefield
I am Nathan Stubblefield
         (*unison*)
I AM NATHAN STUBBLEFIELD
ME
I AM


AND I INVENTED THE—
         (*a cellphone rings*

*all stare at it*
*then, slowly, painfully, loudly, imaginatively,*
*they die*

*the last* NATHAN *standing whispers, with their dying breath:)*
**NATHAN 17.** please, silence your cell phones.
(NATHAN 17 *falls dead.*)
**ALL NATHANS.** (*whispered*) and other noise making devices.

## LABOR TO BE HEARD
by Jeff Augustin

*In the dark, we hear sounds of labored breathing. Suddenly, as if in a doorway, we see a figure in a Safety Hood. Smoke billowing in the light behind him. We now see the source of the breathing. Figures wrapped in cloth, trying to break free, we see hands, faces. Smoke surrounding them as well.*

**A.** We're born from the same spark as you.

**B.** Take breath like you

**C.** Laugh like you

**D.** Love like you

**E.** Feel like you

**A.** And look—

**B.** For the most part—

**C.** Like you

**D.** And yet…

**E.** we labor to be heard.

> (*The breathing grows and grows until lights snap out on them and a tight spot rises on* COAL MINER.)

**COAL MINER.** Down in the mine, we were debating the myth of John Henry. You heard of John Henry? The man…black man I believe, who worked as a steel-driver and beat the steam-powered hammer only to have his heart give out moments later.

We were debating if he were real or not. And if he were real, what happened to his kin. See a fella I know, claims to come from John Henry's lineage. But I never heard of a wife. And just when I was making my point, the earth shook. Rumbled. Like a train was going by. Then rubble fell and black dust filled the air, our eyes, our lungs.

Never heard that many men cry to God.

And as we scratched, pulled at the earth…light broke.

> (*Once again the figure in the gas mask appears, light shining from behind.* COAL MINER *looks at the figure.*)

And for a moment I thought it was God…

> (*A sea of* REPORTERS *fills the stage. Making a ruckus, this is big news, everyone wants the scoop.*)

**ALL REPORTERS.** Over here!

Mr. Morgan, I have a question!

I got a question for you sir!

Over here!

(WHITE GARRETT *appears. Camera lights are snapped.*)

**REPORTER.** Mr. Morgan, what made you go into the mine?

**WHITE GARRETT.** My duty as a citizen

**REPORTER.** Mr. Morgan, did you fear for your life?

**WHITE GARRETT.** No, I had trust in God

**REPORTER.** Did your wife?

(*The* REPORTERS *laugh…it should feel and sound canned.*)

**WHITE GARRETT.** She has more faith in Him than I do. You know what they say

**REPORTER.** What?

**WHITE GARRETT.** A man is only as good as the woman beside him

**REPORTER.** How did you know the gas mask would work?

**WHITE GARRETT.** I didn't.

**REPORTER.** You're so brave!

**WHITE GARRETT.** The miners who fought to stay alive for their families are the brave ones.

**REPORTER.** How did you come up with such a brilliant idea?

**WHITE GARRETT.** It came to me in a dream. That's where most of my ideas come to me. A mentor of mine at Harvard told me to always keep a notebook next to my bed, to train myself in the middle of a dream to recognize an idea and say, loudly "This isn't reality. But this idea could be. Wake up Garrett. Write it down, before it vanishes. Wake up Garrett."

And the night I had that dream—just a few weeks before the mine collapse, thank you Lord—I woke up. I didn't just write it. I drew it, I constructed the gas mask down in my basement. My wife she…

(AMERICAN MARY *appears. More cameras snap.*)

**AMERICAN MARY.** Couldn't believe it. I felt this draft in the middle of the night, and knew, just knew he was down in the basement, working on something brilliant. And the next morning when he showed me the mask…I knew he had changed the course of the world.

**ALL REPORTERS.** Does it ever get lonely? Being with a man who works all the time?

**AMERICAN MARY.** Never. I'm blessed to be with such a brilliant beautiful man.

(*They have a peck.*)

**REPORTERS.** Awwwwwww!

(WHITE GARRETT *and* AMERICAN MARY *exit. The* REPORTERS *follow. We hear as they exit…*)

**ALL REPORTERS.** Over here!

I have tons of questions!

I got many questions for you sir!

Over here!

> (*The figures on the ground resurrect with a breath. Again they continue fighting for air.* BAVARIAN MARY *appears.*)

**BAVARIAN MARY.** John Henry was black and he did have a wife. His true self lived on, not in the folk music that canonized him, but in his wife Polly Anne's memories. Every morning she woke up to the outline of his body that remained deep in their mattress. To his musk that hung in the air. And nightly she would whisper to him as if he were there.

Certain types of women get forgotten in America.

> (*The figure in the safety hood reappears.* BAVARIAN MARY *looks at him. She rises, weaves through the figures. Removes his mask. As she removes the mask...revealing* BLACK GARRETT, *the real* GARRETT. *He lets out a large breath of air. The figures on the ground go still and silent.*)

**COAL MINER.** A black man? Hmmm...

> (COAL MINER *thinks on it.*)

I don't know. It was chaos down in the mine. Wasn't paying that much attention. You know? And he was wearing a mask. Now that I think about it, it was less God like and more...I don't know...more scary. More like death.

> (*A few* REPORTERS *appear...*)

**ALL REPORTERS.** Over here.

Garrett Morgan right? I have a question. Maybe two.

I might have one for you sir.

**GARRETT.** No one wants a photo?

**REPORTER.** Is that why you did it Mr. Morgan? For some sort of recognition

**ANOTHER REPORTER.** Not very American of you

**GARRETT.** No, I did it cause I wanted to help. Save lives

**REPORTER.** Hero complex

**GARRETT.** Not at all.

**REPORTER.** Were you worried that *mask* of yours would do more harm than good?

**GARRETT.** What? No

**REPORTER.** How could you be so sure?

**GARRETT.** The science

**REPORTER.** Did you even go to high school boy?

**ANOTHER REPORTER.** Do you know basic math boy?

**GARRETT.** Ummm...schooling wasn't...it wasn't fair. And I didn't need it

**REPORTER.** You're too good for education?

**GARRETT.** No, I'm self-educated.

**REPORTER.** Oh, so the American education system ain't good enough for you

**GARRETT.** That's not what I'm saying. It's just at the time

**REPORTER.** If you don't like it here. Why don't you and your *immigrant* wife just go back to wherever y'all are from?

**GARRETT.** We do love it here. We both do.

**REPORTER.** Was the mask even your idea? Did you steal it?

**GARRETT.** It's mine. It didn't come to me in a dream. It's been years in the making. When I was ten, I wanted to be a firefighter, even though I knew my people weren't allowed. Whenever there was a fire in the neighborhood, I ran to catch a glimpse of the firemen. There was this one fire, so hot you could see the heat rising off your skin like it was concrete. And the sky was black with smoke. I was coughing just being near it. And I saw these brave men run into that hot, burning building…and all I could think of was the smoke pressing against their chests, them fighting to breathe, fighting to be heard, to live. It took years of studying, of failed experiments and masks. Nights away from my wife…

**BAVARIAN MARY.** It's lonely. Waking up every morning to a cold draft, to the outline of his body. I started to feel like I didn't exist, I didn't matter. You shouldn't have to fight to be remembered, to be seen

**GARRETT.** I wanted to create a system that would keep them alive. Keep future generations alive.

> (*She puts the mask back on* GARRETT, *instantly lights snap out on* BAVARIAN MARY *and the* REPORTERS. *The figures on the ground animate with one large breath. Like before they struggle, searching for air, for joy, for life. As they all collapse, one escapes:* BLACK WOMAN. *She takes the cloth, wraps it, folds it…it becomes a child. She walks towards the light, the doorway, where* GARRETT *once stood. And as she exits, she whispers…*)

**BLACK WOMAN.** (*To the baby.*) We will be heard.
We will be heard.
We will be heard.

> (*Blackout.*)

## HENRIETTAS
by Sarah DeLappe

*four ancient old women with walkers/canes/wheelchairs and white wigs*
*this is peppy and full of dance moves*

**HENRIETTA 1.** Hi. I'm Henrietta.

**HENRIETTA 2.** Hello. I am Henrietta.

**HENRIETTA 3.** Hey. Henrietta.

**HENRIETTA 4.** Henrietta, that's me!

*(they strike a pose)*

**ALL HENRIETTAS.** Hey.

Want a Werther's?

Fuck you!

We're In A Theater.

What was I saying?

Oh, yes.

I'm Henrietta.

I'm an inventor.

And I'm a genius.

*(they do a genius dance)*

**HENRIETTA 1.** I'm 114 years old.

*(to* HENRIETTA 2)

How old are you, Henrietta?

**HENRIETTA 2.** I am 105 years old.

*(to* HENRIETTA 3)

How about you, Henrietta?

**HENRIETTA 3.** Me, I'm 185 years old and two weeks.

**HENRIETTAS 1, 2 & 4.** Happy Belated!

**HENRIETTA 3.** Hey, thanks.

*(to* HENRIETTA 4)

And you, Henrietta?

**HENRIETTA 4.** I'm *[actual age]*.

*(the others look askance)*

J.K. I'm 500!

*(they strike a celebratory pose)*

**ALL HENRIETTAS.** We're Old!

*(barbershop quartet)*

**HENRIETTA 1.** Old

**HENRIETTA 2.** Old

**HENRIETTA 3.** Old

**HENRIETTA 4.** Old

**ALL HENRIETTAS.** We're Really Old!

**HENRIETTA 1.** I'm the Henrietta who invented a torpedo firing system.

**OTHER HENRIETTAS.** Alias: Midcentury Housewife.

**HENRIETTA 2.** I'm the Henrietta who invented a sanitary napkin.

**OTHER HENRIETTAS.** Alias: Turn of the Century Floral Arranger.

**HENRIETTA 3.** I'm the Henrietta who invented an ironing board.

**OTHER HENRIETTAS.** Alias: Reconstruction Era Dressmaker, Mother of Eight.

**HENRIETTA 4.** And I'm the Henrietta who invented the stairs.

*(other* HENRIETTAS *look askance)*

**HENRIETTA 1.** Henrietta.

**HENRIETTA 4.** What?

**HENRIETTA 2.** Remember how each Henrietta invented something

**HENRIETTA 3.** but never got the credit

**HENRIETTA 2.** because we were Henriettas and not like you know

**HENRIETTA 1.** Henrys?

*(slight pause)*

**HENRIETTA 4.** Yeah.

**HENRIETTA 2.** Yeah. Well. That's. Yeah.

**HENRIETTA 4.** Yeah so I invented the stairs?

**HENRIETTA 1.** But—

**HENRIETTA 2.** *(confused)* Like a staircase?

**HENRIETTA 4.** *(duh)* Yes, yeah, like stairs.
Stairs.
You know, stairs?
Stairs?
Stairs?
Sta/irs?

**HENRIETTA 3.** Look. All of OUR inventions were ACTUALLY invented

**HENRIETTA 2.** by ACTUAL Henriettas.

**HENRIETTA 1.** Henrietta Mahim Bradberry—

**HENRIETTA 2.** Henrietta Mary Beatrice Davidson Kenner—

**HENRIETTA 3.** Henrietta Sarah Boone—

**HENRIETTA 1.** So yeah Henrietta if I can just piggyback off of that I think claiming that *you* invented the *stairs* is like super—

**HENRIETTA 2.** Disrespectful?

**HENRIETTA 1.** To those actual Henriettas?

**HENRIETTA 3.** Who were like erased by—

**HENRIETTA 4.** Fine! Fine. Can we just?

*(they throw confetti or a bomb explodes [or a Werther's?])*

**ALL HENRIETTAS.** THIS. IS. WHAT. A. GENIUS. LOOKS. LIKE.

*(they do a little genius dance)*

We are Henriettas.

Henriettas in a Henry's world.

**HENRIETTA 1.** And, sure, we invented some pretty genius stuff.

**HENRIETTA 3.** Sure.

**HENRIETTA 2.** Sure.

**HENRIETTA 4.** But you know what Henrys have invented?

**ALL HENRIETTAS.** Henrys. Can't live with 'em, can't live without

**HENRIETTA 1.** Their stuff!

**HENRIETTA 3.** You can thank a Henry for:

**HENRIETTA 1.** Atomic Bombs

**OTHER HENRIETTAS.** thank you Henry

**HENRIETTA 2.** Garage doors!

**OTHER HENRIETTAS.** thank you Henry

**HENRIETTA 3.** Corn dogs!

**OTHER HENRIETTAS.** thank you Henry

**HENRIETTA 4.** Clip-on ties!

**OTHER HENRIETTAS.** LOOK AT ME

I'M A BABY!

I CAN'T TIE A TIE

I'M A BABY!!

*(it gains speed and volume)*

**HENRIETTA 1.** CAT LITTER!

**ALL HENRIETTAS.** THANK YOU HENRY!

**HENRIETTA 2.** HAND DRIERS!

**ALL HENRIETTAS.** THANK YOU HENRY!

**HENRIETTA 3.** LEAF BLOWERS!

**ALL HENRIETTAS.** THANK YOU HENRY!

**HENRIETTA 4.** TELEPROMPTERS!

**ALL HENRIETTAS.** THANK YOU HENRY!

AUTOMATIC SLIDING DOORS!

THANK YOU HENRY THANK YOU THANKS!

*(it grows and grows)*

HARD DISK DRIVE (THANKYOUHENRY)

LINT ROLLERS (THANKYOUHENRY)

LASERS (THANKYOUHENRY)

SUGAR PACKETS (THANKYOUHENRY)

CARBON FIBER (THANKYOUHENRY)

SPANDEX (THANKYOUHENRY)

THE PILL

HOORAY! THE PILL!

*(it becomes a hushed, ritualistic, witchy chant)*

**HENRIETTAS 2-4.**

| | |
|---|---|
| Spreadsheets (thankyouhenry) | **HENRIETTA 1.** |
| Slushies (thankyouhenry) | *(sung, moaned, ecstatic)* |
| Computer mouse (thankyouhenry) | Thank you Henry |
| Snowboarding (thankyouhenry) | Thank you Henry |
| Compact Discs (thankyouhenry) | Oh, thank you Henry |
| Calculators (thankyouhenry) | Thank you Henry |
| Taser (thankyouhenry) | Thank you Henry |
| Uno (thankyouhenry) | Thank you Henry |
| Email (thankyouhenry) | Thank you Henry |
| GPS (thankyouhenry) | Thank you Henry |
| MRI (thankyouhenry) | Oh, thank you Henry |
| CPR (thankyouhenry) | Thank you Henry |
| Mobile phones (thankyouhenry) | Thank you Henry |
| Voicemail (thankyouhenry) | Thank you Henry |
| Heimlich Maneuver (thankyouhenry) | Thank you Henry |
| Digital Camera (thankyouhenry) | Thank you Henry |
| Microwave Popcorn (thankyouhenry) | Oh, thank you Henry |
| Polar Fleece (thankyouhenry) | Thank you Henry |
| Control-Alt-Delete (thankyouhenry) | Thank you Henry |
| Space Shuttles (thankyouhenry) | Thank you Henry |
| Pinball (thankyouhenry) | Thank you Henry |
| Internet (thankyouhenry) | Thank you Henry |
| Rolling luggage (thankyouhenry) | Oh, thank you Henry |

**HENRIETTA 4.** *(like she's breaking up a wedding)* Hold on.

You know what?

I did invent the stairs.

Yeah.

I am paying homage.

To all the Henriettas who invented the stairs.
Way to go, Henrietta.
Stairs rule.
This Is For You.

> *(she, slowly, stands up from her wheelchair*
> HENRIETTAS 1-3 *gasp!*
> *she shushes them*
>
> *she begins to do the stair mime*
> *she waves goodbye*
> *and disappears*
>
> *the other* HENRIETTAS *look at her*
> *they look at each other*
> *together they ditch their walking devices*
> *and do the stair mime*
> *they wave goodbye)*

**HENRIETTA 3.** I just love the stairs, Henrietta.

**HENRIETTA 2.** Thanks for the stairs, Henrietta.

**HENRIETTA 1.** Henrietta, thanks. Thank you. Thanks.

## THOMAS EDISON TRIES TO WRITE A PLAY
by Claire Kiechel

**1.**

*a beautiful symphony of lights and music*
*warm! sparkling! glamour!*
*we feel like tinsel*
*a woman dressed as a* LIGHTBULB *enters*
*she dances towards the center of the stage*
*a complex little dance*
*a flourish*
*she holds her arms*
*wide for the applause*
*the lights turn fluorescent*
*the* LIGHTBULB *trembles nervously*
*suddenly a trap door opens*
*she is pulled toward it*
*like her body is magnetized*
*she is pulled into it*
*gasping for her failure*

**2.**

*two* SCIENTISTS *enter*
*they should feel like children dressed up like scientists*
**scientist one.** We have a lot to thank Thomas Edison for
**scientist two.** Oh boy, do we ever!
**scientist one.** Practically everything we take for granted today
**scientist two.** Movies!
**scientist one.** Lightbulbs!
**scientist two.** Voice recorders!
**scientist one.** Electronic ballot boxes!
**scientist two.** Phonographs!
**scientist one.** Well we don't use those today, but
**scientist two.** You could still use a phonograph
**scientist one.** But the things that the phonograph inspires, like—
**scientist two.** Discmans!

**scientist one.** well, no, I, this isn't working—do you think like we should make this more musical, you know

**scientist two.** like "how does a bastard, orphan, son of a whore…"

**scientist one.** be serious this needs to be—we—what is this! how do we! we have to—

> (SCIENTIST TWO *slaps* SCIENTIST ONE
> *they exit*)

**3.**

> *two* "OLD" WOMEN *on rocking chairs, smoking pipes*

**one.** did you read this—thomas edison died today

**two.** tom edison was a fat fuck

**one.** you knew him

**two.** I knew him back then

**one.** I once met him in chicago at this fair, I think it was the world's fair

**two.** you met tom
**one.** well I saw him
from a distance
I saw him

**two.** well, I *knew* tom edison back then and I can tell you

**one.** what

**two.** he wasn't all that

**one.** come on

**two.** no I'm serious

**one.** you're just jealous

**two.** he was kind of an asshole

**one.** well yeah but

**two.** well yeah? you don't mind assholes

**one.** not really

**two.** oh not really? an asshole

**one.** don't you think that people are sometimes like

**two.** what

**one.** that some people get to be assholes

**two.** who gets to be an asshole

**one.** some people

**two.** why

**one.** because

**two.** okay whatever

**one.** no no because they know they can be

**two.** yeah

**one.** yeah? you know what I mean

**two.** I guess I know what you mean

**one.** right!?

**two.** yeah he was an asshole because he knew he could be one

**one.** exactly

**two.** but how did he know

**one.** what do you mean

**two.** how did he know he could be an asshole way back when
how did he know that he would be famous for something else
besides his assholery

> *(a pause*
>
> > *they look to the audience*
> >
> > *a buzzer)*

**4.**

### FILM STUDENT.
Lights up
It's a dark night
Thomas is tired
He's young here
seventeen eighteen
just a telegraph operator
He doesn't know who he's going to be yet
but he's like
excited
brow sweaty
there's this other assistant there
Robert
handsome
And Tom he's always liked Robert
They're both on the night shift
but they don't spend it telegraph operating
they experiment

the night of our film
right here in downtown Louisville
they're playing with acid
We'll figure out the logistics later

But you see it—the floor where that hole is going to happen
that acid hole that's going to get him fired
force him to leave Louisville and make a man out of himself
and the question of the movie is:
Why does he come back?
Why does he choose Louisville as the place
of the Southern Exposition?
Why does he light up the whole city
with his bulbs
the first successful nighttime fair
Could it be—
my film posits
could it be because of her!

Now picture her coming up the stairway
the boss's daughter
wearing a nightgown muddy from the fields
She enters the room
sees Thomas and Robert
she's out of breath a little
she's decided tonight is the night

I like to say it's basically *Good Will Hunting* meets *Y Tu Mamá También*
What do you think?

**5.**

*A flash of:* ROBERT, EDISON, *and the* TELEGRAPH
OPERATOR'S DAUGHTER *in a doorway*
*They devour each other*
*Another flash: they pause, the* TELEGRAPH OPERATOR'S
DAUGHTER *looks out:*
**TELEGRAPH OPERATOR'S DAUGHTER.**
I just knew what I wanted
(*Another flash, another pose:*)
His fingers on my volts
(*Another flash, another pose:*)
and as I came, I whispered into his ear my idea
my dream for a centralized electric power distribution system
that could be used to illuminate this great nation
I also chose this moment to whisper the word
*Bamboo*

a detail he would forget until years later
when after 9,999 tries of finding the right material
to make his incandescent light bulb
last
he would finally remember my voice my breath in his ear
*bamboo*
carbonized bamboo filament
I had had the idea for years
but no one would listen to me
I told it to him
because I sensed he was a man who could
scream

(*A scream*)

**6.**

**scientist one.** 9,999 failures is what some would say

**scientist two.** but not Edison

**scientist one.** he would say he found 9,999 ways that do not work

**scientist two.** Was it really 9,999?

**scientist one.** Who knows! It's a good story

**scientist two.** A good story is all it takes.

(*uh oh.* TWO *is upset*)

**scientist one.** What's wrong?

**scientist two.** What if I don't want to be Edison? What if I can't be?

**scientist one.** That's okay.
He had hundreds of us working for him, you know that?
Some of us didn't talk, we just did his work.

**7.**

*the* TELEGRAPH OPERATOR'S DAUGHTER *sits on the floor*
*the woman dressed as a* LIGHTBULB *goes to her*
**LIGHTBULB.**
You okay?
**TELEGRAPH OPERATOR'S DAUGHTER.**
I had a dream
**LIGHTBULB.**
It's okay.

**TELEGRAPH OPERATOR'S DAUGHTER.**

I had a dream that everyone was waiting for something and I was the only one who could give it to them but I didn't know what it was and no one would tell me

**LIGHTBULB.**

It's okay honey, go back to sleep

(*a parade of people carrying lit lightbulbs in their hands*)

**TELEGRAPH OPERATOR'S DAUGHTER.**

Wait, I'm—I can't remember
it's all fading

**LIGHTBULB.** Shhh.
Next time you'll get it.

(*The lightbulbs all go dark. The end.*)

## FINAL FOUR
by Ramiz Monsef

*Four men form a Greek Chorus of* NATHAN STUBBLEFIELDS.
*One looks like Nathan Stubblefield from the pictures on Wikipedia.*
*One looks like Nathan Stubblefield with a hunchback. He is also sort of a mutant. Probably has a tentacle or something.*
*One looks like Nathan Stubblefield but a barbarian. Think Conan. Schwarzenegger, not O'Brien.*
*One looks like a hipster.*

**ALL STUBBLEFIELDS.** I'm Nathan Stubblefield.
We are all different Nathan Stubblefields from different timelines.

**ORIGINAL NATHAN.** I'm the regular Nathan Stubblefield.

**ALL STUBBLEFIELDS.** The one from the Wikipedia page.

**MUTANT NATHAN.** I'm a regular Nathan Stubblefield too.

**OTHER STUBBLEFIELDS.** You're not. Have you seen yourself?

**MUTANT NATHAN.** Rude.

**BARBARIAN NATHAN.** Clearly, I am Nathan Stubblefield. Ruler of the vast mountains of Ta'Gool, fierce in combat...and in the reproductive arts. (*Alternate line: A Master in combat...with a Bachelor's in reproductive arts.*)

**HIPSTER NATHAN.** Uh...Hi, Nate Stubblefield. I was just hanging out in Portland and then there was this flash of light and now I'm here with these...gentlemen.

**ALL STUBBLEFIELDS.** We've all been brought here by Olivia. Olivia who built a time machine.
Olivia who should be coming back any—

(*We hear a great cacophony of sound and a crackling of electricity. A tired but warlike woman enters covered in blood and dragging a bloody sack.*)

**ALL STUBBLEFIELDS.** That's Olivia.
What's in the sack Olivia?

**OLIVIA.** You are.

(OLIVIA *reaches into the sack and pulls out a head. It's a Nathan Stubblefield head. She throws the head to* ORIGINAL NATHAN.)

Catch.

**ALL STUBBLEFIELDS.** This is unexpected.

**ORIGINAL NATHAN.** Miss Olivia I'm starting to feel a mite concerned about what is happening here.

**HIPSTER NATHAN.** I think I'm gonna be sick.

**BARBARIAN NATHAN.** By the Great Gaping Third Mouth of the Nizreen Sea Serpent, you are a splendid warrior, Olivia! I should like to reproduce with you as a partner. I will keep this head as a token of our first mating.

(OLIVIA *threatens* BARBARIAN NATHAN.)

Foreplay!

**HIPSTER NATHAN.** Just want to again say that I don't know these guys so...

**OLIVIA.** At some point in all of your lives you all invented the first version of what would eventually become cell phones. Cell phones have ruined humanity. We're all disconnected, and soulless and we now only know how to express ourselves in 140 characters or less. Art is dying. Empathy is dying. Journalism is dying.

**ALL STUBBLEFIELDS.** Yes, but Pokémon are everywhere!

**OLIVIA.** Exactly.

(OLIVIA *spits on the ground near* ORIGINAL NATHAN.)

**ORIGINAL NATHAN.** My wingtips!

**OLIVIA.** (*Overlapping with* ORIGINAL NATHAN.) So I built a time machine and I have been going to every timeline and executing every Nathan Stubblefield, so the world will never have this technology. You are now the last four.

**HIPSTER NATHAN.** Seems a bit extreme.

**OLIVIA.** ...desperate times...

**HIPSTER NATHAN.** Can we talk about this? I'm only 19 and I haven't invented this "technology" yet, and I'd be glad to maybe...not...if that's what this is all about. There's a lot I still want to do with my life.

**ORIGINAL NATHAN.** This is unacceptable. We are inventors! We bring about progress! My invention will increase connectivity, productivity—

**OLIVIA.** Isolationism. Fear. Fake news sites. Bigotry. Cyberbullying. Slut-shaming. Doxxing. The Alt-right. Nazis—

**BARBARIAN NATHAN.** —roaming hordes of carnivorous lizard people. She has a point. Olivia, how shall we mate? Like dogs or badgers?

(OLIVIA *moves up close to* BARBARIAN. OLIVIA *produces a pen.*)

**OLIVIA.** This is a pen. You use it to express yourself.

(OLIVIA *stabs* BARBARIAN NATHAN *multiple times with the pen à la* American Me. *There should be as much blood as possible.* BARBARIAN NATHAN *dies. The other* NATHANS *stare in shock for a moment— then...*)

**ORIGINAL NATHAN.** Oh my god. Thank you! Thank you!

**HIPSTER NATHAN.** Like badgers? I can't even picture that!

**MUTANT NATHAN.** Did you just kill the inventor of cellular technology with a pen? Talk about a metaphor.

(*Turning to* HIPSTER NATHAN.)

Or is that symbolism? I never know the difference.

**HIPSTER NATHAN.** My god, your breath smells like baby shit.

**MUTANT NATHAN.** Or is that a simile?

**HIPSTER NATHAN.** Please don't talk to me.

**ORIGINAL NATHAN.** You know what? I just remembered I may have left my hat near the ol' time machine. I'm just gonna go take a look and see if it's there. If you'll excuse me...

(OLIVIA *reaches into the bloody sack. She pulls out an old-timey hat drenched in blood.*)

**OLIVIA.** This hat?

**ORIGINAL NATHAN.** Son of a so and so, that's the one! I'm just gonna take this to the water closet and see if I can't clean off some of these...human remains. It's been so nice meeting all of you. Ta!

(ORIGINAL NATHAN *tries to surreptitiously walk to the exit where the time machine is.*)

**OLIVIA.** (*Pointing to the opposite exit.*) Bathroom's that way.

**ORIGINAL NATHAN.** Of course it is. Silly me.

(*He exits.*
*A moment of silence.*
OLIVIA *follows after him.*
*After a moment we hear—*)

**ORIGINAL NATHAN.** (*Offstage.*) Oh god. Look, I'm sorry. I won't invent it. I'll go into accounting or something. Please. I have 10 children. NO!!!! AAAAAA!!!!

(*We hear* ORIGINAL NATHAN *being brutally murdered offstage.*
*The* NATHANS *onstage are frozen in fear.*
*Silence.*
OLIVIA *comes back onstage. She is covered in more blood. She has a bottle of bourbon with her.*)

**OLIVIA.** Who wants a drink.

(*A beat.*)

**HIPSTER NATHAN.** Love one.

**MUTANT NATHAN.** That sounds fantastic. Thank you. I'll get the glasses.

(OLIVIA *points towards the bathroom exit.*)

**OLIVIA.** That way.

**MUTANT NATHAN.** On it.

(MUTANT NATHAN *starts awkwardly shambling towards the exit. He moves excruciatingly awkwardly. It takes a really long time. Maybe he has a tentacle or something. It's just so slow. After it goes on waaaay too long and he has only moved a few feet,* HIPSTER NATHAN *gets proactive.*)

**HIPSTER NATHAN.** How 'bout I get them.

(*He tries exiting towards the time machine.*)

**OLIVIA.** That way.

(*Foiled! He turns and walks towards the bathroom.*)

**HIPSTER NATHAN.** (*As he passes* MUTANT NATHAN.) Excuse me.

**MUTANT NATHAN.** Oh. Well. That's— Look—

(*Calling after* HIPSTER NATHAN.)

The atmosphere is a little more gaseous in my timeline.

(*Turning back to* OLIVIA.)

I'm actually considered quite the looker in my timeline. It's the tentacle. Girls love the tentacle.

**OLIVIA.** I don't care.

(OLIVIA *pulls out a gun and shoots* MUTANT NATHAN. HIPSTER NATHAN *comes back in just as this happens. He immediately turns back around and tries to exit again.*)

**OLIVIA.** Wait.

(HIPSTER NATHAN *freezes.*)

**HIPSTER NATHAN.** Please don't kill me.

**OLIVIA.** Bring those glasses here.

**HIPSTER NATHAN.** Ok, but please don't kill me. I haven't even had sex yet. I told someone I did once but that was a lie.

**OLIVIA.** Bourbon.

(*She pours him a shot. She pours herself a shot. She gives it to him. They clink glasses.
He stares at it for a second. He shoots it.*)

—and cyanide.

**HIPSTER NATHAN.** Fucking hell.

(*He drops dead.
OLIVIA goes to the head that is still lying on stage. She picks it up by the hair with one hand. In the other hand she holds the poison bourbon.*)

**OLIVIA.** I've finally done it. You're welcome, humanity! You'll all thank me one day! One day I will be heralded as the woman who saved the world, who brought reason back to humanity…with a little murder. I did it! I did it! Suck it Nathan Stubblefield!!! AHAHAHAHAHAHAHAHA!!!!!

*(She starts laughing a crazy maniacal laugh in the face of the severed head.*
*The laugh goes on and on until it finally tapers off and she takes a celebratory swig of [poison] bourbon.*
*After a moment she realizes what she has done.*
*She looks at the bottle.)*

**OLIVIA.** Fucking hell.

## BATSON
by Ramiz Monsef
in collaboration with Elijah Jones

*A black man sits at a table. In a circle of light. There is a chess board on the table. He is playing black.*

**JAMES BATSON.** White always moves first. Ain't that some shit. White attacks and Black responds. Constant kung fu. Tai chi. Energy shoots out. Energy gets absorbed, and redirected. Chess. It's a game of innovation. 'Cause no one attacks the same way twice. And you always gotta be inventing new ways to handle attacks. I'm'a tell you a story. I knew a dude. Let's say his name was—

*(A white man enters.)*

**JOE GUTTMAN.** Joe Guttman.

**JAMES BATSON.** And my name is James Batson. I'm from Louisville Kentucky.

*(JOE GUTTMAN moves his D pawn to D4.*
*JAMES BATSON moves a knight to F6.)*

**JOE GUTTMAN.** I mean well. Let's start there. But I'm a lawyer. So, yeah, I mean well, but it takes me a long time to DO well. My JOB right now is to prosecute, and right now I have to prosecute James Batson. For a petty burglary.

*(JOE GUTTMAN moves another pawn to C4.*
*JAMES BATSON moves his G pawn to G6.)*

**JAMES BATSON.** What really happened is I got a DWB. Driving while black. Cops said I "fit a description." So, I get thrown in jail, but let's not forget I'm smart and I know they have no evidence against me, because, hey, I'm no angel, but I'm also no fool, and I'm not perfect, yeah, there are things I did, have done, but this thing they popped me for? I didn't do THAT thing. SO yeah. Lock me up. See what happens. Attack. I redirect.

*(JOE GUTTMAN moves his knight to C3.*
*JAMES BATSON moves his bishop to G7.)*

**JOE GUTTMAN.** I'm 26. I had been a lawyer for six months. I had lost the eight cases I had tried before this one. And yeah, there wasn't much evidence.

*(JOE GUTTMAN moves his pawn to E4.)*

**JAMES BATSON.** There wasn't any evidence.

*(JAMES BATSON moves his pawn to D6.)*

**JOE GUTTMAN.** Witnesses but unreliable ones. The point is, I was a lawyer, but not a very good one. I lost this case.

*(JOE GUTTMAN moves his queen.*

JAMES BATSON *castles kingside [his king winds up at G8, and his king-side rook winds up at F8].*)

**JAMES BATSON.** Hip-hip-hooray.

**JOE GUTTMAN.** Hung jury. Because of one juror who happened to be black.

(*A black* JUROR *enters the edge of the circle and watches the game.*)

**JAMES BATSON.** She wouldn't be swayed by the other jurors to convict me. She believed in my innocence and she was the only thing that kept me out of jail. But wait—let's bring it back to the board. What you see here is called the King's Indian. It's a good defense. It's hard to break through, but there's ways. And a good player can do it. Also, look at the board. What do you see? White has moved up and black is hunkered down in the corner. I mean, a porcupine is only dangerous until you turn him over. Belly soft right? Gimmie a beat.

(*By now, a* JURY *of 12 is in place. They start clapping a beat. At least four jurors are people of color. The rest are white.*)

**JOE GUTTMAN.** So I'm a nine-time loser.

**JAMES BATSON.** Your words not mine.

**JOE GUTTMAN.** But there's something telling me that I could try this case another time.
I think that I could beat my little streak.

**JAMES BATSON.** I think the case you're leaning on is weak. No matter how you swing it.

**JOE GUTTMAN.** Well lemme try taking another tactic.

**JAMES BATSON.** Bring it.

**JOE GUTTMAN.** In a trial, who you gotta prove your point to?

**JURORS.** THE JURY.

**JOE GUTTMAN.** You don't have them on your side what are you dealing with?

**JURORS.** WORRY.

**JOE GUTTMAN.** This time I took the liberty of trying something new.

(*The beat stops.*)

I looked at all jurors of color and I told them, "You're excused."

(*The jurors of color leave the circle.* JAMES BATSON *is the only person of color left onstage.*)

**JAMES BATSON.** Just like a lawyer right? When there's something they don't want you to understand, they either bury it under paperwork and lingo or they try to brush on by it so you just miss it all together. I'm'a break it down for you real quick. See there's two ways you can dismiss a juror.

"Cause," which means, you know, this juror feels they can't be fair in the case or if there's a direct conflict of interest, like the person on trial is your cousin or something. So "cause" right? There's that, or you got something called peremptory challenges. Remember that chess board?

Yeah, well what if before black even got to move, white got to take four of his pieces.

(JOE GUTTMAN *removes four black pieces from the board.*)

What I'm saying is, these peremptory challenges?

(*The beat starts again.*)

They're kinda like…a freebie.

**JOE GUTTMAN.** A gimmie.

**JAMES BATSON.** Take 'em out, no questions asked.

**JOE GUTTMAN.** I used mine on any juror who was black.

**JAMES BATSON.** So here I am again this time I'm feeling less enthused.

**JOE GUTTMAN.** I got a better chance of winning.

**JAMES BATSON.** And I'm certain that I'll lose. I OBJECT!

**JOE GUTTMAN.** Doesn't matter, it's the law.

**JAMES BATSON.** I object!

**JOE GUTTMAN.** Fine, it's pointless.

**JAMES BATSON.** I find your methods circumspect. This ain't a panel that reflects me.

**JOE GUTTMAN.** Maybe not but thems the breaks. Shoulder the weight. What chu want? A jury of your peers?

(*The beat stops.*)

**JAMES BATSON.** I walked in thinking I could shake the case, but I got 20 years.

Damn.

(JOE GUTTMAN *moves a piece putting* JAMES BATSON *in check.*)

**JOE GUTTMAN.** Check.

(JOE GUTTMAN *exits.*)

**JAMES BATSON.** And just like that,

I'm a statistic.

And Goddamn it Joe Guttman you may have found a way to take my soul off the board but you damn sure won't take my spirit.

And I feel it bubbling up in me,

(*Another beat kicks in.*)

My heart is a pummeling piston pounding,

I'm a wolf and I can't stop howling,

But can't see the moon,
A mummy that's clawing his way out the tomb,
RRAH!

Let's keep it one hundred.
I'm black so I'm hunted.
This 20 years I got's the result of the last 200.
I'm being honest
I ain't pullin' no punches—
The jury they look like the Bradys,
Now they hanging niggas in bunches,
Strange fruit
Washed my pain down to the root,
Can't get the jury to hang,
Might as well hang noose,
Back in a box again,
Screaming for oxygen,
Ain't break the law,
How the fuck this my consequence?
RRAH!
I'm just a number, a document—
Occupy squares
In an 8 by 10,
So let 'em claim check,
They ain't toppled the king yet,
And that's real,
I only got one move left,
Appeal.

> (*The stage is empty now except for* JAMES BATSON.)

Appeal.

> (*He claps twice in hopes of getting a response. Nothing.*)

Yelling in a vacuum made of steel and bricks.
And Prison is the loudest loneliest abyss.
Appeal!
I'm'a keep up my holler.
Appeal!
Louder.
Pushing the proper papers past the red tape and the white power.
Appeal!
Put me in the corner, I'm'a clap back.

> (JAMES BATSON *starts clapping a steady single beat.*)

Watch.

Appeal!

> (*Other claps join him. Nine more in fact.*)

Steppin over setbacks,

Written off as a goner,

But I'm gonna tread the water 'til the storm breaks,

'Cause I know I got a strong case,

And I'm'a yell until the walls of Jericho break,

Hell if I don't take a chance on it,

They already dug my grave but it ain't the time to dance on it,

And that's the real,

I'm yelling in the darkness until they hear my voice appeal

Appeal.

Appeal.

Appeal!

APPEAL!!!!

> (*Everything stops.*)

And I'm yelling. Alone in a cell in Danville, Kentucky. And if you ever been to prison, you know how loud it is in there. How even the quietest moment is a cacophony. And I'm yelling over that. And then a miracle happens. The case gets picked up by a man named David Niehaus.

> (DAVID NIEHAUS *comes onstage. He is dressed like a lawyer. He is white.*)

He takes my case and holds it up like a megaphone over the country. He says,

**DAVID NIEHAUS.** "IS ANYONE ELSE LABORING TO BE HEARD???"

**JAMES BATSON.** And so many voices come railing back at him.

> (*From the wings we hear numerous voices yelling "APPEAL!" It starts low at first and then becomes a cacophonic chorus.* JURORS *emerge back out of the shadows and into the light.*)

And those peremptory challenges are being used to strike black jurors all over.

And damn it, it's not right! And, I hate to say it but, if you're yelling and no one is hearing you?

**DAVID NIEHAUS AND JAMES BATSON.** If you're yelling and no one is hearing you!

**DAVID NIEHAUS.** Get a white person to shout with you.

**JAMES BATSON.** Shit, I wish there were more David Niehauses in this world. All of a sudden they hear me. My voice reaches all the way to the Supreme Court. Bam. Those judges look at my case and see—

**JUDGE 1.** —that it clearly violates the 14th Amendment which is equal protection—

**JUDGE 2.** —and the 6th Amendment which is a jury of your peers.

**JUDGE 3.** And it's clear.

**EVERYONE.** It's unarguable.

**JAMES BATSON.** And four months later, I win. And all of a sudden I'm free and there's a new law in the books with my name on it that says it is illegal to reject a juror on the basis of race. A new law was invented because of me, y'all. The Batson Rule. Bam! It's over! Next time someone like me is on trial and some shady lawyer is trying to take away any chance they might have at a fair trial by whitewashing the jury they can stand up and yell, "Your honor, that is a Batson Violation!" Because of me! Attack and respond. Sometimes the response takes time but I tai chi'd the hell out of that mufucker. Boom. Roll credits!

**JAMES BATSON (ALL).**
Victory, victory, victory
Threw the book at me but it didn't stick to me (Ayy)
They tried to come for my neck, thought they had me in check, but instead I made history (Ayy)
Played the game with these crooks (Ayy)
Got my name on the books (Ayy)
All whites up on the jury? (NOPE)
Better change how it looks! (Ayy)

> (JAMES BATSON *starts walking offstage.*
>
> JOE GUTTMAN *enters again. He looks at the chess board and destroys it. The pieces go everywhere. This action is violent. It stops* JAMES BATSON *in his tracks.*)

**JOE GUTTMAN.** I just had to get your attention. Look, the Batson Rule only means you can't strike a juror for racial reasons.
But any other reason? Their address, the look in their eyes, their favorite movie, the color of the sweater they are wearing? All of that becomes fair game.

**JAMES BATSON.** C'mon. I got a law in the law books named after me. It's. a. Law.

**JOE GUTTMAN.** To claim a Batson Violation and have it stick? Well it turns out that it's harder than rowing a boat with dental floss.
Because you can CLAIM racism, but PROVING it is very very difficult.

> (DAVID NIEHAUS *and the black* JUROR *from before enter. They start helping replace the pieces on the board.*)

**JAMES BATSON.** I had so many sleepless nights when I was in. Seeing a chess game on the inside of my eyelids. I had this recurring nightmare. I kept playing the King's Indian. And I kept losing. Every time the board reset, white moved first and every time I'd play that same strategy, like, "this time it's gonna be different." Same response every time. And every time, my opponent would break it. Sometimes my opponent was you. Sometimes it was a C.O. who had come at me out of pocket. Sometimes…sometimes…I was sitting there and the man on the other side of the board…was me. Those were the worst nights. No matter what, part of me will always be a statistic. And that's a hurt that's real hard to erase.

**JOE GUTTMAN.** I thought about what could be done. The best solution I could think of was I had to find you. I had to knock on your door.

**JAMES BATSON.** Let's say I opened it.

**JOE GUTTMAN.** There is a conversation to be had. And it's a conversation that could go on for a long time. So here I am. And I want to know you. And I want to say, I'm sorry. I don't want to be known as being part of creating the Batson Rule. I don't want to be a villain.

**JAMES BATSON.** I mean. You don't get to erase your history. You don't get to walk away from it. Not if I don't.

**JOE GUTTMAN.** That's fine.

**JAMES BATSON.** I'm not forgetful, but I am forgiving. And let's say I'm willing to have that long conversation.

> (*The black* JUROR *and* DAVID NIEHAUS *have the board all set up now and have pulled up chairs to watch the two men play.*)

So yeah, they got my name in the books. Sometimes you are a part of an innovation that should be great. An innovation that should be the cause of a great shift. But sometimes you play the King's Indian against an opponent who knows how to break the strategy. All that means is you gotta go back to the board and practice your game. And I guess now I got someone to practice with.

> (*The board is set up as it was in the beginning of the scene. With* JAMES BATSON *playing black.*)

Wait a minute.

> (JAMES BATSON *rotates the board so that he is now playing white. He moves a pawn up.*)

## I WILL SURVIVE
by Sarah DeLappe

*five disco dancers lip sync and dance (choreographed, tight) to "Love Train"*
*straight out of 1971*
*they wear roller skates*

*music cuts out*
*lights up*

*five workers make disco balls at Omega National Products in Louisville*
YOLANDA *is learning how to do it*

**2.** wow. 1972. can you even believe it?

**3.** crazy

**2.** I know. I'm gonna be 22                    **4.** wow!

**4.** so old!

**3.** makes you want to get out and do something

**2.** yeah, yeah

**1.** yeah you know I've been
thinking about New York City              **YOLANDA.** *(her ball isn't right)*
                                          is this—
                                          *(no one heard her*
**2.** yeah?                    **4.** wow   *so she keeps working)*

**1.** yeah
I dunno
maybe I'll take a Greyhound up
                               **4.** Louisville to Chicago
**3.** with what time          Chicago to N.Y.C.

**1.** I dunno
Christmas or something?
                               **3.** Christmas?
**2.** call in sick or something
                               **3.** you really think your mama's
                               gonna let you miss Christmas?

**1.** yeah I dunno
*(pause)*                       **YOLANDA.** hey I think my
                               adhesive?

**4.** Christmas
at Rockefeller Center          **1.** shit!
wow!
                               **YOLANDA.** sorry
**2.** yeah

**1.** (*helping*) hold on

**4.** I wanna see that tree

           **YOLANDA.** I know

**2.** that's a big tree        sorry

**3.** Michelle's cousin went up   **1.** it's ok

a few years ago

saw that tree         steady hands

           you've got to keep 'em

       **4.** wow   steady

**2.** Bobby?

**3.** yep          there you go

      what'd he say?

**2.** you mean Bobby Jones?

       hey    You know we invented the

            disco ball

**3.** yeah

wait you know that Bobby?   **YOLANDA.** Really? Omega

how do you know that Bobby? hey! National?

**4.** what'd Bobby say about it??


           **1.** that's what they say

           back in the prohibition

**3.** about what??

**4.** that tree!

**3.** oh

well

(*big scoop*) he said it ain't that big.

    (*lights out*

    *music up*

    *now there are nine disco dancers*

    *four new ones roller skate on*

    *they do a huge choreographed dance to "Rock the Boat" or "Kung Fu Fighting"*

    *straight out of 1975*

    *music out*

    *lights up*

    *nine workers make disco balls at Omega National Products in Louisville*)

**2.** wow. 1976. can you even believe it?

          **YOLANDA.** careful

**1.** I know        sharp edges

**2.** I'm gonna be 26!     **6.** right

**4.** so old!

**3.** all these new hires

**4.** babies can't even cut the glass straight

**1.** did you hear Frank
got an order
from New York City?

**2.** no

**1.** a four footer.

**2.** wow  **3.** a four footer?

**1.** I know  **4.** Jesus H Christ

**4.** I love that John Travolta.

**3.** yeah you do

**1.** you know
I've been thinking
about New York City?

**2.** really?

**1.** yeah
maybe I'll take a trip

---

**YOLANDA.** so this is how
we apply the adhesive

**6.** ok

**7.** it's not so hard

**8.** sure took me a while

**9.** the scoring's a bitch

**YOLANDA.**  **8.** so did you hear that
So where you  new record?
from?

**6.** Cleveland.  **7.** *Saturday Night Fever?*
now there's a record

**YOLANDA.**
How are you
liking Louisville? **8.** *Saturday Night Fever?*

**6.** It's ok.  **7.** got it over at Better Days
It's ok.  on Bardstown past the
**YOLANDA.**  cemetery
Steady.
Keep it steady.  **8.** no gosh that's not new
no I'm talking Donna
**6.** Gotcha.
**7.** Donna? who's Donna?
**YOLANDA.**
You know
we invented the **8.** oh jesus
disco ball?  oh jesus
you don't know Donna?

(*lights down*
*music up*

*now there are fourteen disco dancers*
*five new ones roller skate on*
*they do a huge choreographed dance to "Stayin' Alive"*
*straight out of 1979*

*music cuts out*
*lights up*

*fourteen workers make disco balls at Omega National Products in Louisville)*

**2.** wow. 1980. can you even—
**1.** yes.

**4.** time flies when you're

**3.** don't say it jackass
**YOLANDA.** has anyone seen my chapstick?
**6.** haven't seen it
**7.** sorry Yolanda

**YOLANDA.** it's ok

**12.** you know the disco ball was invented in Kentucky

**14.** no way
**12.** yes way
**11.** oh yeah
right here
on this very factory
floor

**8.** you know how many balls I made this week?
**9.** do I care?
**8.** guess
**9.** ugh
**8.** just guess! it's a personal record

**6.** do NOT let her borrow your
**7.** oh I know
**6.** she still has my aquanet
**7.** dang

**2.** oh shit
...
shit
**4.** what
**2.** I'm gonna be 30
**4.** wow
...
shit

**2.** that's supposed to make me feel better?

**14.** at Omega National?
**12.** yuh huh
**14.** wow so
we basically invented disco?
**11.** well—

**9.** ughh
**10.** um um um 20?
**8.** nope higher

**12.** yes
yes we did
**13.** that is such bullshit
**12.** it's not it's a fact
**13.** we did not INVENT the disco ball! we just make them! just slap some mirror on a ball and blammo! disco ball!

**7.** 25?
**8.** higher

**3.** hey at least it's not 40
**1.** yeah

**6.** you made more than 25?

**8.** 32.

**7.** wow!!

**9.** whatever
I made 33 last October

**8.** sure you did

**10.** y'all she made
32 in one day

**11.** SHE MADE 32
IN ONE DAY?!

**12.** that's rad    **8.** one week
                      but

**13.** WHATEVER.
disco sucks

**14.** excuse me?

**13.** disco sucks.
I like Motörhead.

**10.** Motörhead?    **7.** whoa

**11.** you're such a phony

**13.** no I'm not

**11.** I've seen you
listening to the Bee Gees

**7.** everyone likes disco

**8.** except for Nixon
he can rot in hell

**10.** don't use that kind of
language, please

**9.** better than Carter

**12.** hey! I love Carter!

**6.** disco's dead!

**14.** DISCO WILL NEVER DIE!
      *(lights down
      music up*

**3.** you know
who's 30?

**2.** who?

**3.** Stevie Wonder
that's who
so

**1.** Stevie Wonder?

**2.** how do you
know how old
Stevie Wonder is?

**3.** I don't know
how do you
NOT know?

**13.** 3.10 an hour!
thousands a year!

**14.** your strip isn't flat

**13.** what??

**14.** steady. keep 'em
steady.

**13.** shut up.
I taught you that.

**4.** so many new hires

**2.** hey how was New
York?

**1.** it was fine.

**2.** just fine?

**1.** yeah.
kind of dirty.

**3.** yeah?

**1.** yeah.
expensive.

**4.** huh.

*now there are twenty disco dancers*
*six new ones roller skate on*
*they do a huge choreographed dance to "I Will Survive"*
*straight out of 1979*

*it balloons into make-outs and messiness and excessive bacchanalia*

*and then two by two people dance off, leaving* YOLANDA *alone*

YOLANDA *holds a disco ball in the center of it all*
*her awe sours into despair*

*lights up*

YOLANDA *alone in the factory*
*a Top 40 hit on the radio*
*straight out of 2017*

YOLANDA *works on a disco ball for a long while)*
**YOLANDA.** (*to the audience*) It's definitely lonely.

## THE BALLAD OF NATHAN STUBBLEFIELD
by Claire Kiechel
composed by Avi Amon *

NATHAN STUBBLEFIELD *stands in the middle of the stage*
*He fiddles with what looks like a large battery or a small moon*
*He flips a switch*

*Suddenly:* VOICES *from all over the space echo out*

*He searches for them—where are they coming from?*
**VOICES.** nathan! nathan! nathan!

nathan

nathan

nathan

nathan

nathan

nathan nathan nathan

nathan
nay-nay-nay-than nayy
nathan
(NATHAN STUBBLEFIELD *is exhausted*

*The* NARRATOR *enters*)
## NARRATOR.
Behold this tale of woe and gloom
this world this man this afternoon
Please tune your ear to what I say
and every man will have his day
(NATHAN *starts putting his machine together*)
**Nathan?**

---

\* To view or listen to the score for *The Ballad of Nathan Stubblefield*, please visit
aviamon.com/nathanstubblefield.

**VOICES.**
Nathan Nathan Stubblefield—
Stubblefield—Stubblefield—
Mister Nathan Nathan Stubblefield
Is this the way?
Is this the way that you followed?

(NATHAN *continues working*)

Nathan Nathan Nathan Nathan
Nathan      Nathan Nathan      Nathan Nathan
Nathan Nathan Nathan Nathan Nathan Nathan Nathan
Nathan      Nathan      Nathan

**NARRATOR.**
A man's a loser in this game
He's got ten children to his name
and all he does is try to dream
his babes are hungry how they scream

**daddy daddy daddy daddy**

**NARRATOR.**
He had this world he thought he knew
these books they told him "be brand new"
He heard the way from down below

**below below below below**

The earth's crust, the ground he sow

(NATHAN *hears something from below and remembers the ground coils*)

**Nathan Nathan Stubble Nathan Nathan Stubble
Nathan Nathan Stubblefield Stubblefield Nathan Nathan
Stubblefield**

**NARRATOR.**
The poor's got two things they can spare
this mound of dirt this charcoaled air
Machine he made with his own hands
a kind of bridge to distant lands

(NATHAN *builds his machine, winding the coils up tighter and tighter*)

**ism ism ism ism ism ism ism ism ism ism ism ism ism ism ism
ism ism ism ism ism**

**terrestrial**                                **where the voice**

**ism ism ism ism ism ism ism ism ism ism ism ism ism ism ism
ism ism ism ism ism**

**terrestrial**                                **where the voices are!**

ism ism ism ism ism ism ism ism ism ism ism ism ism ism ism
ism ism ism ism ism

terrestrial                                                                                where the voice

ism ism ism ism ism ism ism ism ism ism ism ism ism ism ism
ism ism ism ism ism

terrestrial                                                                                where the voices are

terrestrial magnetism!
                    terrestrial magnetism!

                        using sky using sky
                                using ground ground ground
                        using sky using sky
                                using ground ground ground
                                ground ground ground
                    show me show me show me show me show me show
                    me show me show me

*(he's finished it*
*the* VOICES *echo out in celebration!)*

### NARRATOR.
And he showed it to the people
A metal box an old church steeple
using this dirt this dirt he had
they heard his son call out:

### A CHILD'S VOICE.
                    hey dad

*(silence*
*and then)*

                                                        Nathan! Nathan!

            Nathan!

                                                        Nathan! Nathan!

            Nathan!

(NATHAN *dances in happiness*)

### NARRATOR.
oh! how his chest became so light
oh! how his future burned so bright
Make yourself into someone new
Take their place and point their view

*(But something is wrong)*

**what happened**

what what happened

what happened

where did you go

what happened

what did they say

what happened

what do you know

(NATHAN *looks for a way out*)

**NARRATOR.**
What is it they sometimes say
will ev'ry man have his own day?

**ALL.**
**Nathan Nathan Stubblefield**
**Stubblefield**
**Stubblefield**
**Mister Nathan**

**NARRATOR.**
Nathan Stubblefield
Is this the way?
Is this the way that you followed?

(*He can't find a way to escape*)

**NARRATOR.**
It's harder than you might expect
A man like him we don't select
They shook his hand and gave him cash
when he got home it turned to ash

(NATHAN *is broken*)

**NARRATOR.**
He should have known—a boy like him
the future's night the light is grim
They made sure he was all alone
No one to call his telephone

(NATHAN *starts to pull the coils from the ground*

*Then suddenly:*

*He sees the* NARRATOR *for the first time*

*A moment of recognition between the two of them*

NATHAN *sees the owner of the voice that's been in his head his whole life—it's like looking down a tunnel into a mirror*

*The* NARRATOR *tries to sing, but he finds he can't*

*Instead, a surprised* NATHAN *finds that he has taken the* NARRATOR'*s voice*
*He sings out:)*

### NATHAN.
Behold this tale of woe and glow
this man this knot this horror show

**magnetism magnetism magnetism magnetism**
**magnetism**

The earth it gives it takes away
And ev'ry man will have his day

**terrestrial magnetism terrestrial magnetism**

**terrestrial**
            **terres—to rest to rest—to rest**
                    **terrestrial**
        **magnetism**
            **mag mag mag mag magnetism**
(NATHAN *throws the rope up the branch*
*He puts the rope around the* NARRATOR'*s neck*
*The voices rise in urgency)*


**nathan nathan nathan nathan nathan nathan nathan nathan**
**nathan nathan nathan nathan**
**nathan nathan nathan nathan nathan nathan...**

(NATHAN *pulls the* NARRATOR'*s rope*

*The lights go dark*

*Finally quiet.)*

## HOUSE JOSEPHINE, JOSEPHINE BAKER
by Jeff Augustin

*Dingy dressing room of an underground club.*

**ARLAN.** Where she at?

**ANA MAY CAKE.** (ANA MAY CAKE *types on her phone.*) I'm finding out

**ARLAN.** You ain't talking to her, don't fuck with me Ana May Cake.

(ANA MAY CAKE *shows* ARLAN *their phone.*)

**ANA MAY CAKE.** Dots, fool. You see 'em.

(*Sounds of a received text heard.*)

She's stuck in traffic downtown

**ARLAN.** There's no traffic downtown

**C.** There's a sport ball happening. Cardinals vs. Blue Devils. But a punk-ass fool like you wouldn't know that

**ARLAN.** Stop disrespecting me

**C.** Stop acting like a punk

**ARLAN.** Is that what I am, a Punk?

**C.** Yeah                                    **ANA MAY CAKE.** Yeah

**ARLAN.** Here's a punk for you…y'all disqualified

**ANA MAY CAKE.** Yo, wait up. We were just messing around

**ARLAN.** I'm a very sensitive soul. It may not look like it, 'cause you know I'm all hard and shit. But I like poetry and adopting cats and movies starring Jennifer Lawrence.

**C.** You can't disqualify House Josephine, Josephine Baker. We're the reigning champs. Ain't nobody been better than us for five years.

**ARLAN.** We? Fool didn't you just come from Mexico?

**ANA MAY CAKE.** Yo that's racist.

**ARLAN.** Did your parents not accept their little queer burrito?

**C.** First of all, fuck you. Second of all, fuck. Third of all, I'm from Colombia via Texas. My family loves me 'cause they wanted me—I'm sure your family does not feel the same. I'm just finally being truthful to the queen that has lived inside me since I was four years old.

**ANA MAY CAKE.** Amen.

**C.** And I'm on my way to becoming a member of House Josephine.

**ARLAN.** Let me see your walk

**C.** Walk?

**ARLAN.** Your command of the runway

(C *doesn't have one.*)

Can you vogue?

**C.** ...I'm working on it

    (ARLAN *laughs.*)

**ARLAN.** Do you have a name?

**C.** ...No

**ARLAN.** Then what do you have? Dreams? You should just quit now.

**ANA MAY CAKE.** You don't know shit. You think all those people came out to see the embryos of House Lemonade? Naw, boo boo. They came for us.

**ARLAN.** Who gives a fuck. Y'all not performing, get the hell out of my club.

    (ARLAN *turns to go, and there's* LADY DAY. *Did they just apparate or was they there the whole time? Don't matter.* LADY DAY *is life. No one can move, take up space, demand attention the way* DAY *do—without even trying.* DAY *just is.*)

**LADY DAY.** Arlan.

**ARLAN.** ——

How you doing Lady Day?

**LADY DAY.** You tell me?

**LADY DAY.** ——                        **ARLAN.** ——

**ARLAN.** A day never goes by that you're not looking fine.

**LADY DAY.** Don't feel fine.

    (*She moves towards him.*)

You think I disrespect you?

**ARLAN.** Naw, it's your...(bitches)

**LADY DAY.** Choose your words wisely.

**ARLAN.** Your Josephines. That have been disrespectful

**LADY DAY.** It sounded like it was all in jest.

    (*To* ANA MAY CAKE *and* C.)

Wasn't it?

**ANA MAY CAKE.** Yes, Mother Day. It was    **C.** Yes, Mother Day. It was

**LADY DAY.** Please don't tell me you lost your sense of humor. It was the only sexy thing about you.

**ARLAN.** ...no, no I haven't.

**LADY DAY.** Good.

    (LADY DAY *kisses him. You wish* LADY DAY *was kissing you. It's sensual not to be confused with pornographic. You can tell they had something for a little bit. But you know* LADY DAY...*she don't get too involved. But that's another story for another time.*)

**LADY DAY.** We going to go last. You know they here for us. For me. It'll give me time to get all divine like. Like the people want. Okay?

**ARLAN.** Okay.

**LADY DAY.** Good boy. You can leave us now.

(*He gives a look to* ANA MAY CAKE *and* C *then exits. A beat.*)

Where the hell that hoe at?

**C.** Oh, she stuck in traffic

**ANA MAY CAKE.** Naw that was Day texting me

(*To* LADY DAY.)

What if she back on…

**LADY DAY.** She ain't.

(*A beat.*)

**ANA MAY CAKE.** Is she back with….

**LADY DAY.** Hell no. I think she's just…lost. Searching for some truth. Always got to keep reinventing or there's no point to it at all.

**ANA MAY CAKE.** What if she don't come?

**LADY DAY.** The show gots to go on

**ANA MAY CAKE.** How, we need her. It's a three person routine.

**LADY DAY.** We got a third

(LADY DAY *looks at her.*)

**C.** Me?

**LADY DAY.** Yeah baby

**ANA MAY CAKE.** Oh, fuck no

**C.** I'm not ready

**LADY DAY.** You never are the first time.

**C.** I don't even how to walk

**LADY DAY.** Walk?

**C.** The command of the runway

**LADY DAY.** Where you hearing this shit from?

**C.** Arlan

**LADY DAY.** That fool don't know the hole of his face from the hole of his ass

**ANA MAY CAKE.** But he was making some valid points.

**C.** I don't have a name yet

**LADY DAY.** But you've been thinking about one?

**C.** Yeah.

**ANA MAY CAKE.** What you got?

**C.** They're all stupid

**ANA MAY CAKE.** You can't give fucks about anybody. What they think, what they say. You just got to do you boo boo

**LADY DAY.** You got a name. What is it?

**C.** It's umm…*[SAYS IT SO SOFTLY.]*

**ANA MAY CAKE.** I didn't hear you

**LADY DAY.** With some bass baby

**C.** *[INSERT NAME.]* (*Ideally the actor playing C will create their own name and drag persona.*)

**ANA MAY CAKE.** That's….alright

**C.** Told you

**LADY DAY.** I like it.

**C.** I don't have a persona

**LADY DAY.** Everyone's got a persona. It's why mirrors were made. You get to look at the structure of your face, the curves of your body and create yourself. It's private and it's personal until you're ready to share it with the world.

**C.** What about a costume,

(LADY DAY *goes to the rack…and like magic puts together a costume for* C.)

the routine?

**LADY DAY.** You've been practicing in the shower for days.

**ANA MAY CAKE.** Thank god we going to be lip-synching, 'cause a voice you do not have

**C.** I don't think I can do this.

**LADY DAY.** You can. Come on sit right here.

**C.** That's your chair.

**LADY DAY.** Sit. Go ahead get ready.

**C.** I don't know how—

**LADY DAY.** Yes you do.

(C *looks in the mirror. A moment. C lifts a hand and begins to get ready. Slowly we watch them all get dressed. It's a dance of sorts. If you haven't ever seen a Queen prepare, it is a work of beauty and art. I recommend it for all. When all is done, they look royal.*)

Ready?

(C *nods.*

*A large disco ball drops. Lights change, music begins. And they perform. It is breathtaking. It should feel like that moment during a good play, when the entire audience leans in and stops breathing. And* C…C *is a star in the making.*)

## tina, gena & may
by Claire Kiechel

**tina.** did you bring the candles

**gena.** got 'em

**tina.** did you bring the glitter

**may.** I have two kinds

**tina.** and I brought the donuts

(*TINA arranges things*)

**gena.** why did we need donuts

**tina.** because donuts were her favorite duh

**gena.** according to the internet

**may.** everyone likes donuts gena

**gena.** I just don't think
I don't think she's going to come back here for donuts

**tina.** she's going to come back here for us
donuts are just the icing on the cake

**may.** I should have brought icing

**tina.** it's okay

**may.** we could have spelled her name out on the donuts
Henrietta Mahim Bradberry

**gena.** what was her name before she got married

**may.** I don't know jeez oh gosh is it Mahim is that maybe it

**tina.** guys guys it's all fine it's okay
she doesn't WANT writing

**gena.** you're being really annoying tina
like super bossy

**tina.** because this is my dream!
she came to me in a dream and she told me
she told me to come out here and bring her donuts and glitter and fire
and something would happen
something big

**gena.** you do one presentation on her you think you know her

**may.** that's not fair
I think this is really cool tina
I like being your friend

**tina.** thanks may
okay can we all hold hands

gena?

she wants you here

**gena.** fine

**tina.** Henrietta

thank you for calling us out here

to be your witnesses

this cold November day

**may.** we come here for you

**tina.** that's right

we come here for you

we remember you

gena will you read the excerpt tonight?

**gena.** is this literally your book report?

**may.** shhhh I feel her

**gena.** (*reading*)

"Henrietta Mahim Bradberry was born in Franklin Kentucky in 1903, and

in addition to being an amazing housewife and mother and probably also

lots of other things

she patented two inventions one of which was a torpedo discharge device

because it was 1944 and we were at war and she loved her country even if it

was sometimes hard because she was black and a woman and nobody wanted

to hear her speak"

**tina.** thank you gena

we hear you Henrietta

we feel you

you've always been here

okay say her name with me

Henrietta Mahim Bradberry

**tina & gena & may.** Henrietta Mahim Bradberry

**tina.** we say your name like a spell

we hold it in and we tell

everyone what you did

how you did it

how you stayed

how you hid

how you survived

how you made a mark on the outside

we do what you did

we say out loud—

We Are Magic

**gena & may.** We Are Magic

**tina & gena & may.** We Are Magic
We Are Magic
We Are Magic

**tina.** I tell myself I am magic
because the world tells me I am not

      *(a gust of wind)*

**may.** oh she's here

      *(the candle on the donut goes out)*

## THE DEATH OF KWEEN NATHAN STUBBLEFIELD
by Jeff Augustin

**KWEEN NATHAN STUBBLEFIELD.** How did I, Kween Nathan Stubblefield, die? That seems to be the thing most folks are concerned about. We're fascinated by death and hate mystery.

I've never been fascinated by death, I feared it since the first day I learned of it. When I was a child, when we moved to the poor part—Black part of town, a violent part because folks were so fearful of death—of not getting that 40 hour work week, getting evicted and starving to death. So not having much available to them some went after that quick money. And my first friend in this black part of town Mariah—who if I had the words for gay—not dyke, not faggot—I would've made my girlfriend, she lost a brother trying to make that quick money. A brother whose name I don't remember, but whose smell I can't forget. He smelled like a little boy and an old man—like Old Spice and hot fries. The day he was shot and never came back, I knew death was meant to be feared. That one day you're here and then the next you're gone. Nothing but memories in people's mind and once those people die you become non-existent.

So how did I? Kween Nathan Stubblefield die?

I died the same way Zora Neale Hurston died, an unrecognized genius in an unmarked grave. I died on the Trans-Atlantic voyage, chained and thrown overboard, in a shack in Murray poor as fuck—or was it one of the projects avoided or quickly walked by in Brooklyn, in Silver Lake, on the coasts where every one looks the same, thinks the same, and has a way up. No I died the way my brother died. Shot, alone in a hospital as a John Doe, while I was at some liberal arts college in Massachusetts learning privilege, becoming privileged.

Just kidding. I died quietly in my sleep. Maybe. I don't know.

(*A slight beat.*)

Did you even know I existed?

### End of Play